DATE DUE FOR RETURN

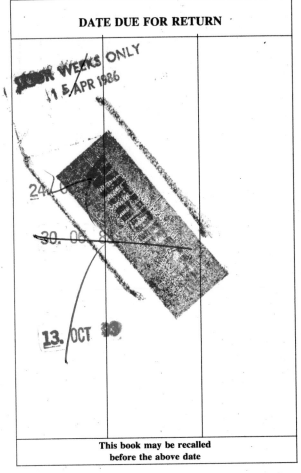

This book may be recalled
before the above date

UL 11b

Perspectives on Development

Foreign aid and industrial development in Pakistan

Perspectives on Development is organized by and
edited from the Centre for Developing-Area Studies, McGill
University, Montreal, Canada. The primary focus of the series
is on economic, social and political development in third world
countries. The series includes works of a broad, comparative
and interpretive character as well as specific institutional and
empirical studies which stem from research activities of the
Centre. However, the series also includes other works judged by
the Editors to be valuable contributions to our understanding
of the development process.

Series Editors

R. Cranford Pratt, Professor of Political Science, University of
    Toronto, Chairman
John A. Barnes, Professor of Sociology, University of Cambridge
Irving Brecher, Professor of Economics, McGill University
Peter C. W. Gutkind, Professor of Anthropology, McGill
    University
Kari Levitt, Associate Professor of Economics, McGill University
Richard F. Salisbury, Professor of Anthropology, McGill
    University

FOREIGN AID AND INDUSTRIAL DEVELOPMENT IN PAKISTAN

by Irving Brecher

Professor of Economics and former Director,
Centre for Developing-Area Studies, McGill University

and S. A. Abbas

Chief, Export Policy Section, Manufacturers Division, United Nations
Conference on Trade and Development

Cambridge : at the University Press 1972

Published by the Syndics of the Cambridge University Press
Bentley House, 200 Euston Road, London NW1 2DB
American Branch: 32 East 57th Street, New York, N.Y.10022

© Cambridge University Press 1972

Library of Congress Catalogue Card Number: 74–166946

ISBN: 0 521 08339 7

Printed in Great Britain
at the University Printing House, Cambridge
(Brooke Crutchley, University Printer)

C

TO OUR WIVES

FOR PATIENCE, SUPPORT AND ENCOURAGEMENT
WELL BEYOND THE CALL OF DUTY

Contents

Tables

Preface

This study was conceived early in 1966, and the basic writing was completed in the summer of 1969. Coverage of the closing phase of the 1960s is relatively brief.

In the broadest sense, the past three years have been the most crucial in Pakistan's history. They have been years of deep social stress and bitter political strife – culminating in the outbreak of an East Pakistan rebellion which threatens to bring national disintegration. This is a real testing time for nation-building in Pakistan.

But the present study has been designed in a narrower setting. Its prime focus is on Pakistan's foreign aid experience from the early 1950s to the end of the Second Five-Year Plan in 1965. And it is chiefly from this perspective that the analysis should be viewed. It will be for others to update the detailed 'foreign aid' story, and to assess the full range of complex interrelations between foreign assistance and Pakistan's national development.

Needless to say, we have not achieved all of our research goals. We are, however, in great debt to those who have helped to make the effort worthwhile – in particular, Dr Moin Baqai, Joint Secretary of the Pakistan Economic Co-ordination and External Assistance Division (and formerly Joint Chief Economist in the Planning Commission), for many important suggestions adopted throughout the work; Professor Edward S. Mason of Harvard University, and Dr Ernest Stern of the United States Agency for International Development, who read and commented critically on the entire manuscript; and Professor Martha F. Loutfi of McGill University, for close collaboration in revising and improving the study. We are also grateful to Drs Hans W. Singer and Meir Merhav, formerly of the United Nations, for sound advice and comments during the planning phase of the research; and to Harold A. Crooks and Claude Lemelin, McGill graduate students, and K. Zaheer Ahmad and Zahoor Alam, M.A. graduates of the Punjab University (Lahore), for valuable research assistance at various stages of the work.

In addition, we are indebted to a host of officials in Pakistan and in the aid-giving countries and agencies, whose co-operation has made it possible to penetrate well beyond the generalities that usually surround foreign aid discussion; and to the United Nations Industrial Development Organization and the McGill University Centre for Developing-Area Studies, which have provided both the financial support and the encouragement essential to the performance of our task. A final word of thanks goes to Miss Rosalind E. Boyd and Miss Grace Goldman for an editorial job well done; to Syed M. Naseer, Mrs Evelyn M. Jones and Miss Christine Ausman for generous assistance on all bibliographic matters; and to Mrs R. G. Barnard and Miss Elinor Fleck for efficiently typing and collating the manuscript.

It remains only to emphasize that responsibility for the analysis and findings presented here lies with the authors; and that this responsibility is not shared by the institutions in which we are or have been employed.

Montreal and Geneva   IRVING BRECHER
March 1971   S. A. ABBAS

Abbreviations

ADBP	Agricultural Development Bank of Pakistan
ADP	Annual Development Programme (Pakistan)
BAW	Federal Office for Manufacturing Industry (West Germany)
CCIE	Chief Controller of Imports and Exports (Pakistan)
CDC	Commonwealth Development Corporation (Great Britain)
CDFC	Commonwealth Development Finance Company Ltd (Great Britain)
CIDA	Canadian International Development Agency
c.i.f.	cost, insurance, freight
CIPCC	Central Investment Promotion and Co-ordination Committee (Pakistan)
CSO	Central Statistical Office (Pakistan)
DAC	Development Assistance Committee of the OECD
DLF	Development Loan Fund (United States)
ECCC	Economic Co-ordination Committee of the Cabinet (Pakistan)
ECNEC	Executive Committee of the National Economic Council (Pakistan)
EPFIDC	East Pakistan Forest Industries Development Corporation
EPIDC	East Pakistan Industrial Development Corporation
EPSIC	East Pakistan Small Industries Corporation
EPWAPDA	East Pakistan Water and Power Development Authority
Eximbank	Export–Import Bank of Washington
FEC	Foreign Exchange Committee (Pakistan)
GAWI	Corporation for the Promotion of the Interests of Developing Countries (West Germany)
IBRD	International Bank for Reconstruction and Development (World Bank)
IDA	International Development Association
IDBP	Industrial Development Bank of Pakistan
IFC	International Finance Corporation
KFW	Reconstruction Loan Corporation (West Germany)
NEC	National Economic Council (Pakistan)
ODM	Ministry of Overseas Development (Great Britain)
OECD	Organization for Economic Co-operation and Development
OGL	Open General Licence Scheme (Pakistan)
PC 1	Planning Commission Form no. 1 (Pakistan)
PICIC	Pakistan Industrial Credit and Investment Corporation
PIDC	Pakistan Industrial Development Corporation
PIFCO	Pakistan Industrial Finance Corporation
PL 480	US Public Law 480
TAC	Technical Advisory Committee of the IDBP
UNCTAD	United Nations Conference on Trade and Development

UNDP   United Nations Development Programme
UNICEF   United Nations Children's Fund
US AID   United States Agency for International Development
WPIDC   West Pakistan Industrial Development Corporation
WPSIC   West Pakistan Small Industries Corporation
WPWAPDA   West Pakistan Water and Power Development Authority

1. Introduction

Foreign aid flows to developing countries began to assume substantial proportions in the early 1950s. Now, some twenty years later, there is clear evidence of widespread unease about the results of these massive flows and their potential for accelerating economic development in the decades ahead.

The 'aid condition'

The Pearson Report has placed the problem in stark perspective:

International support for development is now flagging. In some of the rich countries its feasibility, even its very purpose, is in question. The climate surrounding foreign aid programs is heavy with disillusion and distrust...In the last years of this decade, the volume of foreign official aid has been stagnant. At no time during this period has it kept pace with the growth of national product in the wealthy nations...In much of the developing world [too] there is a sense of disillusion about the very nature of the aid relationship...We have reached a point of crisis.[1]

This is the broad context in which any new study of foreign aid impact must be rooted.

To be sure, the picture is not entirely bleak. In a number of donor countries, such as Canada and West Germany, there appears to be a firm resolve to strengthen and expand foreign assistance programmes. International agencies, such as the World Bank (IBRD) and the United Nations Development Programme (UNDP), are playing an increasingly important role in the search for new directions in aid policy. Even in the United States – where the spirit of disenchantment runs especially deep – there has been a stream of prestigious reports testifying to continuing US concern with problems of aid and development.[2] And yet, despite all this, the blunt fact remains that the overall 'aid condition' is one of malaise; that total foreign assistance stands far below minimum needs in the developing countries; that, in the main, its terms have become harder and more restrictive; and that aid commitments by the United States, much the largest source, have been declining markedly over the past five years.[3]

[1] L. B. Pearson et al., *Partners in Development: Report of the Commission on International Development* (New York, 1969), pp. 4–5.
[2] See, for example, J. A. Perkins et al., 'Development Assistance in the New Administration: Report of the President's General Advisory Committee on Foreign Assistance Programs', mimeo (Washington, D.C., 25 October 1968). And see: Committee for Economic Development, *Assisting Development in Low-Income Countries: Priorities for U.S. Government Policy* (New York, September 1969), and R. A. Peterson et al., *U.S. Foreign Assistance in the 1970s, A New Approach: Report to the President from the Task Force on International Development* (Washington, D.C., 4 March 1970).
[3] The above comments on the international climate of aid refer primarily to the non-socialist donors, which have accounted for the bulk of foreign assistance since 1950. While aid

In considerable measure, the malaise is the product of 'uncertainty and confusion about the nature and purpose of foreign aid. Such uncertainty affects the degree of political support that aid policies receive in donor countries, it obstructs co-operation and co-ordination among donors and strains relations between donors and recipients.'[4]

To disentangle the array of donor motives is no easy task.[5] A reasonable first step is to focus on three goals sought by aid-giving countries: security and commercial gain for themselves, and economic development for the recipients. That is to say, the donors are basically motivated by strategic, commercial and humanitarian considerations, respectively. And the strategic element has loomed largest with the super-powers (the United States and the USSR), commercial factors with the other big powers, and humanitarian factors with the smaller countries.[6]

But this is hardly the full story. For one thing, the security motive is a composite of narrow political advantage and long-run world stability. Secondly, the development motive has been an important theme throughout the aid history of leading donors like the United States and Great Britain. Thirdly, the commercial or profit motive has been far from negligible in the case of smaller countries like Italy and Denmark. Ex-colonial powers like France have placed heavy stress on the narrower forms of political security. There are also the international agencies, ostensibly geared to development, but seldom immune to pressures linked with other goals.

The basic point is that for most donors it is a matter of close interaction among complex, sometimes conflicting, objectives. Frustrations have arisen, inevitably, from a variety of sources; the frequent failure to win political friends and favours; the elusiveness of expected gains from trade and private investment; the search for dramatic development results in programmes dominated by non-developmental goals; the clash between limited success abroad and growing sensitivity to problems of poverty at home. Perhaps most serious of all has been the general tendency, among donors and recipients alike, to make hasty judgments on development performance – judgments that typically derive from inadequate appreciation of foreign aid impact.

It is very difficult, indeed, to promote such understanding through an overview of assistance programmes in the underdeveloped world as a whole. The more solid, though less rapid, route is through in-depth analysis of aid experience in particular developing countries – followed, of course, by a synthesis of the lessons from that experience. The present study of Pakistan is designed as an

---

from the communist countries has risen substantially during the past decade, the sketchy information available on their recent programmes does not seem to warrant taking a different view of the general aid picture. In this connection, see M. I. Goldman, *Soviet Foreign Aid* (New York, 1967), ch. 11. Socialist assistance to Pakistan will be noted in various parts of the present study.

[4] G. Ohlin, *Foreign Aid Policies Reconsidered* (Paris, 1966), p. 13.
[5] See *ibid.* ch. 2; R. F. Mikesell, *The Economics of Foreign Aid* (Chicago, 1968), ch. 1; *Pearson Report*, ch. 1, for a detailed analysis.
[6] For the view that 'politico-military' issues have been at the heart of U.S. aid to Pakistan, see M. Ayoob, 'U.S. Economic Assistance to Pakistan, 1954–1965', *India Quarterly*, April–June 1967.

effort in this direction. It proceeds on the basis of two fundamental assumptions: that economic development is the most meaningful aim of foreign assistance, and that aid can play a significant role in the development process.

'Foreign aid' defined

Chronic underdevelopment, whatever its roots, is necessarily a condition in which the market mechanism – price and profit signals, supply and demand responses, the appropriate economic institutions – is either very weak or virtually nonexistent. Foreign assistance becomes relevant, in this setting, as a device for helping to push the particular economy off 'dead centre'. Consequently, *'aid, properly speaking, refers only to those parts of capital inflow which normal market incentives do not provide'*.[7] And *official* foreign aid – the prime subject of concern here – involves 'a transfer of real resources or immediate claims on resources (for example, foreign exchange) from one country [or group of countries] to another which would not have taken place ... in the absence of specific official action designed to promote the transfer by the donor country'.[8]

Furthermore, it is not only a question of official transfers beyond the range of market forces. There is also the definitional requirement that the specific forms of transfer be development-oriented, i.e., that they represent direct *economic* aid. This means the exclusion of such items as military support and famine relief, while acknowledging their quantitative importance, and even their substantial capacity for indirectly influencing the rate and pattern of the receiving. country's economic development.

What, then, should 'foreign economic aid' embrace for the purposes of this study of Pakistan? There are, in fact, a large number of alternatives from which to choose. Neil Jacoby, for example, defines total US aid allocations as comprising all dollar aid programmes and aid-generated local currency used to finance development.[9] But quite apart from including military assistance, this definition raises the issue of whether local 'counterpart funds' have any real impact on economic development. Hans Singer argues that they are neutral at best because, on the one hand, they are equivalent to the receiving government printing the money and, on the other hand, they permit investment in submarginal projects.[10] This view can be challenged on several grounds: investment of funds absorbed from consumers (by government sales of commodity imports) is not fully analogous to investment financed by printed money; where the inflow of commodity aid is continuous, a once-and-for-all increase in the stock of money may be investible without inflationary effects; to assume that any project which was submarginal before the generation of local currency will continue to be so afterwards, is to say that all opportunities for new capital

[7] P. N. Rosenstein-Rodan, 'International Aid for Underdeveloped Countries', *Review of Economics and Statistics*, May 1961, p. 109.

[8] Mikesell, *Economics of Foreign Aid*, p. 194.

[9] N. H. Jacoby, *United States Aid to Taiwan: A Study of Foreign Aid, Self-Help, and Development* (New York, 1966), ch. 4.

[10] H. W. Singer, *International Development: Growth and Change* (New York, 1964), ch. 15.

formation have been permanently exhausted. Be that as it may, the compelling consideration here is that the development content of counterpart funds remains an open question complex enough to merit intensive treatment elsewhere.

Frederic Benham distinguishes three concepts of economic aid: the UN definition, that is, official grants and net long-term lending for non-military purposes; a much broader, 'donor countries' definition, including private investment and export credit; and Benham's own definition, the UN approach excluding all public lending made on commercial terms.[11] By contrast, the Organization for Economic Co-operation and Development (OECD) measures the 'net flow of official financial resources': cash grants and grants in kind, including technical assistance; sales of commodities against local currencies; government lending (net of repayment of principal) for periods exceeding one year; and grants and capital subscriptions to multilateral aid agencies, as well as net loans from those agencies.[12]

For the most part, the present study will use the OECD-type definition. It has obvious shortcomings, among them the failure to separate the 'aid' component from foreign transfers which impose a burden of repayment on the recipient. But this problem can be mitigated through aid calculations based on 'discounted present value'.[13] And it is a matter of recognizing the fallibility of all such definitions, while judging the OECD approach to be a reasonable compromise between comprehensiveness and analytical soundness.

Scope of the study

It is striking that very little intensive effort has been devoted to defining the central problems of foreign assistance, analysing the aid-giving process, and gauging the economic impact of aid on the recipient countries.[14] Merely to mention this task is, of course, to appreciate how formidable and sensitive an undertaking it is; this helps to explain the reluctance of governments and scholars to plunge deeply into foreign aid analysis. But the issues are no less vital for being complex. It is time to meet them 'head on' by subjecting foreign aid to careful economic assessment on a wide variety of fronts.

There are cogent reasons for making Pakistan a focal point of discussion.

[11] F. Benham, *Economic Aid to Underdeveloped Countries* (London, 1961), ch. 2.

[12] OECD, *The Flow of Financial Resources to Less-Developed Countries, 1961–1965* (Paris, 1967), ch. 8. The OECD figures are chiefly concerned with assistance provided by member countries; coverage is brief for the Sino-Soviet countries (the USSR, Bulgaria, Czechoslovakia, East Germany, Hungary, China, Poland and Rumania), for other non-OECD countries, and for the multilateral aid agencies.

[13] This is attempted in Chapter 3 below. In 1967, OECD itself began to calculate the grant element in foreign aid; see OECD, *The Flow of Financial Resources, 1961–1965*, ch. 6 and annex I. More recently, OECD has distinguished between 'official development assistance' and 'other official flows'; the former characterized by 'concessional terms and development orientation, the latter having trade financing or reserves management as its primary aim'. OECD, *Development Assistance: Efforts and Policies of the Members of the Development Assistance Committee, 1969 Review* (Paris, 1969), p. 43.

[14] See, for example, S. H. Robock, *Brazil's Developing Northeast: A Study of Regional Planning and Foreign Aid* (Washington, D.C., 1963).

In the first place, it is among the oldest and most populous of the new states that have emerged since World War II. Secondly, it has a virtually unbroken record of large-scale and varied economic assistance from abroad. Thirdly, Pakistan provides a vivid illustration of industrial growth in the face of serious economic, social and political obstacles, and with acute problems still to be solved. In addition, it has shown a high degree of political stability during the years associated with its most rapid economic development.[15] Pakistan has a long tradition of overall planning based on a mix of private enterprise and state initiative. Then, too, pertinent statistical and other economic data are comparatively abundant and reliable.

One of the most remarkable features of Pakistani economic development has been the tremendous growth of the industrial sector in a country which, at the time of Partition, had practically no industry worth mentioning. Both government and private business played key positive roles in this process: the latter mainly through heavy reinvestment of profits in expanded output, the former through a sustained incentives policy for increased exports and import substitution. Both, by the same token, bore a considerable responsibility for shortfalls in Pakistan's economic growth, and for the persistence of gross inequities in the distribution of personal and regional incomes.

How and how far foreign aid has affected Pakistan's industrial performance is the fundamental question for this study. As already pointed out, the task is by no means simple. For one thing, there are difficult conceptual problems: defining foreign assistance, distinguishing it from other kinds of international transfer, determining its complementary and competitive effects on domestic investment, deriving meaningful criteria for appraising foreign aid results. And there are parallel difficulties of measurement and statistical testing. Subject to such constraints, the analysis proceeds in terms of the history of aid flows to Pakistan; their interaction with economic growth and planning in the country; the role of foreign aid in the balance of payments and external indebtedness; the reciprocal links between aid on the one hand and income, employment, investment and the structure of Pakistani industry on the other. Emphasis is also placed on the assistance programmes of selected donor countries and institutions, with a view to explaining the aid-giving process and tracing its effects on various segments of Pakistan's industrial activity. An attempt is made to assess costs and benefits of particular foreign-aided projects and, where appropriate, to evaluate such projects in relation to the economy at large. Perhaps the real measure of analytical success will be the ability to provide new signposts for improved public policy in the field of development assistance.

Clearly, this is a substantial undertaking. Considerations of logic and

[15] This, of course, is not to overlook the grave political disturbances that Pakistan experienced in late 1968 and early 1969 (and again in early 1971, after the time of writing). Nor is it to ignore the substantial economic gains recorded in the year 1968/9, despite the disturbances. But the fact remains that Pakistan registered its most impressive economic advance during the first half of the 1960s, when relative political stability prevailed. See K. B. Sayeed, 'The Performance Profile of the Government of Pakistan', unpublished mimeo. (McGill University, Centre for Developing-Area Studies, 1971.)

manageability dictate that certain issues, however interesting and important, be discussed only in subordinate fashion. Such is the case with private foreign aid and investment, agricultural aid, and technical assistance programmes. Each of these topics is a world unto itself and could not be embraced without a massive extension of an already sizable effort. This is also true of aid impact on donor countries: it is the effects on Pakistan as a recipient nation which are of overriding concern here.

Nor are these the only limits imposed on the scope of this study. In particular, there will be no detailed analysis of foreign aid effects on Pakistan's economic infra-structure – power, transportation, communications, natural resource development. The regional implications of the aid inflows will not be treated in any real depth. And reference to socio-political aspects of the inflows will be brief.

In the concluding chapter, it will be emphasized that there is justification – conceptual as well as practical – for leaving such gaps; that it is reasonable to expect them to be filled by other studies in the aid field. But this does not alter the fact that the gaps are very significant indeed, and that the present effort has to be seen as a first-stage, partial approach to aid impact on Pakistan.

2. Towards a theory of foreign aid

Any systematic approach to foreign aid, however partial, must be placed in broad analytical perspective. This chapter explores the role of aid in the growth process, with a view to evaluating the particular experience of Pakistan.

The theory of foreign aid remains quite imperfect. And its application to Pakistan will be less than complete. Consequently, it can hardly be expected that direct, one-to-one links will be drawn between theory and performance. Essentially, what this chapter provides is a fitting-together of certain key variables in the aid–growth relationship, as well as some broad guidelines for assessing the role of aid in Pakistan's industrial development. The framework will have served its basic purpose if it helps to produce a reasonably clear picture of aid effects on Pakistani industry.

Ideally, one should identify every unit of development assistance, determine its direct impact and measure its multiplier effects over time. The real contribution of aid would be viewed in relation to individual consumers and producers, and the extent of aggregate change brought about by aid would be an interesting corollary to these more significant welfare effects. To learn, for example, that the per capita income of a developing country had grown by 100 per cent, without realizing that the condition of the lowest income groups had deteriorated in the same period, would mean being misled on the basic question of economic and social change. Given the empirical constraints, it is natural that distortions of this kind should, in fact, occur. What proves surprising is that most of the literature dealing with the relationship of foreign aid to the development process has been concerned only with the broadest economic results of such assistance.

In addition, considerable woolliness derives from dubious assumptions implicit in the various theories of development. Perhaps the most dangerous assumption is that capital is *the* key to growth.[1] From this it follows that since developing countries are too poor to generate all their own savings, inflows of external capital provide the missing link. The oversimplification becomes evident whenever the development problem is defined solely in terms of producing a level of capital formation sufficient for self-sustained growth. Kenneth Galbraith, by contrast, argues that there are elements just as crucial to development as is foreign capital. And S. M. Fine believes that while some conditions for a satisfactory rate of economic progress 'can be conferred by foreign assistance... perhaps the most critical components must emerge from the society itself'.[2]

[1] In this connection, see M. Friedman, 'Foreign Economic Aid: Means and Objectives', *Yale Review*, June 1958.
[2] See J. K. Galbraith, 'A Positive Approach to Foreign Aid', *Foreign Affairs*, April 1961; S. M. Fine, 'Economic Growth in the Less-Developed Countries', *OECD Observer*, August 1963, p. 26. See also the discussion of prerequisites to development in G. Myrdal, *Asian Drama: An Inquiry Into the Poverty of Nations*, 3 vols. (New York, 1968).

Whether capital inflows play a major role in the growth process, has, indeed, become a matter of intensive debate. This is no less true of private inflows than of official foreign assistance.[3]

The 'take-off' analysis: pre-1914 experience

Kenneth Berrill and A. K. Cairncross regard foreign investment as relatively unimportant in the take-offs experienced by the presently advanced economies.[4] With the usual reservations about conclusions based on inadequate data, Berrill has examined the historical role of foreign capital in the context of two general assumptions: that for most advanced economies, two or three decades can be identified in which certain strategic sectors grew significantly; and that the appropriate take-off periods are those suggested by W. W. Rostow.[5] Foreign capital is observed to have been a very minor part of total capital supply in the periods of take-off before 1914. However, Berrill is careful to note that the limited quantity of foreign capital does not take into account the role of foreign technology, which was important for countries like Japan.

In these terms, Britain, France and Germany are said to have achieved industrialization without foreign borrowing. Similarly, Finland and Japan were able to pass through the take-off period in the absence of foreign capital. Denmark and Sweden relied on external capital only in the late stages of the take-off. Berrill is sceptical about finding a take-off period for Canada, Australia, New Zealand and the United States. But he settles, nevertheless, on 1843–60 for the United States and 1896–1914 for the three other countries; and he concludes that even in those four cases, 'the really heavy foreign investment is after the take-off'.[6]

In essence, both Berrill and Cairncross consider the inflow of foreign capital a result, rather than a cause, of rapid growth as far as the pre-1914 experience is concerned.[7] But Berrill's rather casual treatment of public utilities detracts from the validity of his thesis, since it understates the significance of foreign investment in such enterprises during the take-off stage. Furthermore, both writers neglect the impact of technology and access to foreign markets, two basic components of foreign capital inflow. Perhaps most important of all, the pre-1914 focus is on private foreign capital, and on its automatic response to

---

[3] See R. F. Mikesell, *The Economics of Foreign Aid* (Chicago, 1968), chs. 2–3.

[4] K. E. Berrill, 'Foreign Capital and Take-Off', in *The Economics of Take-Off into Sustained Growth, Proceedings of a Conference held by the International Economic Association*, ed. W. W. Rostow (London, 1963); A. K. Cairncross, *Factors in Economic Development* (London, 1962), ch. 3.

[5] There has, of course, been extensive criticism of the Rostow take-off in the literature. See, for example, S. Kuznets, 'Notes on the Take-Off', in *The Economics of Take-Off into Sustained Growth*.

[6] Berrill, 'Foreign Capital and Take-Off,' p. 295.

[7] 'While foreign investment undoubtedly speeded up the development of these countries, it is more accurate to think of it as accompanying and reinforcing their growth than as preliminary to it...It was a rapid growth in output, more than anything else, that created a shortage of capital...and made it necessary to have recourse to foreign borrowing.' Cairncross, *Factors in Economic Development*, p. 43.

investment opportunities in a dynamic setting; whatever the relevance of this cause–effect relationship for private capital flows, it is quite clear that they differ sharply enough from foreign aid to rule out any simple extension of causal reasoning from one to the other.

Foreign aid and the problem of causality

In fact, foreign assistance must, by definition, have an independent capability for influencing economic growth in the underdeveloped countries. There is nothing automatic about its response to growth needs; and there is much that originates with policy objectives set by the donor. The real question, therefore, is not whether such a causal role exists, but how it is exercised and how far.

No easy answers are to be found, since this is part of the general problem of causality in an interconnected social system. One is led, inevitably, to a host of further aid questions which are hardly more lacking in complexity. Can the rate of economic growth accelerate in the absence of foreign assistance and, if so, for how long? Is it possible to maintain a steady growth rate without continuing aid inflows? Is foreign assistance a necessary condition for getting the growth process under way? What are the most significant contrasts in the role of aid in different countries and at different periods of time? What kinds of impact does economic assistance have on social and political development in the receiving country? To what extent, if any, are the positive effects of aid offset by adverse influence on domestic savings, industrial production and other key variables?

Thus the problem of foreign aid causality is very intricate indeed. The absence of one important input may preclude the possibility of growth. Its presence makes progress possible, but an evaluation of its role is extremely difficult in the context of outputs emerging from a combination of interdependent and simultaneously applied inputs.

The dilemma is well illustrated by considering the inflow of external resources as 'virtually a separate factor of production'.[8] This implies the use of a production function to determine the marginal productivity of the foreign aid factor. Suppose, for example, that one fitted a Cobb–Douglas type of production function.

$$O = \gamma K_D^\alpha L^\beta E^\theta,$$

where O is output, K_D is domestically generated capital, L labour, and E foreign assistance. It would have to be assumed that K_D and E were independent of each other during the period under consideration. But it is far from evident that this should be so (except, perhaps, for the pure dual economy); and it would take a great deal of convincing to refute the judgment that the closest linkages prevail between domestic and foreign capital. Nor is this all; for there is the equally important assumption of relative constancy in the shares of capital and labour; and the validity of that assumption is open to serious

[8] H. B. Chenery and A. M. Strout, 'Foreign Assistance and Economic Development', *American Economic Review*, September 1966, p. 679.

question. In any event, the most accurate measure of the marginal productivity of external resources, θ, would still leave the specifics of foreign aid impact untouched.

The truth is that one can hardly exaggerate the conceptual and quantitative gaps in this field. Nevertheless, a variety of significant analytical efforts continues to be made, particularly on the 'macro' front. The discussion turns now to these advances in foreign aid theory.

The aggregate aid models

The macro approach is strikingly reflected in the aggregate aid models which have appeared with increasing frequency over the past decade.[9] Each model has its own unique characteristics, to be sure. But most of them have a number of important features in common: assuming economic growth to be the only objective of foreign assistance; abstracting from the social and political aspects of the development process; providing an analytical framework for determining how much aid a developing country will require; recommending the policies which such a country should follow in order to achieve a target rate of growth; suggesting or implying broad criteria for evaluating past aid programmes. The Fei–Paauw and Chenery–Strout models give a reasonably representative picture of major strengths and weaknesses in this econometric system.

Fei–Paauw

This is basically an investigation of the quantitative links between external assistance and the mobilization of domestic savings. The authors construct a revised Harrod–Domar model and apply it to a group of thirty-one countries receiving the bulk of United States development aid. 'Self-help', in the form of increased domestic savings, is viewed as the overriding prerequisite to outside assistance; that is to say, the prime test of whether a country should receive aid is its readiness to undertake the 'domestic austerity efforts' necessary 'to achieve self-sufficiency in finance'.[10]

By way of first approximation, the model expresses required investment (I/Y) as a function of the capital–output ratio (k), the target rate of growth of per capita GNP (h), and the population growth rate (r). Thus $I/Y = k(h+r)$; substituting this into $I = S+A$, where S is domestic savings and A is foreign savings, gives $h = (s-rk)/k+a/k$ where s is the average propensity to save and a the aid–income ratio. For fixed values of s, r and k, the target growth

[9] See, for example, H. B. Chenery and M. Bruno, 'Development Alternatives in an Open Economy: The Case of Israel', *Economic Journal*, March 1962; Chenery and I. Adelman, 'Foreign Aid and Economic Development: The Case of Greece', *Review of Economics and Statistics*, February 1966; Chenery and A. MacEwan, 'Optimal Patterns of Growth and Aid: The Case of Pakistan', *Pakistan Development Review*, Summer 1966; N. H. Jacoby, *United States Aid to Taiwan* (New York, 1966), appendices E–G; J. Vanek, *Estimating Foreign Resource Needs for Economic Development: Theory, Method, and a Case Study of Colombia* (New York, 1967).

[10] J. C. H. Fei and D. S. Paauw, 'Foreign Assistance and Self-Help: A Reappraisal of Development Finance', *Review of Economics and Statistics*, August 1965, pp. 261, 263.

rate equation is then represented as a straight line with a slope of $1/k$ and a vertical intercept $s/k - r$.

On this basis, John Fei and Douglas Paauw distinguish between developing countries in terms of a 'favorable' and an 'unfavorable' case. Even in the absence of foreign savings ($a = 0$), per capita GNP will rise if population pressure is 'low' ($s/k > r$); this is the favourable case.[11] If, on the other hand, population pressure is 'high' ($s/k < r$), per capita GNP will fall without foreign savings; this is the unfavourable case.

But this simple extension of Harrod–Domar 'yields the conclusion that the direction of capital movement will continue forever and the volume of the flow will grow at the exponential rate $h+r$'.[12] In an effort to approximate reality more closely, the authors replace the savings assumption ($S = sY$) with a function (u) which takes incremental per capita savings as a constant fraction of increases in per capita income. This they call the 'per capita marginal saving ratio' (PMSR). By incorporating this function into a revised 'open economy' model, they are able to differentiate between three cases of growth in relation to foreign aid. First, there is the favourable case, where no foreign capital is necessary because $h+r$ is less than the initial average savings rate [$s(0)$]; that is, because of a low population growth rate or an unambitious target growth rate, or some combination of the two. Second, there is the intermediate case, where $h+r$ is greater than the initial savings rate but less than the long-run growth rate of capital (u/k); here the developing country will require foreign savings until some finite termination date, after which it will be able to export capital. And third, there is the unfavourable case, where $h+r$ exceeds the long-run growth rate of capital; the need for foreign savings is infinite because of a combination of high target and population growth rates.

The model's five primary parameters turn out to be $s(0)$, u, k, h, and r – i.e., the initial average savings rate, the per capita marginal savings ratio, the capital–output ratio, the target rate of growth of per capita GNP, and the rate of population growth, respectively. Fei and Paauw proceed to estimate the values of these parameters for the thirty-one selected countries, and thereby to solve their 'termination date' equation for each country. Also, by solving their 'foreign savings' equation, they calculate the time-paths of required capital inflows for the eight countries found to have a fixed date when such inflows would end.

The successful countries are the eight with finite termination dates – the intermediate case, comprising Colombia, Greece, Mexico, Pakistan, the Philippines, Taiwan, Thailand and Tunisia.[13] Assuming 'reasonably realistic' values for $s(0)$, k, h and r, the authors suggest that a PMSR (u) of about 35 per cent is an essential condition for self-sufficiency in development finance. 'Roughly

[11] However, choice of a high target rate of growth could make such a country dependent on foreign capital forever. *Ibid.* p. 255.

[12] *Ibid.*

[13] One country, Yugoslavia, has a termination date of zero – the favourable case, requiring no foreign savings.

this level of austerity appears to be needed to qualify a country for gap-filling assistance [that] more or less automatically complements the country's own self-help efforts.'[14]

There are twenty-two countries with a termination date of infinity. These are the unsuccessful countries, or the unfavourable case in the Fei-Paauw model. Most of them require sophisticated and carefully supervised gap-narrowing assistance that will produce 'leverage effects on the growth of domestic savings capacity'.[15]

Chenery–Strout

This is, perhaps, the most comprehensive of the aggregate models, in empirical as well as theoretical terms. It combines all three broad quantitative approaches to foreign aid impact: capital absorptive capacity, the savings–investment gap and the export–import gap.[16]

The authors contend that growth performance in a typical developing country is subject to three major bottlenecks or constraints: the 'skill limit', involving 'the skill formation required of managers, skilled labour, and civil servants in order to increase productive investment'; the 'saving limit', which 'is designed to include not only the marginal propensity to save but the government's ability to increase total saving by changes in the tax structure and by other policies';[17] and the 'trade limit', determined basically by the export growth rate and the marginal import rate. 'By relieving these constraints, foreign assistance can make possible fuller use of domestic resources and hence accelerate growth.'[18]

Development is, in fact, seen as a three-stage process through which a poor country must move if it is to achieve the goal of self-sustained growth. Phases I and II make up investment-limited growth; the operative constraint in Phase I is the country's ability to invest, and in Phase II its capacity for generating the savings required to satisfy investment needs. Phase III, trade-limited growth, reflects 'a country's inability to change its productive structure to meet the changing patterns of internal and external demand'.[19] The total foreign capital required by such an economy can be determined as the sum of its capital needs for each of the three transitional phases.

In symbolic terms, the starting equation for all phases is

$$F_t = I_t - S_t, \tag{1}$$

where F_t represents required foreign assistance (capital) in the year t, I_t the

[14] Fei and Paauw, 'Foreign Assistance and Self-Help', pp. 261, 263.

[15] *Ibid.* p. 261.

[16] The McKinnon model provides a similar synthesis. However, it makes no attempt to quantify absorptive capacity; and it takes a somewhat different view of foreign capital requirements. R. I. McKinnon, 'Foreign Exchange Constraints in Economic Development and Efficient Aid Allocation', *Economic Journal*, June 1964.

[17] Chenery and Strout, 'Foreign Assistance', p. 686.

[18] *Ibid.* p. 680.

[19] *Ibid.* p. 682.

level of gross investment in that year, and S_t the amount of gross domestic savings. The basic conditions of Phase I can be expressed as

$$S_t = S_0 + \alpha'(V_t - V_0), \tag{2}$$
$$I_t = I_0 + \beta k(V_t - V_0), \tag{3}$$

where α' is the marginal savings rate, V is GNP, β the maximum growth rate of investment (the skill limit), and k the incremental capital–output ratio. Combining equations (1), (2) and (3) gives

$$F_t = F_0 + (\beta k - \alpha')(V_t - V_0). \tag{4}$$

Phase I will end when investment reaches a level high enough to sustain the target growth rate of GNP $(\bar{r})$. This requires a rate of investment growth greater than $\bar{r}$, and an inflow of aid to fill the gap between that required rate and the increment in domestic savings.

Having moved into Phase II, the economy must go on investing at a rate adequate to sustain $\bar{r}$. But S remains too small to finance the entire required I, with the result that foreign aid must now fill this second gap. The savings–investment picture can be expressed as follows:

$$I_t = V_0 k\bar{r}(1 + \bar{r}), \tag{5}$$
$$S_t = S_0 + \alpha'V_0(1 + \bar{r}) - \alpha'V_0. \tag{6}$$

Combining equations (1), (5) and (6) gives

$$F_t = V_0 k\bar{r}(1 + \bar{r}) - V_0\alpha_0 - V_0\alpha'\bar{r}, \tag{7}$$

where α is the average savings rate in the initial year. And substituting the equation

$$F_0 = I_0 - S_0 = V_0 k\bar{r} - V_0\alpha_0 = V_0(k\bar{r} - \alpha_0) \tag{8}$$

in (7) gives

$$F_t = F_0 + V_0\bar{r}(k\bar{r} - \alpha'). \tag{9}$$

It is clear that if foreign aid is to decline $(F_t < F_0)$, α' must exceed $k\bar{r}$. In other words, the marginal savings rate must be greater than the target investment rate in order for Phase II to come to an end.

The central problem in Phase III is twofold: heavy import requirements are imposed by the relatively inelastic demand for manufactured goods that arises from their importance in production and from inadequate domestic supply; 'the feasible growth of export earnings...is [also] limited...at any moment in time...by productive capacity as well as organizational and institutional factors'.[20] The import and export limits are expressed in the following equations:

$$\overline{M}_t = \overline{M}_0 + u'(V_t - V_0), \tag{10}$$
$$E_t = E_0(1 + \epsilon)^t, \tag{11}$$

where $\overline{M}$ is required imports of goods and services, u' the marginal import rate, E exports of goods and services, and ϵ the growth rate of exports. Required capital inflows can be denoted

$$F_t = \overline{M}_t - E_t. \tag{12}$$

[20] *Ibid.* pp. 689–90.

Substituting equations (10) and (11) in (12) gives

$$F_t = \overline{M}_0 + u'(V_t - V_0) - E_0(1 + \epsilon)^t. \tag{13}$$

For Phase III to end, either the export growth rate must exceed the target rate of growth in GNP ($\epsilon > \bar{r}$) or the marginal import rate must be substantially below the initial average rate.

This, then, is the Chenery–Strout 'model 1'. It is used to evaluate current development performance and to make five- to ten-year projections of required capital inflow. A supplementary 'model 2' is constructed for longer periods, mainly to allow for import substitution and the consequent reduction in aid requirements for any given pattern of growth.[21] Equation (10) then becomes

$$\overline{M}_t = \overline{M}_0 + u'(V_t - V_0) - M_{mt}, \tag{14}$$

where M_{mt} is the net reduction in import needs at time t. And capital requirements in Phase III can be described as

$$F_t = \overline{M}_0 + u'(V_t - V_0) - M_{mt} - E_0(1 + \epsilon)^t. \tag{15}$$

The authors selected thirty-one developing countries for empirical analysis. Three tests emerge as a basis for measuring progress towards a given rate of self-sustained growth: the 'investment criteria', mainly involving $i > \bar{r}$; the 'saving criteria', particularly $\alpha' > k\bar{r}$; and the 'trade criteria', with emphasis on $\epsilon > \bar{r}$. Ten countries – Israel, Jordan, Malaya, Pakistan, Panama, Peru, the Philippines, Taiwan, Thailand and Trinidad–Tobago – are found to have satisfied all three performance tests during the period 1957–62; in addition, Burma and Korea meet both the saving and trade criteria. Of the remaining nineteen countries, nine (including India) meet the saving or trade criterion, and ten fail to satisfy either test. 'One of the most suggestive features of this grouping of countries is the predominant role played by exports... there is almost no example of a country which has for a long period sustained a growth rate substantially higher than its growth of exports through continuing import substitution.'[22]

Foreign capital requirements in 1970 and 1975 are calculated from alternative estimates for the values of the six basic parameters of model 1 – β, $\bar{r}$, k, α', u' and ϵ. The global figures turn out to be roughly comparable with earlier UN projections. But 'perhaps the most notable feature of this analysis is the sensitivity of aid requirements to variations in internal performance. At historical growth rates, the maximum reduction due to improved performance is about 20 per cent, but at the 6 per cent growth rate, upper-limit performance would reduce external capital needs by 40 per cent.'[23]

Chenery and Strout conclude by drawing a number of important implications for development policy. One is that 'over the whole period of the transition to self-sustaining growth, the use that is made of the successive increments in

[21] Offsetting this reduction, to some extent, would be the lower productivity of capital in import substitution. *Ibid.* p. 698.
[22] *Ibid.* p. 710.
[23] *Ibid.* p. 721.

GNP is likely to be more important than the efficiency with which external assistance was utilized in the first instance'.[24] A second conclusion is that the rapid achievement of a high growth rate, even if it must be supported by heavy capital inflows, is likely to make the most significant contribution to self-sustained development. Thirdly, the focus of public policy in aid-receiving countries 'should vary according to the principal limitations to growth: just as optimal countercyclical policy implies different responses in different phases of the business cycle, optimal growth policy requires different "self-help" measures in different phases of the transition'.[25] Finally, with the increasing availability of reasonably reliable statistics, the project approach to aid-giving and aid assessment should give way to a programme approach based on the recipient's compliance with minimum standards of overall development performance.

Critique of the models

At the empirical level, one can readily identify points of contrast between the Chenery–Strout and Fei–Paauw models. Thus the former does not calculate termination dates for required aid flows to the various countries under study; while the latter does not project capital requirements on a global basis. Then, too, each model's thirty-one country sample contains countries that are not included in the other.[26] Again, three of the successful countries in Fei–Paauw, Colombia, Mexico and Tunisia, fail to satisfy the roughly equivalent saving criterion in Chenery–Strout; while eight countries meeting that test in Chenery–Strout, Argentina, Brazil, Honduras, India, Israel, Nigeria, Panama and Peru, are among the unsuccessful countries in Fei–Paauw.

But it is the theoretical characteristics of the models which are crucial; for differences in empirical results are largely attributable to differing assumptions about the development process; and common conceptual features reveal important shortcomings in the aggregate approach to foreign aid impact. Perhaps the most interesting contrasts involve the role of population growth and the foreign exchange gap between exports and required imports.

Fei–Paauw is, indeed, unique among the aggregate models in taking explicit account of population pressures, by postulating a target growth rate of per capita GNP (h), a rate of population growth (r), and a per capita marginal savings rate (u). The population factor emerges directly as a major constraint on the effectiveness of foreign assistance. On the other hand, Fei–Paauw makes no allowance for a trade gap, presumably on the ground that it must equal the savings–investment gap under conditions of flexible adjustment in an equilibrium system. For Chenery–Strout, there is no necessary 'ex-ante' equality between the two gaps: the 'basic hypothesis is that the equilibrating reactions in investment, savings, and trade behaviour take place over an appreciable period of time and may deviate in varying degrees from optimal instantaneous adjustments'.[27] The two-gap analysis is not without its pitfalls, to be sure; exclusive concern with the 'gap between the gaps' does tend 'to obscure the facts that an investment–saving relationship is implicit in the balance of payments and that this relationship must be consistent with the overall income–expenditure relationship'.[28] But there can be little doubt as to the reality or significance of the trade constraint in the context of underdevelopment and structural disequilibrium.

Nor can there be much question as to the insight gained from the Chenery–Strout 'three-phase' analysis which draws so heavily on the trade-gap problem. Here, too, it is by no means a matter of uncritical acceptance. 'The simple truth is that the theory of economic transition is still in an embryonic stage.'[29] And Chenery–Strout does encourage the inference that sequential growth is a universal phenomenon for developing countries. But there is, in fact, nothing final about the shortage of skills in Phase I of this model, and nothing automatic or logically necessary about the sequence of Phases II and III. The authors are emphatic in pointing out that the only inevitable feature of their growth sequence is that, 'whenever an economy is able to increase its ability to invest capital productively more rapidly than the increase in supply of domestic and foreign financing, there will be a shift from a phase dominated by the absorptive capacity to one dominated by the supply of foreign capital'.[30] The relevance of this stage by stage analysis lies in highlighting major strategic factors that shape the growth process over time, and in suggesting broad policy guidelines to cope with the changing problems of development.

But if the contrasts between Chenery–Strout and Fei–Paauw serve to underscore particular elements of strength in both approaches, their shared features bring out substantial weaknesses in the aggregate models as a whole. In essence, it is a matter of questionable scope and limited causal analysis.

For one thing, 'foreign assistance' is typically defined to include inflows of private investment. Chenery and Strout are quick to acknowledge that such flows do not constitute aid in the sense of unrequited resource transfers: 'the significance of the term as used here is that it represents a governmental decision by lenders and borrowers to secure a given transfer of resources'.[31] However, this does not alter the fact that private foreign investment is basically subject to market forces as reflected in profit potential in the host country; and that model estimates of foreign capital requirements are misleading insofar as they equate self-sustained growth with zero capital inflow.

[27] H. B. Chenery and A. M. Strout, 'Foreign Assistance and Economic Development: Reply', *American Economic Review*, September 1968, p. 913.

[28] H. G. Johnson, *Economic Policies toward Less-Developed Countries* (Washington, D.C., 1967), p. 53. See also H. J. Bruton, 'The Two Gap Approach to Aid and Development: Comment', *American Economic Review*, June 1969.

[29] J. C. H. Fei and G. Ranis, 'Foreign Assistance and Economic Development: Comment', *American Economic Review*, September 1968, p. 907.

[30] Chenery and Strout, 'Foreign Assistance: Reply', p. 914.

[31] Chenery and Strout, 'Foreign Assistance', p. 679.

Much more serious, in the light of the magnitudes involved, is the general tendency to bypass the problem of foreign indebtedness. Aid inflows are viewed in net terms, with the result that for many developing countries, estimates of capital requirements are heavily understated by the amount of external debt service. This means, in effect, that the question of an adequate aid supply is minimized or ignored, as are the basic determinants of a country's own capacity to handle the foreign debt created by such inflows.

The aggregate models also tend to underplay the role of aid in affecting the economic structure of the recipient country. This is especially true for Fei–Paauw, with its broad assumption that the overriding purpose of foreign assistance is to supplement domestic savings. But even the Chenery–Strout model, despite its emphasis on bottleneck constraints and on aid as a separate factor of production, remains quite vague about the process of structural change and the impact of aid on that process. Another way of making this point is to stress that, in the Harrod–Domar tradition, these models assume a constancy and independence of key variables which are unlikely to reflect conditions of the real world. Changing aid inflows, for example, may well exert a strong influence on levels of domestic savings;[32] 'savings are a function of investment in the sense that savings will be forthcoming for profitable...investment opportunities';[33] and structural change implies shifts in absorptive capacity and capital–output ratios, which emerge no less as targets than as constraints in foreign aid policy. Put in still other terms, there is much to be said for the view that 'the really essential issue...is how to facilitate the various learning processes (learning to save, to invest, to export, to engage in efficient import substitution) with the help of foreign aid, rather than how to calculate foreign aid requirements if we know these parameters'.[34]

Unravelling the mystery of these learning processes is a formidable task indeed. To say that the aggregate aid models are not designed to perform the task makes it no less true that they shed little light on this central problem. In the same connection, they abstract from the income distribution and non-economic aspects of development, and they ignore its micro-economic aspects, notably the performance of major sectors and industries in a developing economy.[35] The models, in this sense, are at once too global and too narrow; they provide no answers to some of the key questions of foreign aid impact.

On balance, however, the models reveal much that is important about the

---

[32] For the thesis that foreign aid, when in abundant supply, is apt to be used as a substitute for domestic savings, see M. A. Rahman, 'The Welfare Economics of Foreign Aid', *Pakistan Development Review*, Summer 1967, and 'Foreign Capital and Domestic Savings: A Test of Haavelmo's Hypothesis with Cross-Country Data', *Review of Economics and Statistics*, February 1968.

[33] Mikesell, *Economics of Foreign Aid*, p. 94.

[34] Fei and Ranis, 'Foreign Assistance: Comment', p. 910.

[35] For an interesting attempt to construct a development model which combines the inputs of economic, social and political forces, see I. Adelman and C. T. Morris, 'An Econometric Model of Socio-Economic and Political Change in Underdeveloped Countries', *American Economic Review*, December 1968. Ironically enough, the model takes no account of foreign aid.

role of aid in the complex growth process. They identify a number of strategic growth factors, they explore their implications for the effectiveness of foreign aid, and they draw significant conclusions for overall aid policy.

In addition, it is worth pointing out that related analysis and criticism place the aid models in clearer perspective. A notable example are the disaggregated programming models which have been applied to particular developing countries:[36] 'these multisectoral studies give more logic and empirical content to the import, export, and investment constraints than is possible in an aggregate model'.[37] Equally substantial are the advances that have been made in clarifying the debt problems associated with foreign aid inflows. Three facets of this many-sided relationship deserve special mention in the present context. They are: the rapid accumulation of external debt – typically ignored in the aid models – which has been shown to pose grave problems for developing countries that seek to reduce their long-term reliance on foreign assistance;[38] the concept of 'debt servicing capacity', which has been extended well beyond the debt service–exchange earnings ratio to embrace such basic performance criteria as the GNP growth rate, the capital–output ratio, the marginal propensity to save, and export growth relative to imports;[39] and, with the appropriate simplifying assumptions, the generalization of these tests of economic performance into foreign debt models, e.g., the debt cycle and the critical rate of interest, setting out the conditions under which a country's debt service obligations could become unmanageable.[40]

---

[36] See especially W. Tims, 'Growth Model for the Pakistan Economy', mimeo. (Karachi: Planning Commission, 1965); J. Bergsman and A. S. Manne, 'An Almost Consistent Intertemporal Model for India's Fourth and Fifth Plans', in *The Theory and Design of Economic Development*, eds. I. Adelman and E. Thorbecke (Baltimore, 1966).

[37] Chenery and Strout, 'Foreign Assistance: Reply', p. 913.

[38] These problems are incisively treated in M. A. Rahman, 'The Pakistan Perspective Plan and the Objective of Elimination of Dependence on Foreign Assistance', *Pakistan Development Review*, Autumn 1967, and 'Perspective Planning for Self-Assured Growth: An Approach to Foreign Capital from a Recipient's Point of View', *Pakistan Development Review*, Spring 1968. See also UNCTAD, *The Outlook for Debt Service*, TD/7/Supp. 5 (Geneva, October 1967).

[39] See Mikesell, *Economics of Foreign Aid*, ch. 4.

[40] The 'debt cycle' describes the time pattern that evolves from initial borrowing to final liquidation of foreign indebtedness; alternative assumptions about interest rates, debt maturity, savings and investment will affect the amount of borrowing as well as the period of indebtedness. D. Avramovic et al., *Economic Growth and External Debt* (Baltimore, 1964), ch. 5. The 'critical interest rate' has been defined as the highest rate that a country can afford to pay on external borrowing without producing a faster rise in interest charges than in national income. In symbolic terms, $i'' = [r(s_o^a - s')]/(s_o^a - kr)$, where i'' is the critical interest rate, r the growth rate of Gross Domestic Product, s_o^a the initial average savings rate, s' the marginal savings rate, and k the incremental capital–output ratio; thus, other things equal, the country's ability to manage its foreign debt will vary directly with the marginal savings rate and inversely with the capital–output ratio. See J. P. Hayes, 'Long-Run Growth and Debt Servicing Problems: Projection of Debt Servicing Burdens and the Conditions of Debt Failure', in the same volume, pp. 154–92.

Economic transformation

All things considered, foreign aid can best be viewed as economically productive to the extent that it serves as an instrument for transforming resources within an underdeveloped country. A variety of broad indices are readily available to gauge this impact. There is, for example, Hollis Chenery's 'marginal productivity of assistance – as measured by the ratio of the cumulative increment in GNP over the period to the corresponding increment in capital inflow'.[41] There are also the growth criteria used by Jacoby: the 'target attainment criterion', relating the actual growth of the developing country to the target growth rates set by its government; the 'historical comparison criterion', comparing actual growth rates in the periods before and after development aid began; and the 'contemporary comparison criterion', relating the rise in GNP per dollar of aid to the corresponding increase achieved in comparable countries.[42] These are precise and interesting measures, to be sure. But they give a rather simplistic picture of the effectiveness of aid, for they really beg the question of its causal role in the development process.

The concept of 'economic transformation' is at the heart of the matter. It is, of course, far easier to express than to define. Perhaps the most fruitful first step is to specify a few of the things that transformation is *not* intended to mean. It does not imply, nor does the evidence appear to support the need for, a universal uprooting of basic ownership and operating patterns of production; indeed, one can logically argue that a prime test of the effectiveness of foreign aid is whether it makes rapid and sustained economic growth possible without the massive disruptions occasioned by revolutionary upheaval.[43] Nor does transformation mean 'industrialization', unless the latter term is clearly understood to embrace the entire productive process. Transformation, as against 'industrial development', is 'an economy-wide phenomenon, applying to agriculture and the service trades as well as to manufacturing'.[44] Again, transformation is not a uniform process for all developing countries, or for any such country in all stages of underdevelopment; given the complexities of economic growth, it could hardly be otherwise.

What, then, is the essence of this process? On the basis of the foregoing analysis, it seems reasonable to suggest that economic transformation includes at least four key ingredients: the steady and substantial rise of broad indicators such as real per capita GNP, the marginal savings rate, the export growth rate,

[41] H. B. Chenery, 'Foreign Assistance and Economic Development', in *Capital Movements and Economic Development*, eds. J. H. Adler and P. W. Kuznets (New York, 1967), p. 272.
[42] Jacoby, *United States Aid to Taiwan*, p. 16. The 'contemporary comparison criterion' differs materially from Chenery's 'marginal productivity of assistance'. For one thing, the former is not a measure of marginal product; the aid figure used in the index is a cumulative total, not an increment, for the period in question. Secondly, the Jacoby index does not incorporate the total rise in GNP over the period, but the rise attributable to aid; the relevant figure is that which bears the same ratio to the GNP increase as aid bears to gross investment in the developing country (p. 156).
[43] This is not to deny that a total restructuring of productive activity may be appropriate, or even necessary, in particular circumstances.   [44] Johnson, *Economic Policies*, p. 46.

and the volume of new investment; continuing intersectoral advance marked by improved labour and managerial skills, sizable import substitution, greater capacity to service foreign debt, and systematic absorption of surplus manpower into an expanding work force;[45] a strengthening of attitudes and institutions underlying the increases and shifts in aggregate output; and a sustained rise in productivity, with special significance attaching to the export sphere.[46]

There is also the important question of income distribution. It can hardly be doubted that the persistence of gross inequalities in income is incompatible with any welfare approach to economic transformation; or that such inequalities carry the seeds of extreme social and political instability. There is, however, the further proposition that the 'conventional wisdom' may be in error insofar as it accepts widely skewed incomes as a general precondition for rapid economic growth; it is not at all inconceivable that for many developing countries the most direct route to high savings and rapid growth is not through the narrow band of high-income recipients, but rather through strong consumer demand resting on a broader income base.[47]

The vital point to stress at this juncture is that foreign assistance bears a close reciprocal relationship to economic transformation. At any given time, aid is effective to the degree that it acts as a catalyst in the development process; while over time, the economic change induced by aid, among other inputs, will determine whether and how fast the need for aid can disappear. *If one views foreign aid principally in terms of the transition from economic stagnation to self-sustaining growth, the measure of its success is the behavioural and institutional transformation that the recipient country has undergone during the period of aid inflow.*[48] Moreover, transformation has its non-economic roots too, increasing social mobility, for instance, as well as an expanding range of participation in national decision-making; and aid programmes are most likely to succeed when they are highly responsive to changing requirements throughout the transformation process.

[45] For an illuminating discussion of structural transformation, see W. G. Demas, *The Economics of Development in Small Countries with Special Reference to the Caribbean* (Montreal, 1965), chs. 1–2.

[46] Bruton is very emphatic on this last point: '"Structural [i.e., intersectoral] change" is not enough if new activities have costs above world prices...' If productivity does not rise, 'there will be no increase in exports, there will be only inefficient activities...Productivity growth...indeed would appear to be the central notion rather than structural change.' 'The Two Gap Approach to Aid and Development', Research Memorandum No. 21, unpublished mimeo. (Williamstown, Mass.: Williams College, Center for Development Economics, June 1968), pp. 23–4.

[47] The authors are indebted to Professor C. J. Kurien for a cogent formulation of this demand thesis. See also the following articles reprinted in *The Economics of Underdevelopment*, eds. A. N. Agarwala and S. P. Singh (New York, 1963): P. A. Baran, 'On the Political Economy of Backwardness'; G. M. Meier, 'The Problem of Limited Economic Development'; R. Nurkse, 'Some International Aspects of the Problem of Economic Development'.

[48] It is, of course, possible to argue that self-sustained growth is not necessarily the ideal objective of foreign assistance. There might, for example, be a conflict between that goal and minimum per capita income. But to adopt the income objective could be to imply that aid should go on indefinitely. See G. M. Meier, *The International Economics of Development Theory and Policy* (New York, 1968), p. 119n.

On both sides of the 'aid-transformation' link, the 'micro' dimension is no less significant than the 'macro'. Indeed, the latter merges inevitably into the former, since aid flows and economic change take concrete shape only in relation to particular countries, periods of time, types of assistance and points of impact. This does not mean that every donor's and recipient's aid programme is so unique as to preclude generalization about the role of aid in economic development. It does mean that no theory of foreign aid can be valid without incorporating major micro tests of economic performance.

Jacoby's list covers much of the ground: the 'development strategy' criterion, assessing 'the degree to which allocations of aid and of domestic investment among sectors of the economy approached the optimum'; the 'project selection' criterion, appraising 'the degree to which selections of aid projects approached the optimum'; the 'instrumental structure' criterion, judging the structure of a donor's aid programme in relation to 'statutory purposes, resource inputs, and financial terms'; and the 'administrative policy' criterion, evaluating 'the degree to which actual aid administration conformed to the ideal, given the practical constraints upon policy'.[49] But each of these tests has its limitations.

In the face of practical difficulties with the principle of equi-marginal social return, it becomes necessary to adopt 'proxy criteria' for both inter- and intra-sectoral distribution of foreign resources; but proxies like capital–output ratios, capacity utilization and cost–benefit analysis are by no means free of short-comings.[50] Nor is there much precision in efforts to measure the effectiveness of specific instruments and administrative techniques of foreign aid policy. Furthermore, there are real measurement difficulties in using such important tests as productivity, employment and institutional development in particular industries – the micro counterparts of the above-noted macro tests of economic transformation. And it takes a large amount and variety of micro-analysis, far more than is now available, to paint a concrete picture of foreign aid impact.

In short, while much is already known, a great deal of mystery continues to surround the role of external resources in the development process. This is especially so in regard to the economic and non-economic mainsprings of transformation, as well as the effects of aid-giving on individual industries and income groups in the recipient country. The present study suffers, unavoidably, through reliance on a highly imperfect theoretical framework. Then, too, the study's perspective has been narrowed – by both choice and necessity – through only partial application of that framework to the aid experience of Pakistan.

[49] Jacoby, *United States Aid to Taiwan*, pp. 16–17. See also Mikesell, *Economics of Foreign Aid*, ch. 5.
[50] Judgments on project selection raise some of the more serious conceptual questions. See, for example, H. W. Singer, 'External Aid: For Plans or Projects?', *Economic Journal*, September 1965; A. R. Prest and R. Turvey, 'Cost–Benefit Analysis: A Survey', *Economic Journal*, December 1965; A. O. Hirschman, *Development Projects Observed* (Washington, D.C., 1967), ch. 6.

3. Foreign aid flows to Pakistan: 1950–68

Foreign aid in the present context means grants and loans available on an inter-governmental basis primarily for economic development. In general, therefore, it does not include military assistance or relief supplies.

Major types of foreign aid

Three functional categories of foreign aid can be conveniently distinguished: project aid, technical assistance and commodity (or programme) aid. The first is normally provided for specific projects forming part of a development programme, that is, after a determination of economic and technical feasibility for each project submitted.[1] Project aid falls, in turn, into two classes, capital aid and technical assistance: the former covers the cost of equipment for projects; while the latter includes expert advisory service in the field, training facilities in donor countries, and equipment for instruction and demonstration.[2] Commodity aid comprises food, raw materials and other imports obtained without reference to any particular project. It can make a significant contribution to economic development in several ways, such as increasing the utilization of productive capacity and generating counterpart local funds used for development purposes.

Most of the aid received by Pakistan has been bilateral in nature, and much of it has come from the United States. But multilateral aid has been substantial ever since the World Bank began to support infra-structure investments made under the First Five-Year Plan. And Pakistan now receives most of its foreign economic assistance through the hybrid 'consortium' device organized by IBRD in 1960.[3] The Consortium consists of Belgium, Canada, France, Italy, Japan, the Netherlands, the United Kingdom, the United States, West Germany, the World Bank, and the International Development Association (IDA).

The procedure followed by the Consortium involves two main stages prior to actual commencement of aid flows. There is usually one meeting a year to assess Pakistan's economic performance and its requirements of foreign exchange over the year to come; planned development schemes are scrutinized with

[1] Different procedures are followed by different aid-giving countries and agencies in extending project assistance. Canada and the United States, for example, sign a formal statement with Pakistan describing mutual obligations, the purposes and the work programme relating to every project. On the other hand, Australia and New Zealand require no such formal agreements.

[2] Needless to say, not all technical assistance is linked to a specific project. Foreign school teachers may, for instance, serve on a more flexible basis to help implement a developing country's educational programme. However, the bulk of technical assistance to Pakistan is related to particular projects.

[3] For an excellent discussion of the Pakistan Consortium, see J. White, *Pledged to Development: A Study of International Consortia and the Strategy of Aid* (London, 1967), ch. 3.

a view to deciding the volume of assistance the Consortium members are prepared to offer. A pledging session normally follows, at which each member sets a total aid figure. Then, through bilateral agreements with Pakistan, each donor settles the terms and conditions for financing the project or projects which it selects; this provides the commitment.[4] At that point, the project is ready to be implemented, and the disbursement of aid funds follows.[5]

Aid is also provided by non-Consortium countries, including the USSR, the People's Republic of China, Yugoslavia, Sweden, Czechoslovakia, Poland and Switzerland. They follow a somewhat different procedure. After bilateral negotiations with Pakistan, each donor decides on the amount of aid it will offer. Then there is a pledge known as a 'frame agreement'. Finally, the projects are selected, and commitments are made to finance them.[6]

Trends in foreign aid

Foreign aid has played a key role in the economic development of Pakistan, however difficult it may be to quantify this relationship. Not only did it supply resources which could not be mobilized easily in an economy with low per capita income and savings; more significantly, it put at the disposal of Pakistan scarce foreign exchange without which basic investment and consumption needs could not have been satisfied. It is not surprising, therefore, that foreign aid, investment and national income have moved together over many of the past eighteen years. Table 1 compares six selected years, from pre-plan through Third Plan, and it clearly reveals a rising trend in foreign aid to Pakistan.[7]

The country received little aid until 1951/2. But with the shift towards intense development activity, increased reliance on foreign resources became virtually inevitable. By the beginning of the First Five-Year Plan, about 19 per cent of Pakistan's imports and 35 per cent of its development expenditure were being financed by foreign aid. By the Second Plan, dependence on aid had increased further: in 1959/60, it accounted for 31 per cent of imports and 38 per cent of total development expenditure; more than halfway through the plan, these proportions were 56 and 42 per cent respectively. In 1967/8, the corresponding

[4] In recent years, the Consortium has also been a focal point for stimulating the flow of commodity aid to Pakistan. See Chapter 10 below.

[5] The Consortium procedure tends, in fact, to take much longer than the above sequence suggests. Typically, several months will elapse between the time of US or IBRD pledging and the actual commitment of aid funds. Once the funds are committed, it may be three years before work begins on the selected schemes. The lag between project signing and project disbursement can consume another three years. And there is a sizable lag, again averaging some three years, between conception of the project and its consideration by a Consortium member. (Non-project, or commodity, aid moves somewhat more quickly through the Consortium pipeline.)

[6] It should be noted that Consortium countries have also given assistance to Pakistan outside the Consortium arrangements.

[7] Aid-to-Pakistan figures corrected for price changes are not available; to make such a correction would be an incredibly complex task. The resulting deficiency is, of course, mitigated to the degree that the aid data are expressed as percentages of uncorrected figures on national income, investment spending and related aggregates.

Table 1. *Foreign aid compared with income, development expenditure and imports: selected fiscal years*

Item	1952	1956	1960	1964	1967	1968
Foreign aid (Rs. millions)[a]	5	472	1,068	3,105	3,334	3,570
Proportion of gross national product (%)	0.02	2.1	3.4	7.5	5.7	5.8
Proportion of development expenditure (%)	0.5	34.8	38.1	42.2	37.7	34.0
Proportion of imports (%)	0.1	18.6	31.1	55.8	47.0	49.8

SOURCE: Pakistan Planning Commission.

[a] Includes Indus Basin aid and US surplus agricultural commodities provided under Public Law 480. At the official rate, one Pakistani rupee was worth US $0.30 before 1955 and has equalled $0.21 since then.

ratios were 50 and 34 per cent. Meanwhile, the volume of aid had risen from 2.1 per cent of GNP in 1956 to 7.5 per cent in 1964; this ratio stood at 5.8 per cent in 1968.[8]

As a matter of fact, foreign aid to Pakistan recorded a fairly steady growth until 1965. But the Indo-Pakistan War brought the suspension of US aid; though foreign assistance has risen since 1966, the increase has been modest, and the scale and terms of future aid are in doubt. Tables 2 and 3 present the grant and loan commitments made by all donors between the pre-plan and third plan periods.

Key aid sources and uses

Total economic assistance received by Pakistan up to 31 March 1967 amounted to approximately $4.7 billion, of which $1.3 billion was in the form of grants and $3.4 billion in loans.[9] In the early stages of Pakistan's development, grants

[8] This pattern of change is broad indeed. By way of qualification, it is worth pointing out that the observed trend in aid ratios is partly a function of the particular years selected for comparison; and that on a year to year basis, growth rates in GNP apparently show little correlation with rates of growth in foreign aid since 1963. But Pakistan's continuing high dependence on aid remains clear, regardless of differences traceable to particular benchmark years. Nor should it seem strange to find a low direct correlation between annual growth rates in foreign aid and GNP: for one thing, aid impact would be more likely to show up in a lagged relationship with GNP; in any event, annual fluctuations in so aggregate a figure as GNP are bound to reflect a multitude of changes which obscure or counteract the total effect of aid inflows. For an interesting regression analysis that suggests a substantial positive link between aid and GNP in developing countries generally and Pakistan in particular, see G. F. Papanek and S. C. Jakubiak, 'Aid and Development', a paper presented in June 1970 (after the time of writing) at the Dubrovnik Conference of the Development Advisory Service of Harvard University.

[9] Pakistan CSO, *20 Years of Pakistan in Statistics, 1947–1967* (Karachi, 1968), pp. 322–3. These figures exclude $1.1 billion in PL 480 transfers under Title 1; US AID, *Pakistan's Economic Development and United States Assistance* (Karachi, 1967), p. 22. For a useful brief survey of foreign aid to Pakistan from 1960 to 1968, see F. Kahnert et al., *Agriculture and Related Industries in Pakistan: Prospects and Requirements until 1975* (Paris, 1970), pp. 37–53.

accounted for most of the foreign aid, followed by loans repayable in Pakistani rupees. The chief form of assistance available currently is loans repayable in foreign exchange.

As far as grants are concerned, the largest single contribution was made by the United States, which provided more than three-quarters of the total; Canada was second with roughly one-seventh; and Australia third with about 3 per cent. The contribution of other countries was negligible. The United States was also the leading lender, with nearly half the total, followed by international agencies with some 22 per cent, West Germany 9 per cent, the United Kingdom 7 per cent, and Japan 6 per cent. Table 4 summarizes the picture in terms of major aid sources.

The statistical record of the Second Five-Year Plan reveals that the industrial

Table 2. *Foreign grant commitments to Pakistan, by source up to 31 March 1967* (*thousands of US dollars*)

Country/agency	Before 1st plan	1st plan (1955–60)	2nd plan (1960–5)	3rd plan[a] (1965–70)	Total up to 1966/7
Australia	26,342	2,790	7,090	2,225	38,447
Canada	42,340	62,850	65,515	16,254	186,959
Japan	—	—	834	—	834
New Zealand	3,130	2,490	1,112	—	6,732
Sweden	—	—	3,000	—	3,000
United Kingdom	1,150	3,630	5,696	—	10,476
United States					
Project and non-project grants	123,123	469,538	160,662	9,767	763,090
PL 480, Title II	84,559	36,841	50,159	2,850	174,409
PL 480, Title III	6,003	25,922	20,156	4,993	57,074
UN and specialized agencies	3,470	5,150	4,311	—	12,931
UN Special Fund	—	5,730	6,131	—	11,861
Ford Foundation	—	17,230	19,329	—	36,559
Others	200	4,600	30	—	4,830
TOTAL	*290,317*	*636,771*	*344,025*	*36,089*	*1,307,202*

SOURCE: Pakistan CSO, *20 Years of Pakistan in Statistics, 1947–1967* (Karachi, 1968), pp. 322–3.

[a] Figures relate to the first two years.

sector was the single largest recipient of foreign project aid, closely followed by transport and communications, and then by water and power. Total project assistance committed during that period was about $1.3 billion, of which only $751 million or 58 per cent was disbursed. Some three-fifths of total disbursed aid was used in the public (as against private) sector; 37 per cent was utilized in industry, 35 per cent in transport and communications, and 20 per cent in water and power. Details of sectoral distribution are shown in Table 5.

Non-project aid, by contrast, shows a much more rapid rate of disbursement. Its greatest upsurge occurred during the Second Plan, when commitments

Table 3. *Foreign loan commitments to Pakistan, by source up to 31 March 1967* (*thousands of US dollars*)

Country/agency	Before 1st plan	1st plan (1955–60)	2nd plan (1960–5)	3rd plan (1965–70)[a]	Total up to 1966/7
Belgium	—	—	520	620	1,140
Canada	—	—	12,351	45,362	57,713
China	—	—	30,000	25,710	55,710
Czechoslovakia	—	—	—	17,130	17,130
Denmark	—	—	7,410	2,170	9,580
France	—	—	29,000	24,950	53,950
Italy	—	—	5,910	34,290	40,200
Japan	—	—	147,477	60,000	207,477
Netherlands	—	—	13,180	3,260	16,440
Poland	—	—	—	4,100	4,100
Switzerland	—	—	—	3,300	3,300
Sweden	—	—	—	4,833	4,833
United Kingdom	28,000	28,000	123,420	44,800	224,220
United States					
DLF	—	125,158	97,018	—	222,176
AID	—	—	700,898	240,800	941,698
Eximbank	35,000	70,830	43,910	6,780	156,520
Suppliers' credit	42,290	58,010	52,295	23,480	176,075
USSR	—	—	39,900	32,450	72,350
West Germany	—	—	224,628	70,000	294,628
Yugoslavia	—	—	29,550	26,050	55,600
IBRD	58,230	92,650	209,440	51,500	411,820
IDA	—	—	246,040	83,200	329,240
IFC	—	1,380	9,520	—	10,900
TOTAL	*163,520*	*376,028*	*2,022,467*	*804,785*	*3,366,800*

SOURCE: Pakistan CSO, *20 Years of Pakistan in Statistics, 1947–1967* (Karachi, 1968), pp. 322–3.

[a] Figures relate to the first two years.

Table 4. *Foreign economic assistance to Pakistan by major donors, up to 31 March 1967* (*thousands of US dollars*)

Country/agency	Grants		Loans	
	Amount	% of total	Amount	% of total
Canada	186,959	14.30	57,713	1.71
Japan	834	0.06	207,477	6.16
United Kingdom	10,476	0.80	224,220	6.66
United States[a]	994,573	76.08	1,496,469	44.45
West Germany	—	—	294,628	8.75
International organizations	24,792	1.90	751,960	22.33
Others	89,568	6.85	334,333	9.93
TOTAL	*1,307,202*	*100.00[b]*	*3,366,800*	*100.00[b]*

SOURCE: Pakistan CSO, *20 Years of Pakistan in Statistics, 1947–1967* (Karachi, 1968), pp. 322–3.

[a] Excludes PL 480 assistance under Title I.
[b] Figures do not add up to total because of rounding.

Table 5. *Foreign project aid to Pakistan by sectors: Second Five-Year Plan* (*millions of dollars*)

Sector	Public sector		Private sector		Total	
	Commit-ment	Disburse-ment	Commit-ment	Disburse-ment	Commit-ment	Disburse-ment
Agriculture	17.1	20.0	27.3	0.3	44.4	20.3
Water and power	208.1	122.8	26.1	29.3	234.2	152.1
Industries	137.7	78.9	320.4	202.4	458.1	281.3
Fuels and minerals	30.5	15.1	27.8	9.3	58.3	24.4
Transport and communi-cations	313.1	196.5	108.0	66.9	421.1	263.4
Physical planning and housing	57.1	6.1	—	—	57.1	6.1
Education	13.4	0.3	—	—	13.4	0.3
Health	14.3	2.9	—	—	14.3	2.9
TOTAL	791.3	442.6	509.6	308.2	1,300.9	750.8

SOURCE: Pakistan Ministry of Finance, *The Budget in Brief, 1966–67* (Rawalpindi, 1966), section I, pp. 79–80.

totalled $673.2 million and no less than 96 per cent was actually disbursed.[10] The United States was providing roughly 90 per cent of such assistance in the first year of the plan; by 1964/5, about one-fifth was coming from non-US sources, mainly Canada, West Germany and the United Kingdom.[11]

External debt liability

Given the volume of foreign loans, external debt liability is a function of the repayment period, the rate of interest and the degree of loan-tying.[12] Pakistan was able to secure most of the foreign assistance required during the first plan period in the form of outright grants or 'soft' loans, so that the burden of repayment remained insignificant in those years. But a different trend has developed since 1960, with most foreign aid (apart from PL 480) taking the form of loans repayable in foreign exchange.[13] IDA and US credits aside, the

[10] Pakistan Ministry of Finance, *The Budget in Brief, 1966–67* (Rawalpindi, 1966), p. 79. 'The availability of commodity aid which is flexible and fast disbursing has... been a major factor in the success of the Second Plan and of the import liberalization programme.' Pakistan Ministry of Finance, *Final Evaluation of the Second Five-Year Plan (1960–65)* (Karachi, 1966), p. 28.   [11] *Final Evaluation of the Second Plan*, p. 29.

[12] The link between loan-tying and external debt liability is not a direct one, to be sure. But it does open the door to 'tied prices' well above those prevailing in world markets; this will mean a reduction in the real value of foreign loans (unless the level of available aid is itself assumed to be closely dependent on the tying). To that extent, there will be continuing pressure on the debtor country to increase its external borrowings.

[13] Since 1967/8, an increasing amount of Title I sales under PL 480 must be repaid in US dollars. In November 1970, after the time of writing, Pakistan signed a PL 480 agreement providing for $80.7 million in Title I transfers; the local currency component was only Rs. 99.9 million, the equivalent of roughly $21 million. Pakistan Ministry of Finance, *Pakistan Economic Survey, 1970–71* (Islamabad, 1971), p. 132.

bulk of the loans obtained through the consortium are rather 'hard' in terms of interest rates and repayment periods.[14] As a result, Pakistan's burden of annual repayment increased from $17.2 million in 1960/1 to $95.7 million in 1966/7. Furthermore, the country's foreign exchange position did not improve as rapidly as its debt-servicing liability worsened; consequently, repayment liability rose from 3.6 per cent of foreign exchange earnings in 1960/1 to 13.1 per cent in 1966/7. Table 6 illustrates the severity of this emerging debt problem.

Table 6. *External debt-servicing and foreign exchange earnings in Pakistan: actual figures to 30 June 1967 and projections up to the end of the Third Plan* (*thousands of US dollars*)

Fiscal year	Foreign exchange earnings			External debt service	Debt service ratio %
	Goods	Services	Total		
1961	404,439	71,148	475,587	17,157	3.6
1962	412,587	84,735	497,322	32,618	6.2
1963	478,989	97,818	576,807	47,586	8.2
1964	482,412	93,786	576,198	61,509	10.7
1965	518,889	110,250	629,139	62,223	9.9
1966	581,448	105,336	686,784	73,689	10.7
1967	593,544	136,437	729,981	95,718	13.1
1968	653,562	147,000	800,562	148,023	18.5
1969	755,748	153,300	909,048	169,650	18.7
1970	854,175	157,500	1,011,675	196,100	19.4

SOURCE: Pakistan, *Report of the Working Group on Debt Burden* (Islamabad, 1968), p. 37.

Most of the aid now received by Pakistan is tied to goods and services of the donor.[15] This has been a major cause of aggravated foreign exchange difficulties in the Second Five-Year Plan. The tying of foreign credits is estimated to have raised the average price of procurements for Pakistan by about 12 per cent.[16] More striking is the fact, as shown in Table 7, that major items of iron and steel, representing a large part of non-agricultural commodity assistance, have been overvalued by amounts ranging from 41 to 111 per cent.[17]

[14] See State Bank of Pakistan, *External Debt Servicing Liability* (Karachi, 1965); Pakistan, *Report of the Working Group on Debt Burden* (Islamabad, 1968).

[15] The World Bank Group, IBRD, IDA and IFC, is a notable exception to this rule.

[16] M. Haq, 'Tied Credits – A Quantitative Analysis', in *Capital Movements and Economic Development*, eds. J. Adler and P. W. Kuznets (New York, 1967). For a useful discussion of problems and policy implications of tied aid, see J. N. Bhagwhati, *The Tying of Aid*, a study prepared for the United Nations Conference on Trade and Development, TD/7/Supp. 4 (Geneva, November 1967).

[17] This gross overpricing is not entirely attributable to loan-tying. For some time, the United States has been urging Pakistan to review its procurement procedure and purchase iron and steel elsewhere – precisely because US prices are highly non-competitive. However, the Pakistan government has so far declined to remove iron and steel from the US list of available commodities, on the grounds that it would pose serious administrative problems. Not, apparently, until early 1969 did the government fully grasp this fact of enormous cost and indicate a willingness to consider alternative procurement patterns.

Table 7. *Tied commodity assistance to Pakistan: estimates of overvaluation for iron and steel, 1967 (prices in rupees per long ton)*

Item	Tied source	Cheapest international source	Increase in cost due to tied credit (%)
M.S. billets	633	332	91
M.S. plates	808	469	72
M.S. strips	1,050	430	44
Structurals (channels)	930	555	68
G.P. sheets	1,073	746	44
G.C. sheets	1,066	754	41
Wire rod (6 mm. diam.)	905	429	111
Nail wire (bright 6 s.w.g.)	976	495	97

SOURCE: Pakistan Planning Commission, *Memorandum for the Pakistan Consortium, 1968–69* (Rawalpindi, 1968), p. 71.

For the developing countries generally, it is safe to predict that the debt liability problem will become very grave if vigorous action is not taken to soften and untie foreign loans. Even in Pakistan, where economic performance has been relatively strong, the outlook is far from encouraging. 'Despite some welcome improvement in the terms of credits from a few Consortium members, the average interest rate on loans has gone up, the average repayment period has shrunk, the proportion of tied credits has increased sharply and the grant element in foreign assistance has virtually disappeared.'[18] Furthermore, projections show that the ratio of external debt to foreign exchange earnings will rise to nearly 20 per cent by 1970, about double the ratio in 1965 (Table 6).[19]

[18] Pakistan Planning Commission, *Memorandum for the Pakistan Consortium, 1968–69* (Rawalpindi, 1968), p. 32. See also C. R. Frank, Jr. and W. R. Cline, *Debt Servicing and Foreign Assistance: An Analysis of Problems and Prospects in Less Developed Countries*, US AID Discussion Paper No. 19 (Washington, D.C., June 1969), pp. 21–31.

[19] There are those who regard 20 per cent as an acceptable figure with which any economy should be able to cope – perhaps because it is by no means unusual in the developing world. However, 20 per cent represents a significant problem for Pakistan. In this context, it would be useful to isolate a country's 'free' foreign exchange earnings, and to show that external debt servicing is a much larger proportion of such resources than of total earnings in foreign exchange. But the distinction between free and committed earnings is extremely difficult to draw. In Pakistan's case, one could presumably calculate the free figure by deducting from total earnings such items as export bonus receipts not controlled by the government, exchange required for food imports, barter earnings earmarked for other imports, and government-guaranteed dividend and interest obligations to foreign private investors; the 'adjusted' debt–service ratio would then climb well beyond the 20 per cent level. However, no such figure is presently available for Pakistan. The 'unadjusted' debt service ratio is, for all its shortcomings, a convenient shorthand way of describing the repayment problem.

The real cost of foreign aid

In point of fact, the terms of foreign aid to Pakistan have left much to be desired over the entire period of aid flow. Measuring the 'real cost' incurred by donors provides a revealing picture of this problem.[20]

What is needed is a reasonable criterion for judging donor sacrifice or concession. The choice of a particular criterion is difficult: it must so relate the multitudinous forms and terms of aid that they can be meaningfully aggregated. Valuable work has been done along these lines by John Pincus and Goran Ohlin, among others.[21] Each achieves a common basis by calculating the discounted present values of various types of loans and grants. Pincus' especially useful contribution is his handling of US commodity aid.

The general treatment of loans and grants is quite straightforward in theory. But complications arise in the selection of appropriate discount rates. Ohlin points out that a case can be made for using the social rate of return to capital (or opportunity cost) in the donor country, although he believes that the donor's borrowing rate is probably a more suitable discount rate if the object is to reduce aid to a common denominator rather than seek the actual, but virtually unmeasurable, cost of aid.[22]

Pincus uses the mortgage rate, and the long-term bond rate plus 1 per cent, to obtain the donor's rate of return on capital.[23] The mortgage rate would seem to give a reasonable approximation to the cost of long-term capital. However, it is not a good rate for discounting comparatively short-term loans, for example, those up to ten years; that is, it is important to relate the discount rate to the duration of the loan if accurate discounted present values are to be obtained.

Pincus also discounts loans at 10 per cent, to approximate the rate of return on capital in the less-developed countries; at 7 per cent, the highest average lending rate of any member of the OECD Development Assistance Committee (DAC); and at the IBRD lending rate, in order to obtain a uniform basis for relating loans from donors having different domestic borrowing rates. These produce interesting but not really meaningful results, since they do not measure any donor's actual costs. It may not be possible to discover the ideal rate for discounting, but a figure which represents each donor's cost of capital should yield at least a rough estimate of the real cost of aid for that donor.

[20] It would be a formidable undertaking to calculate the 'real benefits' of foreign assistance to Pakistan. In financial terms, one would have to know the rate of return on capital there; but no single figure would be appropriate, since the range of variation is so wide. Indeed, if one views this financial test as the rate which Pakistan would be required to pay in world commercial markets, it is open to question whether such a rate actually exists.

[21] J. A. Pincus, *Economic Aid and International Cost Sharing* (Baltimore, 1965); G. Ohlin, *Foreign Aid Policies Reconsidered* (Paris, 1966). See Appendix 1 below for further discussion of the literature. And see M. F. Loutfi, 'An Analysis of the Cost of Foreign Aid to the Donor Country: The Case of Japan' – an unpublished Ph.D. dissertation submitted to the University of California (Berkeley) in 1970, after the time of writing.

[22] Ohlin, *Foreign Aid Policies*, p. 72. The opportunity cost of capital in the United States and West Germany has been estimated to be as high as 15 to 20 per cent. See R. Solow, *Capital Theory and the Rate of Interest* (Amsterdam, 1963), lecture III.

[23] Pincus, *Economic Aid*, pp. 124, 131.

It would, of course, be preferable not to use one discount rate per country for its cumulative aid total, but instead to use either one rate to cover aid outstanding at a particular point in time, or a different rate for each loan. However, the latter would be a massive task, and it is very difficult to obtain reliable statistics for the former. Ideally, it would be much better to use opportunity cost, rather than any borrowing rate, but that would be even more impractical.

Typically, no account is taken of the special risk involved in lending to the developing countries. And choosing a single discount rate to allow for this also leads to distortion in judging the cost of aid: a defaulting project or country would have its cost underestimated, and aid to a non-defaulting project or country would have been overly costly by comparison.

Loans and grants of surplus agricultural commodities obviously merit special treatment. Pincus evaluates US transfers under Title I of PL 480 as 80 per cent grant, 20 per cent loan; he does not include local currency counterpart funds as aid.

The tying of aid is not considered for two reasons: virtually all countries tie their aid, so that estimating its cost to the recipient, or its benefit to the donor, would not have much effect on relative donor cost, which is the basis for burden-sharing (although, of course, any country offering untied aid would have its costs undervalued); secondly, in view of commodity differences in quality and function, it is very difficult to estimate the cost imposed on the recipient by tying. Nevertheless, to exclude loan-tying is to produce exaggerated estimates of the real cost of aid to donors.

Tables are provided by Ohlin to illustrate the 'grant element' in loans of varying maturities, discount and interest rates, with grace periods of zero, five and ten years.[24] However, for purposes of greater directness and simplicity, a somewhat different formula is used here to obtain estimates of present cost. Where L is the face value of the loan or grant, i is the interest rate on the loan, r the discount rate, n the duration of the loan, and P its present cost to the donor,

$$P = L\left(1 - \frac{i}{r}\right)[1 - (1 + r)^{-n}].^{25}$$

On this basis, Table 8 shows the frequently striking difference between nominal or stated values and the real cost of loans to Pakistan. While Switzerland and the US Export–Import Bank (Eximbank) appear to be actually profiting by their aid, the United States, Canada, Sweden, Australia, New Zealand and China are nearly or fully as generous as they seem to be. The World Bank and the Netherlands are sacrificing very little, with the ratio of real cost of aid to nominal cost being only 9 per cent for both donors. For most other countries, the real–nominal ratio is between 20 and 57 per cent. The real values change the ranking, but not the membership, of the group of leading official donors:

[24] Ohlin, *Foreign Aid Policies*, pp. 111–12.
[25] See W. E. Schmidt, 'The Economics of Charity: Loans versus Grants', *Journal of Political Economy*, August 1964, for the derivation and further discussion of this formula.

Table 8. *The real cost of foreign aid to Pakistan: total up to 31 March 1967* (*thousands of US dollars*)

Country/agency	Nominal aid			Real cost of aid			Real as % of nominal	
	Loans	Grants	Total	Loans	Grants	Total	Loans	Total
Australia	—	38,447	38,447	—	38,447	38,447	—	100
Belgium	1,140	—	1,140	228	—	228	20	20
Canada	57,713	186,959	244,672	923	186,959	187,882	2	77
China	55,710	—	55,710	50,139	—	50,139	90	90
Czechoslovakia	17,130	—	17,130	9,776	—	9,776	57	57
Denmark	9,580	—	9,580	2,220	—	2,220	23	23
France	53,950	—	53,950	11,405	—	11,405	21	21
Italy	40,200	—	40,200	3,819	—	3,819	10	10
Japan	207,477	834	208,311	64,318	834	65,152	31	31
Netherlands	16,440	—	16,440	1,480	—	1,480	9	9
New Zealand	—	6,732	6,732	—	6,732	6,732	—	100
Poland	4,100	—	4,100	2,319	—	2,319	57	57
Sweden	4,833	3,000	7,833	3,420	3,000	6,420	71	82
Switzerland	3,300	—	3,300	−865	—	−865	−26	−26
United Kingdom	224,220	10,476	234,696	68,992	10,476	79,468	31	34
United States								
Project and non-project grants	—	763,090	763,090	—	763,090	763,090	—	100
DLF	222,176	—	222,176	160,855	—	160,855	72	72
AID	941,698	—	941,698	681,789	—	681,789	72	72
Eximbank	156,520	—	156,520	−18,782	—	−18,782	−12	−12
PL 480, Title II[a]	—	174,409	174,409	—	174,409	174,409	—	100
PL 480, Title III[a]	—	57,074	57,074	—	57,074	57,074	—	100
Suppliers' credit	176,075	—	176,075	0	—	0	0	0
USSR	72,350	—	72,350	40,516	—	40,516	56	56
West Germany	294,628	—	294,628	66,203	—	66,203	22	22
Yugoslavia	55,600	—	55,600	34,750	—	34,750	63	63
IBRD	411,820	—	411,820	35,787	—	35,787	9	9
IDA	329,240	—	329,240	288,085	—	288,085	88	88
IFC	10,900	—	10,900	0	—	0	0	0
UN and specialized agencies	—	12,931	12,931	—	12,931	12,931	—	100
UN Special Fund	—	11,861	11,861	—	11,861	11,861	—	100
Ford Foundation	—	36,559	36,559	—	36,559	36,559	—	100
Others	—	4,830	4,830	—	4,830	4,830	—	100
TOTAL	3,366,800	1,307,202	4,674,002	1,507,377	1,307,202	2,814,579	45	60

SOURCE: Pakistan CSO, *20 Years of Pakistan in Statistics, 1947–1967* (Karachi, 1968), pp. 322–3.

[a] PL 480 assistance under Titles II and III takes the form of outright grants, as against the local currency sales under Title I.

IDA, for example, becomes second only to the United States, Canada rises to third, West Germany falls to fifth, and the World Bank drops from second to tenth.

Loan terms for a few donors have improved more recently, notably Canada's; but as already pointed out, average terms have deteriorated, so that the picture is becoming increasingly bleak. What is more, grants represented 46 per cent of the total real cost of aid, and their virtual elimination in recent years will prove far more serious for Pakistan than the current real figures imply.

While these figures leave much to be desired, they almost certainly understate the difference between the nominal and real cost of aid. In fact, it may well be that the true cost is as low as 20 to 30 per cent of nominal cost, taking into account tied aid and balance-of-payments effects.[26]

[26] For some interesting contrasts, see the grant element figures which have been calculated for the global aid commitments of the sixteen DAC members in 1967. OECD, *Development Assistance: Efforts and Policies of the Members of the Development Assistance Committee, 1968 Review* (Paris, 1968), p. 62.

4. Economic growth in Pakistan

How and to what extent the flow of economic aid to Pakistan has affected the country's development is, as already implied, a question of many facets and great complexity. But clearly, an essential step in such an assessment is to provide a broad review of Pakistan's economic growth experience and prospects.

For purposes of this chapter, the following time periods will be distinguished: 1950–5, pre-plan; 1955–60, the First Five-Year Plan; 1960–5, the Second Five-Year Plan; 1965–70, the Third Five-Year Plan; 1965–85, the Perspective Plan.[1] This is meaningful in the context of both economic performance and available statistical data.[2]

Changes in Gross National Product

In aggregate terms, GNP and its sectoral components are, for all their defects, still the best indicators of economic growth and structural change in Pakistan.

GNP at current prices

Changes in the current price GNP are, of course, a composite of change in both volume and price of output. The relative contribution of each factor is not easily disentangled from such a series. But price changes within the economy tend to obscure sectoral growth as well as the underlying transformation of the economic structure. This is all the more serious because price changes are likely to affect the different sectors of the economy in varying degrees. It is important to correct these distortions and so isolate major changes in the volume of production. And yet, because price and volume changes are so intertwined, it is also important to view them briefly in a joint context.

Current GNP at factor cost increased from Rs. 19.9 billion to Rs. 62.1 billion between 1950 and 1968, a growth rate of some 6.7 per cent per annum. The rates for 1950–5, 1955–60 and 1960–8 were 1.3, 8.5 and 8.9 per cent, respectively.

As would normally be expected, the various sectors contributing to this increase grew at different rates. Mining underwent a phenomenal increase of 13.9 per cent annually, but this was less a matter of inherent strength than of change from a low starting base. The same is true for banking and insurance,

[1] The years 1947–50 made up a rather special and unique period of economic readjustment after the creation of Pakistan.

[2] Unless otherwise noted, GNP and other statistics in this chapter are derived from materials compiled by the Central Statistical Office of Pakistan (CSO) and by the Planning Commission. See especially Pakistan CSO, *20 Years of Pakistan in Statistics, 1947–1967* (Karachi, 1968); Ministry of Finance, *Pakistan Economic Survey, 1967–68* (Islamabad, 1968). In addition, see Pakistan Planning Commission, *The Fourth Five-Year Plan 1970–75* (Islamabad, 1970); this latest Plan was approved in June 1970 and launched in July, after the time of writing.

which grew even faster, at 15.3 per cent annually (although the high growth rate is being sustained). It is remarkable that manufacturing and agriculture did not expand at more divergent rates: the former grew at 9.9 per cent per annum, while agriculture showed a 6.0 per cent increase.[3] It is also worth noting that the rapid rise in the current price GNP did not reflect itself in Pakistan's living standards until 1960: the rate of population growth, while less than half that of current GNP, was high enough to keep per capita real income nearly stationary throughout the previous decade.

GNP at constant prices

Growth in real GNP averaged 3.9 per cent per year over the period 1950–68; it was 2.7 per cent for the years 1950–5, 2.4 per cent for 1955–60, and 5.5 per cent for 1960–8.[4] The Second Five-Year Plan witnessed a near-doubling in the pace of expansion as compared with the First Plan; this assumes even greater significance when it is realized that, for the first time in Pakistan, GNP outstripped the growth of population. Since 1960, per capita real income has increased by 25 per cent, or 2.8 per cent a year in average terms.

Most of the economy gives clear evidence of this steep upward trend. But again, different sectors have contributed in varying degrees to the overall growth rate. And the result has been a substantial change in the composition of GNP over the period.

The most striking development has been the growth of the manufacturing sector, which expanded at the rate of 9.2 per cent per annum in the years 1950–5, 5.7 per cent in 1955–60 and 8.8 per cent in 1960–8.[5] Manufacturing increased at an average annual rate of 8.1 per cent in 1950–68. Equally prominent is the fact of slow progress in the agricultural sector, which grew at an average annual rate of 2.4 per cent, with rates of 1.6, 1.4 and 3.5 per cent, respectively, for 1950–5, 1955–60 and 1960–8.[6]

This being so, there is expected to be a sharp reversal in the contribution of these sectors to the economy by the end of the Perspective Plan. In 1950, agriculture accounted for 60 per cent, and manufacturing 6 per cent, of GNP; the planners see the former declining to 36 per cent by 1985, and the latter rising to 21 per cent. Agriculture continues, nevertheless, to be Pakistan's largest single sector, with GNP fluctuating in the same direction as farm output.[7]

Here the question arises as to how the sectoral growth rates recorded so far

[3] Agriculture grew at 8.0 per cent annually in 1960–8. However, a substantial part of this improvement came in 1967, when an increase of 17 per cent was recorded. Apparently, much of this increase stemmed from the rise in food prices caused partly by the suspension of US PL 480 shipments.

[4] GNP in 1959 prices rose from Rs. 24.5 billion in 1950 to Rs. 48.3 billion in 1968. The 1968 figure is being revised upwards.

[5] The figure for the third period includes a 9.8 per cent annual increase in 1960–5 and a 7.0 per cent increase in 1965–8.

[6] The figure for 1960–8 reflects a rate of 3.2 per cent for the first five years, a poor 1 per cent in 1967, and a dramatic 9 per cent in 1968. No clear trend has yet emerged.

[7] In 1965, some 49 per cent of GNP still derived from agriculture.

Table 9. *Production of selected manufacturing industries in Pakistan: annual compound growth rates, 1955–65 (percentages)*

Industry	1955–60	1960–5	1955–65
Ammonium nitrate	—	n.a.	11.58[e]
Ammonium sulphate	n.a.	−3.24	9.47[a]
Board			
Chip	n.a.	19.28	34.16[a]
Paper	n.a.	11.16	12.19[a]
Straw	n.a.	6.90	2.98[a]
Cement	10.46	8.45	9.45
Cigarettes	15.53	17.22	16.37
Cotton cloth	6.77 (30.35)[b]	2.72	4.73
Cotton yarn	8.29 (41.71)[b]	4.30	6.28
Diesel oil			
High-speed	8.45	69.95	35.76
Low-speed	5.48	0.42	2.92
Furnace oil	−0.72	64.17	27.67
Jute goods	20.80	7.13	13.76
Kerosene oil	15.28	72.71	41.10
Motor spirit	8.00	31.46	19.15
Paints and varnishes (cwt.)	n.a.	3.48	n.a.
Paints and varnishes (gallons)	n.a.	16.05	n.a.
Paper			
Newsprint	n.a.	11.82	n.a.
Packing and other	2.40	0.61	1.50
Printing	20.46	4.80	12.35
Writing	0.38	16.02	7.92
Safety matches	20.22	6.08	12.93
Sea salt	1.87	−0.35	0.76
Silk and rayon cloth	21.80	4.24	12.68
Soda ash	−1.37	4.41	1.48
Sole leather	−3.53	15.88[c]	4.66[d]
Steel ingots	—	1.76	0.87
Steel re-rolling	5.04	30.84[c]	15.81[d]
Sugar	8.86	13.43	11.12
Sulphuric acid	n.a.	10.85	18.40[a]
Super-phosphates	n.a.	18.17	35.09[a]
Tea	−4.57	7.10	1.10
Tyres and tubes	7.74	12.52	10.10
Upper leather (tanned)	16.82	29.80[c]	22.42[d]
Urea	—	n.a.	32.00[e]
Vegetable oil	18.79	23.99	21.36
Woollen, worsted yarn	11.58	—[c]	6.28[d]

— = negligible or zero.   n.a. = figure not available.
SOURCE: Pakistan Ministry of Finance, *Pakistan Economic Survey, 1965–66* (Rawalpindi, 1966), statistical section, pp. 18–20.
[a] 1958–65; [b] 1949–55; [c] 1960–4; [d] 1955–64; [e] 1962–5.

compare with those which have been projected in the Perspective Plan.[8] In fact, the changes in most sectors are too erratic for reliable interpretation. Only two conclusions can be drawn on a firm basis. First, the rate of growth in the industrial sector has been extremely high: the period 1950–5 shows rapid expansion, and while there seems to have been a slowing down during the First Five-Year Plan, new surges of activity occurred during the Second Plan and beyond. Thus the industrial growth rate projected for 1965–85 may not be very wide of the mark. But it is no less clear that the rapid growth of the past was in part a direct outcome of the prevailing low level of economic development in Pakistan, and particularly the low level of industrialization; to maintain this rate will require a massive and sustained effort.

The second conclusion relates to the low annual growth rates recorded in the agricultural sector during 1950–5 and 1955–60. An appreciable increase occurred in 1960–8, and the projections made by the Planning Commission for 1965–85 have been considerably influenced by this upturn. To some extent, the increase has been a consequence of favourable weather conditions and may not reflect a sizable change in productivity. Indeed, while West Pakistani agriculture appears to have experienced notable increases in productivity, it is well to realize that East Pakistan has made little progress in this respect. A low growth rate in 1950–60 and constant or declining productivity in preceding decades merit more serious attention than they have received – especially because an expansion rate lower than the projected one would also affect the industrial sector adversely through reduced levels of raw material supply, foreign exchange and domestic demand.

Other key indicators of change

And yet, notwithstanding such doubts, the facts of output growth within the industrial sector of Pakistan are dramatic indeed. Table 9 provides a sectoral breakdown for 1955–65, and it shows very rapid advance for a variety of industries including diesel oil, chipboard, super-phosphates and steel re-rolling.[9]

Another way of looking at structural change in the economy is to take into account variations in the employment pattern. In 1950, agriculture employed about 75 per cent of the labour force; in 1984/5, it will employ only 49 per cent, according to the Perspective Plan.[10] Other non-industrial activities will undergo a corresponding expansion, as implied in Table 10.

There has also been a remarkably high rate of capital formation in Pakistan. In 1950–5 investment totalled Rs. 10.3 billion, or 7.5 per cent of GNP; in 1955–60, Rs. 14.9 billion or 9.8 per cent; and in 1960–5, Rs. 26 billion or 13.9

[8] It is difficult to make such a comparison because the Planning Commission has changed its sectoral classification from one plan to another, and even for the same plan. However, figures for 1950–65 are available from CSO, and for 1965–85 from the Planning Commission.
[9] A number of trend lines have been fitted to these data in order to correct for irregular movements. The results are charted in Appendix 2 below.
[10] These figures make no allowance for the serious underemployment which pervades the agricultural sector.

Table 10. *Sectoral composition of employment in Pakistan, 1951–85 (percentages)*

Fiscal year	Industrial[a]	Non-industrial[a]	Total
1951	22.67[b]	77.33	100
1961	23.98[b]	76.02	100
1965	17.19	82.81	100
1970	19.20	80.80	100
1985	22.92	77.08	100

SOURCES: Data for 1951 and 1961 from the Population Census; data for 1965, 1970 and 1985 from the Planning Commission.
[a] Includes part of the service sector.
[b] Under revision.

per cent. Capital stock per employed person for the same periods was Rs. 455.2, Rs. 585.2 and Rs. 860.9, respectively.

On the other hand, the productivity picture is less encouraging. It is not easy to find comparable data for the various sectors, but evidence can be pieced together to give an indication as to the direction of change in Pakistan. In the manufacturing sector, the index of productivity per head declined from 115 in 1953 to 103 in 1959/60 (taking 1954 as the base year); furthermore, 1959/60 shows an improvement over the intervening years.[11] For the agricultural sector, there seems to have been a productivity increase of 1.6 per cent per year; but this may well be the consequence of an unreliable estimate of employment in the agricultural sector. The projected long-term increases for both industry and agriculture, as noted in Table 11, appear difficult to defend on grounds of logic or experience. And the overall productivity estimate is high in the light of results obtained in most other countries.

Table 11. *Productivity per worker in Pakistan: projected annual increases, 1965–85*

Sector	%
Agriculture	2.9
Construction	2.4
Manufacturing	4.2
Mining	4.1
Public utilities	3.7
Transport	2.6
Other services	1.5
All sectors combined	2.7

SOURCE: Pakistan Planning Commission.

Economic planning and performance

The first four years of Pakistan's existence were devoted to the rehabilitation of the economy and to overcoming the distortions caused by partition of the sub-continent. Considerable progress during this period and the timely Korean

[11] Pakistan CSO, *Census of Manufacturing Industries, 1959–60* (Karachi, 1962).

War boom produced the image of a strong, expanding and buoyant economy. The crash that followed not only shattered this image but also exposed the inherent weakness of the system and the narrow base on which it was operating. It became clear that a transformation of the economy would be necessary if Pakistan was to provide a reasonable and rising standard of living for its growing population; also that given the available resources, governmental economic planning would have to be a major instrument for achieving these goals.[12]

The pre-plan period, 1950–5

Planning operations actually began during these 'pre-plan' years, but modestly and with very limited impact. A six-year development plan was prepared by the Development Board and went into effect from the middle of 1951. The plan provided for a total investment of Rs. 2.6 billion in the public sector, of which Rs. 1.4 billion were to be financed from internal resources. During the first five years of the plan period, public sector investments actually amounted to Rs. 3 billion; private investment was an estimated Rs. 2.3 billion; and the publicly owned Pakistan Industrial Development Corporation (PIDC) spent Rs. 620 million. Thus investment outlays in 1951–5 totalled about Rs. 6 billion, or Rs. 1.2 billion annually.

The First Five-Year Plan

The First Plan covered the period 1955–60. Its objectives were an increase in national and per capita income, self-sufficiency in food, an improved balance of payments, increased employment opportunities, expanded social services, and regional balance in economic development especially between East and West Pakistan.

Total outlays under the First Five-Year Plan were Rs. 10.8 billion: Rs. 7.5 billion in the public sector and Rs. 3.3 billion in the private sector. It aimed at raising national income by 15 per cent in five years. As the annual rate of population growth was assumed to be 1.4 per cent, an increase of 7 per cent in per capita income was expected during the plan period. It was estimated that the labour force would increase by about 2 million; the employment target involved providing jobs for those new entrants, so as not to accentuate the prevailing unemployment and underemployment.

The allocation of investment in the public sector was as follows: agriculture and village aid, 16.1 per cent; water and power development, 28.8 per cent; industry, 17.4 per cent; transport and communications, 17.8 per cent; and social services, 19.9 per cent. In the private sector, 33 per cent was expected to go into industry, 25 per cent into housing and construction, and the rest into transport equipment, agriculture, services, and trade and commerce. It was

[12] For an illuminating general survey of economic policies, problems and progress in Pakistan since Partition, see G. F. Papanek, *Pakistan's Development: Social Goals and Private Incentives* (Cambridge, Mass., 1967); S. R. Lewis, Jr., *Economic Policy and Industrial Growth in Pakistan* (London, 1969); L. B. Pearson et al., *Partners in Development: Report of the Commission on International Development* (New York, 1969), pp. 302–17.

maintained that 'while the Government cannot determine precisely the magnitude or the kind of private investment that will actually be made, it can, by suitable policies and its import licensing powers, greatly influence the magnitude of private investment, and ensure that it does not go into fields considered undesirable or of lower priority'.[13]

Production increases envisaged for the agricultural sector under the First Five-Year Plan were: foodgrains, 9 per cent; sugar cane, 33 per cent; cotton, 21 per cent; jute, 15 per cent; and tea, 15 per cent. This was to be achieved by extending irrigation to an additional 1.6 million acres, by improving the facilities for the 4.2 million acres already under irrigation, and by increasing the use of fertilizers. Also, an ambitious extension programme, covering about one-quarter of the total rural population, was formulated under 'village aid'.

For the industrial sector, an increase of 60 per cent in output was planned. Among the production targets were: cotton textiles, 28 per cent; sugar, 104 per cent; cement, 91 per cent; cigarettes, 104 per cent; and jute goods, 71 per cent. Substantial new industries, particularly fertilizers and natural gas, were also begun under the plan. And to support the industrial programme, a 570-megawatt increase in the power supply capacity was arranged.

The plan was to be financed by public savings to the extent of Rs. 1 billion; by private savings, Rs. 5.6 billion; and by external resources, Rs. 4.2 billion. Details of the proposed financing appear in Table 12.

Table 12. *Financing of the First Five-Year Plan: current prices*

Source	Rs. millions	% of total investment
Domestic resources		
Public saving	730	6.8
Additional saving	270	2.5
Capital receipts	1,200	11.1
Borrowing from the banks	1,500	13.8
Domestic private savings	2,900	26.9
Total	*6,600*	*61.1*
Foreign resources		
Aid and loans	3,800	35.2
Foreign private investment	400	3.7
Total	*4,200*	*38.9*
TOTAL	*10,800*	*100.0*

SOURCE: Pakistan National Planning Board, *The First Five-Year Plan, 1955–60* (Karachi, 1958).

Total foreign exchange requirements for the plan period were projected at Rs. 16.6 billion. Aid, loans, investments and foodgrain assistance were expected to yield Rs. 6.1 billion, with domestic earnings of foreign exchange estimated

[13] Pakistan National Planning Board, *The First Five-Year Plan, 1955–60* (Karachi, 1958), p. 16.

at Rs. 10.5 billion. In fact, the First Five-Year Plan sounded very optimistic about the foreign exchange position: 'If agricultural production is increased as proposed in the Plan, by the beginning of the next Plan period the country's dependence on external aid for development purposes will be substantially reduced.'[14]

The First Five-Year Plan did not prove to be a success; nor did it appear in published form until the fourth year of the planning period. Even the modest plan targets were not attained. Real national income in 1958/9 was only moderately above that of 1954/5; and because of the increase in population, per capita income had actually declined.[15] Investment totalled Rs. 10.3 billion, as against Rs. 10.8 billion proposed by the plan; in monetary terms the shortfall was only about 5 per cent, but it was 33 per cent in real terms. The public sector, which had been viewed as the main channel for growth policy, showed a shortfall of Rs. 340 million; and the private sector, Rs. 140 million. There is no evidence that the First Plan resulted in any significant increase in the level of investment over the five-year pre-plan period. In fact, some estimates indicate a decline in real investment during the First Plan.

The estimates of public savings and foreign aid diverged widely from the realized figures: actual public savings were Rs. 430 million, as against the estimated Rs. 1.0 billion; total domestic savings were Rs. 4.2 billion, against the estimated Rs. 6.6 billion; total foreign resources were Rs. 3.3 billion, against the estimated Rs. 4.2 billion. An unprecedented increase in prices was recorded during the plan period: in 1959/60, they were at least 40 per cent higher than in 1955/6; this increased the cost of ongoing projects and adversely affected both savings and exports.

Although the First Plan claimed top priority for agriculture, less than half the proposed programme in this sector was actually implemented. Fertilizers and improved seeds recorded especially large shortfalls. Even in the irrigation projects, where the targets were generally achieved, much of the effort was wasted by failure to undertake settlement speedily.

In some respects, to be sure, the plan did bring positive results. It provided much of the infra-structure urgently needed at that stage of Pakistan's economic development. Also, in a few sectors, notably industry and water and power, there were substantial increases in investment, output and employment. But on the whole, the First Five-Year Plan was a disappointing effort. Economic policies had switched abruptly from one extreme to another, guided primarily by the short-run demands of the situation rather than by the strategy of economic growth. The economy was still consumption-oriented, failure in the key agricultural sector was fatal, and the foreign exchange position continued to be precarious. In short, at the end of the First Plan the country remained far from its basic professed objective of self-sustained growth.

[14] *Ibid.* p. 14.
[15] Population growth was considerably underestimated: the 1961 Census reported an increase of 2.1 per cent, as against 1.4 per cent assumed by the plan; some recent studies indicate an even greater increase in population during that period.

The poor performance was by no means entirely of Pakistan's own making. Adverse weather conditions and deterioration in the terms of trade took a heavy toll. It seems clear, nonetheless, that the chief causes were the absence of a sustained effort to cut down non-developmental expenditure, failure to resist the temptation of excessive deficit budgeting for current needs, inadequate measures to strengthen export potential, and failure to gear economic policy to the needs of development.

The Second Five-Year Plan

The Second Plan (1960–5) was launched under more favourable circumstances. The new government which assumed power in 1958 not only brought political stability to the country but also laid the basis for a vigorous growth policy by giving full attention and support to development activity. The plan was, therefore, prepared in an atmosphere when doubts and misgivings about the capacity of the country to pursue a successful development policy had been largely dispelled and when the evidence of its viability had become apparent.

The Second Five-Year Plan aimed at increasing GNP by 24 per cent, and per capita income by 15 per cent (assuming a 1.8 per cent annual increase in population). Total investment was estimated at Rs. 23 billion or 13.5 per cent of GNP, with Rs. 14.6 billion in the public sector and Rs. 8.4 billion in the private sector.[16] In financial terms, the plan was roughly twice the size of the First Five-Year Plan; in real terms, the increase was around 50 per cent owing to the steep rise in prices. Of the total investment, Rs. 14 billion were allocated to West Pakistan and Rs. 9 billion to East Pakistan.

Table 13. *Allocation of investment in the First and Second Five-Year Plans, by sectors in current prices*

| Sector | Second plan proposed investment | | | | First plan[a] (%) | |
	Public	Private	Total (Rs. millions)	Target[a] (%)	Actual	Target
Agriculture and village aid	2,451	969	3,420	17.2	11.9	16.1
Water and power	4,140	250	4,390	28.4	21.1	28.8
Industry	1,460	3,660	5,120	10.0	14.1	17.4
Fuel and minerals	450	550	1,000	3.1		
Transport and communications	2,725	1,325	4,050	18.6	25.8	17.8
Housing and settlements	1,885	1,525	3,410	12.9	9.6	9.2
Education and training, health, manpower and social welfare	1,445	165	1,610	9.8	7.5	10.7
TOTAL	*14,556*	*8,444*	*23,000*	*100.0*	*90.0*	*100.0*

SOURCE: Pakistan Planning Commission.
[a] Figures apply to the public sector. Allocations in the private sector are not available for the First Plan.

[16] These and subsequent figures relate to the revised Second Plan; the total investment target was raised from Rs. 19 billion, mainly in order to take account of sharply rising prices.

Table 14. *Financing of the Second Five-Year Plan: current prices*

Source	Rs. millions	% of total investment
Domestic resources		
Revenue surplus	1,220	5.3
Capital receipts	1,400	6.1
New taxation	1,750	7.6
Local bodies	200	0.9
Customs on commodity aid	700	3.0
PL 480 counterpart funds	600	2.6
Private savings (including public corporations' own resources)	6,180	26.9
Total	*12,050*	*52.4*
Foreign resources		
Commodity aid	3,500	15.2
Project aid and loans	6,850	29.8
Foreign private investment	600	2.6
Total	*10,950*	*47.6*
TOTAL	*23,000*	*100.00*

SOURCE: Pakistan Planning Commission, *Final Evaluation of the Second Five-Year Plan (1960–65)* (Karachi, 1966).

Table 13 compares public sector outlays under the two plans. It can be seen that there were few significant changes in the pattern of allocation: the shares of agriculture and transport and communications increased slightly, while water and power as well as 'human resource' spending (education, health, manpower and social welfare) underwent small declines; only the shares of industry and housing recorded sizable shifts, the former downward and the latter upward. The comparative pattern becomes quite different, however, when private sector outlays are included. In particular, agriculture's share of total expenditure shows a striking increase in the Second Plan, industry only a modest drop, and housing a substantial decline.

Of total plan outlays, some Rs. 12.1 billion were estimated as local currency expenditure and Rs. 10.9 billion as the foreign exchange component. In addition, the Indus Basin Replacement Works were expected to cost Rs. 3.3 billion, of which Rs. 1.4 billion were to be in local currency and Rs. 1.9 billion in foreign exchange. Total domestic resources to be mobilized during the Second Plan, therefore, were Rs. 13.5 billion. Some Rs. 2.5 billion in balance-of-payments support were also envisaged. Thus total foreign exchange requirements of the plan worked out at Rs. 15.3 billion. Table 14 shows how the necessary financial resources were to be secured.

In the industrial sector, the Second-Five Year Plan aimed at increasing output in some of the major industries as follows: sugar, 233 per cent; vegetable ghee, 127 per cent; jute manufacturing, 76 per cent; super-phosphates, 1,100 per cent; soda ash, 196 per cent; caustic soda, 678 per cent. New industries

Table 15. *Industrial production targets in the Second Five-Year Plan (thousands of tons)*

Industry	Base period production (1959/60)	Production target (1960–5)	Increase (%)
Food manufacturing			
White sugar	150	500	233
Edible vegetable oils	150	250	67
Vegetable ghee	22	50	127
Tea	27	32	19
Textiles			
Cotton spinning	190	260	37
Jute manufacturing	250	440	76
Paper and board			
Paper	40	80	100
Board	13	25	92
Chemical industries			
Ammonium sulphate	42	50	19
Super-phosphate	1.5	18	1,100
Ammonium nitrate	—	103	—
Urea	—	176	—
Soda ash	25	74	196
Caustic soda	4.5	350	678
Non-metallic minerals			
Cement	1,050	4,000	281

SOURCES: Pakistan Planning Commission, *The Second Five-Year Plan, 1960–65* (Karachi, 1960), p. 259; *Final Evaluation of the Second Five-Year Plan (1960–65)* (Karachi, 1966), p. 188.

would produce ammonium nitrate and urea. To support this programme, a 40 per cent increase in power capacity was required. The production plans are presented in Table 15.

The Second Five-Year Plan was completed in June 1965. National income rose 29 per cent over the plan period, as against the target increase of 24 per cent. Total planned investment was surpassed by Rs. 2.5 billion. The agricultural sector recorded an annual increase in output of 3.2 per cent, as compared with the increase of 1.4 per cent under the First Plan. In the industrial sector, output expanded by 8.8 per cent a year, as against 7.4 per cent under the First Plan. In consequence, the share of manufacturing increased from 9.3 per cent of GNP in 1960 to 11.5 per cent in 1965.

Gross investment in 1965 stood at 15.8 per cent of GNP, as compared with 10.9 per cent in 1960. This amounts to an increase of 86 per cent in investment over the plan period. In the private sector, the investment target was over-fulfilled by 47 per cent, whereas the public sector showed a shortfall of 10 per cent. As a result, the private sector share of total development expenditure reached 48 per cent, as compared with the planned share of 37 per cent; for the public sector, the shares were 52 and 66 per cent, respectively.

One of the most remarkable changes involved the relative shares of domestic and foreign resources in development financing. Domestic savings increased from 5.9 per cent of GNP in 1960 to 9.5 per cent in 1965. This produced a foreign resources contribution to gross investment of 41 per cent, as against the projected 50 per cent. The actual share of foreign resources in the First Plan had been 44 per cent. Thus greater support came from domestic resources during the Second Five-Year Plan, despite a substantial increase in development activity. It should be added that the enlarged domestic effort rested partly on an export performance which far exceeded the planned figures.

In sum, Pakistan attained a respectable rate of growth in national income during the Second Plan; per capita income rose considerably as well. In a country where average living standards had stubbornly resisted improvement for about fifteen years, this was no insignificant achievement. However important the qualifications may prove to be, it can hardly be doubted that massive foreign aid inflows played a key stimulative role in this period of rapid economic growth.[17] On the other hand, it seems equally clear that more careful domestic planning, a sustained entrepreneurial effort and judicious government policies supplied ingredients without which Pakistan could not have recorded its impressive advance.

The Third Five-Year Plan

The Third Plan (1965–70) seeks an increase of 37 per cent in real GNP over the plan period, that is, a growth rate of 6.5 per cent per year.[18] Per capita income is projected to increase by 17 per cent, assuming population growth at 2.6 per cent per annum. The total size of the Third Plan is Rs. 52 billion, with Rs. 30 billion for the public sector and Rs. 22 billion for the private sector.

Of total plan investment, East Pakistan has been allocated Rs. 27 billion and West Pakistan Rs. 25 billion, as compared with Rs. 9 billion and Rs. 14 billion, respectively, in the Second Plan. Thus, the Third Five-Year Plan marks an increase of 200 per cent for the East Wing and 78 per cent for the West. The intention is to reduce the existing regional disparities in conformity with Article 145 of the Pakistan Constitution; it guarantees the elimination of East–West differences in per capita income by 1985.

Domestic resources are to account for Rs. 35.5 billion and foreign resources for Rs. 16.5 billion. The latter would therefore contribute only 32 per cent of the total programme. Table 16 gives the details of plan financing.

[17] See E. S. Mason, *Economic Development in India and Pakistan* (Cambridge, Mass., 1966). And see the *Pearson Report* for the view that Pakistan's experience in the 1960s reflects 'a close positive correlation between levels of savings and investment, and foreign aid inflows' (p. 314).

[18] A revised plan was published in March 1967. The broad targets were retained, but changes were made in phasing and sectoral priorities. See Pakistan Planning Commission, *Revised Phasing, Sectoral Priorities and Allocations of the Third Five-Year Plan (1965–70)* (March 1967), appended to *The Third Five-Year Plan, 1965–70* (Karachi, 1965); W. Tims, *Analytical Techniques for Development Planning: A Case Study of Pakistan's Third Five-Year Plan (1965–70)* (Karachi, 1968). And see Pakistan Planning Commission, *The Mid-Plan Review of the Third Five-Year Plan (1965–70)* (Rawalpindi, 1968) and *Memorandum for the Pakistan Consortium, 1969–70* (Islamabad, 1969).

Table 16. *Financing of the Third Five-Year Plan: current prices*

	Rs. millions		% of total investment	
Source	Original	Revised	Original	Revised
Domestic resources				
Additional taxation	3,000	6,000	5.8	11.5
Revenue receipts	8,600	6,315	16.5	12.1
Net capital receipts	2,400	3,185	4.6	6.1
Deficit financing	1,500	3,000	2.9	5.8
Additional resources	1,000	1,000	1.9	1.9
Private domestic savings	19,000	16,000	36.5	30.8
Total	*35,500*	*35,500*	*68.2*	*68.2*
Foreign resources				
Commodity loans	5,500		10.6	
Project loans (including technical assistance)	7,000		13.5	
PL 480 counterpart funds	1,000		1.9	
Foreign loans and credits to private sector	2,300		4.4	
Foreign private investment	700		1.3	
Total	*16,500*		*31.7*	
TOTAL	*52,000*		*100.00[a]*	

SOURCE: Pakistan Planning Commission, *The Third Five-Year Plan, 1965–70* (Karachi, 1965), pp. 66, 75, and *Revised Phasing, Sectoral Priorities and Allocations of The Third Five-Year Plan (1965–70)* (March 1967), pp. 3–5 (appended to report cited).
[a] Percentages do not add up to total because of rounding.

There have been some interesting developments in sector allocation policy. The original Third Plan continues the upward trend in agriculture's share of total outlays, but much less markedly so than between the first two plans. Human resource spending is to rise substantially, after a second plan decline; while transport and communications show a slight increase over the two previous plans. For industry and housing, the trend continues steadily downward from the pre-plan period; while water and power register a decline from their second plan peak. Table 17 presents the varying sectoral allocations from pre-plan through the Third Five-Year Plan.

In the revised Third Plan, by contrast, both agriculture and industry have had their shares in the original plan reduced as far as the public sector is concerned. Transport and communications are projected to increase (as before), but so are water and power. There is to be a slight decline for both housing and human resources. The revised and original allocations for the public sector are compared in Table 18. Apparently, the Pakistan government is looking to the private sector for offsetting increases in agriculture and industry; this would imply still greater reliance on economic expansion rooted in domestic resources.

The production increases envisaged in the plan for individual industries include: sugar, 175 per cent; jute goods, 218 per cent; writing and printing

Table 17. *Sectoral priorities in development expenditure, 1950–70*

Sector	Pre-plan (% of total investment)	First Plan (% of total investment)	Second Plan (% of total investment)	Third Plan[a] (Rs. millions)	Third Plan[a] (% of total investment)
Agriculture	6	7	13	8,670	15
Industry, fuels and minerals	36	31	28	14,210	25
Water and power	13	17	19	9,050	16
Transport and communications	14	17	17	10,360	18
Physical planning and housing	22	20	15	7,025	12
Education	5	6	4	3,030	5
Health	3	2	1	1,370	2
Manpower and social welfare	1	—	Neg.	285	1
Works programme	—	—	3	2,500	4
TOTAL	100	100	100	56,500	100[b]
Less expected shortfall				−4,500	
				52,000	

SOURCE: Pakistan Planning Commission, *The Third Five-Year Plan, 1965–70* (Karachi, 1965), pp. 43, 45, 48.
[a] These figures have since been revised; but the private sector changes are not available, and therefore the original figures are given. See Table 18.
[b] Percentages do not add up to total because of rounding.

Table 18. *Public sector allocations in the original and revised Third Five-Year Plans*

Sector	Original plan allocation, May 1965 Rs. millions	Original plan allocation, May 1965 % of total	Revised plan allocation, December 1966 Rs. millions	Revised plan allocation, December 1966 % of total
Agriculture	4,670	13.5	4,115	13.3
Water and power	8,400	24.3	8,047	26.0
Industry, fuels and minerals	5,160	15.9	4,105	13.2
Transport and communications	6,460	18.7	6,711	21.6
Physical planning and housing	3,025	8.8	2,477	8.0
Education and training	2,730	7.9	2,374	7.7
Health	1,330	3.9	1,175	3.8
Social welfare	125	0.4	90	0.3
Manpower	100	0.3	86	0.3
Works programme	2,500	7.2	1,820	5.9
Total	34,500	100.0[a]	31,000	100.0[a]
Less expected shortfall	4,500		1,000	
TOTAL (net)	30,000		30,000	

SOURCE: Pakistan Planning Commission, *Revised Phasing, Sectoral Priorities and Allocations of the Third Five-Year Plan (1965–70)* (March 1967), appended to *The Third Five-Year Plan, 1965–70* (Karachi, 1965), p. 5.
[a] Percentages do not add up to total because of rounding.

Table 19. *Production targets of principal industries in the Third Five-Year Plan*

Industry	Base year production 1964/5 (000 tons)	Third Plan target 1969/70 (000 tons)	Growth planned (%)	Achieve-ment in 1966/7 (000 tons)	Achievement in 1966/7 as % of target
White sugar	233	640	174.7	416	65.0
Vegetable ghee	95	140	47.4	88	62.9
Tea	31	37	19.4	34	91.9
Sea salt	216	400	85.2	360	90.0
Jute goods	289	920	218.3	404	43.9
Cotton yarn	259	360	39.0	266	73.9
Cotton cloth (m. yds.)	764	—	—	739	—
Writing and printing paper	32	100	212.5	25	25.0
Newsprint and mechanical paper	47	100	112.8	45	45.0
Board	24	100	316.7	26	26.0
Nitrogenous fertilizer	393	2,500	536.1	335[a]	—
Cement	1,685	6,000	256.1	2,009	33.5
Caustic soda	10	90	800.0	17	18.9
Soda ash	34	172	405.9	31	18.0
Sulphuric acid	21	600	2,757.1	22	3.7
Cycle rubber tyres and tubes (000 nos.)	6,849	—	—	7,012	—

SOURCE: Pakistan Ministry of Finance, *Pakistan Economic Survey, 1967–68* (Islamabad, 1968), pp. 29–30.
[a] Data for ammonium nitrate are not available.

paper, 213 per cent; nitrogenous fertilizers, 536 per cent; soda ash, 406 per cent; sulphuric acid, 2,757 per cent.; cement, 256 per cent. Table 19 shows the physical targets and achievements.

Given the record of solid performance under the Second Plan, it is reasonable to expect a large-scale fulfilment of third plan targets. However, the 1965 Indo-Pakistan War brought serious dislocation to Pakistan (as it did to India): it diverted scarce resources, weakened productive capacity, and interrupted aid inflows. These problems have by no means disappeared. Indeed, they have been compounded by the political disruptions of 1969; much will depend on the resilience and flexibility of the Pakistan economy in 1969 and 1970.

But the sudden decline in foreign aid, and the concurrent increase in defence expenditures, did force increased emphasis on quick-yielding low-import investments. GNP increased 8.3 per cent in 1967/8; the average annual increase in the first three years of the Third Plan was 6 per cent, as compared with the 6.5 per cent target. In agriculture, the first two years showed a growth rate of only 1.4 per cent, far below the 5 per cent target; however, the first three years will average about 3.2 per cent (compared with a second plan rate of 3.4 per cent). The growth of large-scale industry declined from 15 per cent in the Second Plan to 6, 11 and 13 per cent in the first three years of the Third Plan; but these lower rates were largely due to bottlenecks which now seem to be less serious (for example, under-utilization of excess capacity and raw material shortages).

Import liberalization retrogressed in 1965/6 because of the reduced aid and the increased need for imported food and defence materials. But the upward trend resumed in 1966/7. By January 1968, more than 90 per cent of all imports of industrial raw materials were free from controls; their effective prices were substantially raised in order to prevent imports from increasing too rapidly. This has had a favourable impact on industrial investment in particular.

Pakistan's public sector has seen more of a shortfall than the private sector. By the end of the first three years of the Third Plan, only 41 per cent of the total allocation for public development expenditure had been spent. The completed plan is expected to have a shortfall of at least 17 per cent. Taxes have already been raised.

The private sector had reached 56 per cent of the plan target by the end of the third year. The third year brought the best results because of the increased availability of foreign credits.

Performance within the industrial sphere has been quite uneven. As of the fiscal year 1967, some of the principal industries with ambitious targets had done fairly well: white sugar (65 per cent of a 175 per cent target increase), jute goods (44 per cent of a 218 per cent target), and cement (34 per cent of a 256 per cent target). But other ambitious hopes had not been fulfilled: writing and printing paper (25 per cent of a 213 per cent target), caustic soda (19 per cent of an 800 per cent target), soda ash (18 per cent of a 406 per cent target), and sulphuric acid (4 per cent of a 2,757 per cent target). In general, the most modest targets came nearest to achievement, for example tea (92 per cent of a 19 per cent target) and cotton yarn (74 per cent of a 39 per cent target). Given the constraints, it is encouraging that already established industries were able to make such gains. And performance appears to have been improving at a faster rate since the second year of the Third Plan. But it is still not clear how close to the target the industrial sector is likely to come by the end of the plan.

As for progress in reducing the regional imbalance, East Pakistan received about 52 per cent of total public sector outlays and 51 per cent of total foreign project assistance in the first three years of the Third Plan. But the gap in per capita income is not narrowing, mainly because of the low level of private activity in the East Wing (22 per cent of total private spending), as well as its slow rate of growth in agriculture.

Foreign aid commitments have fallen very short of required inflows. From 1966 to 1968, an average of about $400 million was pledged annually, as against the plan target of $550 million. This has probably compelled the government to seek short-run gains at the expense of long-term growth. On the other hand, it is quite possible that the lower rate of industrial investment will be offset by increased efficiency through greater selectivity in aided investments; that is to say, the less generous aid now being made available is likely to be used in more productive ways. But the fact remains that continuing shortages in aid inflow could have damaging consequences for the Pakistan economy.

Long-term prospects

The government of Pakistan has formulated a Perspective Plan which aims at tripling GNP by 1985. Table 20 summarizes the basic projections.

Table 20. *GNP, investment, savings and external resources in the Perspective Plan: constant prices (1964/5)*

Item	1964/5	1969/70	1974/5	1979/80	1984/5	Annual compound rate, 1965–85 (%)
		Millions of rupees				
GNP (market prices)	45,540	62,765	89,815	129,690	187,300	7.2
Gross plan investments	8,400	12,700	19,180	28,650	42,800	8.5
Gross domestic savings	4,710	8,515	15,180	26,150	40,800	11.4
External resources	3,690	4,185	4,000	2,500	2,000	−3.0
Exports	3,050	4,800	7,300	11,000	14,000	7.9
Imports	6,990[a]	8,985	11,300	13,500	16,000	4.2
		As a percentage of GNP				
Gross plan investments	18.4	20.2	21.4	22.1	22.9	
Gross domestic savings	10.3	13.6	16.9	20.2	21.8	
External resources	8.1	6.6	4.5	1.9	1.1	
Exports	6.7	7.6	8.1	8.5	7.5	
Imports	15.3	14.2	12.6	10.4	8.6	

SOURCE: Pakistan Planning Commission, *The Third Five-Year Plan, 1965–70* (Karachi, 1965), p. 19.
[a] Of these imports, Rs. 250 million were financed by drawing on foreign exchange reserves.

It has been assumed that population grew at 2.6 per cent during the Second Plan and will rise to 2.7 per cent in the Third; that it will increase to 2.8 per cent in the Fourth Five-Year Plan; and that it will decline to 2.6 per cent in the Fifth Plan and 2.1 per cent in the Sixth. Since a major target of the Perspective Plan is a per capita real income of around $200 in 1985 (as against the 1965 figure of about $85), GNP for the year must be as projected, namely, Rs. 187 billion.

Full employment is also a target for the plan period. It would involve creating some 30 million jobs – 25 million for the absorption of new entrants into the labour force and 5 million for the backlog of unemployment.[19]

Elimination of dependence on foreign assistance is a third 1985 objective. By the end of the Sixth Five-Year Plan, Pakistan is expected to develop entirely on the basis of its own financial and foreign exchange resources.

In the context of past experience, the GNP target does not seem unreasonable. But the anticipated increase in per capita income may well be excessive, since the Planning Commission has assumed a relatively low population in the base year and a low rate of long-term increase. The full employment target may also be unrealistic, for several reasons: the estimated employment potential of the

[19] The Planning Commission defines 'full employment' as a 'reasonable minimum' of unemployment – 4 per cent of the labour force, or roughly 2.5 million people. Pakistan Planning Commission, *The Third Plan*, p. 25.

proposed investments appears to be on the high side; the projected shift towards capital-intensive industries and techniques of production could be a further aggravating influence; the labour force may very possibly rise more than expected by the Planning Commission. Then, too, the plan ratios of domestic to foreign resources may not be firmly based; in fact, they rest on rather heroic assumptions about export growth, import substitution and external debt.[20]

More generally, it seems clear that much of the Perspective Plan is now open to question. This is hardly surprising in view of unforeseen developments since mid-1965; the Indo-Pakistan War, the crisis in international aid-giving, Pakistan's political turmoil in 1969, and so on. Against this background, it is indeed hazardous to look ahead to 1985, and all the more so when the socio-political problems of Pakistani development are given the strong emphasis which they deserve.[21]

[20] Appendix 3 below provides a discussion of Pakistan's foreign aid requirements in the coming decades.
[21] See Pakistan Planning Commission, *Socio-Economic Objectives of the Fourth Five-Year Plan (1970–75)* (Islamabad, 1968). And see *The Fourth Plan.*

5. Foreign aid and Pakistan's balance of payments

Some of the balance-of-payments implications of foreign aid to Pakistan have been touched on in earlier chapters. It is appropriate, now, to treat them in a more intensive fashion.

Changes in the 'payments' structure

The international payments position of Pakistan has been a cause of serious concern for more than a decade. Table 21 traces the broad pattern of export and import flows back to 1948, while Tables 22 and 23 highlight changing commodity shares in trade since 1955.

Pakistan's first ten years were largely a period of favourable trade balance.[1] Sterling devaluation in September 1949 brought the earliest deficit, but severe

Table 21. *Foreign trade of Pakistan, 1947–66[a]* (*millions of rupees*)

Year (July–June)	Exports	Imports	Balance	Exports as % of imports
1947/8	717	269	+448	267
1948/9	1,870	1,487	+383	126
1949/50	1,218	1,284	−66	95
1950/1	2,554	1,620	+934	139
1951/2	2,009	2,237	−228	90
1952/3	1,510	1,383	+127	109
1953/4	1,286	1,118	+168	115
1954/5	1,223	1,103	+120	111
1955/6	1,784	1,325	+459	135
1956/7	1,608	2,335	−727	69
1957/8	1,422	2,050	−628	69
1958/9	1,325	1,578	−253	84
1959/60	1,843	2,461	−618	75
1960/1	1,799	3,188	−1,389	56
1961/2	1,843	3,109	−1,266	59
1962/3	2,247	3,819	−1,572	59
1963/4	2,299	4,430	−2,131	52
1964/5	2,408	5,374	−2,966	45
1965/6	2,718	4,208	−1,490	65
1966/7	3,006	5,192	−2,186	58

SOURCE: Pakistan CSO, *20 Years of Pakistan in Statistics, 1947–1967* (Karachi, 1968), p. 107.
[a] Data on sea-borne trade with India are included since April 1948, and data on land-borne trade since July 1948; for Iran, statistics on land-borne trade date from July 1949; exports to Afghanistan are also included since July 1949, and imports from March 1951.

[1] Unless otherwise noted, figures in this chapter are derived from the Central Statistical Office and the Planning Commission of the Government of Pakistan.

Table 22. *Exports of Pakistan: selected years (percentages of total)*

Item	1954/5	1959/60	1964/5
Carpets	0.01	0.33	1.20
Cotton piece goods	0.06	3.04	5.51
Cotton twist and yarn	0.05	9.52	5.78
Fish excluding canned	2.25	2.53	3.52
Footwear	0.03	0.23	0.75
Hides and skins	—	—	0.18
Jute goods	1.95	12.33	12.47
Leather and leather goods	0.005	0.71	2.43
Raw cotton	25.36	10.24	11.91
Raw hides	0.74	0.83	0.21
Raw jute	51.18	39.56	35.07
Raw skins	1.65	3.67	1.08
Raw wool	4.28	4.09	2.43
Rice	6.36	3.69	4.95
Sports goods	0.51	0.64	0.54
Tea	4.77	1.93	0.42
Wheat	0.005	—	—
Other exports	0.79	6.66	11.55
TOTAL	100.00	100.00	100.00

SOURCE: Pakistan Central Statistical Office.

Table 23. *Imports of Pakistan: selected years (percentages of total)*

Item	1954/5	1959/60	1964/5
Art silk yarn	1.35	0.96	0.69
Chemicals	2.01	2.48	2.00
Cotton piece goods	3.98	0.17	0.08
Cotton twist and yarn	3.07	0.35	0.37
Drugs and medicines	3.24	3.26	2.15
Dyes and colours	2.00	1.78	2.19
Electrical goods	2.18	3.02	6.12
Grain, pulses and flour	0.01	18.67	12.65
Iron and steel, and manufactures	7.66	8.73	16.36
Machinery	34.54	22.39	17.40
Non-ferrous metals and manufactures	1.05	1.73	1.98
Oil minerals	11.73	9.68	2.33
Oil vegetable	0.41	2.33	3.81
Paper, paste board and stationery	2.13	1.25	0.86
Rubber and rubber manufactures	1.23	1.21	1.30
Transport equipment	4.83	6.21	9.99
Woollen yarn and manufactures	0.33	0.03	0.12
Other imports	18.25	15.75	19.60
TOTAL	100.00	100.00	100.00

SOURCE: Pakistan Central Statistical Office.

import restrictions kept it well below Rs. 100 million. Only a year later, there was a surplus of no less than Rs. 934 million – primarily due to huge export increases generated by the Korean War.

However, the cessation of hostilities resulted in a drastic fall in Pakistani exports, and a rather weak trade balance persisted during the next few years. Rupee devaluation in July 1955 produced a substantial but short-lived recovery. By 1958, exports had declined 20 per cent; their slow growth since then – along with the sharp rise in imports – has yielded an unbroken record of trade deficits, most of them very large.

The first plan years

The First Five-Year Plan projected earnings of foreign exchange at Rs. 10.5 billion, and foreign exchange expenditure on consumer and development goods at Rs. 16.6 billion. Assuming no change in reserves, this left a balance of Rs. 6.1 billion which was to be financed by foreign aid and private foreign investment. Since private foreign investment was expected to be limited (Rs. 500 million), the bulk of the gap, Rs. 5.6 billion, would have to be met through capital and commodity aid as well as technical assistance.

Table 24. *Foreign exchange earnings during the first plan period* (*millions of rupees*)

Item	1955/6[a]	1956/7	1957/8	1958/9	1959/60	Total
Raw jute	941	808	858	790	818	4,215
Jute manufactures	85	102	133	145	220	685
Raw cotton	510	362	246	223	168	1,509
Cotton manufactures	32	95	34	68	200	429
Hides and skins	49	51	50	61	40	251
Wool	85	96	78	81	77	417
Tea	31	48	20	16	40	155
Miscellaneous exports	203	138	109	145	200	795
Invisible receipts	195	209	198	289	207	1,098
TOTAL	2,131	1,909	1,726	1,818	1,970	9,554

SOURCE: Pakistan Planning Commission, *The Second Five-Year Plan, 1960–5* (Karachi, 1960), p. 83.
[a] Adjusted for devaluation of the Pakistan rupee in 1955.

Table 24 shows actual foreign exchange earnings over the period 1955–60. It can be seen that, in total, they fell short of the first plan projection by about one billion rupees. As already indicated, the stimulus of devaluation proved temporary, and export performance was weak during those years. The improvement of 1959/60 can be attributed mainly to the introduction of the Export Bonus Scheme, under which exporters of specified commodities were given negotiable import licences equivalent to 20 to 40 per cent of the value of their exports. Since the licences commanded a high premium in the open market, this served as a strong incentive to export activity. In effect, the scheme amounted to a selective further devaluation of the rupee, or (alternatively) to a system of export subsidies for certain commodities.[2]

It is also apparent that Pakistan was continuing to rely heavily on jute and cotton as major export items. In 1960, they provided some 71 per cent of total foreign exchange earnings, roughly the same proportion as in 1956. For both commodities, however, a significant shift had occurred from raw materials to manufactured and semi-manufactured exports.

In any event, the flow of foreign aid was about a billion rupees below the expected level; actual imports substantially exceeded the projected figure. A marked reduction of both developmental and other imports became necessary. In fact, the import gap was cut from the projected Rs. 6.1 billion to Rs. 4.9 billion; but the economic consequences were very serious indeed. Considerable excess capacity developed in some industries for want of raw materials, ongoing projects were delayed, and investment priorities suffered. In the private sector, funds were diverted from profitable industrial production to the construction of luxury houses, office buildings and factories.

Notwithstanding the shortfall, foreign aid financed over half of the total development expenditure, and about a third of total imports in the first plan period. For the most part, however, plan expectations remained unfulfilled. It follows that large aid inflows failed, overall, to produce rapid economic growth in Pakistan during those years. But it does not follow that the inflows played an insignificant role in achieving the positive results which were, in fact, recorded; the evidence on infra-structure and industrial expansion points to the contrary judgment. Furthermore, even the broadest inspection of the balance-of-payments picture suggests that major adverse effects probably would have stemmed from a greater shortfall in aid than actually occurred. Although some might argue that aid can have a detrimental effect by inducing the recipient to avoid hard policy decisions, the implication is quite clear that additional aid, by preventing crucial import cuts, could have pushed Pakistan's economic performance closer to the first plan targets.

Second plan growth

In the Second Five-Year Plan, foreign exchange earnings were expected to reach Rs. 11.3 billion, compared with Rs. 9.6 billion during 1955–60; total imports were projected at Rs. 22.2 billion. The resultant import gap of Rs. 10.9 billion was to be covered by external resources.

As shown in Table 25, actual foreign exchange earnings over the plan period amounted to some Rs. 13.3 billion and so exceeded the plan target by 18 per cent; the annual rate of increase was 7 per cent, as against the 3 per cent projected in the plan. Meanwhile, total imports turned out to be Rs. 21.3 billion, or 4 per cent less than the projected figure. The actual import gap was therefore Rs. 8.1 billion, as compared with the planned Rs. 10.9 billion.

Much impressed by these statistics, the Planning Commission concluded

---

[2] For a detailed analysis of this policy, see H. J. Bruton and S. R. Bose, *The Pakistan Export Bonus Scheme* (Karachi, 1963).

Table 25. *Foreign exchange earnings during the second plan period (millions of rupees)*

Item	Second Plan actual						Second Plan projections	Difference
	1960/1	1961/2	1962/3	1963/4	1964/5	Total		
Raw jute	872	870	848	776	820	4,186	4,100	+86
Jute manufactures	320	339	317	341	350	1,667	1,600	+67
Raw cotton	195	163	401	443	400	1,602	1,100	+502
Cotton manufactures	122	50	92	115	170	549	800	−251
Hides and skins	74	90	81	76	70	391	350	+41
Wool	83	87	91	97	90	448	400	+48
Rice	54	112	125	71	140			
Fish	56	72	106	82	90	2,144	1,500	+644
Paper and newsprint	6	10	6	6	20			
Other exports	142	172	214	290	370			
Invisibles	409	464	500	514	530	2,417	1,400	+1,017
Total	2,333	2,429	2,781	2,811	3,050	13,404	11,250	+2,154
Adjustment for double counting of freight	−47	−45	−33	−26	—	−151	—	—
TOTAL	2,286	2,384	2,748	2,785	3,050	13,253	11,250	+2,003

SOURCE: Pakistan Planning Commission, *Memorandum for the Pakistan Consortium, 1965–6* (Karachi, 1965), p. 179.

that 'one of the outstanding features of the Second Plan has been its success in stabilizing and improving the balance of payments situation in the country'.[3] The full facts are somewhat less reassuring, however. For one thing, the plan's balance-of-payments goals were modest in relation to growth needs, though the caution is understandable in the light of first plan performance. More important, 'the gap between the country's foreign exchange earnings and payments for imports grew, both in absolute terms, and as a proportion of Pakistan's gross national product'.[4]

On the import side, the great increases were a natural concomitant of rapid growth in an economy able to generate, by itself, far less than the required economic resources. There can be little doubt that, in this broad sense, the record inflows of foreign assistance during the Second Plan – building, in turn, on a foreign-aided industrial base – played 'a decisive role in accelerating the rate of investment...and...raising growth rates [in Pakistan]'.[5] By the same token, the inflows mirrored a continuing climb in imports and a growing debt service problem, which could produce a chronic balance-of-payments crisis.

On the export side, a closer look reveals that only in 1962/3 and 1964/5 did the growth of merchandise exports exceed the actual plan period average; the lower growth rate target was not even reached in the other plan years. More specifically, the truth is that the manufacturing sector contributed little to the relative improvement in foreign exchange earnings. The prime boost came from

[3] Pakistan Planning Commission, *The Third Five-Year Plan, 1965–70* (Karachi, 1965), p. 79.
[4] B. Glassburner, 'The Balance of Payments and External Resources in Pakistan's Third Five Year Plan', *Pakistan Development Review*, Autumn 1965, p. 497.
[5] Pakistan Planning Commission, *The Third Plan*, p. 8.

agriculture and services: in particular, raw cotton exports produced Rs. 1.6 billion, as compared with the estimated Rs. 1.1 billion; fish and rice maintained a high degree of buoyancy; and invisibles (including private remittances and transportation and insurance) exceeded the plan target by more than one billion rupees. Exports of cotton manufactures, by contrast, recorded a shortfall of Rs. 251 million; and in general, the other manufacturing groups did not fare much better.

This export pattern clearly underlines the inward-looking, import-substituting nature of industrial expansion in Pakistan during the second plan years. It also brings into focus the high cost structure of industry established on the basis of a protected market, and the paradox that the sector claiming a substantial proportion of the available foreign exchange resources for development imports was unable to make a strong contribution to export growth.

To be sure, industrialization has changed the character of Pakistan's trade in a number of ways since the early and middle 1950s. Imports shifted markedly in favour of capital goods and industrial raw materials and against consumer goods: as noted in Table 26, consumer goods dropped from 63 per cent of total imports in 1951 to 30 per cent in 1965, while the intermediate items rose correspondingly over those years. There were interesting export shifts as well: raw jute and raw cotton shrank from 77 per cent of total exports in 1955 to 47 per cent in 1965, while jute and cotton manufactures grew from 2 to 24 per cent of the total; increases in such exports as carpets and leather goods were also recorded. However, export concentration remained very high, with the jute and cotton group accounting for 71 per cent of total exports in 1965 (as against 79 per cent in 1955); the other increases in manufactured exports were of a modest order. There seems no escape from the conclusion that Pakistan's rapid industrialization during the Second Plan failed to make any deep impact on the export sector.

Third plan problems

In the face of these balance-of-payments pressures and uncertainties, the Third Five-Year Plan projects a development programme of unprecedented size and seeks to reduce external resources from the Second Plan's 38 per cent of total outlay to 32 per cent in 1965–70. This would have been a most difficult undertaking even without a disruptive Indo-Pakistan War and the suspension of Consortium discussions which followed, for the plan envisaged not only a very substantial advance from a rather shaky export base, but also a decline in the rate of import growth far more drastic than the experience of the 1960s appeared to justify. With the war and its aftermath, the task becomes one of truly heroic proportions.

But the plan has undergone substantial revision in terms of accelerated spending in later years, greater concentration on agriculture, and a more intensive effort to utilize existing industrial capacity. There are also encouraging signs of progress during the plan's first three years. What the final record will show, however, remains very much an open question – all the more so because

Table 26. *Pakistan's imports of capital goods, industrial raw materials, and consumer goods, 1951–65*[a]

Fiscal year	Capital goods		Industrial raw materials		Consumer goods		Total	
	Amount (Rs. millions)	%	Amount (Rs. millions)	%	Amount (Rs. millions)	%	Amount (Rs. millions)	%
1951	140.8	8.98	436.0	27.80	991.8	63.22	1,568.6	100.00
1952	173.0	9.98	527.4	30.43	1,032.7	59.59	1,733.1	100.00
1953	119.4	19.00	178.4	28.39	330.6	52.61	628.4	100.00
1954	274.5	30.26	223.3	24.62	409.2	45.12	907.0	100.00
1955	250.1	26.67	229.7	24.49	458.0	48.84	937.8	100.00
1956	182.9	18.60	279.1	28.38	521.3	53.02	983.3	100.00
1957	318.2	15.18	459.5	21.92	1,318.8	62.90	2,096.5	100.00
1958	314.0	16.63	493.0	26.12	1,080.8	57.25	1,887.8	100.00
1959	337.9	20.10	382.3	22.74	960.8	57.16	1,681.0	100.00
1960	634.4	20.39	680.3	21.86	1,797.3	57.75	3,112.0	100.00
1961	631.0	20.62	1,217.6	39.85	1,207.7	39.53	3,056.3	100.00
1962	1,113.2	31.67	1,248.0	35.51	1,153.5	32.82	3,514.7	100.00
1963	1,140.1	26.94	1,416.1	33.46	1,675.6	39.60	4,231.8	100.00
1964	1,454.7	30.63	1,565.0	32.95	1,730.0	36.42	4,749.7	100.00
1965	1,884.6	37.94	1,575.8	31.73	1,506.6	30.33	4,967.0	100.00

SOURCE: Pakistan Central Statistical Office.
[a] Data up to 1956 cover purchases on private account only; since 1957, imports on government account as well.

of deep political tensions during the latter phases of the plan, and a mounting concern over the problems posed by Pakistan's growing foreign indebtedness.

The burden of foreign debt

Whereas external financing of the First Five-Year Plan had been chiefly grant-based, some 80 per cent of commitments over the second plan period took the form of loans.[6] As of June 1965, the total externally held public debt of Pakistan stood at around Rs. 9.5 billion or roughly $2 billion.[7] Debt service obligations amounted to $74 million in 1965/6, nearly 11 per cent of foreign exchange earnings during that year. By June 1967, the total debt had increased to $2.9 billion; servicing costs were $96 million or 13 per cent of exchange earnings.

Net of external debt service, the total foreign aid requirements of the Third Plan are expected to be about 61 per cent higher than those of the Second; foreign exchange earnings are to increase by some 51 per cent over the second plan figure. All things considered, neither a decline in the debt service ratio

[6] Pakistan Ministry of Finance, *Pakistan Economic Survey, 1964–5* (Karachi, 1965), p. 196.
[7] State Bank of Pakistan, *External Debt Servicing Liability* (Karachi, 1965), p. vi. Foreign debt figures in the present section are derived mainly from this source and from Pakistan, *Report of the Working Group on Debt Burden* (Islamabad, 1968), and also from unpublished World Bank materials.

nor a narrowing of the external resource gap appears likely during the next few years. What is more, if present trends continue, the Pakistani debt service may well exceed 20 per cent of its export earnings by 1975 and may approach 25 per cent by 1980.

A comprehensive study of the country's foreign debt has been made by the State Bank of Pakistan. The study is based on 209 foreign loans and credits contracted up to June 1965; it does not take into account the external debts discharged prior to that date. 'Starting with the payable balance of the principal amount of [Rs. 4.3 billion] at the beginning of the fiscal year 1965–6 and taking cognizance of foreign assistance in [the] pipeline, it brings out the size of half-yearly and yearly payments of principal and interest till the entire debt is amortized by 2014–15.'[8] This involves an estimated outflow of foreign exchange equivalent to Rs. 9.5 billion as principal and Rs. 3.3 billion as interest. Annual outflows begin at Rs. 432 million in 1965/6, rise to Rs. 558 million in 1969/70, and then gradually taper off until the year 2014/15. New loans would, of course, affect the total debt liability and would probably cause a shift in the peak period.

In June 1965, seventeen countries and agencies were providing external finance for Pakistan. The repayment position on these loans is shown in Table 27. The figures give an interesting picture: the total interest works out to 34.4 per cent of the overall principal; the major lenders are the United States (Rs. 3.7 billion), IBRD (Rs. 1.4 billion), IDA (Rs. 1.3 billion), Germany (Rs. 961.7 million), Japan (Rs. 741.9 million), and the United Kingdom (Rs. 737.1 million). Interest as a percentage of the principal amounts to 62.3 per cent for Great Britain, 52 for the Netherlands, 50.1 for IBRD, 48.4 for IFC, 47.2 for Canada and 41 for Germany. The Chinese loan is interest-free, and very low rates are recorded by the other socialist countries (12.4 per cent for Yugoslavia and 14.7 per cent for the Soviet Union); IDA, French and US credits occupy an intermediate position between the interest rate extremes.

These State Bank estimates suffer from two limitations. First, they have a cut-off date at mid-1965 and so do not take into account the appreciable lending to Pakistan since that time. Secondly, the estimates do not attempt to separate out the 'concessionary' part of the loans; they are not, therefore, a full measure of real resource transfer to Pakistan.

The real cost estimates of Chapter 3 are based on loan data as of March 1967. They reveal that the most liberal lenders are the United States, IDA and China; and that relatively generous lending terms are also provided by the socialist countries apart from China. But the post-1965 period is notable chiefly for the substantial overall hardening of loans to Pakistan.[9] There can be no doubt as to the growing seriousness of the foreign debt problem. Glassburner has summarized it well in the following words:

This alarmingly rapid rate of increase of servicing obligations is one of the main reasons why the [Third] Plan seeks to reduce relative dependence on aid as rapidly

[8] Pakistan, *External Debt Servicing Liability*, pp. v–vi.
[9] See especially Pakistan, *Report on Debt Burden*, pp. 53–5.

Table 27. *Foreign loans to Pakistan by source, up to June 1965 (millions of rupees)*

Country/agency	No. of loans/ credits	Principal repayable	Interest payable	Amount	Interest as % of principal
Canada	2	54.4	25.7	80.1	47.24
China	1	114.3	—	114.3	—
Denmark	2	31.2	9.8	41.0	31.41
France	26	119.8	28.9	148.7	24.12
Italy	1	14.6	4.6	19.2	31.51
Japan	9	741.9	292.7	1,034.6	39.45
Netherlands	7	72.3	37.6	109.9	52.00
United Kingdom	14	737.1	459.3	1,196.4	62.31
United States AID	38	3,377.0	885.5	4,262.5	26.22
United States Eximbank	9	247.4	73.6	321.0	29.75
United States other	2	28.6	4.1	32.7	14.34
USSR	2	181.1	26.6	207.7	14.68
West Germany	45	961.7	394.3	1,356.0	41.00
Yugoslavia	9	96.1	11.9	108.0	12.38
IBRD	19	1,429.2	716.3	2,145.5	50.12
IDA	17	1,284.7	287.5	1,572.2	22.38
IFC	6	48.1	23.3	71.4	48.44
TOTAL	209	9,539.5	3,281.7	12,821.2	34.40

SOURCE: State Bank of Pakistan, *External Debt Servicing Liability* (Karachi, 1965), p. vi.

as possible. But this is the other horn of a serious dilemma which is common to many underdeveloped countries: difficulties in marshalling internal resources make foreign economic assistance tremendously attractive; but, although it is (compared to commercial capital resources) very cheap, its continued increase inevitably entails the drain of a rising proportion of foreign exchange resources into debt servicing. If the pace of development is to be maintained, then, more and more must be borrowed for the purpose of meeting these costs, at least for a time.[10]

In the end, though, concern over the foreign debt leads back to the wider question of Pakistan's long-term balance-of-payments prospects. Both dependence on aid and capacity to service the debt will, in large degree, be a function of export performance and import substitution in the decades ahead. But the sobering fact is that, on the one hand, rapid growth in export manufactures is bound to prove difficult for various reasons, including stiff world competition, widespread trade restrictions, and high cost production in Pakistan; and that, on the other hand, vigorous import substitution will be constrained by its own necessity to feed on capital goods and raw material imports. There is also the complex issue of how far Pakistani commercial policy will promote the desired export–import goals. And meanwhile, a sharply rising external debt will itself impose a continuing heavy burden on domestic efforts to build a viable foreign exchange position. In short, there is no simple answer to the balance-of-payments question for Pakistan; perhaps there is no single answer either.

[10] Glassburner, 'Balance of Payments', pp. 520–1.

6. Selected aid programmes: national and international donors

In the Pakistan context, each of the main sources of foreign aid is a world unto itself. Taking only the period after the start of the Second Plan, one finds that no less than five countries – the United States, West Germany, Japan, the United Kingdom and Canada – as well as two international agencies – the World Bank and the International Development Association – had each committed aid funds well in excess of $100 million by 1967.[1] Three socialist nations, the USSR, China and Yugoslavia, had provided combined assistance exceeding $200 million. The US programme alone totalled more than $2 billion;[2] while the World Bank Group (IBRD, IDA and IFC) had committed nearly $600 million and West Germany about $295 million.[3]

But it is not simply a matter of scale. Some of these programmes are so varied and complex as to defy analysis in depth at any level beyond the individual donor country or international agency. And even for the vast programmes, it is open to question whether known techniques can yield a meaningful evaluation of single donor impact on Pakistan's economic development.

This study is not intended as a detailed probing of bilateral and multilateral aid programmes in Pakistan. Nor is it designed to reach precise conclusions on the performance of particular branches of each donor's aid effort. The major aid-givers are surveyed in order to point up broad parallels and contrasts among these programmes; to highlight the aid-giving process from the donor's perspective; and, in the light of experience in selected Pakistani industries and projects, to draw inferences about strengths and weaknesses of donor programmes.[4]

[1] See Appendix 4 below for details on aid to Pakistan by national and international origin; also Pakistan, *Report of the Working Group on Debt Burden* (Islamabad, 1968); and US AID, *Pakistan's Economic Development and United States Assistance* (Karachi, 1967). For a global review of foreign aid flows to the manufacturing sector of developing countries, see United Nations Industrial Development Organization, *Industrial Development Survey*, ID/CONF. 1/46* (Vienna, September 1967), ch. 3 (section B). And for a broad survey of donor country assistance programmes, see OECD, *Resources for the Developing World: The Flow of Financial Resources to Less-Developed Countries, 1962–68* (Paris, 1970). In general, 1967 is the terminal year for the aid statistics cited in the present chapter. At the time of writing, the relevant data were not available in as much detail for the period since 1967. In any event, it is the comparative aspects of the aid flows, not the absolute figures for each donor, which are of prime concern in the discussion that follows.

[2] Total US aid figures here exceed those given in Chapter 3 largely because the latter exclude PL 480 assistance under Title 1.

[3] Aid figures throughout this chapter are expressed in nominal, rather than real cost, terms. As noted in Chapter 3, donor rankings are not necessarily the same in both cases.

[4] Commodity assistance is a special case. It is treated separately in Chapters 9 and 10 because of both its large dimensions and its virtual confinement, until recently, to the aid programmes of the United States and Canada.

United States economic aid to Pakistan

Pakistan received a total of $3.5 billion in economic assistance from the United States over the fifteen-year period 1952–67. This was more than three times the combined aid provided by West Germany, Canada, Great Britain and Japan. Loans accounted for 38 per cent of the US total, PL 480 'grants' 37 per cent, and other grants 25 per cent. Much of the aid has been heavily concentrated in industrial commodities, power and irrigation, and the transport sector; PL 480 aside, these items made up over half of all US economic aid to Pakistan. Regional aid concentration was especially high: West Pakistan received more than five times as much US assistance as East Pakistan.[5]

The changing pattern of aid flow

But great size and concentration are only two of many important broad characteristics of US economic aid to Pakistan during those fifteen years. It is equally interesting to view the programme in terms of changes in aid flow over time.

While there are peaks and valleys throughout the period, the trend is, in the main, strikingly upward, from a total of less than $20 million in 1952 to about $260 million in 1959 and more than $550 million in 1965.[6] But the flow shrank in 1966 to the lowest level in more than ten years, a product of the unsettled circumstances associated with the 1965 Indo-Pakistan War; subsequent US flows have fallen well short of pre-war figures dating from 1963.

Some 60 per cent of all US economic assistance to Pakistan up to 1965 was provided during the Second Five-Year Plan, that is, in the last third of the period beginning in 1950. This, in turn, reflected a remarkable shift in the relative importance of development grants and loans in the US programme: non-PL 480 grants declined by about a third between the first and second plans, while loans underwent a more than fourfold increase; this meant a drop from 40 to 27 per cent in the grant share of the two successive plans, as compared with a rise from 19 to 45 per cent in the loan share.[7]

Only a handful of Pakistani industrial sector projects received US assistance during the 1950s – the grant-aided Pak-American Fertilizer Factory at Daudkhel,

---

[5] This is a rough estimate based on information contained in US AID, *U.S. AID in East Pakistan* (Dacca, 1966). The same report notes that US project loans and commodity aid 'comprise approximately 50 per cent of total capital assistance received by East Pakistan from all aid donors since 1960, [and that] counting only project assistance, AID's contribution is about 25 per cent' (p. 29). There is no published statistical breakdown of total US aid between the two wings of Pakistan. Nor is there available any assessment of indirect effects produced in each wing by direct aid to the other.

[6] US AID, *Pakistan Briefing Book* (Lahore, 15 November 1966), chart on 'U.S. Economic Assistance to Pakistan'. Unless otherwise noted, US aid figures in this chapter are derived from the *Briefing Book*, also from US AID, *Pakistan's Economic Development*, and *Statistical Fact Book: Selected Economic and Social Data on Pakistan* (Karachi, June 1966).

[7] PL 480 flows nearly doubled between the two plans, thereby maintaining a constant share of total US financing.

for example, and the loan-aided Pakistan International Airlines. By contrast, the 1960s have brought a substantial number and variety of US loans to industrial projects: the General Tyre and Rubber Co. in Karachi; the Rafhan Maize Products Co. in Lyallpur; the Singer Sewing Machine Co. in Karachi; the Intercontinental Hotels in Karachi, Dacca, Lahore and Rawalpindi; the Pakistan Industrial Credit and Investment Corporation (PICIC), for re-lending to private industry; and so on. In addition, there has been a series of US initiatives aimed at increasing the effectiveness of technical assistance to industrial enterprise: the establishment of the Pakistan Investment Advisory Centre in 1963, with a view to advising potential investors 'on [the] soundness of proposed new investments, [assisting them] in formulating proposals, [and studying] prospective industrial sectors for investment feasibility'; assistance towards high quality operation in the securities market by the Investment Corporation of Pakistan established in 1966 to assist in broadening the country's capital market; and expert staff to enable the East Pakistan Small Industries Corporation (EPSIC) to 'fulfill its function of appraising loan applications and assessing the feasibility of projects'.[8]

But having said this about US project aid to Pakistan industry, it is also necessary to emphasize that it still ranks far below infra-structure financing in terms of both size and breadth of impact. US AID, in fact, has made virtually no dollar loans to industrial firms;[9] nor has any US agency made a dollar loan to PICIC since 1961.[10] Only the Export–Import Bank of Washington (Eximbank) has provided direct dollar loans to Pakistan's industrial sector, which amounted to $65.7 million;[11] and since 1961, only Eximbank has made dollar 're-lending' loans to a major financial institution, the Industrial Development Bank of Pakistan (IDBP). Direct US loans to cover local industry costs are financed from the relatively small 'Cooley Fund' comprising rupees from PL 480 sales; as of March 1966, a total of Rs. 68.9 million ($14.5 million) had helped to finance building and production costs of twenty-six Pakistani firms linked (as required by law) to a US business partner.[12] Finally, whatever

[8] US AID, *Briefing Book*, p. 23. The US grant to EPSIC for improved loan appraisal is of special interest in this connection. By mid-1967, seven Pakistani commercial banks, with more than 575 East Wing branches, had joined in a 'consortium' arrangement with EPSIC to increase and make more effective the flow of financial resources to small-scale industry in East Pakistan; this represents a substantial, and therefore promising, mobilization of regional capital and skills. See P. Perera, *Development Finance: Institutions, Problems, and Prospects* (New York, 1968), pp. 346–51.

[9] In recent years, a $35 million AID loan was under consideration with respect to a Pakistan proposal for a steel mill in Karachi. Foreign aid negotiations on this huge project have now been suspended indefinitely. See Chapters 7 and 8 below for a detailed study of specific projects.

[10] The fact that, as of June 1968, there were still around $2 million in undisbursed US loans, undoubtedly helps to explain the drying-up of assistance to PICIC. And yet non-US lenders have been extending large credits to PICIC since 1961.

[11] This is an unpublished 1967 figure which includes terminated loans; it was obtained directly from Eximbank.

[12] Pharmaceutical and hotel firms accounted for fifteen of the Cooley loans. The Pakistan Fabric Co., a jute-bagging firm in East Pakistan, received three loans totalling $1.1 million.

might be inferred about the overall effects of US technical assistance to private industry in Pakistan, there can be no doubt as to its negligible size in the context of the whole US aid programme.[13]

By far the largest flow of US aid to industry has taken the form of raw materials, machinery and spare parts financed by development loans on a long-term basis. Massive commodity assistance of this kind really dates no further back than 1959: between 1950 and 1958, it totalled $189.5 million, most of which came towards the end of the period; from 1959 to 1966, $1.02 billion went to Pakistan as general commodity loans, and they never fell below $100 million in any fiscal year after 1959.[14] This, of course, was bound to reflect itself in a variety of shifting aid patterns. In general, though, it signalled a policy of continuing heavy emphasis on non-project lending in the face of an approximate doubling of US assistance between the first and second plans.[15]

The aid-giving process

Here one is dealing with a vast aid network that has undergone significant change in programme size, content and direction. The discussion will be confined to the US aid-giving process as it relates to Pakistan.

The Agency for International Development is very much at the centre of the stage, for it has exclusive authority over development loans and grants, joint jurisdiction (with the Department of Agriculture) over PL 480, and close working links with other institutional branches of the aid programme. It is also AID which serves as the major US channel for co-ordination with the programmes of other donor countries and the relevant international agencies.

For present purposes, perhaps the most interesting fact is that AID has developed its techniques of loan appraisal and review by the recipient country to a level of sophistication which no other donor, with the possible exception of the World Bank, can match.[16] Strong emphasis is placed on the economic, as well as technical, soundness of the activity to be financed, on the viability and consistency of the recipient's development plan, and on its ability to undertake the self-help measures which are necessary to ensure satisfactory economic performance. In the Pakistan context, important aid decisions frequently emerge from a process of intimate give-and-take between Washington headquarters and one of the largest AID field missions in the underdeveloped

The General Tyre and Rubber Co., noted above, obtained the largest single loan – $1.4 million for construction of a tyre and tube plant in Karachi.

[13] Industry and mining together received $6 million in US technical assistance during the second plan period. However, this did account for nearly 14 per cent of all such assistance in those years.

[14] These figures were provided by the Statistics and Reports Division of US AID. They do not include assistance given under PL 480; and they are made up chiefly of loans to Pakistan's industrial sector.

[15] Non-project, or programme, aid rose from about 38 per cent to 40 per cent of total US assistance to Pakistan in the second half of the decade 1956–66. Its relative importance increased sharply in 1967 and 1968.

[16] For a concise account of agency programming, see US AID, *Principles of Foreign Economic Assistance* (Washington, 1965).

world; between US officials and their Pakistani counterparts; and between all those groups on the one hand and international bodies like the IBRD Consortium on the other. Furthermore, AID lending terms are invariably liberal in their rate of interest (0.75 to 2.50 per cent), the grace period (ten years), and the repayment period (thirty years).[17]

This, however, is not the whole story. For one thing, the very fact of care in loan assessment has given a large 'time dimension' to projects aided by the United States; indeed, it is fair to generalize that they are frequently among the slowest to reach the stage of implementation or final rejection. Secondly, there is, surprisingly enough, little systematic AID follow-up on the operating efficiency and impact of assisted projects; in this respect, the agency is no less vigilant than other donors, but not much more so either. In the third place – and more particularly for this study – AID gives very little dollar support to public sector projects in Pakistan industry, or to local financial institutions (like IDBP) under majority government ownerships.[18] While couched in terms of productivity, this policy may well have deeper roots in ideology, that is, in the philosophy of promoting private, as against public, enterprise.[19]

In fact, there is only one form in which AID provides regular project assistance to industrial firms in Pakistan – the modest rupee loans financed by the Cooley Fund.[20] And the irony is that the careful process of agency loan appraisal characteristic of infra-structure projects seems to have had little place in the Cooley scheme of things. This is not to say that no strict formal requirements are laid down for prospective borrowers, but rather that, in practice, Cooley loans are typically approved on the basis of relatively thin evidence as to the borrowers' capacity for profitable business operation.[21]

The final point to be made, in this regard, is that where US dollar loans are

---

[17] State Bank of Pakistan, *External Debt Servicing Liability* (Karachi, 1965), p. 46; Pakistan, *Report on Debt Burden*, p. 184. The State Bank classifies all AID loans to Pakistan as 'soft' – along with all IDA loans, a few West German credits, and an Eximbank wheat loan; all other foreign loans are considered 'hard'. *External Debt Servicing Liability*, pp. 50–2.

[18] The above-noted technical assistance to EPSIC is one of the few examples of such support; so too the aid extended to the Agricultural Development Corporations, and to the ammunition-producing Wah factory.

[19] 'Government operation of all a country's major productive activities is usually inefficient and may lead to controls and policies inconsistent with free and open societies. However, this does not mean that the United States will refuse requests to assist governmental activities. The question is whether, in a specific country, the measures taken are justifiable from the viewpoint of economic growth and are consistent with efforts to create a viable free political and social system.' US AID, *Foreign Economic Assistance*, p. 16. It remains to ask why, in the case of Pakistan, practically no AID funds have been channelled to industrial projects in the public sector.

[20] This being so, there would appear to be a policy bias against allocating aid directly to individual industrial firms, whether public or private. Therefore, it seems that ideological considerations may account for much but not all of the low level of US assistance to public sector industrial projects in Pakistan.

[21] Cooley support has been under consideration for three new fertilizer plants in Pakistan, each involving a loan of $10–12 million. It is a fair assumption that assessment procedures on these projects are unusually thorough.

actually extended to Pakistani industrial firms, it is the Eximbank's appraisal criteria which prevail, not AID's. The strength of Eximbank's lending tests can hardly be doubted. What seems equally clear, however, is that they differ from those of AID in both orientation and terms of repayment:

There is no sharp distinction between A.I.D. Development Loans and Export-Import Bank long-term loans in terms of recipient countries or purposes for which funds are available...However, the...Bank finances only U.S. dollar costs while A.I.D., when circumstances warrant, can finance a share of local costs. The Bank usually lends for industrial or public utility projects needing considerable machinery from the United States while A.I.D. lends for a broader range of purposes. The [Bank's] loan terms are geared to the nature of the project itself; A.I.D. takes the nature of the project into account but adjusts the terms of its loans to the repayment capacity of the country.[22]

For Pakistan, this has meant that only five of Eximbank's thirteen industrial loans made between 1957 and 1966 were directly for plant construction, four of these being hotels; that all the loans carry the maximum rate of interest (5.75 per cent) permitted under US law; that none provide a grace period exceeding five years or a total repayment period exceeding twenty; and that several of the loans require repayment in eight years or less.[23]

The World Bank Group

As of June 1967, the World Bank Group had committed a total of some $774 million in loans and investments to Pakistan – slightly more than a fifth of the country's aggregate economic aid inflows from the United States.[24] In terms of overall size, the Group's commitments to Pakistan ranked third only to those in India ($1.9 billion) and Japan ($857 million).

Major types and dimensions of Group assistance

Of the three Group members, the World Bank has operated the oldest and largest programme in Pakistan: since 1952, IBRD has made twenty-three loans worth $425.3 million, or roughly 55 per cent of the Group total. The IDA programme began in 1962, about two years after the organization was created; it has since extended the same number of credits, amounting to $331 million or 43 per cent of all Group financing. From 1958, also two years after its establishment, IFC has made eight investments worth $17.8 million and accounting for the other 2 per cent of the Group figure.

As a matter of fact, the flow of Group assistance to Pakistan is an even more recent phenomenon than these IDA and IFC statistics suggest. While

[22] US AID, *Foreign Economic Assistance*, p. 44.
[23] While the differences between AID and Eximbank's appraisal criteria are real, they should not be exaggerated. AID does not appear to have financed any local costs in Pakistan (apart from PL 480 transactions). And the tying of AID loans has necessarily meant heavy Pakistani purchases of machinery from the United States.
[24] IBRD and IDA, *Annual Report 1966/67* (Washington, 1967), p. 69; IFC, *Annual Report 1966/67* (Washington, 1967), p. 26. Unless otherwise specified, Group statistics are derived from these sources and from IBRD, IFC and IDA, *The World Bank Group in Pakistan* (Washington, 1965).

IBRD lending shows no clear trend over the past fifteen years, the second half of the period has been the more active one by far; approximately 70 per cent of the flow has occurred in the 1960s, and around half during the years 1961–4.[25] Furthermore, IDA credits were relatively modest in the first two years, with the 1964/5 flows providing nearly three-quarters of the total. And substantial IFC financing did not begin until 1962, with the years 1965–7 producing two-thirds of all commitments.

Each member of the Group has developed its own pattern of sectoral concentration in Pakistan. For the World Bank, it is transportation, industry, and power and irrigation (including the Indus Basin), in descending order of magnitude; indeed, those sectors absorbed virtually the entire portfolio of IBRD financing in Pakistan between 1952 and 1965. For IDA, it is transportation, agriculture and the Indus Basin, which together accounted for almost four-fifths of total credits. And for IFC, it has been exclusively the industrial sector from the very beginning.

Focusing on industry alone, one finds, again, that each institution has played its own special role in the Pakistan setting. As of 1965, IBRD had made seven loans in all, totalling $113.4 million. With one exception, they went (for re-lending) to PICIC, a privately owned development finance company established in 1957 largely on the advice of the World Bank.[26] The sole case of direct IBRD support to an industrial firm, and the first IBRD loan to Pakistan industry, is that of Karnaphuli Paper, which received $4.2 million in 1955 towards construction of an integrated pulp and paper mill in East Pakistan.

By 1965, in contrast, IDA had extended only one credit to the industrial sector. The 1962 'industrial estates' loan of $6.5 million is particularly interesting, however, for it represents a pioneer donor effort to stimulate the growth of a wide variety of small- and medium-scale industries in West Pakistan. Then, too, IDA provided two significant credits in 1966: $25 million in January, to finance imports of components and spare parts for commercial vehicles assembled in domestic plants; and another $25 million in December, to finance import requirements of several Pakistani capital goods industries, including steel castings, diesel engines, and electrical and tubewell equipment. These mark the first year that the World Bank Group provided commodity aid designed for expanded utilization of plant capacity in Pakistan's industrial sector.[27]

As for IFC, it has been (since 1955) the one member of the Group to make direct project loans to industry. By 1967, it had become involved in loan and equity financing with six private manufacturing enterprises. Ismail Cement Industries Ltd has the largest IFC participation ($5.7 million in two commit-

[25] Annual Group data are taken from US AID, *Statistical Fact Book*, table 9.3.
[26] By March 1969, the World Bank had made a total of eight PICIC loans amounting to $184.2 million. IBRD, Bank Press Release No. 69/16 (Washington, D.C., 19 March 1969), pp. 1–2.
[27] It should be noted that, in the Pakistan Consortium, the Group had previously done much to convince donors of the prime importance of commodity assistance as an instrument of foreign aid policy. See Chapter 10 below.

ments), followed by Pakistan Paper Corporation Ltd (a 1967 investment of $5.2 million) and Packages Ltd (a paper product investment of $3.2 million).[28] In addition, IFC is a 5 per cent shareholder in PICIC, and both have undertaken a number of joint industrial investments.[29]

Group techniques of aid-giving

There is no easy way to describe the aid-giving process of the World Bank Group. Even the broadest inspection would point up considerable divergencies in terms of individual Group members, time periods and economic sectors. It is proposed, here, to spell out a few of these differences, but at the same time to highlight features in common; and to note some striking contrasts and similarities between the Group on the one side and US aid-giving on the other.

It seems appropriate to begin with the Group's own assessment of its special strengths as a source of development aid:

As multilateral institutions with a broad mandate from...governments, the World Bank Group has certain advantages in the administration of development finance. The [fact of member-government ownership] creates the possibility of an unusually close and co-operative relationship between the Bank Group and the developing countries. After 21 years of operations and with an international staff chosen strictly on professional merits, the Group has acquired special experience and expertise in the development field. It has no political, commercial or other non-development objectives to distract it from its function of assisting the economic growth of its developing member countries. In providing external finance for projects of high economic priority, and in offering advice on a wide range of development problems in the less developed countries, the Bank Group may help bring about a more effective use of domestic resources and of assistance made available under bilateral programs.[30]

There can be little doubt as to the general cogency of this reasoning.

All three agencies, for example, provide their funds in untied form. Indeed, borrowers from IBRD and IDA are required to purchase their materials and equipment in those member countries (or Switzerland) which offer the best value. This is in sharp contrast to the predominant aid-tying enforced by the United States and most other donors. More important, it has probably meant substantial savings in foreign exchange costs for many developing countries including Pakistan.

Equally clear is the fact that the World Bank Group, like US AID, has become a veritable treasure house of information and understanding on problems and prospects of the Pakistan economy. In large part, this is the product of long-time IBRD (and AID) concern with basic issues of economic planning and policy in the country – the kind of concern which culminated in a widespread

---

[28] These figures represent the 'original principal amount', as against the 'credit amount' given in Appendix 4 below. Pakistan Paper is a joint venture with a German industrial consortium and Pakistani private investors. A $25 million integrated pulp and paper mill is to be established. IFC, *Annual Report, 1966/67*, p. 15.

[29] As of March 1969, these involved five Pakistani enterprises and $22.2 million in total financing. IBRD, Press Release No. 69/16, p. 2.

[30] IBRD and IDA, *Annual Report, 1966/67*, pp. 6–7.

new appreciation of the role of commodity aid in economic development. It is also the result of a sophisticated loan appraisal system carefully nurtured over the past two decades.

The World Bank (like AID) has built up elaborate, and generally painstaking, procedures for judging the 'cost-benefit' effects and the creditworthiness of infra-structure and agricultural projects, in Pakistan specifically and throughout the underdeveloped world.[31] The IFC, on the other hand, has been responsible for detailed appraisal and supervision of all Group projects relating to manufacturing industry, mining and development finance companies.[32] Pursuant to these tasks, both agencies maintain close contact with Pakistani projects by sending special missions abroad for on-the-spot discussion and investigation.

This whole process of policy and project appraisal has reached its highest point through the device of the Aid Consortium. Here, undoubtedly, is one of the major innovations in the development field over the past ten years.[33] The Consortium formed by IBRD in 1960 has revolutionized the giving and use of foreign aid in Pakistan. Duplication and overlapping of donor programmes has been substantially reduced; an effective forum has been created for comprehensive discussion of the country's problems by donors and recipient alike; the technique of collective aid-pledging has broadened the time horizon of Pakistan's planning authorities; increasing reliance on performance tests has raised levels of expertise and strengthened efforts towards sound implementation of policy.

It would, of course, be a mistake to attribute these Consortium results exclusively to World Bank action; US AID, for instance, has played a constructive and significant role in the total setting. Nor would it be correct to assume unqualified Consortium success, for serious problems of overall financing and aid utilization remain to be solved.[34]

And there are other factors to be weighed in the balance as far as the process of the World Bank's aid-giving is concerned. In the first place, the cost of detailed technical analysis of proposed Pakistani development schemes has, as in the US case, frequently been prolonged delay between submission and execution of the project. Secondly, there is reason to believe that, in general,

[31] For an intensive analysis of project appraisal techniques based on IBRD experience, see J. A. King, Jr., *Economic Development Projects and Their Appraisal: Cases and Principles from the Experience of the World Bank* (Baltimore, 1967).

[32] Effective 1 November 1968, the Development Finance Companies Department was transferred from IFC to the World Bank. In October 1969, IBRD established an Industrial Projects Department, whose purpose 'will be both to expand Bank lending in the industrial sector, and to make practical recommendations to the developing countries as to how they can best accelerate their industrial growth', IBRD, Bank Press Release (Washington, D.C., 2 October 1969).

[33] See J. White, *Pledged to Development: A Study of International Consortia and the Strategy of Aid* (London, 1967).

[34] There is clear evidence of Pakistani disquiet over the levels, terms and procedures of Consortium financing in recent years. 'Unfortunately, there has been a gradual change in the original concept of the Consortium since 1965 which has affected its utility as an enlightened framework for foreign assistance on a multilateral basis.' Pakistan Planning Commission, *Memorandum for the Pakistan Consortium, 1969–70* (Islamabad, 1969), p. 37.

the indirect – that is, secondary or linkage – economic effects of major schemes are given little consideration, particularly as regards projects in the industrial sector. Thirdly, evaluation of ongoing and completed projects appears to be neither regular nor intense; in this connection, it is worth noting that the Bank Group, by contrast with AID, maintains a very small field staff in Pakistan which, however influential it might be on policy issues, is not equipped to play a continuing follow up role.

Nor is this all. It needs to be added that, aid-tying aside, IDA is the only member of the Group to compare favourably with US AID in the liberality of its loan terms for Pakistan (0.75 per cent interest, ten-year grace period, forty years for repayment).[35] And except for Karnaphuli Paper and the Agricultural Development Bank of Pakistan (ADBP), there have been no Group loans to industrial or financial companies in Pakistan's public sector;[36] the AID parallel here is particularly striking, and in both cases the question remains whether it is considerations of productive efficiency or social philosophy that are paramount.

West Germany

The West German foreign aid programme is a relatively recent development. It resulted from a conscious decision on the part of the German authorities to achieve an international position commensurate with the country's economic power and political interests. The highly successful reconstruction of the West German economy provided the Federal Republic with the means to embark on aid diplomacy. Once the decision had been taken in 1960, the programme increased at a phenomenal rate. Within a year, total disbursements of bilateral capital and technical assistance had risen from very modest levels to some US $242 million; they have increased regularly since then and reached $493 million in 1967.[37] Germany now ranks third among donor countries on a world-wide basis, immediately after the United States and France.

German aid to Pakistan also shows a striking growth pattern. In 1960, about $160,000 were disbursed in grants for technical assistance. Within a year that figure had jumped to $1.1 million and had been supplemented by $4.2 million in resource transfers through commodity sales for local currency. A surge of

[35] Pakistan, *External Debt Servicing Liability*, pp. 44–5; and *Report on Debt Burden*, p. 184. Interest on IBRD loans to Pakistan varies from 4.625 to 6 per cent, the grace period from zero to six years, and the repayment period from seven-and-a-half to twenty years. For IFC investments, the corresponding figures are 7 to 8 per cent, three to five-and-a-half years, and four to eleven years.

[36] IDA has extended three agricultural credits to ADBP since its creation in 1961; the third credit, totalling $27.7 million, was provided in June 1969. IDA, Press Release No. 69/25 (Washington, D.C., 26 June 1969), p. 2. In February 1970, IDA announced a $20 million credit to IDBP. IDA, Press Release No. 70/5 (Washington, D.C., 11 February 1970).

[37] OECD, *Geographical Distribution of Financial Flows to Less Developed Countries, 1960–1964* (Paris, 1966), p. 12; and *Development Assistance: Efforts and Policies of the Members of the Development Assistance Committee, 1969 Review* (Paris, 1969), pp. 300–1. Unless otherwise specified, figures in this section are derived from OECD sources, and from Pakistan, *Report on Debt Burden*.

development loans brought commitments of German aid up to about $90 million in 1962. There was a sharp decline in 1963, but with sizable continuing credits, annual assistance has since ranged between $30 million and $70 million. Over the whole second plan period (1960–5), German aid commitments amounted to $216 million, or 10.9 per cent of all (non-PL 480) foreign resources made available to Pakistan in those years.[38] At the end of 1967, total German aid to Pakistan exceeded $300 million. This has meant third rank for Germany, after the United States and the World Bank Group.

In 1966, Pakistan received only $1.4 million worth of German grants, that is, less than one per cent of the Federal Republic's total grant outlays. However, new development loans of $37 million, more than 10 per cent of the total, were directed to Pakistan. Germany also committed itself to accept almost $1 million of Pakistan currency in exchange for goods and services.

Roughly 85 per cent of the 1966 capital assistance (including export credits) was allocated to specific Pakistani projects. Most of these involved the develop ment of energy resources, transport and communications. Three projects in the manufacturing sector received $8.7 million. Non-project aid accounted for about $9 million, chiefly in the form of current import financing.

Development loans have made up the greater part of German aid to Pakistan. They are normally tied to German sources of supply, despite the continuing strength of the country's balance of payments. Of the six loans extended in 1966, four were earmarked for infra-structure and 'investment' projects; these carried interest charges of 3 per cent, were to mature in slightly more than twenty-five years, and provided a grace period of seven-and-a-half years. On the other hand, the $7.5 million commodity loan carried an interest charge of 5.5 per cent, was to mature in twenty years, and had a grace period of five-and-a-half years.

It might appear that the German government has so arranged its loan terms as to encourage Pakistan to use external resources for long-run projects rather than for financing current imports. Yet Germany is one of the few donor countries to devote a substantial amount of its aid to commodity lending. And the government has stated that 'capital aid credits to secure the supply of raw materials, semi-finished products and spare parts required for the utilization of existing production capacities (maintenance support) are to be granted to countries enjoying advanced economic development to promote a smooth functioning of the economy'.[39] In fact, according to John White, the 'technical requirements of economic development are constantly at the forefront [in the administration of the German aid programme]; the practice of aid-giving is constantly under scrutiny by the sole yardstick of its contribution to development'.[40]

[38] Pakistan Planning Commission, *Memorandum for the Pakistan Consortium, 1966–67* (Karachi, 1966), pp. 108–10.
[39] West Germany, 'Memorandum to the OECD Development Assistance Committee', unpublished mimeo. (Paris, 1967), p. 4.
[40] J. White, *German Aid: A Survey of the Sources, Policy and Structure of German Aid* (London, 1965), p. 9.

But there is no unified German control over foreign aid. Since 1961, a Federal Ministry for Economic Co-operation (BMZ) has been responsible for overall development policy as well as technical assistance. Two other departments, however, retain substantial aid authority: the Ministry for Economics oversees the planning and processing of capital assistance projects; whereas the Ministry for Foreign Affairs takes the political decisions on aid policy and co-ordination. This division of responsibilities does not seem to make for smooth administration. White gives several instances of tension and conflict among the three departments, which may well have weakened the entire aid-giving process.[41]

Three specialized agencies administer the aid programme: the Reconstruction Loan Corporation (KFW), the German Corporation for the Promotion of The Interests of Developing Countries (GAWI), and the Federal Office for Manufacturing Industry (BAW). KFW handles all bilateral assistance; it has acquired considerable expertise over the years since 1948, when it was set up to help finance Germany's economic recovery and to make loans to German exporters. The other two agencies are responsible for the selection and appointment of German experts going overseas on technical assistance missions.[42]

Canada

Canadian aid to Pakistan had its start nearly twenty years ago, and the flow has been sizable ever since. From 1950 to 1967, Pakistan received approximately Cdn $227 million under the Colombo Plan, or nearly a third of total Canadian disbursements under the plan.[43] In addition, about $42 million in Canadian long-term export lending has been provided for Pakistan since 1962, under Section 21 A of the Export Credits Insurance Act. Canada now ranks fourth, after the United States, the World Bank Group and West Germany, among the official donors of aid to the Pakistan economy.

For the most part, Canada's foreign assistance has taken the form of outright grants. Indeed, Canadian lending under the Colombo Plan did not begin until 1964. By 1967, however, some $31 million worth of development loans had gone to Pakistan. Both the grants and loans are tied mainly to Canadian goods and services. Combined aid commitments over the second plan period amounted to $82 million for Canada, or roughly 4 per cent of Pakistan's aid from all donors.

[41] *Ibid.* ch. 3.

[42] In 1970, after the time of writing, the West German Government introduced a number of organizational changes designed to broaden the role of the Ministry for Economic Co-operation and to effect a clearer delineation of responsibilities among the various aid agencies. See 'Reshaping German Development Aid: Interview with Professor Karl-Heinz Sohn, Parliamentary Secretary of State in the Federal Ministry for Economic Co-operation, Bonn', *Inter Economics*, September 1970.

[43] Canada External Aid Office, *Annual Review, 1966–67* (Ottawa, 1967), p. 23. Figures in this section (all in Canadian dollars) are obtained from this source, from unpublished materials of the External Aid Office (renamed the Canadian International Development Agency in September 1968), and from the above-cited 1966–67 *Memorandum for the Pakistan Consortium* (Pakistan Planning Commission).

Canadian assistance has been heavily concentrated in three sectors: electric power, food aid and industrial commodities. Prior to 1959, power projects like the Warsak Dam absorbed more than half the aid total. Warsak alone accounted for $37.8 million and has become a major source of power in West Pakistan. During the Second Plan there was much less emphasis on power, but more recently it has again assumed very large proportions.[44]

A significant part of Canadian aid to Pakistan has been allocated to food assistance, ranging from about 13 per cent during the Second Plan to 20 per cent over the past few years. But perhaps the most important change has been the growth of non-food commodity flows since 1959. In that year, Canada provided Pakistan with copper and wood pulp valued at less than half a million dollars. Since then, both the range and dimensions of commodity aid have increased substantially. Copper shipments totalled some $11 million between 1959 and 1966; and wood pulp more than $8 million. In addition, Canada has shipped $14 million worth of aluminum and more than $11 million in fertilizers to Pakistan, together with considerable quantities of tin plate, tallow and nylon twine.

Other types of Canadian aid flow have been relatively small, for example: $15.8 million in varied agricultural assistance; $14.5 million for Pakistani manufacturing industry; $6.7 million for the transport sector; $4 million to develop the country's fisheries; $3.4 million to finance aerial surveys of its land and resources. In the present context, it seems worth stressing the fact that Canada has assigned a low priority to industrial projects, presumably on the grounds that 'industries producing primary materials for local manufactures or basic construction can be...considered as accessory to infrastructure, and thereby make a...secondary claim on aid funds'.[45] Only five industrial projects in the developing countries were approved over the entire period 1950–65; and Pakistan accounted for the three largest schemes, namely, the Maple Leaf cement plant at Daudkhel and the newsprint mill and hard-board plant at Khulna.

The Canadian aid programme is administered by the Canadian International Development Agency (CIDA), formerly the External Aid Office, set up in 1960 as a semi-autonomous federal body responsible to the Minister for External Affairs. Broad policy formulation is the task of a Canadian International Development Board comprising the president of CIDA (ex officio chairman) and senior officials of the Bank of Canada and the departments of Finance, External Affairs, and Industry, Trade and Commerce. CIDA maintains close liaison with other agencies concerned with aid, such as the federal Export Development Corporation (successor to the Export Credits Insurance Corporation in October 1969).

Canada, in fact, was one of the first donor countries to streamline and co-ordinate its administration of foreign assistance. It is also an active member

[44] The Kanupp Nuclear Power Project, designed to provide electricity for Karachi, is the largest Pakistan venture financed chiefly by Canadian aid funds. Canada has undertaken to contribute $48 million of a total estimated cost of $60 million for the project.
[45] K. Spicer, *A Samaritan State? External Aid in Canada's Foreign Policy* (Toronto, 1966), p. 170. Spicer gives an incisive analysis of Canada's foreign aid programme.

of the Pakistan and India Consortia, the Development Assistance Committee of OECD, the United Nations Development Programme, and an increasing number of consultative groups organized by the World Bank. And yet despite these strong multilateral links – or perhaps because of them – Canada has not developed the sophisticated aid-appraisal machinery, nor the on-the-spot 'aid mission' expertise, which one might expect to be an integral part of any sizable foreign aid programme.[46]

The United Kingdom

During the colonial era, Britain had developed deep economic and political interests in the Indian subcontinent. It was natural that, with Partition, these historical links should produce substantial UK economic aid for both India and Pakistan. In fact, Britain committed $124.3 million in development assistance to Pakistan over the second plan period, i.e., 6.3 per cent of all foreign financing for the plan.[47] Between 1950 and 1967, British aid totalled about $235 million, placing the United Kingdom among the top five official donors.[48]

Until the early 1960s, UK assistance to Pakistan comprised mainly long-term credits for infra-structure and for the purchase of British jute machinery; for the most part, it was neither specific project nor general commodity aid in the conventional sense, but something in between.[49] Since 1964, however, there have been substantial project and commodity flows – the former partly a reflection of a growing British desire to do things which could be visibly associated with the aid-giver.[50] A large proportion of recent British credits has been used to finance the purchase of a mixed bag of capital goods and industrial raw materials: buses, railway rolling stock, electrical equipment, steel billets, chemicals, dye-making machinery, and so on. These shipments give effect to the official UK view that 'there is a long-term need for increased "non-project" aid which results from the massive industrial investment already undertaken. This is generating increasingly heavy demand for imports needed to maintain economic levels of activity.'[51]

In general, British aid to Pakistan takes the form of tied credits under the

[46] Heavy Canadian reliance appears to be placed on IBRD assessment of aid projects and development policies in Pakistan and elsewhere. Quite apart from the merits of IBRD appraisal, it is at least open to question whether such a high degree of external dependence is best calculated to maximize the effectiveness of a substantial donor country programme. In May 1970, after the time of writing, the Government of Canada established an International Development Research Centre. The new Centre could well produce major improvements in the quality of Canadian aid-giving.

[47] Pakistan Planning Commission, *Memorandum for the Pakistan Consortium, 1966–67*, pp. 108–10.

[48] Pakistan CSO, *20 Years of Pakistan in Statistics, 1947–67* (Karachi, 1968), pp. 322–3. See also Pakistan, *External Debt Servicing Liability*; United Kingdom, *Overseas Development: The Work in Hand* (London, January 1967).

[49] Britain has also financed the purchase of machinery for the Pakistani sugar mills at Kushtia and Rajshahi.

[50] Electrification of the Lahore–Multan railway provides a project case in point.

[51] United Kingdom, *Overseas Development*, p. 92.

Export Guarantees Act of 1949. Loan terms vary over a wide range: from zero to 6.125 per cent interest, from no grace period to seven years, and from six to eighteen years for repayment. Like Canada, Britain has traditionally extended its assistance as a response to formal Pakistani requests, with little or no UK initiative and very limited economic appraisal of aid feasibility and results.[52] There are indications, however, that the British government (as well as the Canadian) has begun to ask more of its own aid questions; and this trend is likely to grow stronger under the stimulus of a special Ministry of Overseas Development (ODM).[53]

The ODM assumed responsibility for the UK aid programme in 1964. This role had previously been shared by the Treasury, the Foreign Office, the Commonwealth Relations Office, the Colonial Office and the Department of Technical Co-operation. Now it is ODM which works out broad aid policy, the terms and conditions of capital aid, the principles of technical assistance, the geographical distribution of aid, and British relations with international aid organizations.[54]

ODM is arranged administratively on the basis of area, subject and functional duties. The geographical departments are, in effect, regional study groups that assess the needs of individual countries and control the detailed deployment of financial and manpower resources allocated to the aid programme. The subject departments, such as education and medicine, serve as contact agencies for personnel involved in professional and technical assistance. As for the functional departments, they handle a variety of tasks including overseas appointments and co-operation with other aid donors. There is also an economic planning staff which cuts across all three stages; 'it is responsible for providing economic and statistical services for the Ministry, and for the formulation from the economic standpoint of the Ministry's views on development questions'.[55]

On behalf of ODM, overseas officers in British diplomatic missions seek to maintain close relations with agencies of the recipient governments. As of May 1966, there were thirty-six such officers, ranking from counsellor to third secretary, who were concerned exclusively with aid matters.[56] But ODM operates only two field missions on its own account, one regional development division in the Caribbean, the other in the Middle East, which advise UK aid authorities and help organize technical assistance activities. Accordingly, the home-based professional and technical staff and advisers of ODM travel extensively in connection with the preparation of programmes and the elaboration and execution of particular projects.

There is also the Commonwealth Development Finance Company Ltd

---

[52] This is doubtless a factor in the general popularity of British and Canadian aid among senior civil servants in Pakistan.

[53] In November 1970, after the time of writing, the Conservative Government transformed ODM into a functional unit of the Foreign and Commonwealth Office. The new agency was renamed the Overseas Development Administration (ODA). See ODA, *Aid for Development: Fact Sheet*, no. 1 (London, November 1970).

[54] The Treasury continues to deal with the World Bank, in consultation with the ODM.

[55] United Kingdom, *Overseas Development*, p. 35.   [56] *Ibid.* p. 37.

(CDFC), which was set up in 1953 as an instrument for joint government–private aid to the private sector of developing Commonwealth countries. Its funds are provided by the Bank of England, some Commonwealth central banks, and about ninety British industrial and commercial enterprises. As of 1967, CDFC had varied investments or commitments in more than forty enterprises in South and Southeast Asia. However, its total lending to Pakistan amounted to only $4.8 million; nearly half went to the Pakistan Paper Corporation (in co-operation with IFC, among other lenders), the balance being mostly for sugar mills and jute industries. CDFC's normal loan terms are 7.5 to 8 per cent interest, repayable within five to seven years. Its loans are not generally included in UK aid totals since they have only recently been reported to the Economic Affairs Division of the government of Pakistan. CDFC equity investments in Pakistan total $3.1 million; $2.6 million have gone to the Sui Gas Transmission Co., the rest to PICIC and sugar mills.[57]

In addition, the United Kingdom has a Commonwealth Development Corporation (CDC), financed entirely by government funds and established in 1948 to promote economic development in the private sector of the dependent territories. In 1963, it was authorized to invest in Commonwealth countries which had become independent after August 1948; Pakistan, therefore, remained beyond the scope of CDC financing. In 1969, the CDC was empowered to operate in all developing countries. CDC investments now represent approximately 5 per cent of total UK aid.[58]

It seems clear that ODM has done much to instill a new sense of expertise in British aid. There also appears to be substantial room for further administrative reform.[59]

Japan

Because of the ambiguities in Japan's approach to foreign aid, it is very difficult to be exact about the volume of Japanese assistance to Pakistan (and to other countries as well).[60] According to official Pakistan figures, Japan provided some $208 million in aid over the years 1950–67.[61] During the Second Five-Year Plan, Japanese aid is recorded at approximately $144 million, or 7.3 per cent of total foreign resources received in those years; annual commitments ranged between $20 and 38 million.[62] The great bulk of this assistance has gone to Pakistan's

---

[57] See Pakistan, *Report on Debt Burden*, p. 62; and United Kingdom Central Office of Information, *Britain and the Developing Countries: South and South-East Asia* (London, July 1968), p. 16.

[58] See Overseas Development Institute, *British Development Policies: Needs and Prospects, 1968* (London, 1968), pp. 41, 72–4; also CDC, *Report and Accounts 1968* (London, 1969); and ODM, *Aid for Development: Fact Sheet*, New Series no. 7 (London, August 1969).

[59] See, for example, T. Soper, *Aid Management Overseas* (London, 1967); J. Lambe, ed., *British Development Policies: Needs and Prospects, 1969* (London, 1969).

[60] See J. White, *Japanese Aid* (London, 1964), ch. 3.

[61] Pakistan CSO, *20 Years of Pakistan in Statistics*, pp. 322–3.

[62] Pakistan Planning Commission, *Memorandum for the Pakistan Consortium, 1966–67*, pp. 108–10.

industrial sector – mostly in support of particular projects, and with a strong emphasis on steel, fertilizer and chemicals.

Japan's foreign aid programme developed haphazardly out of the highly successful export promotion activities which, in recent years, have established that country as one of the world's leading exporters of industrial products. The Japanese government had used its World War II reparations debt as an instrument for improving the country's competitive position in world markets, especially those of Asia. Consequently, the line between war reparations, export financing and foreign aid became irretrievably blurred.

Most Japanese grants to developing nations have been made under reparations agreements to countries in the Far East and Southeast Asia which were occupied by Japan during World War II, such as Korea, the Philippines, Burma, Indonesia and Indo-China. Thus, Japanese grants to Pakistan since 1960 amount to less than $3 million, all in the form of technical assistance.[63] In addition, the Japanese government has disbursed approximately $60 million in development loans to Pakistan; this figure is far less [than the sum of yen credits committed since 1961. In 1966, Japan transferred about $500,000 in grants, mostly for technical assistance, and it extended more than $20 million in project loans.

The first yen credit to Pakistan was given in 1961 and amounted to $19.9 million. It was followed two years later by two credits totalling $53.4 million. Since 1963, Japan has extended three more yen credits to Pakistan; the last one in 1967, and each in the amount of $30 million.

Most Japanese loans are tied to Japanese sources of supply. The authorities justify this by reference to the country's highly unstable balance of payments. It is also contended that the tying of loans does not increase development costs since contracts are arranged at internationally competitive prices.

The terms offered by Japan for these official credits have generally been less favourable than those of many donors, though they have gradually improved. As of 1965, interest payable on nine Japanese credits represented 39 per cent of the principal.[64] It is now the declared policy of the Japanese government to soften 'terms of aid in compliance with the objectives stated in the 1965 DAC "Recommendations of Financial Terms and Conditions"'.[65]

Administrative control over foreign aid in Japan is shared by three government departments: the Foreign Ministry and the ministries of Finance and International Trade and Industry. They operate directly or through such organizations as the Export–Import Bank of Japan and the Overseas Technical Co-operations Agency. The autonomous Economic Planning Agency is also involved in the aid-giving process through the Overseas Economic Co-operation Fund.

[63] OECD, *Geographical Distribution of Financial Flows to Less Developed Countries*, p. 138, and unpublished OECD materials. Unless otherwise noted, figures in the rest of this section are derived from these sources, and from *Report on Debt Burden*.

[64] Pakistan, *External Debt Servicing Liability*, p. vi.

[65] Japan, 'Memorandum to the OECD Development Assistance Committee', unpublished mimeo. (Paris, 1967), p. 1.

Grants are usually negotiated by the Foreign Ministry with the recipient country, since until recently they were extended within the wider framework of the war reparations agreements. Requests for development loans are typically handled by the Export–Import Bank, subject to the approval of the Finance Ministry; processing is complex and irregular, because it usually involves the contracting firms, and often private banks which underwrite part of most loans.

Japan has no permanent aid mission in Pakistan, nor in any other country. However, Japanese firms awarded contracts for yen-financed projects generally appear to take great care in training nationals of the receiving country, and Japanese follow up procedures seem to be superior to those of many other donor countries.[66]

France

Although France is a major Western donor, having devoted 0.7 per cent of GNP to foreign aid in 1967, the bulk of its effort is concentrated in the 'zone franc'.[67] Consequently, French development aid to Pakistan has been modest; during the second plan period, France committed about $25 million in long-term credit, or 1 per cent of all external aid for the plan.[68] In fact, French aid to Pakistan did not begin until 1960: by 1967 it had reached $54 million.[69]

But even this limited contribution is noteworthy as evidence of France's aim, in recent years, to extend assistance well beyond the 'zone franc' to such countries as India, Pakistan and Mexico. Another recent trend has been an increase in loans relative to grants. It also appears that the French government is seeking to shift resources from 'soutien budgetaire', or maintenance support, to technical assistance. At the same time, both loans and grants are to move upward with rising public expenditures.

A number of French credits have been extended to finance the development of Pakistan's chemical industry; for example, the construction of a streptomycin plant at Chittagong and a DDT factory at Khulna. The largest single French investment is in petroleum; substantial aid has also gone to Pakistani sugar mills, and France has joined with Switzerland and Italy to finance the construction of a machine tool plant at Landhi. All thirty-nine French credits are tied, and none provide a grace period; most carry an interest rate of 5 per cent, and all the repayment periods range between ten and thirteen years.

French aid administration has undergone much refinement over the years.

---

[66] Interviews with senior government officials in Pakistan underscore the relative on-the-spot efficiency of projects aided by the Japanese.

[67] OECD, *Development Assistance: Efforts and Policies, 1969 Review*, p. 308. For an account of France's foreign aid programme, see France, *L'Aide Française au Développement*, Mémorandum de la France au Comité d'aide au développement de l'OCDE (Paris, 27 June 1966), and France, *L'Aide de la France aux Pays en Voie de Développement, 1966* (Paris, 1967).

[68] Pakistan Planning Commission, *Memorandum for the Pakistan Consortium, 1966–67*, pp. 108–10.

[69] Pakistan CSO, *20 Years of Pakistan in Statistics*, pp. 322–3.

Since 1966, all executive and administrative powers in this field have been regrouped within the Ministry of Foreign Affairs, under the Secretary of State in charge of 'coopération'. Funds for countries of the 'zone franc' are usually channelled through special agencies like the 'Fonds d'Aide et de Coopération' for French Africa and the Malagasy Republic. The 'Caisse Centrale de Coopération Economique' handles non-'zone franc' countries that have special relations with France, such as Tunisia and Morocco; while grants and loans to other countries, like Pakistan, are processed directly by the 'Direction Générale de Coopération Technique et Culturelle' in the Ministry of Foreign Affairs. France has established permanent aid missions in countries which receive a substantial portion of French assistance; in other countries the French Ambassador is usually assisted, as in Pakistan, by an aid attaché who is a full-fledged member of the diplomatic service.

The socialist donors

It is difficult to be precise about the foreign aid programmes of the USSR, the socialist countries of Eastern Europe, and China. Economic and statistical information is relatively scarce and fragmented; furthermore, the available figures are seldom fully comparable with those of the Western donors.[70]

The USSR

Soviet aid is by far the most extensive of the socialist group. Over the period 1953–66, the USSR provided a total of around $5 billion in economic assistance to the non-socialist developing countries – the great bulk of it in the form of low interest credits financing the development of public sector industry, and repayable in twelve years beginning one year after delivery of Soviet machinery and equipment. Pakistan's share of this aid was very small, about $72 million or less than 2 per cent.[71]

By mid-1965, only two development credits had gone to Pakistan. The first, in 1961, amounted to $30 million; it served to finance oil prospecting activities by Soviet technicians and the delivery of drilling equipment and related construction materials. A second loan, $11 million in 1964, financed the importation of agricultural machinery. Between 1965 and 1967 credits totalling $36 million were extended largely for construction equipment, power, land

---

[70] Among the important sources of aid data in this section are: K. Müller, *The Foreign Aid Programs of the Soviet Bloc and Communist China: An Analysis* (New York, 1967) and M. I. Goldman, *Soviet Foreign Aid* (New York, 1967). See also: L. Tansky, 'Soviet Foreign Aid to the Less Developed Countries', and (no author given) 'The U.S.S.R. and the Developing Countries: Economic Cooperation', in *The Soviet Economy: A Collection of Western and Soviet Views*, ed. H. G. Shaffer, 2nd ed. (New York, 1969); V. Vassilev, *Policy in the Soviet Bloc on Aid to Developing Countries* (Paris, 1969); OECD, *Resources for the Developing World*, annex II.

[71] 'The geographic distribution of Soviet economic assistance is highly concentrated; three countries – Afghanistan, India, and the United Arab Republic...account for 51 per cent of the total aid extended by the U.S.S.R.' L. Tansky, *U.S. and U.S.S.R. Aid to Developing Countries: A Comparative Study of India, Turkey, and the U.A.R.* (New York, 1966), p. 17.

and airport improvement, and industrial machinery.[72] All the Soviet credits carry interest rates of 2.5 or 3 per cent.

In 1966, Pakistan and the USSR concluded an agreement on economic and technical co-operation valid until 1972. The agreement provides for the delivery of Soviet equipment to various sectors of the Pakistan economy including power, transport, construction and communications. It is not clear, however, whether these shipments represent purely commercial transactions or subsidized exports.

In point of fact, the aid and trade aspects are typically bound together in the Soviet assistance programme; for example, payment of both principal and interest on USSR credits is often made in commodities exported by the recipient countries. That is to say, a basic Soviet objective is to encourage the development of socialist-type productive enterprises, and thereby to promote a steady flow of capital goods exports to, and raw material imports from, the developing nations.

There appears to be little USSR concern with the integration of aid into the borrower's overall development programme. Industrialization is viewed as primarily a matter of building heavy industry in the public sector – with Soviet project assistance in capital and know-how playing an important catalytic role in this process. Other routes to economic development are given either a secondary role (the agricultural sector, for instance) or virtually none at all (non-project industrial commodity aid). And USSR lending terms have yet to reflect any substantial concern over the possibility that short repayment periods will confront borrowers with serious debt servicing problems.

In this context, the question arises whether Soviet economic assistance to Pakistan is likely to expand significantly in the years ahead. The plain truth is that no one really knows, despite Pakistan's recent success in securing more aid from outside the World Bank Consortium.

Other socialist donors

Yugoslavia has been the leading East European source of socialist aid to Pakistan: eighteen loans totalling $58.5 million had been made by 1967; all carry an interest rate of 3 per cent, none provide a grace period, and repayment ranges from eight to thirteen years; interestingly enough, six of the credits financed factory construction in the private sector.[73] Czechoslovakia has extended four loans to Pakistan totalling $43.8 million, in order to finance a sugar mill and three power plants; these credits carry 2.5 per cent interest and are repayable in eight years. Poland has made two loans, amounting to $4.1 million, at 2.5 per cent interest and repayable in nine years. All of the East European donors apparently follow the Soviet emphasis on low-interest, medium-term project aid to industry, though, it is clear, not necessarily aid to the public sector.

By far the largest single socialist credit to Pakistan is the $60 million loan

---

[72] Pakistan, *Report on Debt Burden*, pp. 141–2.
[73] Yugoslav aid commitments totalled $30.1 million during the second plan period. Pakistan Planning Commission, *Memorandum for the Pakistan Consortium, 1966–67*, pp. 108–10.

made by China in 1965; half the credit is project assistance and the other half commodities. In addition, a loan of $6.9 million was made early in 1967 to finance the import of foodgrains. Both credits are interest-free, provide a grace period of ten years and are repayable in ten years. In December 1967, China extended a third interest-free, long-term loan, in the amount of $40 million. Commodity and raw material imports absorbed $15 million of it, and the remaining $25 million is being used to establish a brick manufacturing plant, a sugar mill, a fertilizer factory, and a foundry and forge plant.[74] Given these terms, as well as current relations between the two countries, it would not be surprising if Pakistan intensified its efforts to obtain Chinese economic assistance in the coming decade.[75]

[74] *Pakistan News Digest*, Karachi, 5 April 1970, p. 3. Then, too, the first ordnance factories in East Pakistan were completed in 1970 with Chinese assistance (see p. 1).

[75] Actually, by 1968 Pakistan had become the largest recipient of Chinese aid to the non-socialist developing countries. Pakistan's $109 million, together with the United Arab Republic's $106 million and Indonesia's $105 million, accounted for one-third of total Chinese commitments. OECD, *Resources for the Developing World*, pp. 304–5.

7. Case studies: the public sector

One of the basic objectives of this work is to examine the formulation of aid requests, aid negotiations and the utilization of aid in the industrial sector, with a view to discovering how these processes can be made more effective. Accordingly, close scrutiny has been given to many projects in the public and private sectors of both East and West Pakistan. The analysis in this chapter and the next is based on this broad survey, although relatively few projects have been used as specific examples.[1]

Such a survey is, in the nature of things, concerned with sensitive issues of public policy. The information derives mainly from personal interviews and unpublished materials in Pakistan and the donor countries. In large part, it was the availability of such information which determined the choice of projects. In addition, considerable emphasis is placed on project difficulties in order to draw the most useful lessons from past experiences.

Procedural intricacies, and consequently the time lags between aid request and aid agreement on the one hand and aid agreement and aid disbursement on the other, depend to a great extent on the type of aid sought. As a broad proposition, it can be maintained that the least complicated procedure involves commodity and programme assistance. The processing of project aid, by contrast, is cumbersome, time-consuming and complex. Technical assistance projects occupy an intermediate position in this respect. In the industrial sector, all types of aid – long-term project assistance, commodity aid, technical assistance and suppliers' credit – have been used. The immediate concern here is with long-term project aid and suppliers' credit, both of which have loomed large in the total picture.

Suppliers' credit

Suppliers' credits pose their own special problems. While it would be correct to say that they place the heaviest burden and the most stringent conditions upon the borrowing country, there are wide variations in practice from country to country.[2]

Belgian suppliers' credit, for example, has been available at about 7 per cent

---

[1] For a comprehensive list of industrial and other projects financed by foreign loans, see Pakistan, *Report of the Working Group on Debt Burden* (Islamabad, 1968); also State Bank of Pakistan, *External Debt Servicing Liability* (Karachi, 1965), appendices i-vii; Pakistan Planning Commission, *Memorandum for the Pakistan Consortium, 1969–70* (Islamabad, 1969), Statistical Appendix, part c. In addition, see Appendix 5 below for a list of foreign loan-financed industrial projects classified by public and private sector.

[2] One feature common to many of these credits is the requirement of a 10 per cent advance payment. For a general review of such financing, see IBRD, *Suppliers' Credits from Industrialized to Developing Countries* (Washington, D.C., 1967). See also J. G. Smith, 'External Assistance, Industrialization and Economic Development: A Case Study of Medium-Term

and is repayable in twenty equal semi-annual instalments. Under no circumstances is the total repayment period extended beyond twelve years after the orders are placed for import of goods. The procedure of utilization of Belgian credits is extremely cumbersome. A Pakistan importer must first contact a Belgian supplier and finalize the details of his proposed deal, and then submit the proposed contract to Nationale du Ducroire asking for the insurance cover. The supplier will simultaneously approach Credit Export, an autonomous body which is the main source of financing in Belgium. The proposal is then considered by Ducroire and, if approved, concurrence of the recipient government is sought to charge the project against the pledge made for the country at the Aid Consortium. At the same time, Ducroire gives an undertaking to provide insurance cover to the supplier and asks him to obtain permission for funds from Credit Export, finalize the contract and submit it to them. After this has been done, the insurance cover is issued and funds are made available by Credit Export. This procedure has often produced several years' delay in getting projects started.

The general complaint against Canadian suppliers' credit is the slow process of project evaluation. It is reported, for instance, that the Export Credits Insurance Corporation of Canada took more than three years to appraise the ill-fated Sylhet pulp and paper mills project.

French suppliers' credit lays down the condition that the minimum value of each contract reserved for projects should not be less than one million dollars. The credits carry an interest rate of 5.25 to 5.50 per cent per annum and are repayable in ten years. Repayment starts six months after the final shipment of the goods.

West German export credits are repayable over ten years without any grace period and carry interest of 6.25 to 6.50 per cent. These stringent conditions, coupled with a slow and complicated procedure for appraisal of projects, have resulted in substantial uncommitted pledges of German credit.

Italian credits carry interest of 6 per cent and are repayable in ten years. The real problem with the Italian credits is that there are no special financial institutions or associations of exporters to process the export credits; the importer has to establish contact on his own with an Italian exporter who is willing to sell on credit. The absence of an appropriate credit framework, together with the high prices of capital goods in Italy, has seriously hampered the acceptance of Italian credit made available through the Consortium.

Over the years, Japan has improved the terms and conditions of its export credits to Pakistan. The credits offered in the early period of Japanese assistance carried interest of 5.75 per cent per year and were repayable in eight years. Later, although available at 6 per cent, credits were repayable in ten years and also had a grace period of five years. At the first Consortium meeting in 1961, Japan offered credit repayable in fifteen years, with a grace period of five years and bearing a 6 per cent interest rate. On subsequent credits, the interest rate was

Finance and Suppliers' Credit to Ghana, 1957–1966', unpublished mimeo. (McGill University, Centre for Developing-Area Studies, 1968.)

reduced to 5.75 per cent; still later, the repayment period was increased to eighteen years and then lowered to ten years at 6 per cent interest. Japanese credit currently available to Pakistan has been quite popular with the aid-receiving agencies.

Suppliers' credits from the Netherlands took a long time to materialize. The Dutch government had not specified the terms and conditions of credit and had left it open to be settled through negotiation. It was only after considerable delay that a financial house could be found to assist projects under the Dutch credits. The credits are now repayable in ten years and carry a rate of interest of 5.75 to 7 per cent.

Current British credits bear an interest rate 0.25 per cent higher than the rate charged by the UK Treasury on borrowings from consolidated funds for a comparable period. In effect, this rate has worked out at 5.75 to 6 per cent per annum. The repayment period is now fixed at ten years with no grace period.

Project aid[3]

Donors claim that deficiencies in the preparation of requests for aid constitute a major impediment to the flow of aid and are responsible for long delays. The projects are not well conceived, and aid requests are sometimes nothing more than shopping lists. Some of the aid-giving institutions have therefore insisted on viewing project assistance as an integral part of a development plan, so that it may be possible to assess whether or not particular projects are in accordance with a clear and soundly conceived development policy. The obvious advantage of considering project aid in the context of a sound development programme is that it does, on the one hand, establish a set of national priorities and, on the other, provide clear evidence of feasibility. There can hardly be any doubt that this procedure brings into proper perspective the priority of a project, its technical feasibility and financial viability, and the capacity of the economy to implement the programme in terms of its institutional system. The World Bank and US AID have adopted this approach to project appraisal. However, it should be realized that their appraisals are the slowest among all the institutions providing assistance to Pakistan. The relative economic success of Pakistan, its streamlined planning machinery, and its long association with IBRD and US AID call for changes in this procedure so as to overcome the delays in starting industrial projects.

It goes without saying that such delays can be very frustrating to aid donors and recipients alike. Commitments can be held up for lack of timely action by the sponsoring authorities, or, still worse, on account of conflicting opinion on vital issues where more than one agency is involved. This seems to have been the position in June 1963, particularly in East Pakistan where some of the major projects were facing a situation of uncertainty: inac-

---

[3] The line between suppliers' credit and long-term project assistance is often very difficult to draw. Both are subsumed under the term 'project aid' for the purposes of this chapter.

tion and disagreement among sponsors had put the aid to these projects in jeopardy; this caused concern even at the highest levels of government in Pakistan.

To cite a few examples, commitments were held up by France, since a contract with PIDC for a DDT factory at Khulna ($1 million) was under revision and negotiations had not been completed on a streptomycin factory at Chittagong ($2.9 million). IBRD and IDA assistance for the Chandpur irrigation scheme ($9 million) could not be finalized, as the aid-giving agencies did not agree with some provisions of the proposed water rates ordinance which was to come into effect after completion of the project, and timely action had not been taken by the East Pakistan Water and Power Development Authority (EPWAPDA) to sort out this issue with the donors. West German export credit for lift pumps ($1.5 million) occasioned great difficulties because the negotiations with the suppliers had not been concluded. US AID was not willing to process an aid request for three transmission lines east of the Brahma-putra ($5 million), since EPWAPDA had apparently furnished conflicting information on certain aspects of the project and had no firm plans for power generation in the province; in this setting, transmission lines seemed unnecessary and an obvious waste.

As far as the utilization of aid is concerned, a better phasing-out of projects is needed. Slackened activity in the early part of the first and second plans, because of slow aid inflow, and feverish activity to exhaust aid allocation towards the end of the plan periods in order to justify increased aid, have very often resulted in distortion of priorities. It may appear to be sound logic for the authorities to press for full utilization of annual aid commitments so as to avoid weakening their case for further aid; but this is certainly poor economics in that it is likely to tie up resources, in marginal projects.

The main inadequacies of project planning in Pakistan would seem to be the following:

There is a tendency to underestimate project cost, presumably so as to get approval for inclusion in the development programme. Low costs are readily shown to reflect a low capital–output ratio, a low capital–employment ratio, and a favourable foreign exchange earnings–investment ratio in the case of exportable items. Once the project is initiated, it becomes an ongoing enterprise with priority over new projects; irrespective of complaints, resources continue to flow into the project. The fact that its final cost turns out to be several times the estimated cost is very often much less a consequence of price increases or errors in judgment than the result of a calculated mistake.[4]

Little demand analysis is undertaken for most of the industrial projects. Even in the case of projects where economies of scale are very important and where a thorough technical appraisal is undertaken, demand estimates are made in the most perfunctory manner. In planning a steel mill, for instance, careful demand projections are important for determining the size of the

[4] Needless to say, with direct costing of projects being so inadequate, little or no effort is made to gauge the long-run international competitiveness of these projects.

project. Yet the Krupps' feasibility report on the Chittagong steel mill based its projections merely on the existing per capita consumption of steel in Pakistan (6 kg) and on what was regarded as adequate for 1969/70 (9 kg) and 1973–5 (13 kg). The demand projections for the Kalabagh steel mill are based on what is termed 'the United Nations formula':

$$x = y.0.17+0.5733,$$

where x is the annual steel requirement per inhabitant in kg, and y is the annual per capita gross product in US dollars. Annual per capita consumption of steel is thus worked out on the basis of expected growth in per capita income and is finally multiplied by population to obtain aggregate demand.[5]

Inter-industry relations are not considered at all in project planning, with the result that the vital question of the origin of inputs and the destination of outputs is ignored. At Pakistan's stage of economic development, many industries are not producing for final consumption, and therefore the problem of inter-industry demand needs strong emphasis. It is important to analyse interrelated flows within the industrial sector in order to arrive at a more rational allocation of resources.

In estimating project costs, landed cost plus import duty are often taken as the ceiling. As a matter of fact, the import duties used in many such cases are not a protective device but were imposed for revenue or balance-of-payments reasons. In those circumstances, the real frame of reference should be landed cost alone; otherwise, there is wide latitude for lavish costing and inefficient operation.

With few exceptions, little attention has been paid to the careful training of technicians and managers at the project level. As a result, serious bottlenecks have frequently emerged in operating or maintaining the factories. Training of counterparts to shoulder the responsibility is an essential function of foreign advisers and technicians and should receive the emphasis that it deserves.

Progress reporting and the review process for industrial projects are wholly inadequate. The quarterly Pakistani reports are extremely vague and use neutral terms which neither generate confidence nor contain any warning of impending difficulties. Such reporting is, in fact, done in a routine fashion and serves no real purpose. If major mistakes in execution of the projects are to be avoided, a more efficient and meaningful system of progress reporting will have to be evolved. Periodic joint reviews by foreign consulting engineers and their Pakistani counterparts during the construction period, and by management consultants and Pakistani managers during the operation of the project, could help to solve many of the problems and to prevent disputes that are otherwise likely to occur.[6]

[5] Because East and West Pakistan have no present domestic steel production, their sizable market demand is easily defined by import statistics. However, it is still necessary to make a sophisticated quantitative assessment of future market demand.
[6] On the whole, progress reporting and evaluation in the donor countries is also very weak. Even the United States and the World Bank, for all their sophistication in aid analysis, devote relatively scant resources to continuing follow up on accepted or rejected projects and

The Khulna newsprint mill and hard-board plant

An interesting example of how serious difficulties might well have been avoided through sound project evaluation is provided by the Khulna newsprint mill and hard-board plant.

In June 1954, Messrs Sandwell and Co., Consultants, Ltd, of Vancouver, Canada, were commissioned by PIDC, the sponsoring agency of the project, to undertake a technical and economic feasibility study for the establishment of a newsprint mill in Khulna, East Pakistan, based on the resources of the adjoining Sunderban forests. The report was submitted in December 1954 and was approved by the appropriate authorities. Under an agreement with PIDC dated 12 July, 1955, the firm of Sandwell was appointed engineering consultant to the project and was made responsible for the following services: preliminary engineering, such as carrying out of a field survey, selection of site, determination of process and equipment, and preparation of cost estimates; design engineering, preparation of detailed working drawings for construction and installation, and supervision of construction and installation work; and other engineering, in connection with consultation and advice on the engineering aspects of operation and management problems, and on design for plant improvement and extension.

The feasibility report was revised in December 1955 to take into account the effects of devaluation of the Pakistan rupee in July 1955 and the increase in duties on imported material. The net result of these changes was a substantial rise in the cost of the project. The total cost was Rs. 49.5 million, of which Rs. 28.5 million (Cdn $6.2 million) in imported inputs were provided by Canadian credits under the Colombo Plan. The Canadian General Electric Company supplied the equipment, with financing arranged by the Export Credits Insurance Corporation. The rupee cost of the project was met through the use of counterpart funds.

The engineering consultancy agreement with Sandwell and Co. expired on the completion and installation of the Khulna newsprint mill in June 1959. But meanwhile, in April 1957, a management consultancy agreement had already been signed with Messrs Sandwell International Ltd, a subsidiary of Sandwell and Co., to provide for the management of the mill from the first day of its operation until 31 December 1960, with particular reference to the following services: (1) to advise upon, and to supervise in management and operating matters in connection with, the procurement of wood for the mill; and (2) to advise upon, and to supervise the arrangements for, placing the project in operation and bringing it to the rated capacity.

In March 1959 certain amendments were made in the 1957 agreement in respect of the scope of work as well as the terms of payment. In October 1960, before the expiry of the contract for the management consultancy, a fresh three-year agreement was signed which, in addition to the services hitherto

programmes. There is often an abundance of reports – AID if anything has too many – but the essential problem is their superficial quality.

provided, included responsibility for the sales programme and the development of markets and marketing methods inside and outside Pakistan. This was further renewed in July 1963 for a period of three years and was to expire in December 1966.

Sandwell and Co. was thus associated with the project for over ten years – in planning, execution, operation and marketing. The fact that its agreements were revised again and again provides prima facie evidence of satisfactory service. Furthermore, it was entrusted with the task of expanding the mill, and an agreement for rendering engineering services in connection with such expansion was entered into in July 1962. In the context of such a long association covering a wide variety of operations, one would have expected a smooth relationship between the consultants and PIDC. Yet serious difficulties arose between the parties towards the end of the contract period – culminating in the termination of the contract in December 1965, one year earlier than originally envisaged.

PIDC considered the performance of the firm unsatisfactory in terms of the care, skill and diligence normally provided by professional engineers. An expert investigation was said to have revealed various deficiencies and to have shown that the expansion work had fallen short of the required standard. PIDC claimed damages of Rs. 8.4 million, payable in Canadian dollars. It served legal notice on the consultants, demanding payment within one month of the receipt of notice, and set out the items which in its opinion were defective or unserviceable.[7]

The consultants argued that the inspection was carried out long after the completion of the additional capacity and after the expiry of the management agreement. They were not associated with the inspection and had no reasonable opportunity to observe and explain defects, if any; such defects might have been a consequence of faulty maintenance by the Pakistani engineers. A further contention was that the contract was terminated because demand for newsprint from the mill was very high at that time, owing to large orders from the US forces in Vietnam, with the result that the mill authorities found the contract for expansion of foreign and domestic markets to be redundant.

There is, apparently, more to the background of this dispute between PIDC and Sandwell. In 1960, when Sandwell and Co. was working as management consultant to the Khulna newsprint mill, a proposal was made by PIDC to start a hard-board plant adjacent to, but independent of, the newsprint mill.

---

[7]   The largest item in the claim, Rs. 7.7 million, related to the 'toilet tissue converter' which, it was maintained, was an obsolete piece of equipment that the mill was not able to operate. Another significant item, Rs. 270,000, involved two new 'autoclaves' which PIDC charged had defects in design and in the door-to-door sealing device. The autoclave body and piping were allegedly made of a substandard material which could not withstand the conditions of cooking, and the constant leakage of the door made it impossible to maintain the cooking pressure. A third important item in the claim, Rs. 250,000, was for the corrosion and erosion of the casing and wearplates of the pumps through faulty selection of material and manufacturing defects. Other small items – relating to tissue conversion equipment, turbines, grinder plant, and the crack speed of one paper machine and the drive motor of another – accounted for Rs. 170,000.

On the basis of the economic and technical feasibility report by Sandwell, the scheme was submitted to the Pakistan government in October 1960 and approved by the National Economic Council in May 1961. The total cost of the factory, excluding forest operations, was estimated as Rs. 8.3 million. The government of Canada agreed to finance it under the Colombo Plan.

The Canadian government, however, did not agree to the appointment of Sandwell and Co. as the consultant and suggested instead H. A. Simons (Int.) Ltd of Vancouver. Because of the difference of opinion on the consultants, the project was considerably delayed, and it was only in July 1963 that a 'memorandum of understanding' between Pakistan and Canada was signed in respect of assistance to the project.

The hard-board scheme, as revised by Simons, involved a cost of Rs. 14.3 million – Rs. 10.5 million in foreign exchange (Canadian dollars) and Rs. 3.8 million in rupees to be financed from counterpart funds. The substantial increase in cost was the result of: a change in the production process from 'batch' to 'continuous' in order to ensure better quality, uniform standards and minimum losses; inclusion of a steam plant; and the purchase of eight barges to transport raw materials from the Sunderban forests.

The project moved very slowly and was not completed on schedule. It has run into difficulties because of labour disputes and the lack of trained personnel. Very little attention seems to have been paid to providing managerial training, with the result that power and responsibility have become centralized at the highest level and the most senior policy-makers have been overburdened with day-to-day management problems.

The Fenchuganj fertilizer factory

There are also examples of projects which have progressed well enough in planning and execution but have faced serious problems in operational terms. The Fenchuganj fertilizer factory in East Pakistan provides one of the best illustrations of this. It was undertaken in 1958 with the assistance of a Japanese credit of $20.6 million from Messrs Kobe Steelworks Ltd, and a credit of $4.6 million was received from Mitsubishi Heavy Industries in 1959. No particular problems seem to have cropped up during the execution of the project; it was completed and put into operation on schedule. Repayment of the loans has been made regularly as envisaged in the contracts.

The tragic mistake was made in 1963 when, under pressure from the East Pakistan Agricultural Corporation for quick deliveries of fertilizer, the factory was operated at 98 per cent of capacity without any overhaul. This resulted in breakdowns, to such an extent that the factory reached only 33 per cent of its rated capacity in 1964. Replacement parts were not easily available, since by then the equipment had become obsolete through a rapid change in the technology of chemical fertilizers; consequently, parts had to be specially made. The failure to undertake an overhaul in time and the absence of proper provision for spares nearly ruined a very successful project.

The sugar mills at Kushtia and Rajshahi

An illuminating example of the many facets of foreign aid projects is the proposal to establish sugar mills at Kushtia and Rajshahi in East Pakistan. After approval of the scheme, the government of Pakistan allocated French credit for these mills. EPIDC, the sponsoring agency, argued in favour of West German credit, on the ground that the cost was 50 per cent lower. The basis of this judgment appears to have been the tender floated for machinery for the Kushtia sugar mills.

There is no doubt that the lowest French bid was 50 per cent higher than the lowest German bid – although there were wide variations within the German bids, with the highest being more than 100 per cent above the lowest. However, EPIDC was given to understand that the German credits had all been used up, and that the choice lay between not undertaking the project at all and going ahead with the French credits. It seems that EPIDC had become reconciled to French financing – and preparations were under way to establish sugar mills at Rajshahi and Kushtia financed by French credits – when EPIDC and the government of East Pakistan learned that, as a matter of fact, German credit was available for sugar mills but had been allocated to West Pakistan for mills at Bannu, Badin or Mardan. In the context of intense political pressures for parity between East and West Pakistan, the allocation of the preferred German credits to West Pakistan sugar mills became an explosive issue. To put the record straight, the real problem consisted in the refusal of the Germans to finance the sugar mills at Kushtia and Rajshahi, and not in the central government's failure to recognize the interests or wishes of East Pakistan.

A German aid mission (the KFW Mission) had visited Pakistan in 1960, and had travelled extensively, in order to obtain first-hand information on the country's economic development and to determine the industries and sectors in which Germany might provide assistance. On the basis of this survey, the Germans showed interest in the Karachi steel mill, sugar mills in West Pakistan, the supply of ships to the National Shipping Corporation, and in assisting the Khulna shipyard in East Pakistan. On that occasion, one of the senior officers of PIDC seems to have impressed upon the mission the necessity of locating sugar factories not at Kushtia or Rajshahi, but at Kalichapra, near Chittagong. The officer concerned had no authority to suggest a change in the proposed location of the mills, but the Germans were obviously impressed by the alternative site and believed that the original location could not be defended on economic grounds. The KFW Mission had itself made an appraisal of the Kalichapra project and found it economically and technically feasible. The Germans, therefore, felt justified in insisting that they would finance the sugar mills only if they were located in Kalichapra. Thus the government of Pakistan was confronted with a situation in which its whole system of requesting and processing aid was being undermined by an unauthorized action by a senior officer of PIDC. At no stage was a request made to the German government by PIDC or the Ministry of Economic Affairs for assistance for a sugar factory at Kalichapra. In spite of much diplomatic activity at the highest level, the Germans did not change their position, and this compelled the central government to allocate French credits for sugar mills at Kushtia and Rajshahi.

At one point, it was suggested that Germany make assistance available to sugar factories at all three locations. It was argued that crushing capacity in East Pakistan was below the plan target; and that since the existing sugar factories in East Pakistan, formerly running below capacity, were now operating at full capacity and earning a good profit, East Pakistan could support a mill at Kalichapra in addition to those proposed at Kushtia and Rajshahi. The Germans were not impressed by this argument; the idea of an additional sugar factory at Kalichapra did not find favour with them for two reasons. First, Germany was operating with fixed budgets of aid for the two wings, that is, with a ceiling on funds which could be made available to East Pakistan; and secondly, the Germans had by then hardened their position on the Kushtia–Rajshahi project and termed it unsound.

Meanwhile, with the problems of sugar mill location and German financing under debate in EPIDC, the Economic Committee of the Cabinet, Pakistan's Embassy in Bonn and the Ministry of Economic Affairs, the French learned of the controversy and lost their enthusiasm for the mills at Kushtia and Rajshahi. They did not withdraw entirely, but adopted a 'go-slow' policy in making effective commitments. It appeared at one stage that the project would have to be abandoned for want of assistance from abroad.

The central government, caught in this political squeeze, proceeded to negotiate aid for sugar factories in East Pakistan with several other foreign governments. The Minister of Finance, on the occasion of one of his visits to Britain, raised this issue with the British Chancellor of the Exchequer. The Chancellor noted that he would find it easier to contemplate increased aid for Pakistan if requests were made for those goods for which there was surplus capacity in the United Kingdom. Fortunately, the machinery for sugar mills fell in this category, and assistance of $4.9 million for the import of machinery for sugar mills was approved in June 1963. This assistance was allocated to the sugar mills at Kushtia and Rajshahi. It was further agreed that unused resources, if any, could go towards balancing or expanding the sugar factory at Thakurgaon, also in East Pakistan.

The streptomycin factory at Chittagong

For certain projects, particularly in the pharmaceutical industries, lack of technical know-how and patent rights has created serious problems. In February 1962, the government of Pakistan approved a scheme for establishing a streptomycin factory at Chittagong, in East Pakistan, with a production capacity of fifteen tons per year. In the first instance it proved difficult to find assistance for the project; but even when in June 1963 French credit of $2.9 million became available, no substantial progress could be made on the project, as no French firm with patent rights and technical know-how was willing to supply the required machinery. Indeed, because of the patent rights, only a few firms were in a position to provide assistance, and their refusal to do so made the utilization of the tied credit impossible. The essential weakness in planning this project consisted in not visualizing the type of difficulties which are bound to arise in a highly specialized industry protected by patent rights.

The penicillin factory at Daudkhel

The availability of technical know-how, patent rights and assistance is by no means a guarantee that a pharmaceutical project will succeed. A cogent example of failure even when these conditions are fulfilled is the penicillin factory at Daudkhel, West Pakistan.

The project was originally sponsored by the Central Ministry of Health and Social Welfare and was approved by the National Economic Council (NEC) in April 1957. On the basis of this approval, the Ministry of Health entered into an agreement with the United Nations Children's Fund (UNICEF) to establish a penicillin factory and sell the product at cost. The estimated cost of the project, with a production capacity of 6.8 million mega units, was about Rs. 10 million. In 1960, when the scheme was in an advanced stage of implementation, the Ministry of Health submitted a revised pro forma with a cost increase of Rs. 2.2 million, of which Rs. 1.8 million were to be provided by UNICEF in the form of machinery for manufacturing penicillin and Rs. 390,000 by the UN Technical Assistance Administration in expert assistance. The increase in cost was defended by the sponsoring authority on the plea of increase in prices, as well as on the basis that it was an entirely new venture for which no one in Pakistan was qualified to prepare a plan. As usual, there was little scrutiny of the revised estimates, and the proposal proceeded as an ongoing project. Even for the Central Development Working Party, which evaluated the whole scheme, this became essentially a matter of ex post facto approval.

It seems that having twice escaped with inadequate planning in terms of the cost and benefit of the project, the factory management became bolder and submitted, in September 1962, a plan for expanding the factory with a view to increasing its production from 6.8 million to 10.8 million mega units, at a cost of Rs. 5.2 million. In July 1963 the project was once again approved by NEC, but no progress was made until June 1965.

The delay has been attributed to a difference of opinion among three UNICEF experts. The first expert had recommended expansion of the factory on the basis of the existing techniques of production. A second expert advised against plant expansion and recommended instead the use of a better strain of raw materials to increase output. In view of this contradictory advice, the Pakistan authorities asked UNICEF to send a third expert to advise them on the appropriate course of action. He visited the factory in March 1965 and in fact opposed its expansion altogether. He also suggested certain improvements in operation which could materially reduce costs.

The most interesting aspect of the third expert's report was its demonstration that the original scheme was utterly misconceived. He maintained that, at the optimum level of production, imported inputs would account for two-thirds of the total production cost of 30 paisa per mega unit, i.e., 20 paisa per mega unit. The c.i.f. price of imported penicillin was 10 paisa per mega unit; and the report logically concluded that Pakistan should have continued to import penicillin rather than manufacture it. This point about cost is so basic that it seems incredible that it was not taken into account at any stage of project preparation. The sponsoring agency has tried to meet the argument by suggesting that the cost of production of penicillin in foreign countries is high, but that they are able to sell or export penicillin at a lower price by distributing the cost among the other pharmaceuticals which they manufacture. Sufficient information is not available to contradict or confirm this contention; but even if it is true, it could hardly change the fact that the rational choice for Pakistan was to import, not manufacture, penicillin.[8]

The DDT factory at Khulna

The failure to appreciate the tied nature of credit sometimes causes unnecessary difficulties. PIDC concluded an agreement with an American firm for the supply of machinery, against French credits, for a DDT factory at Khulna. It was agreed that the US firm would receive payment in French francs. But PIDC discovered, only at a fairly late stage, that the French government was unwilling to approve the agreement and insisted that the suppliers must have a registered office in France. PIDC then negotiated, and finally entered into, an agreement with a French firm for the supply of equipment for a DDT factory on a 'turn-key' basis.[9] This agreement was approved by the governments of France and Pakistan in March 1964. By June 1965, the loan had been fully utilized and repayment had already started. However, the executing agency's apparent misunderstanding as to the nature of tied aid delayed the project by about one-and-a-half years. This created a serious problem for the malaria eradication programme, which was supposed to use the DDT produced by the new factory.

The Chittagong steel mill

Japan has been particularly active in assisting industry in East Pakistan. The Chittagong steel mill has made a real contribution and has promoted Pakistani

[8] In a broad welfare sense, one could argue that distorted costing by foreign producers may warrant the establishment of domestic firms with lower real costs. But there is no evidence to suggest that the cost of producing penicillin in Pakistan was lower than the real foreign cost. Nor is it at all clear – given the problem of scarce foreign exchange – that Pakistan would have been wise to manufacture penicillin even if domestic cost had been less than the real cost of the subsidized foreign product.

[9] Under a turn-key arrangement, the supplier of machinery undertakes to carry out trial production and guarantees that the factory will be operational as soon as it is transferred to the relevant authorities.

confidence in Japanese machinery and skills. The mill was set up with an annual production capacity of 150,000 tons of steel ingot, and a corresponding production of 108,000 tons of steel per year. Since 1961 it has been financed by a number of Japanese credits totalling some $36 million and offered through the Consortium. These credits resulted in completion of the project without any major difficulty as well as expansion of its productive capacity.

Two distinguishing features of the project have been a keen appreciation of local conditions by the Japanese, and their emphasis on training. More than a quarter of the total labour was trained in Japan. A close liaison was maintained between the Japanese and Pakistani technicians at the time of the erection of the factory as well as when it started trial operations; this resulted in an effective transfer of technology and skills. Keeping in mind the nature of the industry, construction proceeded at a rapid rate: the first Japanese contract was signed in March 1963, and the mill went into production in October 1967.[10]

But while the Chittagong steel mill has been a success in the sense that it was completed smoothly and on schedule, from the planning point of view it has been a problem project. The original cost of the project was estimated at Rs. 114 million for a plant of 100,000 tons capacity. The tenders invited in 1962 pushed the cost up to Rs. 138 million. Revision of the project to 150,000 tons capacity raised costs further to Rs. 271 million. Actual costs have exceeded Rs. 300 million, giving a high capital cost of $420 per ton-year capacity. To be sure, the open hearth furnace technology used by the mill is out of date; but costs should not have gone beyond $250 per ton-year capacity. The main cause of the high cost of production is the size of the mill. A steel mill with a capacity of 100,000 tons per year could not have been sustained, but even at its present capacity of 150,000 tons the unit is uneconomic. This has adversely affected the industries which use its output. It is doubtful whether, in an industry like steel where economies of scale are important, it was a sound decision to build a unit with such a limited capacity.

The Pak-American fertilizer factory at Daudkhel

That the absence of proper cost and demand analysis may create serious problems and prevent full advantage being taken of the economies of scale is also borne out by the experience of the Pak-American fertilizer factory at Daudkhel. In the 1950s, when this factory was built (with US assistance), demand in West Pakistan was only 10,000 tons per annum. Since the projections of demand were based on historical trends in the use of fertilizers rather than on proposed structural changes in the economy, a factory with a planned output of 50,000 tons per annum was considered sufficient. A unit of this size was less than optimum, but the low level of demand was viewed as a constraint.

[10] By contrast, some projects have long been in a preliminary stage for lack of proper preparation: for example, the Khulna shipyard expansion, for which a German loan of $1.2 million was available, and the triple phosphate factory at Chittagong, which has made very slow progress with $1.9 million in French credits.

PIDC had to propose an extension of the factory when it found that, instead of an expected surplus, there was in fact a shortage of fertilizer, and that annual production needed to be expanded to 90,000 tons per year. This would have brought economies of scale, because the cost of production would have declined from Rs. 280 to Rs. 232 per ton. The scheme would take about three years to complete, and during this period, fertilizer would have to be imported if production targets in the agricultural sector were to be fulfilled.

Even for a scheme of such high priority it took a long time to obtain foreign assistance, as it had to go through the slow moving machinery of the aid-giving institutions. This points to rigidity in existing aid procedures, which do not discriminate between important and less urgent projects. On the Pakistani side things seem to have moved quickly; the scheme was submitted on 20 November 1962 and approved on 6 January 1963. Since Belgian credits were allocated to the project, consultants had to be appointed in agreement with the Nationale du Ducroire. This was not done until September 1963. The original offer of aid by Credit Export carried a high rate of interest; and more time was lost in negotiating a lower interest rate, which was not settled until June 1964. Draft inquiries for purchase of plant and machinery were made in September 1964, and tender inquiries in March 1965. Negotiations with suppliers were concluded by September 1965, and the contract finalized in December 1965. Bank guarantees were issued, and a letter of credit was opened in March 1966. Delivery of the machinery began in December 1966, but the main units were not delivered until May 1967.[11]

This sequence of events is all the more revealing because it involved an important ongoing project for which no feasibility report was required. It is not difficult to conceive of the damage to the economy through such delays: prolonged imports, loss of direct output of the unit concerned, and loss of direct and indirect output of other units through non-availability of foreign exchange.

The natural gas fertilizer factory at Multan

This West Pakistan project has been a cause of concern to the country's planners for some time. The original cost estimate submitted in October 1956 was Rs. 168.9 million for the production of 103,000 tons of ammonium nitrate and 59,200 tons of urea. The factory was planned for completion by 1961. The Economic Committee of the Cabinet approved the scheme in August 1957, and aid worth $10 million was made available by the United States. Within a few months of approval, a revised scheme was submitted to the NEC with a cost estimate of Rs. 239 million, that is, over 40 per cent higher than the original estimate. NEC was naturally reluctant to approve such an increase, but the scheme was eventually approved with a directive to the sponsoring agency

---

[11] Meanwhile, a Japanese credit of $1.5 million had been extended to Pak-American in October 1964, two French credits totalling $2.5 million in December 1965, and an Italian credit of $294,000 in January 1966.

(PIDC) to find ways and means of reducing the cost. The directive apparently reached PIDC after the project had been completed. A contract was made with ENSA of France for installation on a turn-key basis.

Although the factory was scheduled to go into production in October 1961, only a trial run was possible by that time, and the plant had to be closed down because of leakage in the pipelines. ENSA brought two plane loads of accessories to replace the defective parts, but only a marginal increase in production could be achieved. At one stage, Montecatini of Italy was appointed to give its advice on equipment, design and workmanship; but the dispute between ENSA and the sponsoring agency could not be resolved. It is not clear what final solution was reached, but the project was handed over to PIDC on 10 April 1963, with the ammonium nitrate plant working at 73.2 per cent of capacity and the urea plant at only 48.7 per cent. As a result, the cost of production of fertilizers has been very high. The failure of PIDC to set up an economically viable plant for producing fertilizer, even with the huge investment of Rs. 239 million, is extremely unfortunate, particularly at a time when government policy has been according a very high priority to the development of agriculture.[12]

The machine tool factory at Landhi

In certain projects which need a high level of technical know-how, it has been found useful to have not only foreign assistance and consultants but also foreign equity participation. The project for a machine tool factory at Landhi (near Karachi) was conceived by the Central Policy Board for Heavy Industries in 1962. In 1964, the Executive Committee of NEC approved the scheme for Rs. 96.1 million, with a foreign exchange component of Rs. 41.2 million. It has been possible to secure Rs. 18.4 million in French credits for the project, along with Swiss loans totalling Rs. 15.3 million and an Italian credit of Rs. 1.3 million. A foreign engineering firm is assisting the project on a consultancy basis, but while operations have begun, it has not been possible to find a foreign equity participant.

Efforts to persuade the consultants to undertake such participation have not succeeded, whereas the firms which might have been interested are unable to participate because they were not involved at the planning stage of the project. Here, again, is a good example of how an ill-conceived plan can create problems by committing resources in an inefficient manner.

The Zeal-Pak cement factory at Hyderabad

In view of the high rate of construction activity in development projects as well as in housing, there has been a heavy demand for cement in West Pakistan. According to WPIDC, in June 1961 the supply of cement lagged behind

[12] In July 1966, the Netherlands provided a loan of $572,000 to finance expansion of the Multan factory; this was followed by a West German export credit of $1.9 million in March 1967.

demand by about one million tons. It therefore proposed an extension of its Zeal-Pak factory at Hyderabad by the addition of two kilns with a productive capacity of 700 tons per day. There were distinct advantages in expanding the unit, since after expansion the cost of production would be Rs. 58.5 per ton as against Rs. 65 for a new smaller unit elsewhere. The estimated total cost was Rs. 67 million, of which Rs. 38 million would be in foreign exchange. The total saving in foreign exchange would be Rs. 34.9 million per year, which is the c.i.f. cost of 400,000 tons of cement imports in West Pakistan. Despite the critical supply shortage, it was not until mid-1964 that financing was obtained for the project, in the form of a $6.7 million suppliers' credit from Denmark.[13]

The Karachi steel mill

This mill has been the subject of serious controversy between Pakistan and the United States. There have, in fact, been two proposed Karachi steel mills. And there is a great deal to be learned from this enormous project.

The Karachi steel mill was planned for a production capacity of 575,000 ingot tons. Its total cost was estimated at $260 million, with an import content of around $167 million. Originally, the project was to be based on imported pig iron and scrap. Its rupee requirements were to be raised by National Steel of Pakistan Ltd (a private sector corporation organized in 1962), the government of Pakistan and local financial institutions. There were successive amendments to the scheme with respect to scale and investment as well as ownership, but the real bottleneck remained high cost and non-availability of finance. A loan of about $120 million was under negotiation with Eximbank of Washington, and roughly $35 million of this total was to be obtained from US AID; but these discussions have been terminated.

The cost figures, drawn up by US experts (H. K. Ferguson Co. and Arthur G. McKee and Co., consulting engineers for National Steel Corporation of Pittsburgh and Armco Steel Corporation, respectively), were found to be low, and it was this which caused the breakdown in negotiations. An AID 'Project Committee' had concluded that the total cost was underestimated by $45 million ($32 million in foreign exchange). At this point the Karachi steel mill was already marginal, because the cost was very high, the mill would be dependent on imported scrap (coming almost exclusively from the United States), the loans from AID and Eximbank were transferable to other projects, and friction had developed from the over-lengthy negotiations. In fact, discussions

[13] A West German credit of $1.1 million had been extended to the Zeal-Pak factory in February 1961; also, France, Germany and Sweden have made loans to the factory since the Danish credit. The Planning Commission has meanwhile revised its estimates of the total requirement of cement in West Pakistan. According to these estimates, a capital investment of Rs. 2,500 in development requires one ton of cement. On this basis, cement requirements in the Third Five-Year Plan have been worked out at six million tons for the whole of Pakistan, out of which four million tons would be produced in West Pakistan. Two WPIDC schemes for expansion, one for the Rohri cement factory and the other for the Wah cement factory, were submitted to the Consortium in 1965/6; Japanese credits totalling $6.5 million were received in 1966 and 1967.

about a Karachi steel mill date back to 1950, and a number of feasibility studies have been made since then. The Eximbank was first approached in 1962.

In spite of the increased cost, the profit in full capacity years was calculated at 9.5 per cent of invested capital (7.75 per cent over the full twenty years of the project), which was a respectable rate of return and comparable to US steel industry profit rates. This can partly be explained by the consultants' 15 per cent underestimation of the selling prices of the finished products. And with profitability adjusted to reflect the project's costs and benefits to Pakistan, the cash return over the project's useful life would be 15 per cent of invested capital, a satisfactory rate in overall economic terms. The debt service capacity of the project was found to be more than adequate, there would be a $24 million annual foreign exchange saving, and extensive peripheral benefits would accrue through the multiplier process.

However, important problems remained. The cost figures required more careful scrutiny, the breadth of the product-mix had to be reconsidered, and the US interest in keeping the project in the private sector had to be evaluated.

After negotiations with AID and Eximbank broke off, their funds were used for other purposes; and two new reports were obtained by the government of Pakistan, one from National Steel of Pakistan (previously associated with the original US project group) and the other from Investment Management Ltd (a private company possibly backed by the Aga Khan's interests). Both reports involved an integrated mill based only on imported ore. Dependence on scrap was felt to be undesirable since it would have increased reliance on the United States. The reports were favourable, and the government is going ahead with planning for the integrated mill. The Pakistan Steel Corporation was set up as a government agency to establish the Karachi steel mill in partnership with the private sector. No new negotiations have yet begun with the United States to finance this redesigned project, and it seems improbable that they will. Apparently better sources exist, and it is not unlikely that Investment Management Ltd will participate.

A number of lessons may be drawn from this experience. For one thing, a great deal of time has been consumed at considerable expense and so far with no tangible results. Expensive US experts were employed, yielding inaccurate and often careless reports; this was an important source of irritation to both the United States and Pakistan. Confidence in foreign experts is not always well placed.

The circumstances of the breakdown are not completely clear, but there are considerable political overtones. Initially, the Karachi steel mill was seen by Pakistan largely as a prestige symbol; this tended to cloud its economic evaluation. Within the range of its absorptive capacity, the supply of foreign capital at that time was virtually unlimited, enabling Pakistan to avoid careful economic and financial scrutiny. But as foreign funds became relatively scarce, the Planning Commission tended towards much greater economic rationality and realism; a very expensive mill, based on imported ore and scrap, financed on hard terms and with political strings, now looked like a rather poor idea.

In addition, favourable reports on the Kalabagh field (also in West Pakistan) made it apparent that there was an alternative, cheaper way of obtaining a steel mill. As for the United States, it was continually concerned that the mill should be primarily in the private sector, whether that was economically desirable or not; and fears were often voiced that the government of Pakistan might take full control before very long.

Currently, prospects for the new Karachi steel mill keep changing. The short-fall in domestic and foreign resources has caused closer scrutiny to be applied to prospective import-based industries such as the mill. Potential import sub-stitution through such projects is generally giving way to increased emphasis on agricultural production as a substitute for food imports. PL 480 assistance has not always been available when needed, and future PL 480 imports may be repayable only in foreign exchange. Furthermore, basing a major industry on imported raw materials is not necessarily sound.[14]

The Kalabagh steel mill

The Kalabagh mill project differs from the Karachi steel mill in that it involves a plant based on domestic ore, and it is fully in the public sector. It would seem that Kalabagh had been treated more or less as a substitute for Karachi: optimistic expectations about the Karachi mill relegated the Kalabagh project to the background, and disappointments in the availability of aid for the Karachi project brought it back into prominence.

The real problem with Kalabagh has been the poor quality of the domestic ore. But several tests of the ore have been made, and finally a revised plan was submitted on the basis of a full industrial scale test by Salzigitters of West Germany. The tests were considered very successful by a UN panel which met in Pakistan in May 1967. It is estimated that the project, with production capacity of about 815,000 tons of rolled steel products, would cost some Rs. 1.4 billion and would have a foreign exchange component of Rs. 878.1 million. The average cost of production would be Rs. 628.1 per ton, as against the c.i.f. cost of imported steel at Rs. 613.6 per ton. However, the cost of shipping steel to the main market in northern West Pakistan more than makes up for the price advantage of imported steel. The revised project is still awaiting approval by the government. The Soviet Union is doing a feasibility study and has agreed to finance the mill if the results are favourable. This is not surprising, given the fact that steel mills are the USSR's preferred field of assistance, and taking into account the attractiveness of its lending terms, the growing economic relationship between the Soviet Union and Pakistan, and the recent efforts of the Pakistan government to seek more assistance from non-Consortium sources, particularly the USSR and the socialist countries of eastern Europe.

[14] In June 1970, after the time of writing, the Soviet Union agreed to extend a $200 million credit for a one million ton steel mill to be built near Karachi. This was the result of a five-day visit to the USSR by President Yahya Khan. *Pakistan News Digest*, Karachi, 1 July 1970, p. 1.

The present thinking in Pakistan seems to be that both the Kalabagh and Karachi steel mills can and should be undertaken. Indeed, the government also appears to be planning a second steel mill in East Pakistan, as well as further expansion of the Chittagong steel mill.

The machinery plants at Taxila

An electrical machinery complex at Taxila (near Rawalpindi), costing about Rs. 131 million, has been under negotiation with the Soviet Union over the past few years. The original feasibility study for this project was carried out by the British Associated Electrical Industries (AEI), and during 1966 considerable progress was made in negotiating a loan from Britain with a contract to AEI. But a bilateral agreement between the USSR and Pakistan in September 1966 superseded these negotiations and put AEI completely out of the picture. A second feasibility study of the project has since been done by the USSR.

The People's Republic of China is also interested in Taxila. It is, in fact, already providing equipment and advisers for a heavy machinery complex which is to cost Rs. 121 million and will come into operation in 1970.[15] Pakistan seems well satisfied with the Chinese assistance. The project is being financed by an interest-free loan, repayable in twenty years. Chinese equipment for the complex is costing 20 to 50 per cent of what would be paid for corresponding imports from Western Europe or the United States. In addition, China has agreed to supply Pakistan, on a long-term credit basis, with all the raw materials to be used during the first few years of the project's operation.

More recently, China has undertaken to finance a Rs. 211 million foundry and forge project at Taxila, designed to supply both its own and the Soviet machinery plants there. This represents a noteworthy example of Soviet–Chinese aid co-operation in public sector heavy industry.

[15] Trial production began in July 1970. *Pakistan News Digest*, Karachi, 15 April 1970, p. 1.

8. Case studies: the private sector

In some ways, Pakistan's private sector is even more difficult to deal with in terms of case studies than the public sector. The range of private industrial activity is extremely wide, the machinery of central co-ordination rather loose, and detailed operational data particularly difficult to obtain. Then, too, a very substantial amount of foreign assistance is channelled through intermediate Pakistani financial institutions which, in turn, make key decisions on the allocation of such funds to specific industries and enterprises.

With these considerations in mind, seven cases have been selected for discussion here. Three are companies that have received financial support from the World Bank or the affiliated IFC: Karnaphuli Paper Mills, Ismail Cement Industries and Packages Ltd. Two cases are the IDBP and PICIC, both development finance institutions. And the two other cases are the industrial estates project financed by the IDA, and the rupee loan-financing provided by the United States under the Cooley Amendment to PL 480. Brief reference will also be made to US technical assistance to Pakistani industry.[1]

Karnaphuli Paper Mills Ltd

This project represents the only direct World Bank loan to Pakistani industry. The loan, made in 1955, did not actually go to the private sector but to the publicly owned PIDC. In line with its general policy of disinvestment, PIDC later transferred the company to a private entrepreneur. The loan is now classified as a private sector credit – which in fact it is, if not by design then by accident.

Negotiations for the loan began in 1950. The project to establish a paper mill at Karnaphuli (East Pakistan), with a production capacity of 30,000 tons of paper per year, was initiated by the Industries Ministry of the government of Pakistan. Discussions proceeded at a slow pace as IBRD preferred to make a loan to an industrial development bank if such an institution could be set up by Pakistan in a manner satisfactory to IBRD. Agreement could not be reached on this; but meanwhile (in 1952) PIDC had been established, and it took over the project with a renewed request to IBRD for a loan under the public sector programme. The World Bank insisted that the scheme have a corporate structure designed to attract private investors. But by 1953 it appeared

---

[1] Special emphasis is given to IDBP and PICIC, each a major response to the needs of industrial development in Pakistan. Commercial bank resources there (as in many countries) consist chiefly of short-term demand deposits, and flexibility of investments is ensured by concentration on short-term, self-liquidating commercial loans. A network evolved quite early to meet the requirements of trade and other short-term credit in medium-sized industry. But only institutions like IDBP and PICIC could provide the vital long-term financing needed by large-scale and smaller firms alike.

that IBRD had decided not to back the project – primarily on the ground that the estimated cost of production was very high as compared with the major paper-producing countries; and that although the mill was about to start manufacturing, it lacked senior operating personnel.

By the beginning of 1954, two of the major World Bank conditions, which had led to a stalemate in negotiations, were being met by the company. Following a report by the president of a Canadian paper company to IBRD that although the mill was well conceived and well engineered it could not operate successfully unless substantial changes in the managerial, technical and supervisory staff were made, a major reorganization of personnel in these categories was undertaken. Also, towards the end of 1953, the company sold about 70 per cent of its holdings to the public at a 25 per cent premium. In view of these developments, the World Bank again started taking an interest in the project; but before the loan negotiations (resumed in 1954) could be completed, serious riots broke out in the industrial areas of East Pakistan. In the mill itself, the acting general manager and several workers were killed in March 1954. Although the plant remained undamaged, construction work and production were suspended. An air of uncertainty prevailed in East Pakistan, and, upset by these developments, some foreign technical and managerial staff left the mill. Under the circumstances, and by mutual consent of IBRD and the government of Pakistan, aid negotiations were suspended until complete order could be restored.

By late 1954, industrial calm had returned to the province, and a general manager, a managerial staff of about twenty-five, a local supervisor and technicians had been appointed. As a result of this reorganization, production reached 75 per cent of capacity. Negotiations with the World Bank were reopened, and they continued until the middle of 1955. In May 1955, IBRD and the government of Pakistan concluded an exchange of views on Pakistan's economic and financial situation; and finally, talks in Washington produced a $4.2 million loan repayable in fourteen-and-a-half years at an interest rate of 4.625 per cent per annum.

The Karnaphuli project provides a striking example of how a viable scheme can be jeopardized by political instability. The period of loan negotiation was marked by political upheavals, lack of development discipline and labour riots. In this general atmosphere of uncertainty, the World Bank was understandably hesitant to commit resources even for a project which was based on local raw material (bamboo), provided direct employment for about 3,000 people and involved foreign exchange savings estimated at $3.5 million a year.[2]

[2] For further discussion of Karnaphuli, see A. O. Hirschman, *Development Projects Observed* (Washington, 1967). In January 1969, the IFC announced a $5 million loan to the company, along with an equity investment of $630,000 and a contingency loan of $600,000. This, as well as a PICIC loan of $3.4 million, formed a major part of a $17 million expansion programme designed to increase Karnaphuli's production capacity to 50,000 tons of paper by 1971. IFC, *Annual Report 1969* (Washington, 1969), pp. 27–8.

Ismail Cement Industries Ltd

Ismail Cement Industries was sponsored by a group of Pakistani industrialists, known as the Naseer A. Shaikh Group, who owned about 40 per cent of the share capital.[3] Another 40 per cent was subscribed by the public, while PICIC and IFC accounted for the remaining 20 per cent of the holdings. The original project envisaged establishing a cement plant at Gharibwal, between Rawalpindi and Lahore, at an estimated cost of $12.8 million for two kilns with a capacity to produce about 416,000 tons of Portland cement per annum. The plant was intended to supply cement to the northwest region of West Pakistan, particularly to the Mangla Dam which was under construction as a part of the Indus Basin replacement works.

In terms of the possible market for its output, the plant was well conceived. The Second Five-Year Plan had specified a production target of three million tons for 1965. However, the plan target was not realized, and the supply situation remained unsatisfactory. The Third Five-Year Plan, as already noted, estimates demand at six million tons by the end of 1970, of which about four million tons are to come from West Pakistan.

Prior to the establishment of Ismail Cement Industries, two surveys of cement demand in Pakistan were conducted. The first was sponsored by PICIC and was undertaken in 1960 by a well-known firm of consultants. In 1961 another survey was conducted by the Economist Intelligence Unit (EIU) for IFC. Whereas the results of the first survey were considered to be on the high side, the demand estimates of EIU turned out to be too conservative. The EIU survey placed the actual consumption of cement in West Pakistan at about one million tons in 1960; and it projected 1.2 million tons for 1961, 1.8 million for 1965, and 2.5 million for 1970. That survey further projected the demand for cement in northern West Pakistan at one million tons in 1965 and 1.5 million tons in 1970; for the Gharibwal area, assumed to be the company's natural market, the estimates were 645,000 tons for 1965 and 770,000 tons for 1970. Taking West Pakistan as a whole, these projections meant an increase of 150 per cent during the period 1960–70. But actual development of construction activity, and hence the demand for cement, far exceeded expectations, as evidenced by serious shortages during this period.

However, doubts were expressed as to the feasibility of expanding output at Ismail Cement – in the face of a falling-off of demand in the area with completion of the Mangla Dam, and the fact that two additional cement units were being financed by PICIC in the same region. These doubts were valid insofar as they emphasized the need to balance supply and demand in the northwestern part of West Pakistan: export of any sizable surplus of cement from this area is inconceivable due to the high cost of internal transport. But such reasoning failed to appreciate that, in view of past performance in this sector, the estimated demand for 1970 was not high; and that even if all

[3] For a more general review of the Ismail experience, see J. C. Baker, *The International Finance Corporation: Origins, Operations, and Evaluation* (New York, 1968), pp. 105–10.

the proposed units went into production, demand would exceed supply by a substantial margin. Furthermore, the effect of the fall in demand through completion of Mangla would be more than offset by the new demand for the Tarbela Dam. When construction at Tarbela went into full swing, one would expect the area to develop a shortage of cement rather than a surplus.

Meanwhile, Ismail Cement had begun production in June 1964 with its first kiln in operation. At the end of 1967, the factory, with two kilns operating, was producing at the rate of 200,000 tons of cement a year. It is administered by a managing agency, Naseer Mughis Ltd, which receives a fee equivalent to 7.5 per cent of Ismail's net profits before tax. Sales, financial matters and accounts are handled by the Lahore office of the managing agency, while the mill is actually run by a foreign resident manager.

IFC's original participation in Ismail amounted to $4 million in 1961. This was provided in conjunction with a foreign exchange loan of $3 million by PICIC. In 1964, the company proposed the addition of a third kiln at an estimated cost of $4.8 million. It also planned to meet an estimated rupee over-run on the project of $1.3 million; the over-run represented mainly increased freight charges on machinery and equipment imported into Pakistan, as well as the cost of reinforcing various structures to make them resistant to possible damage from earthquakes.[4] Rated capacity was expected to increase from 1,200 tons per day to 1,800 tons, that is, from 416,000 to 624,000 tons of cement per year. Actual production was expected to increase from 360,000 to 540,000 tons per annum.

The factory was favourably located with respect to raw materials and employed the mining lease of the adjoining area. At that time the limestone was carried in trucks, but a proposed ropeway would dispense with the trucking and thereby possibly achieve economies in cost. (The ropeway was completed in 1965 and has, in fact, brought substantial economies.) Further cost savings might come through the shift from oil to gas as a source of energy following completion of the Sui Northern Gas pipeline.

Ismail approached IFC for additional financing of $1.7 million to assist in the planned expansion programme. The progress made by the original project during the construction period gave solid grounds for IFC confidence in the management of the company and in the soundness of such an investment. Accordingly, the request was approved – in terms of some $400,000 in equity participation and a $1.3 million loan at 7.5 per cent interest repayable in ten years. This made the IFC's total Ismail commitment their largest investment in Asia. PICIC joined in the venture for a second time, with loan-equity financing of approximately $1.5 million.[5]

[4] PICIC had already provided about $280,000 to meet this need.
[5] The demand for cement continues to pose no real problem for Ismail. The central question is whether it will be able to supply the cement at a competitive price. In this context, it may be worth noting the Shaikh Group's dissatisfaction with the financial treatment accorded Ismail by PICIC. Among the grievances cited are wasteful loan procedures, corruption in the lower PICIC ranks, and politically rooted discrimination. It has not been possible to determine how far such complaints are borne out by the facts.

Packages Ltd

Packages Ltd was incorporated in February 1956 in Lahore by a group of Pakistanis, the Wazir Ali Group, who now own 73 per cent of the share capital, in co-operation with a Swedish company, Akerlund & Rausing, which holds the rest of the equity.[6] Both participants have vast business holdings and experience. The Wazir Ali Group controls major Pakistan companies in the fields of textiles, edible oils, soap, razor blades, insurance and the assembly of cars, tractors and scooters. The Swedish firm is a specialist in the manufacturing and packaging of pulp and paper, and it has a large number of subsidiary companies throughout the world.

Packages has been a highly successful operation, partly because of good management and partly because, as the only unit of its kind in Pakistan, it enjoyed a sheltered market from the very beginning. A comparison between 1958 (the first year) and 1963 (when the company decided to expand with the assistance of an IFC loan) reveals remarkable progress. Sales rose from Rs. 6.6 million to Rs. 21.6 million, and net income before tax from Rs. 300,000 to Rs. 2.8 million. Packages declared dividends annually from 1960 to 1963, and in 1962 it capitalized reserves amounting to Rs. 3 million. By September 1964 it had accumulated reserves of over Rs. 4.5 million.

An important factor contributing to the company's success is the sensible division of labour between the Pakistani and Swedish collaborators. The Swedish group has full responsibility for technical matters, including local basic training of personnel by the Swedish staff seconded to Packages, and advanced training in Sweden or other countries in Europe. The Pakistanis are responsible for financial matters and general management. The board of directors consists of four Pakistanis and three Swedes and is presided over by one of the co-owners of the Swedish company. Both the managing director and the general manager of the company are Pakistani. Thus the joint venture system has provided not only equity capital and foreign exchange, but also the vast experience and technical expertise of a leading international company in the particular line of manufacturing. In return for their technical assistance and training services, the Swedish collaborators receive a royalty fee of one per cent of sales.

In 1964, Packages sought a loan of $3.2 million from IFC to undertake a plant expansion involving a total investment of $12.7 million. An integrated pulp and board-making plant was to be installed, and conversion facilities were to be extended. The expansion was designed to overcome the limiting factor of raw material supplies; the production capacity would be 10,500 tons of chip board and duplex board, and 4,500 tons of specialty board. In the specialty field, the major product would be tetra paper board, a specially laminated board developed by Akerlund & Rausing for use in milk packaging by dairies. The new project was to be jointly financed by the sponsors, PICIC and IFC.

PICIC had involved itself much earlier in the financing of Packages: in 1958

---

[6] G.-Man, the leading ink manufacturer in northern Europe, was also a founding participant. See Baker, *The International Finance Corporation*, pp. 115-18.

it had made a loan of Rs. 2.2 million to enable the company to expand its capacity. There was substantial repayment, and little doubt as to recovery of the outstanding balance. PICIC made its second loan, Rs. 1.8 million, in 1963. Packages then applied for joint financing of its expansion by PICIC and IFC. In order to raise more share capital, it offered to convert itself into a public limited company and allocated a large proportion of its shares for public subscription. For a firm with the reputation of Packages, such a conversion raised no real problems. If past experience was any guide, it seemed quite certain that as and when the shares were put on the market, they would be oversubscribed.

The company arranged for a total equity capital of Rs. 22.5 million, of which Rs. 14.5 million was to be in local currency: Rs. 4.5 million of the local currency would be subscribed by the Wazir Ali Group, and Rs. 10 million by the public; the Rs. 8 million in foreign exchange equity capital was to be provided, half each, by IFC and Akerlund & Rausing. The project also involved foreign exchange credits of Rs. 12 million from PICIC and Rs. 11 million from IFC, and rupee credits of Rs. 3.5 million from local financial institutions.

Both equity and loan financing were, in fact, secured. The PICIC and IFC credits carry an interest rate of 7.75 per cent, and they are repayable in ten years commencing in 1969.

IFC agreed to participate on several grounds. First, the proposed increase in output could easily be absorbed by the market and was essential to meet the expected demand. Secondly, the production of tetra paper board would facilitate the establishment of a modern and hygienic dairy industry in Pakistan. Thirdly, Packages had been a profitable and well-run enterprise, and it had good prospects for growth in view of the effective collaboration between Pakistani enterprise and foreign technical skill.

It may be well to add that the future is not entirely unclouded. For one thing, the 1965 war with India and the ensuing climate of uncertainty produced a tightness in the rupee capital market which has yet to be dissipated. Secondly, the war induced some migration of trained labour from Packages to safer mills at Wazirabad and Nowshehra, with the result that expansion plans have not gone ahead as rapidly as expected. Thirdly, Packages is not a low cost producer by international standards; in any event, it now faces stiff domestic competition in the field of packing papers. Then, too, there is considerable risk in the production of tetra paper: while it has clear advantages over traditional packings, it does involve a real change in consumer habits.

The Industrial Development Bank of Pakistan

IDBP was set up in 1961 as a successor to the Pakistan Industrial Finance Corporation (PIFCO). As a matter of fact, IDBP came into existence through the reorganization of PIFCO, inheriting its assets and liabilities, and should therefore be considered a continuation of PIFCO operations.

The PIFCO experience

PIFCO started its activities in June 1949 with a paid-up capital of Rs. 20 million, of which 51 per cent was subscribed by the government of Pakistan and 49 per cent by private and institutional investors. It provided loans to industrial, mining and utility enterprises against the security of their existing assets for a period not exceeding twenty years. This, in effect, meant that PIFCO could assist in modernization, expansion and balancing of existing units but could not finance the establishment of new ventures.

PIFCO suffered from other serious constraints on its operations. Until 1953, it could provide assistance only to public limited companies, and except for its last year of operation, it had no foreign exchange resources at its disposal. After the public companies restriction was removed, and private limited companies and partnerships brought under PIFCO's purview, the volume of lending increased substantially, reaching a level of about Rs. 21 million per year by 1956. But in 1957, PICIC emerged as an outlet for foreign exchange loans by agencies like the World Bank and US AID. This relegated PIFCO to a subordinate financial role. It appears that at this particular stage of development in Pakistan, the limiting factor for private industry was not rupee financing but the availability of foreign exchange. When PICIC began its operations with foreign exchange loans available at about 7.5 per cent, few borrowers were attracted by rupee credit at 6 per cent from PIFCO, since the scarcity value of foreign exchange more than compensated for the differential in interest rates.

Over the period 1948–60, PIFCO loans to private industry totalled Rs. 293 million or about Rs. 25 million per year. The bulk of the funds (56 per cent) went to jute and cotton textiles, and the rest to thirty-three other categories including shipping, cement and glass. Most of the loans were extended to large entrepreneurs and were concentrated in a few big business interests.

Structure and resources of IDBP

IDBP was set up to remedy the defects of PIFCO, mainly with respect to its inability to lend to new enterprises, its lack of foreign exchange resources and its involvement with only large firms. Contrary to the practice of PIFCO, IDBP offered small and medium-sized industrial enterprises a wide range of services, including short-, medium- and long-term loans, guarantees, and assistance in carrying out surveys and research.

The central and provincial governments control, directly or indirectly, 61.2 per cent of IDBP's total stock. The remaining eighteen major shareholders are: a total of twelve Pakistani banks, insurance companies, provident funds and private industrial interests, with 15.2 per cent of the shares; and six foreign institutions, with 10.7 per cent of the shares. The balance of 13 per cent is held by fewer than 200 shareholders. The turnover of shares is relatively small.[7]

[7] In terms of stock control, IDBP could, of course, be treated as a public sector enterprise. It is here included among the private sector cases for several reasons: the substantial

Table 28. *Financial resources of IDBP, up to 30 June 1967*

Source of funds	Rs. millions
Capital, reserve and special fund	59.58
Borrowings from government and counter finance for advances to PWSR	74.44
Domestic credit lines	130.00
Deposits	82.22
Total rupee resources	346.24
Total foreign exchange resources	1,330.32
	1,676.56

SOURCE: IDBP, *Six Years of IDBP* (Karachi, 1967), pp. 9–10.

IDBP started with the capitalization and resources of PIFCO. Gradually, it proceeded to build up its own strength, and the results are shown in Table 28. IDBP's foreign currency loans comprise allocations by the Pakistan government from credits obtained abroad. Details of these allocations are given in Table 29.

Most of the foreign exchange resources allocated to IDBP are tied credits requiring that purchases be made in the lending countries. In certain cases, the credits are also tied to the purchase of specific types of equipment; as of June 1967, for instance, UK credits of Rs. 242.6 million were tied to the purchase of jute machinery, and Rs. 44.7 million to the purchase of textile machinery; again, Japanese credits of Rs. 109.3 million were tied to the purchase of textile machinery. All IDBP-allocated loans have been obtained by the government of Pakistan at interest rates varying from 3 to around 6 per cent a year, with maturities ranging from five to twenty-two years. The foreign exchange risk on the loans is borne by the ultimate borrower.

Scope and terms of IDBP lending

IDBP is authorized to make loans to a wide variety of enterprises engaged or seeking to be engaged in industry. The loans may be extended for construction, expansion and purchase of industrial equipment as well as for working capital, provided the working capital component does not exceed 25 per cent of the total loan. IDBP may also undertake certain commercial banking activities, such as accepting deposits, making inter-bank call loans, and buying and selling domestic and foreign bills of exchange.[8] It may guarantee loans provided their term does not exceed twenty years. And it may subscribe directly to the equity capital of any industrial concern subject to government approval.

Originally, IDBP's upper lending limit was one million rupees, but with the increase in capital goods prices, it was raised to Rs. 2.5 million in 1964/5, including a foreign exchange ceiling of Rs. 1.5 million; in April 1967, the foreign exchange ceiling was increased to Rs. 2 million. For jute, cotton,

private ownership of IDBP shares; its prime role in channelling funds to the private sector; the importance of direct comparison with the privately controlled PICIC.

[8] A programme of deposit banking was launched by IDBP in 1966/7.

Table 29. *Foreign currency loans by IDBP, as of 30 June 1967*

Source of credits	Allocations to industry (Rs. millions)				
	Unspecified	Jute	Textile	Other	Total
Belgium	31.7	—	12.0	—	43.7
China	4.8	—	—	—	4.8
Denmark	4.8	—	—	—	4.8
France	21.1	—	—	9.5	30.6
Italy	22.3	—	—	9.5	31.8
Japanese yen	42.3	—	—	27.2	69.5
Japanese suppliers	—	—	109.3	—	109.3
Poland	4.8	—	—	—	4.8
Switzerland	6.6	—	—	—	6.6
United Kingdom	36.4	242.6	5.8	—	284.8
Platt Bros. (UK)	—	—	38.9	—	38.9
US Eximbank	39.2	—	—	53.1	92.3
USSR	9.6	—	24.0	—	33.6
West Germany	118.4	—	—	—	118.4
West German exports	—	—	—	120.0	120.0
Yugoslavia	5.3	—	—	40.3	45.6
IDA	19.1	—	—	—	19.1
TOTAL	*366.4*	*242.6*	*190.0*	*259.6*	*1,058.6*

Allocation for unspecified industries	366.4	
Allocation for specified industries	692.2	1,058.6
Less: Loans and guarantees outstanding	687.2	
Letters of credit outstanding	123.7	810.9
Resources available		247.7
Less: Sanctions by IDBP	248.7	
Specific allocation by the government	29.7	278.4
Shortfall		30.7

SOURCE: IDBP, *Sixth Annual Report, 1966–67* (Karachi, 1967), appendix C.

inland transport and mining, however, there is no upper limit. With the permission of the government, specific industries can be, and have been, added to the no-ceiling list. IDBP has concentrated on small investors in order to encourage small and medium enterprise. As of 1967, about 80 per cent of all loans in East Pakistan and 82 per cent in West Pakistan were for Rs. 500,000 or less. Table 30 shows the number of IDBP loans in different size categories in East and West Pakistan.

By June 1967, IDBP had sanctioned over one billion rupees in loans to set up 1,897 new industrial units, of which 970 were in East Pakistan and 927 in West Pakistan. During the same period, Rs. 417 million went to existing units for balancing, modernization and expansion designed to improve utilization of existing industrial capacity.

Although a large proportion of IDBP credit is concentrated in jute and cotton textiles and ancillary industries, the loans range widely over Pakistan industry. Table 31 illustrates this broad coverage.

Table 30. *IDBP loans, by size, in East and West Pakistan, as of 30 June 1966*

Size of loans including foreign currency	East Pakistan		West Pakistan		Total	
	No. of cases	%	No. of cases	%	No. of cases	%
Up to Rs. 0.5 million	872	80	1,367	84	2,239	82
Rs. 0.5–1 million	126	11	143	9	269	10
Over Rs. 1 million	94	9	116	7	210	8
TOTAL	*1,092*	*100*	*1,626*	*100*	*2,718*	*100*

SOURCE: IDBP, *Five Years of IDBP* (Karachi, 1966), p. 9.

Interest on IDBP foreign currency loans has been fixed by the government at 7.5 per cent per year, while interest on rupee loans varies from 7 to 8 per cent per year. The date of interest is always related to the amount of the loan; that is, higher rates are charged on larger loans. There are also technical assistance, documentation and commitment fees, at 0.25 per cent each, on the amount of loan sanctioned but not utilized. On foreign currency loans, there is a letter of credit charge of 0.125 to 0.25 per cent per quarter, with effect from the date

Table 31. *Distribution of IDBP loans by industry and province, 1 August 1961 to 30 June 1967*

Industry	East Pakistan		West Pakistan	
	Rs. millions	%	Rs. millions	%
Textiles (other than jute)	197.7	29.2	335.2	43.4
Jute manufactures	255.2	37.7	—	—
Food products	49.4	7.3	74.0	9.6
Engineering	25.1	3.7	43.3	5.6
Natural gas	0.5	—	50.7	6.6
Chemicals	7.3	1.1	35.9	4.7
Non-metallic mineral products	20.7	3.0	19.9	2.6
River transport	31.6	4.7	—	—
Sea transport	0.9	0.1	30.1	3.9
Film studio and production	12.5	1.9	16.4	2.1
Cotton ginning	—	—	24.7	3.2
Printing and publishing	6.5	1.0	17.8	2.3
Paper and stationery	7.5	1.1	13.0	1.7
Oil storage and distribution	5.7	0.8	11.4	1.5
Electrical equipment	6.4	1.0	8.6	1.1
Wood products	7.5	1.1	6.8	0.9
Hotels	8.7	1.3	4.6	0.6
Road transport	5.1	0.8	8.1	1.0
Small industries	9.3	1.4	44.6	5.8
Others	19.1	2.8	26.7	3.4
TOTAL	*676.7*	*100.0*	*771.8*	*100.0*

SOURCE: IDBP, *Six Years of IDBP* (Karachi, 1967), p. 20.

the letter of credit is opened until the date it expires.[9] As far as security is concerned, IDBP covers its loans by a first mortgage on the fixed assets of the enterprise. In some cases, mortgages on other properties of the borrower, interim bank guarantees, and personal guarantees of the directors of private limited companies are also required.

Loan appraisal

All loan applications to IDBP are made by way of response to an extensive questionnaire covering the financial and technical aspects of the proposed venture, as well as the security pledged against the loan. On this basis, the Bank's regional office carries out a comprehensive project appraisal. The report is submitted by the manager of the Project Department to a regional Staff Loan Committee. If the requested loan is less than Rs. 200,000, it is submitted, after examination and approval, directly to the regional Technical Advisory Committee (TAC); if above this limit, it must be submitted for preliminary approval to the head office, which, if it approves, returns the loan to the regional TAC. After a favourable decision by TAC, every loan is sent to the head office for submission to the board of directors. This is a rather cumbersome and time-consuming procedure; it takes from six months to a year to complete the formalities, which undoubtedly discourages prospective borrowers. Furthermore, the procedure is the same for small, medium and large enterprises, and virtually irrespective of the amount involved, with the result that the time of IDBP's limited appraisal staff is spread thinly over cases that are often of little or no importance.

Inadequate control is maintained over sanctioned loans – this despite a system of quarterly progress reports and ad hoc inspection reports. As of March 1966, IDBP's list of deferred cases included forty-eight accounts with the instalments ranging from Rs. 1,000 to Rs. 300,000. Also, seventy-seven loans for cotton-ginning factories – aggregating Rs. 8.5 million – had defaulted in payments. The deferred cases were estimated at 8 per cent of the total portfolio. This appears to be due to weak appraisal and failure to grant a satisfactory grace period. To a certain extent, it reflects the fact that IDBP works out the repayment of its loans in terms of the maturities it will have to meet on its own borrowing, rather than on the basis of a realistic estimate of cash generation in the particular enterprise.

Although IDBP advances credit against valid collateral, it works on a very high debt–equity ratio. Its 18.5:1 ratio is far in excess of the 5:1 prescribed by ordinance, and of the average normally accepted by international financial institutions. Moreover, IDBP has apparently been unable to insulate itself against political pressures, particularly in East Pakistan. Perhaps this is the price it must pay for rapid growth and for undertaking pioneering tasks seldom performed by a financial institution.

[9] See IDBP, *How to Apply for Loans* (Dacca, 1966), pp. 3–4.

Relations with IBRD

Early in 1963 the government of Pakistan approached the World Bank for a loan to IDBP. Pursuant to initial negotiations, a fact-finding mission was sent to Pakistan by IBRD. The mission agreed that IDBP had a major role to play in the industrial development of Pakistan, but it made World Bank assistance conditional on an improved financial position, increased profitability, strengthened organization and more efficient operations. The prerequisites included, specifically: transfer of control of IDBP to private hands; reorganization of IDBP's capital structure, particularly with a view to bringing the financial ratios within the limits of prudent investment banking practice; a firm policy for collecting loans and enforcing security; and operational emphasis on business principles rather than social policy.

Agreement could not be reached on the role of IDBP as seen by the IBRD mission and by the authorities in Pakistan. Consequently, the IBRD assistance never materialized. Meanwhile, IDBP has been developing along the lines charted during its early years.

The Pakistan Industrial Credit and Investment Corporation

In 1956 a World Bank mission led by Mr George D. Woods, then Chairman of the First Boston Corporation, visited Pakistan to study the feasibility of establishing a privately owned institution for credit extension to industry. It was envisaged that the proposed institution would make equity investments, underwrite and distribute securities, and provide technical advice and managerial service to industrial enterprises. The institution would be able to borrow capital abroad and lend in both domestic and foreign currency. The World Bank had already helped to set up similar institutions in Turkey (1950) and India (1955), and assistance to industrial finance companies has since become a major field of interest to the IFC, an affiliate of IBRD.

Structure and resources

On World Bank advice, PICIC was incorporated in 1957 with an initial paid-up capital of Rs. 20 million; this was raised to Rs. 30 million in 1961 and Rs. 40 million in 1963.[10] IFC participated in the 1963 issue by purchasing, at a 7 per cent premium, 200,000 shares with a total par value of Rs. 2 million. Sixty per cent of the total capital has been subscribed by Pakistani investors; the remaining 40 per cent is held by foreign shareholders, with the United States accounting for 10.9 per cent, the United Kingdom 10.8, Japan 7.3, Germany 6 and IFC 5 per cent.

As of March 1967, the paid-up capital and reserves of PICIC stood at Rs. 72 million. It had received two loans from the government of Pakistan totalling Rs. 60 million. The first loan, Rs. 30 million, was made in 1957 free of interest,

[10] For a broader survey of PICIC operations, see P. Perera, *Development Finance: Institutions, Problems, and Prospects* (New York, 1968), pp. 259–64.

Table 32. *Foreign exchange resources and allocations of PICIC, as of 31 March 1967*

Lender[a]	Year of loan agreement	Amount ($ millions)	Loans approved by PICIC[b] ($ millions)	Interest rate	Repayment
Belgium	1967	5.00	—	6	
Czechoslovakia	1964	2.94	2.94	5.5	
France	1963	7.72	7.06	6	Linked to projects
	1967	2.50	—	6	
Italy	1965	3.10	3.10	6	
	1967	6.00	—	6	
Japan	1961	4.97	4.97	6	1967–76
	1963	2.49	2.48	6	1967–78
	1963	3.00	2.99	5.75	1970–82
	1964	5.00	3.45	5.75	
	1967	3.50	—	5.75	Linked to projects
Poland	1964	2.94	2.94	5.5	
United Kingdom	1962	2.50	2.49	0.125 over U.K.	1965–79
UK shipping	1964	7.84	8.37	Treasury rate	Linked to projects
US AID	1958	4.20	4.20	5	1959–64
	1960	9.90	9.90	5.5	1960–4
	1961	7.50	7.47	5	1963–9
West Germany	1962	17.50	17.42	5.5	
	1963	5.00	4.92	5.5	
	1964	2.50	2.41	5.5	Linked to projects
	1965	2.50	2.49	5.5	
	1966	3.75	—	5.5	
	—	3.00	—	5.5	
IBRD	1957	4.08	4.08	5.75	1962–72
	1959	9.93	9.93	varying	1962–79
	1961	14.79	14.79	—	
	1963	20.00	19.97	—	Linked to projects
	1964	30.00	29.86	—	
	1965	30.00	30.00	5.5	
TOTAL		224.15	240.34[c]		

SOURCE: Pakistan Industrial Credit and Investment Corporation.
[a] Loans are completely tied to the lending agency except in the case of Germany (two-thirds) and the IBRD.
[b] IBRD, US AID and Germany all require prior approval of major sub-projects.
[c] Total includes approvals not yet allocated to source.

with a repayment period of thirty years and fifteen years' grace. The second (equal) loan, granted in 1960, bears interest at 4 per cent, is repayable in forty years, and provides four years of grace. In 1966, PICIC arranged a Rs. 30 million loan from US AID. The loan is to be subordinated to all foreign indebtedness but has precedence over share capital; it carries an interest rate of 5 per cent, and the repayment period is twenty years with ten years' grace.

Foreign currency credits available to PICIC in March 1967 are shown in

Table 33. *Assets, capital and liabilities of PICIC, as of 31 March 1967*

Assets	Rs. millions	Capital and liabilities	Rs. millions
Foreign currency loans	483.48	Issued share capital	40.00
Local currency loans	9.69	Reserves	31.97
Equity investments	40.67	Foreign currency borrowings	451.02
Current assets	80.17	Local currency borrowings	70.60
Fixed assets	0.75	Current liabilities	21.17
TOTAL	*614.76*		*614.76*

SOURCE: Pakistan Industrial Credit and Investment Corporation.

Table 32. It will be noted that total foreign credits amount to $224.2 million but that PICIC had sanctioned foreign currency loans of $240.3 million – a shortfall of $16.1 million – presumably in anticipation of new loans.

In the early stages, the major areas of interest for PICIC loans were textiles and food products and processing, but in recent years engineering, chemicals, paper and paper products have shown marked strength. With a leading role assigned to the private sector in the Third Five-Year Plan, the pattern of loan allocation will undergo substantial further change as Pakistan achieves higher levels of industrialization.

Assessment

Table 33 provides a recent picture of PICIC's balance sheet position. The corporation has given a solid financial performance. Its reserves and unappropriated earnings increased from about 30 per cent of share capital at the end of 1964 to 69 per cent at the end of 1966. In relation to portfolio loans and investment, they showed an increase from 4 per cent in 1964 to 5.5 per cent in 1966. PICIC's shares, which had a face value of Rs. 10 each, had reached Rs. 14.6 by the end of 1965 and Rs. 16.9 by the end of 1966. There has been a steady improvement in dividends: in 1966 they were raised from 7.5 to 8 per cent, representing about 26 per cent of net profit as compared with 33 per cent in 1965. The ratio of debt to equity stood at 7.5:1 in March 1967.

More generally, it seems clear that PICIC has had a considerable impact on the industrial development of Pakistan. Its loans and other operations are estimated to have helped finance some Rs. 1.8 billion in total investment. When all PICIC-approved projects (up to mid-1967) have been completed, they will provide an aggregate investment of roughly Rs. 3.2 billion. PICIC loan disbursements and direct equity investments during the second plan period represent about one-tenth of private investment in Pakistan during those years, and total investments in PICIC-assisted projects about one-third.

Nor does there seem to be any escape from the conclusion that PICIC has made a greater contribution than IDBP to Pakistan's industrial development. This can be attributed partly to PICIC's better management and partly to its different institutional structure. PICIC has a natural advantage in dealing with established clientele as well as obtaining favourable lines of credit from abroad. A typical borrower from PICIC is an entrepreneur with substantial resources. Even if a prospective borrower does not actually need a loan, he may approach PICIC as the only feasible means of securing foreign exchange – which often commands a premium of 150 per cent on the open market. PICIC's 'success story', therefore, is in part a matter of more efficient use of resources, and in part a question of more favourable circumstances beyond its (or IDBP's) control.

The industrial estates project[11]

By contrast with the substantial flow of foreign resources to large-scale industries in both the public and private sectors, inflows to small industry in Pakistan have been almost negligible.[12] A prime example of the latter is the $6.5 million IDA credit for establishing industrial estates at Gujranwala and Sialkot in West Pakistan.[13] The scheme involved settling 677 small- to medium-sized industrial enterprises on the two estates, with supporting technical service and training centres at Gujranwala, Sialkot and Nizamabad and an institute in Lahore. The total cost of the project (including financial facilities for the entrepreneurs) was estimated at $13 million, half of which was to be met from the IDA credit that took effect in March 1963. The government of Pakistan asked the Battelle Institute of Frankfurt, West Germany, to be consultants on the project, and they began operations in April 1963.

The project made very slow progress. By the end of 1965, six months before the closing date of the loan, only $1.5 million in credits had been utilized, of which $600,000 represented the consultancy fee; direct use of the credit had thus been only $900,000. By March 1966, another $160,000 were utilized, bringing total withdrawals to nearly $1.7 million. Only six enterprises had commenced operation – two at Sialkot and four at Gujranwala – as against the target of 677 units; and there was hardly any alternative available to IDA but to accede to the request of the government of Pakistan, made in December 1965, that the credit be extended to 31 December 1967 to permit complete disbursement of the loan.

The project seemed to be in trouble from the beginning. An IDA Supervisory Mission visiting Pakistan in October 1964 found ample evidence of inadequate co-operation and co-ordination among the organizations involved in the project, that is, the consultants, the small industries, and the Industrial Development

---

[11] This scheme is sometimes classified as a public sector project since foreign assistance went directly to the government of Pakistan (State Bank of Pakistan, *External Debt Servicing Liability* (Karachi, 1965), p. 55.) However, the project is here treated in private sector terms on the grounds that the foreign funds were to be used for the development of private enterprises.

[12] For further analysis of small industry financing in less-developed countries, see R. W. Davenport, *Financing the Small Manufacturer in Developing Countries* (New York, 1967); W. F. Harwood et al., *Encouraging the Growth of Small Industry in Pakistan* (Stanford, 1963).

[13] In June 1970, after the time of writing, IDA provided a second credit, $3 million, for small industry development in Pakistan. IBRD and IDA, *Annual Report 1970* (Washington, 1970), pp. 23, 108.

Bank of Pakistan. In particular, IDBP had imposed stringent security conditions on the small enterprises which they were not in a position to satisfy. Consequently, the mission recommended a system of cash allocations to stimulate the project. These recommendations were still in process of implementation when, under a scheme of reorganization, the functions of the West Pakistan Industrial Development Corporation (WPIDC) with respect to small industries were transferred to a newly created autonomous body called the West Pakistan Small Industries Corporation (WPSIC). Then, in September 1965, while the board of directors of WPSIC was busy formulating its policies, war broke out between India and Pakistan. Not only did the war affect overall economic policy in Pakistan; it had a very direct impact on this project as severe damage was inflicted on Sialkot.

In the context of the unsatisfactory record, the extraordinary situation created by the war and the Pakistan government's request to extend the credit, another Supervisory Mission visited the country in February 1966 to review the project, investigate the causes of insufficient progress and suggest remedial measures. The mission emphasized that:

> The small-industries development in Pakistan, both East and West, must be considered from its present state of development to be a failure. The two industrial estates at Sialkot and Gujranwala, in which IDA is involved, can never be more than a partial success. In December 1967, when it is expected that all the IDA credit will have been disbursed, only about 40 % of the sites on these estates will be occupied, provided the recommendations made to WPSIC and the Provincial and Central Governments are observed and implemented.[14]

The following factors were considered primarily responsible for the poor performance of the project: the problem of small-scale industries was not well understood, as evidenced by inadequate planning to secure a phased development of the project; instead of concentrating on a small area, efforts were dissipated over a wide field; neither WPSIC nor the consultants ever thought of making the estates economically viable in terms of profitability; the structure of taxation was not geared to the needs of the small-scale industries; IDA's credit was committed too soon, resulting in slow disbursement and slow utilization; several organizations involved in the project lacked the will to co-operate. On balance, the mission concluded, 'the project is a bold one and is essentially sound in its objective. However, it has been ill-conceived.'[15]

Largely following its recommendations, a reorganization of the project was undertaken and substantial progress has since been reported. It is estimated that by the credit expiry date of 31 December 1967, 'some 250 manufacturing units will be under construction or already in production. The industrial area at Gujranwala is fully allocated and the Sialkot estate is 50 % occupied.'[16]

[14] IDA and IFC, 'Report of the Supervisory Mission to Pakistan Regarding IDA Credit PAK 30, Industrial Estates Project – February 1–16, 1966', unpublished mimeo. (Washington, D.C., March 1966), section A, p. 3.   [15] Ibid. p. 8.

[16] IDA and IFC, 'Report of the Supervisory Mission to Pakistan: Credit No. Pak-30, Small Industries Estates Project – November 14–30, 1966', unpublished mimeo. (Washington, D.C., December 1966), p. 13.

Although these figures would be more meaningful if the units in production had been separated from those under construction, and if the figures for Sialkot and Gujranwala had been made comparable, this does provide evidence of rapid progress as compared with the state of affairs prevailing in June 1965.

Progress on the two IDA-financed industrial estates was also appreciable relative to developments on the six West Pakistan estates financed only by IDBP loans. By December 1967, the former apparently had fifty-five factories, 8.1 per cent of the proposed total (677), under actual or trial production; while the latter had achieved only 1.3 per cent of the overall target, i.e., twenty-one factories out of a planned 1,652. There is little doubt that the IDA estates have reaped considerable advantage from easier access to much-needed foreign exchange. On the other hand, they can hardly be deemed a success in terms of their own objectives.

A realistic assessment of the problems and prospects of industrial estates is all the more necessary in view of the fact that in both West and East Pakistan new industrial estates have been under serious consideration. The West Pakistan experience seems to warn against high consultancy fees, over-designed factory buildings, under-utilization of space, superficial appraisal of loan applications, lack of control over the project after sanctioning, and the involvement of a multiplicity of organizations causing unnecessary delays and problems of jurisdiction.

Major responsibility for the disappointing West Pakistan results, on the IDA and non-IDA estates alike, would seem to rest with both the planners who misconceived the scheme and the administrators who mismanaged it. In particular, there continues to be a singular lack of understanding among the WPSIC authorities implementing the programme, despite a recent reorganization to simplify procedures for project formulation, appraisal and approval. Few officials appear to have acquired the motivation or technical know-how essential for success in this type of venture.

Cooley loans

The flow of surplus US agricultural commodities to Pakistan under PL 480 (Title 1) has led to a large accumulation of rupees as counterpart funds in favour of the government of the United States. As noted earlier, one of the uses to which these funds have been put is AID lending to qualified borrowers to develop private business enterprise in Pakistan.

Cooley loans are available to US citizens, partnerships, associations and corporations which have their principal place of business in the United States and a majority of US ownership; also to affiliates of US firms, provided the US firm, by virtue of its equity interest or operating ties, has substantial control and influence over the policy of the affiliate. Non-US interests or interests not affiliated with the United States, that is, purely Pakistani firms, are eligible for Cooley loans only if the loan would lead to an expansion of the market for US agricultural products in Pakistan or abroad.

There is, apparently, little stringency in the conditions of Cooley loan financing. Loans can be made for procurement of fixed assets (including land, buildings, plant, equipment and shares), as well as for operating expenses, inventory accumulation and industrial training. The repayment period is flexible, and interest rates are comparable to those charged by local financial institutions. One constraint on these loans is that they cannot support the manufacture of commodities exportable to the United States if such exports compete with US goods. Also, they are not available for production which would compete with US agricultural commodities in Pakistan, the United States or third markets. Since the loans are in local currency, they cannot, of course, be used to import capital goods, raw materials or spare parts; it is only the local costs of investment, expansion and operation which can be Cooley-financed.

Besides pertinent data on the applicant's interest and experience, the loan application asks for a breakdown of capital and operating expenses, data on the applicant's existing capitalization, a statement on sources and uses of funds, current cash flows, balance sheets and profit-and-loss accounts over five years, and details of all proposed borrowing and other financing. Also required are market studies, export projections, estimates of the internal benefits and external economies generated by the enterprise, and (in the case of Pakistani firms) a detailed account of how the proposed loan would promote the expansion of markets for US agricultural products.

One would expect that such loan materials would, by permitting careful evaluation, minimize the chances of project failure and produce mainly successful business operations. The record, however, belies such expectations. Of the thirty-three Cooley loans granted to Pakistan by 1967, only twenty-four had been disbursed; and of the disbursed loans, sixteen or two-thirds involved serious difficulties. The most common problem has been the borrower's failure to generate enough resources to make the repayment of principal and interest possible. Rescheduling of repayment, increased borrowing, capitalizing the interest defaulted, deferring the principal – these have been common features of Cooley loan performance. Debt adjustment had to be undertaken in the case of Wyeth Laboratories (a Rs. 1.8 million loan), Singer Sewing Machine Co. (Rs. 5 million), Shezan International (Rs. 2.4 million), and Intercontinental Hotels Corporation in Karachi (Rs. 4.7 million) and Dacca (Rs. 3.5 million). More drastic measures had to be adopted in other cases, for instance, legal proceedings against Pakistan Fabrics for recovery of three loans totalling Rs. 5.3 million.

On the whole, the Cooley loans have not been a success in Pakistan. The specific causes of failure differ from one enterprise to another; but the firms generally fall into two categories – those based on faulty planning and those which have been adversely affected by factors beyond the control of the enterprise. A clear instance of the former is Arbor Acres Pakistan, which was set up as a US affiliate to undertake poultry breeding in Karachi with an annual output of 350,000 broiler chickens plus some layer pullet chickens and table eggs. A decision (which had to be reversed later) to concentrate on the production of eggs rather than broilers, coupled with the low quality and high cost of feed, brought substantial losses; as a result, not only did principal and interest payments for March and September 1967 remain unpaid, but the company had to request a new loan of Rs. 400,000 to modify the design of the poultry houses, produce feed internally and eliminate unprofitable operations. The case of General Tyre Pakistan, an affiliate of the General Tire and Rubber Co. in the United States, falls chiefly in the category of 'outside factors'. A period of initial losses caused by liberalized competing imports created serious problems and considerably delayed the break-even point in operations; also, the company's supply of imported raw materials has been adversely affected by the shortage of foreign exchange.[17]

In two fields, pharmaceuticals and hotels, Cooley loans do seem to have produced positive results. The hotel development is of special interest. In association with Pan American Airways, Pakistan International Airways and the National Bank of Pakistan, the Intercontinental Hotel Corporation has already established first-class hotels in Karachi, Dacca, Rawalpindi and Lahore; new hotels are planned for Chittagong and Peshawar. This represents the largest concentration of Intercontinental Hotels in any single country. Insofar as a high percentage of the accommodation available remains booked, the hotels have been a success in Pakistan. They are also expected to provide a broad stimulus to the country's tourist industry.

In the main, however, the evidence points up a sharp contrast between liberal Cooley loan commitment and thoroughgoing, even cumbersome, rules of appraisal. One can reasonably infer that solid US policy has yet to emerge in this sphere.

*   *

It remains only to note that the United States has attempted to play an important role in providing technical assistance to Pakistani industry. Marked success has thus far eluded the US programme, apparently for a wide variety of reasons, including insufficient project planning, limited management training, inadequate coverage of East Pakistan, shortage of competent local staff, and weak links with Pakistani government authorities.

---

[17] The problem of imports raises the question as to whether General Tyre Pakistan was, in fact, a well-conceived project. It appears that the value added by the project has been negligible – that all of the company's equipment and raw materials have had to be imported, and that the cost of these imports has been more or less equal to the import cost of the finished product.

9. Commodity aid to Pakistan: a general review

Commodity aid, in the form of industrial materials, can be viewed as an inflow of foreign economic resources designed to remove some of the obstacles to self-sustaining growth. Such assistance is usually classified either as programme aid or more specifically as maintenance imports. It has received increasing donor emphasis over the past half decade.

'Programme' versus 'project' aid

The basic distinction between programme and project aid stems from the fact that the former is usually not tied to specific undertakings but framed in terms of total development requirements. Consequently, there exists some flexibility in allocating non-project assistance, the limits being set by presently installed capacity. For instance, when sulphur is given to Pakistan, it can be used for either papermaking, fertilizer production or textile manufactures (or all three industries); while a loan made for the Karachi Nuclear Power Plant will not be available for a transmission line between Siddhirganj and Ishurdi.

Where rapid economic growth and transformation are political necessities, certain obvious constraints emerge from the impossibility of moving smoothly upward from one level of economic activity to another. Therefore, at some point in the course of the drive towards take-off, the economy will be unable to sustain itself without external resources. Recurrent deficits will show up in the foreign account as import coefficients increase and available raw materials and spare parts prove inadequate to the needs of installed industrial capacity. In this context, the developmental role of commodity assistance can be both immediate and crucial; for it is intended to combat under-utilization by maintaining existing capacity when there is insufficient foreign exchange available for the purchase of certain key materials. Without such aid, the implementation of plans for continuous expansion in the industrial base of a poor economy must be left in abeyance.

Project aid, by contrast, has the effect of increasing productive capacity. And there is a real possibility that a developing country will continue to accept such assistance at a time when non-project needs are not being fully met by the available foreign exchange – thereby aggravating the problem of under-utilized capacity.[1] But this is not the whole story. Project aid does permit the donor to gauge the recipient's absorptive strength in particular fields, as well

---

[1] Programme aid can also bring additions to installed capacity – through raw materials for capital goods industries, for example. This is notably true for India, which has a large capital goods manufacturing sector. In the case of Pakistan, however, the great bulk of non-project assistance has gone towards increased use of existing productive capacity. Accordingly, the capacity-creating aspect of programme aid will not be analysed here.

as its ability to perform a concrete task. Furthermore, carefully planned project assistance can promote self-sustained growth by helping to expand and re-shape the receiving country's productive structure. And programme aid, indiscriminately provided, can be an impediment to self-sustaining growth.

Alan Carlin observes that in the absence of any useful performance criterion, programme aid has a tendency to be allocated among recipient countries solely on the basis of deficits incurred in the budget or the balance of payments, or in both.[2] He sees such aid as a device for creating negative incentives; it is almost a contradiction in terms, for all that is being accomplished is to buttress a condition that is supposedly the object of change. In other words, development through economic transformation is not taking place; the aid is merely serving to narrow or close gaps arising from historical and contemporary relationships between poor and rich economies. This form of assistance, Carlin argues, prevents aid from inducing the change necessary for higher sustainable levels of economic activity.

The constraints on development can, in fact, be categorized in terms of the time horizon over which economic transformation is expected to occur. At any point in time, there are both bottleneck (short-run) and structural (long-run) constraints. In the former case, the inability of the economy to acquire essential goods or services prevents efficient use of available resources, thereby stunting potential growth; while in the latter instance, the failure to transform the productive structure relegates an open, poor economy to continued heavy dependence on external sources.

What all this means is that commodity assistance, despite its direct link to the immediate bottlenecks, should be not only a gap-filler but also an integral part of development plans designed to encourage those changes necessary for eventual self-sustained growth. It is not enough to provide for the fullest utilization of existing capacity; installed productive capability must be so strengthened as to become the foundation for the achievement of structural change. It is in these terms that commodity aid can have its greatest impact.

The size and pattern of commodity aid flows to Pakistan

The most significant commodity flows to Pakistan come from the United States under the AID programme; approximately $1.2 billion worth of non-PL 480 imports had been financed by AID and its predecessor agencies by 1966.[3] Canada, though giving a much smaller proportion of non-food aid, has been the second ranking donor as far as this category is concerned; by 1966 it had provided some $51.7 million.[4]

---

[2] A. Carlin, 'Project Versus Programme Aid: From the Donor's Viewpoint', *Economic Journal*, March 1967.

[3] US commodity aid figures are derived from: US AID Statistics and Reports Division (Washington, D.C.); *U.S. Overseas Loans and Grants and Assistance from International Organizations* (Washington, D.C., 17 March 1967), p. 18.

[4] Canada, unpublished CIDA materials. Australia and Great Britain are the only other donors which were giving commodity assistance as early as 1960. During the past few

Table 34. *US AID-financed commodity flows and total US economic aid to Pakistan, 1949–66 (millions of US dollars)*

Fiscal year	Commodity flow,* nominal value (I)	Net obligation and loan authorization — Total A*	Net obligation and loan authorization — Total B†	I as % of A	I as % of B
1949–52	—	10.6	11.1	—	—
1953–7	132.8	330.3	556.3	40.2	23.4
1958	56.5	92.9	158.2	60.8	35.7
1959	76.7	162.7	229.5	47.0	33.3
1960	111.9	198.6	291.8	56.3	38.3
1961	118.0	124.2	167.8	95.0	70.3
1962	112.6	240.1	422.2	46.9	26.6
1963	159.2	174.3	355.2	91.3	44.8
1964	145.1	213.9	380.1	67.8	38.1
1965	181.0	182.3	348.2	99.3	51.9
1966	115.0	114.1	141.6	100.9	81.2
TOTAL	*1,208.8*	*1,844.0*	*3,062.0*	*65.6*	*39.5*

A = total aid flow, excluding PL 480 and Export–Import Bank loans.
B = total aid flow.
SOURCES: * Unpublished materials from the US AID Statistics and Reports Division (Washington, D.C.). † US AID, *U.S. Overseas Loans and Grants and Assistance from International Organizations* (Washinton, D.C., 17 March 1967), p. 18.

The United States programme

Non-PL 480 commodity assistance represents the largest proportion of total US economic aid to Pakistan – roughly 40 per cent over the period 1953–66. Table 34 shows the dimensions of commodity aid in the overall US programme. While those statistics do not reveal any systematic trends in the relative importance of the commodity flows, more recent figures reflect a sharp rise in their share of total US assistance to Pakistan.

This non-PL 480 commodity aid embraces a very wide range of goods, the most important of which can be grouped into 'raw materials and semi-finished products' and 'machinery and vehicles'. As can be seen in Table 35, these two categories have together represented between 75 and 93 per cent of US commodity aid flows since 1955. Machinery and equipment have been the major item in the 'machinery and vehicles' category; and chemicals and iron and steel mill products have predominated in the 'raw materials and semi-finished products' group.[5] From 1955 to 1961, the two main categories of aid-

years, there has been a sizable increase in commodity aid to Pakistan from other donors, notably West Germany, China, Japan and IDA. In this connection, see Pakistan Planning Commission, *Final Evaluation of the Second Five-Year Plan (1960–65)* (Karachi, 1966), pp. 28–9, 172; Pakistan, *Report of the Working Group on Debt Burden* (Islamabad, 1968), pp. 99–151; Planning Commission, *The Mid-Plan Review of the Third Five-Year Plan (1965–70)* (Rawalpindi, 1968), pp. 31–2, 188, and *Memorandum for the Pakistan Consortium, 1969–70* (Islamabad, 1969), pp. 70–3.
[5] See Appendix 6 below for detailed statistics on US commodity aid flows.

Table 35. *Major types of non-PL 480 commodity assistance to Pakistan: US AID and predecessor agencies, 1955–66 (thousands of US dollars)*

Fiscal year	Raw materials and semi-finished products (A)	Machinery and vehicles (B)	A+B (I)	Total commodities (II)	I as % of II
1955	7,270	7,371	14,641	17,759	82
1956	18,948	18,617	37,565	49,549	75
1957	21,124	18,052	39,176	47,719	82
1958	18,580	28,030	46,610	56,492	82
1959	32,565	30,785	63,350	76,650	82
1960	48,454	47,808	96,262	111,967	85
1961	55,428	46,340	101,768	118,091	86
1962	62,642	26,121	88,765	112,635	78
1963	100,207	37,706	137,913	159,229	86
1964	92,641	43,732	136,373	145,163	93
1965	139,292	29,087	168,379	181,089	92
1966	64,200	39,996	104,196	115,064	90

SOURCE: Unpublished materials from the US AID Statistics and Reports Division (Washington, D.C.).

financed non-PL 480 imports – that is, raw materials and semi-finished products, and machinery and vehicles – differed relatively little in value. However, the former greatly exceeded the latter over the years 1962–6. Outside of these groupings, petroleum and fertilizer have been the most important products going to Pakistan, again in terms of nominal value.

The Canadian programme[6]

The commodity flows of Canadian aid to the industrial sector of Pakistan comprise a wide variety of products, including aluminum, copper, sulphur, woodpulp, nylon twine and tallow. The aluminum, which is given in ingot form, is fabricated into sheets and rods in Pakistan's own mills and used for general manufacturing purposes. Because of recent difficulties experienced in obtaining copper, aluminum has begun to be used for transmission wires and cables as well. Canadian copper rod is processed into bare and insulated wire and cable for the electrical industry. The sulphur, though applied chiefly in the preparation of fertilizer, is sometimes also used in the textile and paper-making industries. The wood pulp, of which Pakistan produces little, is used mainly for the manufacture of paper. Nylon twine goes to the manufacturers of fish nets. And tallow is allocated among nearly twenty manufacturers of soap.

Table 36 summarizes Canada's non-food commodity aid flows to Pakistan since the inception of the programme in 1955. In value terms, aluminum, fertilizer, copper and woodpulp have been the most important components of the

[6] In this connection, see K. Spicer, *A Samaritan State? External Aid in Canada's Foreign Policy* (Toronto, 1966), ch. 7.

commodity aid programme. And all but fertilizer have been made available to Pakistan over a longer period than the other commodities – copper since 1955, aluminum since 1957, and woodpulp since 1959.

Criteria for appraising non-food commodity assistance

Aid in general

When applying economic criteria to determine the efficacy of foreign assistance, one should be conscious of the distinction between general and partial analysis of cause–effect relationships. In any economy characterized by close inter-dependence, partial analysis cannot be expected to yield the total effect of

Table 36. *Canadian non-food commodity aid to Pakistan, 1955–66 (long tons, Canadian dollars)*

Commodities	1955	1956	1957	1959[a]	1960	1961
Aluminum						
Quantity	—	—	500	—	5,085	1,963
Value	—	—.	258,822	—	2,411,193	979,717
Copper						
Quantity	300	300	—	200	502	—
Value	285,600	314,496	—	129,922	377,262	—
Tinplate						
Quantity	—	—	—	—	8,507	172
Value	—	—	—	—	1,731,697	36,130
Mild steel						
Quantity	—	—	—	—	6,433	235
Value	—	—	—	—	598,205	21,853
Galv. steel						
Quantity	—	—	—	—	174	1,326
Value	—	—	—	—	35,378	268,851
Fertilizers						
Quantity	—	—	—	—	30,509	40,718
Value	—	—	—	—	1,313,131	2,738,766
Sulphur						
Quantity	—	—	—	—	—	—
Value	—	—	—	—	—	—
Woodpulp						
Quantity	—	—	—	3,001	1,998	10,028
Value	—	—	—	345,676	253,212	1,088,517
Tallow						
Quantity	—	—	—	—	—	—
Value	—	—	—	—	—	—
Nylon twine						
Quantity	—	—	—	—	—	—
Value	—	—	—	—	—	—
TOTALS						
Quantity	*300*	*300*	*500*	*3,201*	*53,208*	*54,442*
Value	*285,600*	*314,496*	*258,822*	*475,598*	*6,720,078*	*5,133,834*

Table 36 (*cont.*)

Commodities	1962	1963	1964	1965	1966	Totals
Aluminum						
Quantity	2,930	5,411	4,511	1,805	3,643	25,848
Value	1,513,010	2,780,049	2,477,914	1,016,271	2,641,311	14,078,287
Copper						
Quantity	1,997	1,498	3,790	2,609	1,746	12,942
Value	1,467,703	1,082,502	2,822,182	3,144,812	1,866,771	11,491,250
Tinplate						
Quantity	—	—	—	—	—	8,679
Value	—	—	—	—	—	1,767,827
Mild steel						
Quantity	—	—	—	—	—	6,668
Value	—	—	—	—	—	620,058
Galv. steel						
Quantity	—	—	—	—	—	1,500
Value	—	—	—	—	—	304,229
Fertilizers						
Quantity	60,270	53,955	21,195	10,000	9,000	225,647
Value	2,997,329	2,709,799	960,703	414,563	394,130	11,528,421
Sulphur						
Quantity	—	—	11,676	—	—	11,676
Value	—	—	218,782	—	—	218,782
Woodpulp						
Quantity	11,291	11,128	13,845	2,457	15,066	68,814
Value	1,299,601	1,299,967	1,895,925	372,556	1,837,012	8,392,466
Tallow						
Quantity	—	—	—	324	7,454	7,778
Value	—	—	—	76,506	1,758,970	1,835,476
Nylon twine						
Quantity	—	—	—	232	257	489
Value	—	—	—	653,869	760,978	1,414,847
TOTALS						
Quantity	*76,488*	*71,992*	*55,017*	*17,427*	*37,166*	*370,041*
Value	*7,277,643*	*7,872,317*	*8,375,506*	*5,678,577*	*9,259,172*	*51,651,643*

SOURCE: Unpublished materials from the Canadian International Development Agency.
[a] Canada provided no non-food commodity aid to Pakistan in 1958.

resource transfers from donor to recipient country. In large measure, this is because the initial impact is typically carried well beyond the point of entry to other segments of the economy.

An important related cause of divergence between the apparent and real effects of aid is the phenomenon of 'fungibility'. Consider the example of three aid-financed projects, X, Y and Z, and assume that the donor ties the aid to project X. Is it justifiable to assess aid impact in terms of the performance of X? This seems doubtful, since the recipient government might well have undertaken X even if there had been no aid at all. In that event, the effects of the foreign resources would be attributable to either Y or Z, or both, and not to the project with which the aid is contractually identified; X was never the marginal project.

Carlin argues that the 'fungibility' problem has been overemphasized, and that it is possible for every project to be a marginal one, thereby eliminating any distortion on this account. 'As long as the sum of available free foreign exchange plus untied programme aid is less than essential maintenance imports, no project requiring substantial amounts of foreign exchange will normally be undertaken without some public or private international financing.'[7] On the other hand, Singer contends that

> the developmental impact of any good expenditure plan plus policy package is maximized if these expenditures and policies are properly related to others and taken as a whole...The identification of a marginal project for purposes of tying aid to it without illusion or deception does not only require a high degree of sophistication but is really inherently impossible except in rare cases.[8]

It is also important to note Singer's emphasis on the behaviour of the policy-makers. In fact, a crucial index of aid performance is the resourcefulness of the recipient government in allocating available resources in terms of an expanded input base. As T. C. Schelling observes, 'the results of an aid process depend...on the behaviour of governments'.[9] This point is intimately linked to the argument that it is at the macro-economic level that aid can be most accurately identified with certain desired goals of developmental planning. Accordingly, economic evaluation of aid impact may well be more meaningful in the general rather than the particular case.

Commodity aid – major criteria

As already noted, commodity assistance – unlike project aid – tends to be allocated on a macro-economic basis for general development purposes.[10] And import requirements for maintaining and utilizing installed capacity provide much of the rationale for requests and offers of non-project aid.

Under-utilization, as well as misuse, of existing resources is an inherent feature of underdevelopment. Commodity assistance has a role to play in promoting the use of existing capacity without jeopardizing planned development projects. Indeed, the extent to which such aid prevents under-utilization of already installed industrial capability is a key test by which its performance may be judged.

---

[7] Carlin, 'Project Versus Programme Aid', p. 51.

[8] H. W. Singer, 'External Aid: For Plans or Projects?', *Economic Journal*, September 1965, p. 543.   [9] T. C. Schelling, *International Economics* (Boston, 1958), p. 453.

[10] 'A significant part of United States aid is based on an assessment of total resource requirements and availabilities of the recipient country...This approach [aid-financed commodity imports] provides the recipient country with maximum flexibility to meet individual resource needs and to choose imports in ways which...may result in reduced expenditures. Often, spare parts or industrial raw materials are more critically needed for the success of the development programme than new projects.' M. C. Gay, 'Problems in the Integration of Foreign Aid with National Plans', in *Planning the External Sector: Techniques, Problems and Policies, Report on the First Interregional Seminar on Development Planning*, United Nations, ST/TAO/Ser. C/91 (New York, 1967), p. 202.

This leads to the question how capacity utilization is to be measured. If the technical structure of every industrial unit were known, one could derive from the capital–output and capital–labour ratios that amount of output and labour which represented full capacity utilization for the industrial sector. Given reliable statistics, actual employment and output levels over the relevant period of time would be known. The latter figures would show the extent of resource utilization on an industrial base inclusive of commodity aid. Finally, depending on a variety of assumptions, it would be possible to estimate the hypothetical level of utilization that would have been attained without the aid.

Let the measures be denoted the potential level (P), the actual level with aid (A), and the hypothetical level without aid (H), respectively. These categories suggest several indexes of the contribution of aid-financed commodities: (i) The gap between P and A expressed as a percentage of P over the aid period. This, of course, provides a measure of unused capacity in relation to full potential – the 'potential–actual' gap. (ii) The gap between A and H expressed as a percentage of P. This may be described as the 'aid–no aid' gap in relation to full capacity. It is algebraically identical to the difference between what might be called the 'potential–no aid' gap ($P - H$) and the potential–actual gap ($P - A$), both with respect to P. (iii) The aid–no aid gap expressed as a percentage of A. This is essentially an estimate of the difference between performance with and without aid. In dynamic terms, such a measure can be fully accurate only at the macro-economic level; but a partial analysis, sector by sector or industry by industry, would give an approximation of the direct impact of aid on employment and output levels.

These three indexes can be written in the following manner:

(i) $$\left(\frac{P-A}{P} \times 100\right)_t \text{ where } t = 1, \ldots, n,$$

(ii) $$\left(\frac{A-H}{P} \times 100\right)_t = \left[\left(\frac{P-H}{P} - \frac{P-A}{P}\right) \times 100\right]_t,$$

(iii) $$\left(\frac{A-H}{A} \times 100\right)_t.$$

All three performance indexes are relevant to a total assessment of commodity aid on the basis of industrial capacity. They are also extremely difficult to apply.

In any event, there would seem to be at least four major criteria for evaluating the effects of commodity assistance on industrial development:

The capacity criterion. At this stage it is almost unnecessary to note the impossibility of making accurate estimates of the capital–output and capital–labour ratios for Pakistani industry. However, if one assumes that available industrial supply does not exceed effective demand, rises in employment and output can be equated with increases in utilization of industrial capacity – once account is taken of the installation of new capacity in any given time period. The degree to which potential capacity is approached is reflected in employment and output levels over time. This could be measured for each industry into which commodity assistance has flowed directly, and for the industrial sector taken as a whole. By taking the aid–no aid gap, by itself or as a percentage of actual utilization, one could make some approximation of the extent to which use of capacity had been augmented due to the availability of aid-financed imports.

This performance test would have to be applied with the usual warning about partial analysis; for instance, if Pakistan's sulphur-using industries have been experiencing shortages of this particular input, then one would expect this constraint to be a cause of diminishing demand for other inputs (including labour), as well as a cause of fluctuations in output – not only for these specific industries but, to some degree, for the industrial sector as a whole. More to the point, there are wide gaps in available data on employment and output; and it is necessary to be far less precise in measuring commodity aid impact than even this one test would imply.

The balance-of-payments criterion. In the most immediate sense, the importance of commodity aid results from its role in relieving the foreign exchange constraint on the development possibilities of the recipient economy. Thus, a second criterion for judging the efficacy of this form of assistance is linked to the balance-of-payments position of the recipient. The central question to be posed is: how much foreign exchange savings resulted from the aid? A related measure would express these savings as a percentage of the current account balance (deficit) from year to year. Still another measure would be the proportion of total imports financed by the aid. As a matter of fact, a considerable variety of indexes can be devised for this purpose.[11]

The structure criterion. Although the short-run developmental role of commodity aid has been stressed (in relation to bottleneck constraints), such aid obviously exerts its influence over an extended period as well. The long run is nothing more or less than the summation of its component short runs. Misallocation of resources in any one year and misinterpretation of immediate needs compound themselves by contributing, over time, to the formation of an undesirable structure of production for both domestically sold and exported goods and services. To describe the role of aid-financed imports solely in terms of current foreign exchange shortages is, therefore, to neglect its potential role in the development process. Gap-filling alone does not permit this form of economic assistance to realize its complete potential. It is through an overall import policy, for export- and aid-financed imports, that commodity aid becomes an important instrument of development planning; for it then affects the whole course of industrial transformation.[12]

[11] For an interesting analysis of the impact of PL 480 commodity aid on the Greek balance of payments, see G. Coutsoumaris et al., *Analysis and Assessment of the Economic Effects of the U.S. PL 480 Program in Greece*, Center of Planning and Economic Research (Athens, 1965), ch. 10.

[12] This must be distinguished from the test of donor influence on the recipient country's import policies. The political test is discussed below; here external pressures on the aid-receiving government are not considered.

For the long run, a strong balance-of-payments position is of central importance. Efficient import policy will create priorities allowing for the growth of those industrial undertakings which lead to greater import substitution and export expansion. By acquiring the raw materials and spare parts for such enterprises at the expense of those which do not promote economic transformation, import policy (including requests for commodity aid) reaches towards maximum effectiveness. A further requirement is that, given the available and expected domestic resources, the import policy encourage the kind of factor intensity most conducive to industrial growth.[13]

It is necessary to take account of changes in the structure of production over the aid period. The changing pattern of imports, as among capital, intermediate and consumer goods, is a primary index for judging the effects of commodity aid on economic transformation. In particular, an increasing proportion of capital and intermediate goods could be regarded as evidence of growing industrialization, since this would imply an enlargement of the importing country's industrial base.[14] More generally, the structural test implies measurement of the changing composition of both aggregate and industrial output – as between agriculture and industry, foreign and domestic supply, exports and production for the home market, large- and small-scale manufacturing, consumer and producer goods industries.

The political criterion. When applying the first three criteria, it would be quite unreasonable to assume that the only constraints on the achievement of an optimal productive and distributive structure are economic in nature. The economic system under consideration is not, after all, operating autonomously and pushing itself towards higher levels of economic activity; it is rather a complex system where economic growth is planned within a political framework. Consequently, the analysis must allow for the developmental constraints posed by the political process. It is characteristic of development efforts in poor countries that most of the stimuli – and impediments – to economic growth originate at the political rather than the entrepreneurial level. In a very real sense, therefore, commodity assistance has a part to play in removing political bottlenecks – inadequate or burdensome legislation, wasteful allocation and distribution of resources, bureaucratic delays, and so on.

---

[13] There has been some criticism of Pakistan's import policy on the grounds that it has not sufficiently encouraged labour-intensive production. 'Overall, the impact of import policy combined with other policies such as interest rate and credit policy, has been antithetical to labour-intensive investment, so that one must conclude that this particular goal of national planning has not been meaningfully translated into any part of current import policies.' P. S. Thomas, 'Import Licensing and Import Liberalization in Pakistan: A Critical Evaluation', unpublished mimeo. (US AID, n.p., n.d.), p. 51. It remains, of course, an open question whether emphasis on labour-intensive industry is desirable, even for a capital-scarce, densely populated country.

[14] On the other hand, a relative decline in consumer goods imports resulting from restrictive policies might well produce a rate of import substitution in consumer goods industries which would be inefficient in terms of both current investment and the long-run pattern of industrial production.

There are two distinct roles for aid at the political level. One may be seen in terms of expected gains in diplomatic influence or leverage by the donor over the recipient. In this case, the aid-giver is attempting to impose its notion of desirable political behaviour for the recipient in the latter's domestic and international affairs. Secondly, there is the donor's political leverage aimed at producing certain kinds of economic policy. It is this second form of leverage which receives attention here.[15] And it is relevant even where the aid transfers are completely untied, for there is normally an understanding that these resources should be used as efficiently as possible so that development efforts will bear a close relationship to the recipient's own social goals.[16]

Rational economic planning requires that the design of commodity assistance programmes be an integral part of overall import policy. In political terms, the impact of commodity aid can be assessed by examining the evidence of broad shifts in Pakistan's economic policies, especially in regard to imports and productive efficiency.

Establishing an import policy in such matters as licensing procedures, tariff levels and import liberalization is a key aspect of long-run development planning. If such planning is to approach an optimal impact – in both an immediate and a long-run sense – there are certain goals that planners should be attempting to achieve.

In the short run, they should be so requesting and distributing imports (commodity aid and normal commercial purchases) as to yield the most efficient allocation of available foreign exchange resources. This requires consideration of such matters as economies of scale in the purchase of foreign materials: licences permitting the acquisition of limited quantities of imports may not produce as low a price as would otherwise be obtained; on the other hand, licences that allow very large quantities to be imported by individual corporations may lead to undesirable monopolies and the consequent inefficient distribution of resources in terms of long-run social returns. Over a longer planning period, as elaborated above, such considerations as sound industrial transformation and a favourable balance-of-payments position enter into policy decisions involving imports. In all these respects – short as well as long run – it remains valid to distinguish between two interrelated issues: the policies actually implemented by the recipient government and the donor's role in bringing these policies into effect.

[15] There is, of course, also the role of aid in improving policy implementation through the transfer of expertise to a developing country. But this is not 'leverage' in the sense of bargaining power associated with the provision of aid.

[16] The other side of this coin is to argue that non-project aid is of questionable value precisely because it can influence basic economic policies in the developing country, and thereby create serious tensions between donor and recipient. See A. O. Hirschman and R. M. Bird, *Foreign Aid – A Critique and A Proposal*, Essays in International Finance, no. 69 (Princeton University, July 1968), pp. 3–14. At least in the Pakistan context, the cogency of this view would seem to be doubtful.

10. Impact of commodity aid on Pakistan's industry

The discussion in Chapter 9 leads to certain presumptions as to the impact of non-food commodity aid on the growth of the Pakistan economy in general and on the development of its industrial sector in particular. Commodity and project aid, it has been reasoned, are neither mutually exclusive nor perfect substitutes; but the former has distinct features which argue in favour of its continued, and perhaps increasing, use as an instrument of international resource transfer.

For one thing, commodity assistance enables a developing country to exploit an often neglected source of growth – idle capacity. It also improves the country's balance-of-payments position in a unique way – by not only increasing available resources but also easing the management of the external accounts. Given its effective integration into a development programme, commodity aid broadens the range and quickens the pace of industrial transformation in a developing economy. Finally, commodity assistance is an especially strong instrument of donor influence on the economic policies of recipient governments.

What follows is an attempt to test the validity of these propositions by examining the empirical evidence available for Pakistan.

Impact on capacity utilization

As in the case of many developing countries, foreign aid programmes in Pakistan have, until recently, tended to emphasize 'capacity-building' over 'capacity-using' imports, partly on the assumption that the former make a greater contribution to economic development. Yet the success of any industrialization programme depends on maintaining a careful balance between both types of imports. This is particularly true when development goods are supplied in large degree from foreign sources and when the process of industrialization is subject to a strict foreign exchange constraint. If so much new plant capacity is installed that relatively little foreign exchange is left to feed into it the necessary imported inputs, then the bulk of these capital costs will have been wasted, the foreign exchange resources will have been inefficiently deployed, and the growth rate of industrial output will not have been maximized. This, in turn, will weaken the country's overall ability to service its external debt. Conversely, if exchange and/or import controls link commodity imports too closely to plant capacity, businessmen may decide to expand their plant mainly to obtain additional import quotas, with the result that the allocation of investible resources will be only loosely related to either the industrialization programme or the internal pattern of demand.

It is clear that Pakistan's authorities have become aware of the waste that can arise from the wrong mix of development imports. Indeed, the new industrial policy formulated by the Planning Commission seeks explicitly to maximize the growth of output rather than the growth of capacity. It rests on a cost–benefit approach which 'tacitly assumes that the new capacity to be created will also be utilized to the full extent. If there is no assurance that new capacity can be fully utilized, it should not be created.'[1]

Allowance is made for a small margin of under-utilization, which is likely to correct itself in the short run if growth in demand takes place and if import policy makes 'sufficient raw materials available to operate the existing capacity to the best advantage of the economy'. However, if there is large under-utilization, 'it would be wise...to be reluctant in granting new sanctions for investment... even if the benefits per unit of imports seem relatively high'.[2]

The evidence

There is, nevertheless, impressive evidence of under-utilization of capacity in the Pakistan economy. In his review of Consortium experience, John White states that prior to 1963, 'actual production was in many cases more than 50 per cent below capacity'.[3] This observation is consistent with unpublished surveys conducted by the US AID Mission in Pakistan.

Nural Islam has found a significant cost disadvantage for most domestic industrial goods as against imports, and he attributes this in part to the prevalence of capacity under-utilization. 'There is a considerable excess capacity in the manufacturing industries in Pakistan. About 60 per cent of the industries examined worked below 40 per cent of their installed capacity.'[4] The proportion of industries working below 40 per cent of capacity was less than average (50 per cent) for capital goods and above average (78 per cent) for intermediate goods; but such differences are regarded as insignificant in terms of explaining inter-industry cost differences between domestic and imported products.

Table 37 gives a frequency distribution of Pakistani industries with respect to the degree of capacity utilization. Such widespread under-utilization cannot, of course, be traced to any single factor like the shortage of imported raw materials and spare parts. Thus the US AID Mission in Pakistan has reported that in 1964, when the flow of commodity aid was on the increase, the main reason given by managers of a small sample of industries was not inadequate supplies of foreign raw materials, but rather a scarcity of skilled workers, foremen and managerial personnel.[5]

---

[1] Pakistan Ministry of Finance, *Industrial Policy and Import Liabilities* (Rawalpindi, 1967), p. 10.   [2] *Ibid.*

[3] J. White, *Pledged to Development: A Study of International Consortia and the Strategy of Aid* (London, 1967), p. 79.

[4] N. Islam, 'Comparative Costs, Factor Proportions, and Industrial Efficiency in Pakistan', *Pakistan Development Review*, Summer 1967, pp. 229–30. Islam's figures on excess capacity are not without shortcomings. He defines it as the difference between actual output and installed capacity as assessed by the Pakistan Tariff Commission. But he notes that many important industries have not been subject to investigation by the commission. Furthermore, there is no precise indication of the number of shifts involved in the measurement of installed capacity. And the excess capacity figures are broad aggregates which relate to different industries at different points in time.   [5] Unpublished US AID Mission materials.

Table 37. *Utilization of capacity in Pakistan's manufacturing industries*

% of capacity utilization	% of industries		
	Consumer goods	Intermediate goods	Capital goods
0–20	27.60	34.80	11.10
20–40	34.50	43.50	38.90
40–60	10.30	17.40	22.20
60–80	10.30	—	22.20
80–100	17.30	4.30	5.60

SOURCE: N. Islam, 'Comparative Costs, Factor Proportions, and Industrial Efficiency in Pakistan', *Pakistan Development Review*, Summer 1967, p. 230.

Closely connected to the manpower shortage is the prevalence of single shift operations. Both AID and the World Bank have referred, on several occasions, to this drag on the growth of output.[6] Despite the shortage and high cost of equipment, production targets are set chiefly on a single shift basis; textiles are an exception, along with a few other industries using indigenous raw materials. Two-shift operations would not only double production but would drastically reduce overheads; and they would permit the use of scarce senior management to much better advantage.[7]

Notwithstanding these other factors, however, it is clear that the under-utilization of capacity is 'engendered partly by a lack of coordination between industrial investment licensing and the licensing of imports of raw materials and spare parts'.[8] The magnitude and direction of commodity aid flows are highly relevant in this context.

Precise measurement of their impact would involve a thoroughgoing investigation. For each industry, detailed information would be required as to year-to-year changes in output, capacity utilization, total variable costs and the import component of such costs. If the composition of commodity aid flows were unspecified, the analysis could proceed in terms of an assumed allocation of resource transfer – the assumption that commodity aid is channelled to those sectors where it yields the maximum increment in output. But since donors usually tie aid credits to specific types of commodities, the flow would have to be disaggregated by actual end use. Details on the composition of investment would also be necessary, as well as substantial data on the volume of development imports actually financed by domestic and foreign resources.

Given all this information, a number of important relationships could be quantified: the increment in output (from greater capacity utilization) which could have been achieved without commodity aid, that is, with imports financed

---

[6] Unpublished materials provided by US AID and IBRD.

[7] Other important output bottlenecks are lack of market demand and uneconomic size and location of plant. Obviously, commodity assistance can do little, if anything, to overcome such constraints.

[8] Islam, 'Comparative Costs', p. 238.

Table 38. *Import intensity and capacity utilization in Pakistan*

Industry	Import intensity*	Capacity utilization[a]†	
		East Pakistan	West Pakistan
Highly import-intensive products			
Grain milling	62.7	A	A
Basic metals	35.2	L	L
Perfumes, cosmetics and soap	26.6	A	L
Metal goods	24.2	A	L
Plastic goods	24.1	L	L
Paints and varnishes	20.5	L	L
Rubber and rubber products	19.6	A	L
Woollen textiles	18.7	H	A
Electrical goods	18.0	L	L
Transport equipment	18.0	A	L
Non-electrical machinery	17.4	A	L
Silk and art silk	17.1	A	L
Pharmaceutical products	12.8	L	L
Construction	12.8	n.a.	n.a.
Printing and publishing	11.6	H	L
Paper and board	10.9	H	L
Moderately import-intensive products			
Tanning and leather finishing	9.1	H	A
Coal and petroleum products	8.4	—	H
Edible oil and fat	7.3	H	A
Electricity, gas, water and sanitary services	6.6	H	H
Dying, printing and finishing of textiles	5.6	H	H
Non-metallic mineral products	5.0	—	A
Wood, cork and furniture products	4.5	L	A
Articles of paper and board	4.5	—	L
Thread and thread-ball making	4.3	H	H
Cotton textiles	4.1	H	H
Less-than-average import-intensive products			
Small-scale industries	3.7	n.a.	n.a.
Jute textiles	3.5	H	—
Footwear	3.3	H	A
Knitting	3.1	H	L
Bakery products and confectionery	2.6	L	A
Chemical fertilizers	2.0	H	H
Mining and quarrying	1.5	n.a.	n.a.
Matches	1.3	H	H
Cotton ginning	1.3	A	A
Services not otherwise classified	1.2	n.a.	n.a.
Cotton growing	0.8	n.a.	n.a.
Salt	0.6	L	A
Other agriculture not otherwise classified	0.4	n.a.	n.a.
Tea	0.3	L	A
Sugar refining	0.3	H	H
Jute growing	nil	n.a.	n.a.
Jute pressing	nil	n.a.	n.a.

For footnotes see facing page.

solely out of Pakistan's foreign exchange earnings and reserves; the increase in output that can be attributed to the commodity aid inflows; the increments in output achievable through increases in commodity aid. Needless to say, the required information is not fully available; nor would the statistical task be at all simple even if it were. There is, however, enough material at hand to make a rough assessment of commodity aid impact possible.

Import intensity and capacity utilization

A major question is whether the more import-intensive industries suffer from a greater under-utilization of capacity. Islam reports that 'no strong correlation is discernible'. This he finds plausible in view of an alleged 'bias towards a more liberal licensing for the import intensive industries, especially if they are successful in the export markets'.[9]

But other data have appeared more recently on this issue, and they are worth analysing here. The measure of import intensity chosen is the value of imports of intermediate goods in each industry expressed as a percentage of the industry's gross value of product.[10] For purposes of capacity utilization, use is made of an index computed by the Pakistan Planning Commission.[11]

Table 38 lists the industries in descending order of import intensity, together with the corresponding capacity utilization in East and West Pakistan. Three categories of import intensity have been distinguished: industries with an intensity below that for total intermediate sales (4 per cent) have been designated as 'less than average'; those with an intensity ranging from 4 to 10 per cent as 'moderate'; and the remaining industries as 'high'. There are also three classes of capacity utilization: low, average and high, as explained in the table.

Table 39 presents this information in summary form. It points to a definite relationship between industrial import intensity and the extent to which productive capacity is utilized. In East Pakistan, 80 per cent of the highly import-intensive industries were operating at or below 80 per cent of capacity, as against 14 per cent of the moderately intensive industries and 40 per cent of those with less-than-average intensity. The link is even more apparent in West Pakistan: in thirteen of the fifteen highly import-intensive industries – more than 86 per cent – capacity utilization was below 60 per cent of potential; by contrast, only 11 per cent of the less import-intensive industries operated

---

SOURCES: * Computed from W. Tims and J. Stern, 'Pakistan Inter-Industry Flow Table (Revised), 1963–64', unpublished mimeo. (Harvard University Center for International Affairs, 1967). †Pakistan Ministry of Finance, *Industrial Policy and Import Liabilities* (Rawalpindi, 1967), pp. 13–22.

[a] Capacity utilization below 60 per cent is denoted by L (low); utilization between 60 and 80 per cent by A (average); and above 80 per cent by H (high).

[9] *Ibid.* p. 230.

[10] This measure was derived from W. Tims and J. Stern, 'Pakistan Inter-Industry Flow Table (Revised), 1963–64', unpublished mimeo. (Harvard University Center for International Affairs, 1967).

[11] Pakistan Ministry of Finance, *Industrial Policy and Import Liabilities.* The index is based on production statistics for the calendar year 1965 and the fiscal year 1965/6.

Table 39. *Distribution of Pakistan industries by import intensity and capacity utilization*

Capacity utilization†	High (above 10 %)		Moderate (4–10 %)		Less than average (less than 4 %)	
	No.	%	No.	%	No.	%
East Pakistan						
Low (below 60 %)	5	33.3	1	14.3	3	30.0
Average (60–80 %)	7	46.6	—	—	1	10.0
High (above 80 %)	3	20.1	6	85.7	6	60.0
Total (no. of industries)	*15*	*100.0*	*7*	*100.0*	*10*	*100.0*
West Pakistan						
Low (below 60 %)	13	86.6	1	10.0	1	11.1
Average (60–80 %)	2	13.4	4	40.0	5	55.6
High (above 80 %)	—	—	5	50.0	3	33.3
Total (no. of industries)	*15*	*100.0*	*10*	*100.0*	*9*	*100.0*

Import intensity*

SOURCES: * Computed from W. Tims and J. Stern, 'Pakistan Inter-Industry Flow Table (Revised), 1963–64', unpublished mimeo. (Harvard University Center for International Affairs, 1967). † Pakistan Ministry of Finance, *Industrial Policy and Import Liabilities* (Rawalpindi, 1967), pp. 13–22.

at below 60 per cent capacity; again, seventeen of the nineteen less-than-average and moderately import-intensive industries – 94 per cent – had above-average or average capacity utilization.[12] The relationship is the more remarkable since it prevailed at a time when both the availability of imported goods and the volume of commodity aid were greater than ever – shortly after the import liberalization programme had reached its peak, and before the impact of commodity aid curtailment following the Indo-Pakistan War could be felt in any substantial degree.

In Table 40 one sees the broad significance of this relationship, and consequently the very real basis for expecting adequate supplies of development imports (however financed) to have a strong impact on the growth of both total and industrial output. Sixteen highly import-intensive industries account for over 43 per cent of the gross value of total product. If the gross product of the primary sector (agriculture, mines and quarries) is excluded, the industries with high import intensity make up nearly 70 per cent of non-primary gross product.

Commodity aid effects

As will be seen below, increased foreign aid – and, in particular, a greater emphasis on commodity aid within the Pakistan Consortium – was a major

---

[12] It may well be that West Pakistan's greater extent of industrialization means wider scope for excess capacity than in East Pakistan, regardless of the degree of import intensity.

Table 40. *Distribution of Pakistan industries by import intensity*

	No. of industries		Gross value of product	
Import intensity	Total	For which capacity index is available	Rs. millions (current prices)	%
High (above 10 %)	16	15	45,669.78	42.7
Moderate (4–10 %)	10	10	4,755.30	4.4
Less than average (less than 4 %)	17	10	56,398.61	52.8
TOTAL	43	35	106,930.69[a]	100.0[a]

SOURCES: Computed from Pakistan, *Industrial Policy and Import Liabilities* (Rawalpindi, 1967), pp. 13–22; and from W. Tims and J. Stern, 'Pakistan Inter-Industry Flow Table (Revised), 1963–64', unpublished mimeo. (Harvard University Center for International Affairs, 1967).

[a] Includes nine very small sectors, whose gross product was valued at Rs. 107 million in 1963/4.

factor in the liberalization of import controls which began in 1960 and was gradually extended until 1965. This liberalization brought a substantial rise in commodity imports: in the last half of 1964 imports under the 'free list' (which included most of the raw materials and capital goods Pakistan requires from abroad) had increased by 46 per cent over the same period in 1963, more than three times as much as total imports.[13]

It has been shown, in the previous section, that such an increase in commodity imports *should* have led to a substantial rise in capacity utilization in many industries and consequently to a significant increase in total output; but it remains to establish that in fact it *has*. This central issue will now be considered.[14]

In his comments on import liberalization, White notes that in the second half of 1963, 'utilization of plant capacity, which had fallen to 53 per cent when the liberalization programme began, allegedly rose above 80 per cent within 18 months'.[15] According to the IDA, 'when imports were liberalized in 1964, production increased immediately and installed capacity was used more fully'.[16] These statements are entirely consistent with survey findings of the US AID Mission in Pakistan.[17]

One of these surveys covered the period from January to December 1964. It was confined to nineteen steel-using firms in the Karachi area, since the most important liberalization measure in that year had been the inclusion of

[13] Unpublished figures obtained from the World Bank.
[14] Even a strong correlation between import intensity and capacity utilization does not necessarily mean that large commodity aid inflows will substantially increase utilization of capacity. As already noted, much will depend on the strength of factors other than import intensity.
[15] White, *Pledged to Development*, p. 80.
[16] IDA, Press Release no. 66/22: $25 Million Loan to Pakistan for Industrial Imports (Washington, 23 December 1966), p. 2.
[17] Unpublished materials made available by AID.

four items of iron and steel in the free list for imports. Of the fifteen companies replying, only one reported no change in capacity utilization – because a key raw material was not on the free list; a second noted an increase from one to three working shifts; and the other thirteen firms reported that single-shift capacity utilization had increased, on the average, from 47 to 96 per cent. Although the survey cannot be considered statistically significant for the whole of Pakistan, the overall impression has been confirmed in discussions between various members of the mission and businessmen, government officials and others in West Pakistan.

Another AID survey covered sixty-five industrial plants in East and West Pakistan, each importing over 90 per cent of its raw materials. Between July 1963 and March 1965, capacity utilization in these plants increased by almost 30 percentage points (or more than 50 per cent) – from 53 per cent in July–December 1963 to 82 per cent in February–March 1965. The increase was slightly more in the East Wing (31 percentage points) and slightly less in the West (27 percentage points), perhaps because the previous allocation of import licences had favoured importers from West Pakistan. This survey, of course, may not be representative of the industrial sector as a whole, since only a fraction of industrial plants obtain as much as 90 per cent of their raw materials from foreign sources. Also, it has not been possible to ascertain what proportion of total industrial output can be attributed to the sixty-five plants. But in view of the breadth and magnitude of the increase in capacity utilization, it seems reasonable to infer that the commodity aid-financed programme of import liberalization had a significant impact on the rate of industrial activity in Pakistan – an impact presumably proportional to the reliance of each plant on imported raw materials.[18]

The balance of payments

The role of foreign aid in Pakistan's balance of payments was reviewed in Chapter 5. But commodity assistance, as already noted, has several distinct features, and these merit special consideration here. For one thing, it is more immediately connected with the short-term growth of output than is project aid, which is mainly geared to the expansion of productive capacity. For another, commodity aid directly relieves the foreign exchange constraint that is a constant source of concern to the planners of a developing country set on achieving a given rate of growth. Again, insofar as such aid is less rigidly tied to particular

[18] The fact remains that, because of inadequate data, the foregoing analysis of commodity aid impact on capacity utilization is somewhat sketchy. Indeed, it is apparent that the tests formulated in Chapter 9 have not been fully applied.

In this connection, an interesting attempt has been made by Wouter Tims to estimate the multiplier effects of commodity assistance on Pakistan's industrial production. He found that for each rupee of decline in commodity aid there is likely to be a reduction of about Rs. 2.5 in national product. That is to say, a Rs. 400 million decrease in commodity aid inflows would reduce the annual growth rate of GNP by about 1.7 percentage points. See W. Tims, 'Import Projections and Commodity Aid', unpublished mimeo. (Rawalpindi, 1968).

Table 41. *Pakistan's commodity aid and trade, 1955–64 (millions of US dollars)*[a]

Fiscal year	Total imports (I)	Commodity aid (II)	Imports otherwise financed (I minus II)	Total exports
1955	278.3	18.1	260.2	374.6
1956	490.4	51.3	439.1	337.7
1957	430.5	50.1	380.4	298.6
1958	331.4	62.7	268.7	278.3
1959	516.8	85.6	431.2	287.0
1960	669.5	122.0	547.5	377.8
1961	652.9	127.3	525.6	387.0
1962	802.0	119.4	682.6	471.9
1963	930.3	167.2	763.1	629.8
1964	1,128.5	156.7	971.8	508.2

SOURCES: Import and export figures were obtained from Pakistan's Central Statistical Office; commodity aid flows from unpublished materials provided by the US Agency for International Development and the Canadian International Development Agency.

[a] Imports and exports have been converted from Pakistan rupees into US dollars at the official exchange rate of $0.21 per rupee.

supplies – if not suppliers – and shipments are more easily delayed or advanced, greater autonomy and flexibility in development planning rest with the recipient country's authorities.

For these reasons, it seems useful to provide an index of commodity aid importance in the Pakistani balance of payments. First, aid flows from the United States and Canada, the preponderant donors, were aggregated in value terms for the period 1955–64; then aid-financed imports were subtracted from total commodity imports in order to obtain the value of imports financed by other means; these two sets of figures are shown in Table 41, along with total merchandise imports and exports. Finally, the 'effective' trade deficit was computed by deducting non-aid-financed imports from total commodity exports; Table 42 compares this deficit with the 'nominal' deficit on merchandise account.[19]

To be sure, this approach has limited analytical significance. It assumes that both exports and imports would have been unchanged in the absence of commodity assistance – an assumption which may be valid with respect to the former but certainly not the latter. It also assumes that all specific entries in Pakistan's external accounts are independent of each other – which is hardly the case; for instance, while project and commodity aid may be imperfect substitutes for each other, they are substitutable, and it is unlikely that the upward trend in commodity aid flows would have had no effect on project aid commitments.

[19] In definitional terms, the larger the amount of commodity aid, the more the two deficits will diverge. They will coincide in the extreme case where such aid is zero. Other relevant indexes – one based on total current account imports, for example – could, of course, be constructed, and the inclusion of all aid donors would naturally increase the accuracy of any such index.

Table 42. *Pakistan's commodity trade deficits, 1955–64*

Fiscal year	Nominal deficit		Effective deficit[a]	
	US $ (millions)	% of imports	US $ (millions)	% of imports
1955	+96.3	+34.9	+114.4	+41.1
1956	152.7	31.1	101.4	20.6
1957	131.9	30.6	81.8	19.0
1958	53.1	16.0	+9.6	+2.9
1959	229.8	44.4	114.2	22.1
1960	291.7	43.5	169.7	25.3
1961	265.9	46.7	138.6	21.2
1962	330.1	41.1	210.7	26.2
1963	300.5	32.4	133.3	14.3
1964	620.3	54.9	463.6	41.0

SOURCE: All figures were computed from Table 41.
[a] Total commodity exports minus imports otherwise financed.

Nonetheless, the comparison between the nominal and effective trade deficits does have value, for it yields a rough measure of the increments in Pakistan's resources which can be attributed to commodity aid. Thus, Table 42 shows that over the years 1955–64, the flow of commodity aid reduced Pakistan's aggregate trade deficit by about 40 per cent. That is to say, the effective deficit averaged roughly 60 per cent of the nominal deficit during that period; in these terms, Pakistan would have incurred a trade deficit two-thirds larger than the one actually produced with commodity aid. When the deficit is expressed as a percentage of overall imports, the average reduction amounts to some 16 percentage points – from 31 to 15 per cent; before 1958, it was of the order of 10 percentage points a year, and after that it ranged from 14 to 25 points.

But as already implied, Pakistan would probably have been unable to sustain the larger deficit without commodity aid. In that sense, the effective deficit serves as an index of increased import capacity: between 1955 and 1964, Pakistan can be said to have acquired approximately 16 per cent more of total imports than would otherwise have been possible.[20]

The industrial structure

In the context of W. W. Rostow's analysis, John Power has emphasized 'three different but inter-related structural disequilibria that give the take-off period [of a newly-developing country] a specific character:...the agriculture sectoral disequilibrium;...the structural disequilibrium at the factor level between the growth of labour supply and saving;...and the disequilibrium between imports and exports'. The first of these disequilibria involves a significant reallocation of labour from agriculture to industry; this must take place before

[20] Bearing in mind the sharp rise in US commodity assistance to Pakistan in recent years, it would be surprising if this index did not record a substantial increase for the late 1960s.

the productivity of labour in agriculture even begins to approach that of labour in industry. Secondly, given the growth of the labour force, a sharp rise in the rate of saving is required if output per man is to grow. And thirdly, growth 'implies a rapidly rising potential balance-of-trade deficit that must be met eventually by import substitution and promotion of new – presumably manufactured – exports, even if in the short run foreign aid can fill a part of the gap; this need reinforces the urgency of industrialization stemming from the first disequilibrium'.[21]

In short, structural transformation in a developing economy is evidenced initially by changes in the composition of domestic output and the deployment of labour between agriculture and industry, by a marked increase in the rate of saving, and by the substitution of domestically produced consumer and investment goods for imports. Ultimately, moreover, these shifts will bring about a significant expansion in exports.

To the extent that commodity aid speeds up the growth of the industrial sector, it will contribute towards a more rapid change in the composition of output. In this respect, perhaps the strongest effects are felt through a more intensive use of existing plant capacity in key industries; and it has already been seen that for Pakistan this impact has been positive. By increasing aggregate domestic output, commodity assistance can also substantially raise the economic surplus available for investment. Then, too, commodity aid – as part of an overall import policy – can narrow the trade gap in such a way as to accelerate the process of import substitution and export growth.

The import pattern

The previous chapter cited the pattern of imports as a primary index for assessing the structural impact of commodity aid. Table 43 shows that changes in this pattern have been quite pronounced in the case of Pakistan. In 1951, more than 63 per cent of the country's imports were consumer goods; in 1966 the proportion was 23 per cent. The decline was rather irregular: consumption imports as a percentage of total imports actually increased from 1954 to 1957, remained fairly stable until 1960 and increased again from 1962 to 1963. But the ratio fell sharply after 1963, and from 1961 on, capital goods and industrial raw materials accounted for 60 to 77 per cent of total annual imports.[22]

Clearly, a process of substitution was at work. But it was not a simple one. In part, the changing import pattern reflected an expansion in Pakistani consumer goods production supplying domestic needs. However, it was also a matter of aid-supported government priorities in import policy; and the import pattern mirrored a very considerable increase in investment and output in the intermediate and capital goods industries.

Two further observations are worth making in this connection. First, capital

[21] J. H. Power, 'Industrialization in Pakistan: A Case of Frustrated Take-Off?', *Pakistan Development Review*, Summer 1963, pp. 193–4.
[22] The record 77 per cent ratio of 1966 was doubtless linked to the special circumstances arising from the Indo-Pakistan War.

Table 43. *The structure of commodity imports into Pakistan 1951–66*

Fiscal year	% of total imports		
	Consumer goods	Industrial raw materials	Capital goods
1951	63.22	27.80	8.98
1952	59.59	30.43	9.98
1953	52.61	28.39	19.00
1954	45.12	24.62	30.26
1955	48.84	24.49	26.67
1956	53.02	28.38	18.60
1957	62.90	21.92	15.18
1958	57.25	26.12	16.63
1959	57.16	22.74	20.10
1960	57.75	21.86	20.39
1961	39.53	39.85	20.62
1962	32.82	35.51	31.67
1963	39.60	33.46	26.94
1964	36.42	32.95	30.63
1965	30.33	31.73	37.94
1966	22.94	36.61	40.45

SOURCE: Pakistan Central Statistical Office.

goods imports increased proportionally more than raw material imports over the years 1951–66; although since 1963, with increasing commodity aid inflows, the latter have grown somewhat more rapidly than before. Secondly, the import liberalization measures adopted since 1963 have not caused any increase in the proportion of consumer goods imported; though they have somewhat slowed down the rate of decline, at least as compared with the period 1960–2.

The composition of domestic output

There is evidence, too, of major related changes in the composition of Pakistan's output. Taufiq Khan and Asbjorn Bergan have observed 'a clear structural change in favour of non-agricultural sectors. Though structural changes have taken place also within the agricultural sectors, these are more pronounced in the case of non-agricultural sectors such as large-scale manufacturing.'[23]

Table 44 shows that between 1949/50 and 1963/4 agriculture's share of gross value added fell from approximately 60 to 50 per cent; and that the expansion of non-agricultural output was due mainly to large-scale manufacturing and the construction industry. In fact, the non-agricultural sector grew at a rate twice as high as that of agriculture; hence its relative gain year by year. And there is some indication that not only growth rates but also growth patterns changed around 1959/60.

[23] T. M. Khan and A. Bergan, 'Measurement of Structural Change in the Pakistan Economy: A Review of the National Income Estimates, 1949/50 to 1963/64', *Pakistan Development Review*, Summer 1966, p. 176.

Table 44. *Sectoral gross value added as a percentage of GNP in Pakistan, 1949–64*

Sector	1949/50	1954/5	1959/60	1963/4
Agriculture	59.9	56.1	53.3	49.9
Non-agriculture	40.1	43.9	46.7	50.1
Manufacturing	5.8	8.0	9.3	10.5
(*a*) Large-scale	1.4	3.6	5.0	6.5
(*b*) Small-scale	4.4	4.4	4.3	4.0
Construction	0.9	1.5	2.1	3.9
Transportation, storage and communication	5.1	5.7	5.9	6.0
Wholesale and retail trade	11.7	11.7	11.7	12.5

SOURCE: Computed from T. M. Khan and A. Bergan, 'Measurement of Structural Change in the Pakistan Economy: A Review of the National Income Estimates, 1949/50 to 1963/64', *Pakistan Development Review*, Summer 1966, pp. 203–4.

Frustrated take-off?

Unquestionably, then, structural transformation has been taking place in Pakistan since 1950. Doubts have been raised, however, as to the contribution of these changes to economic growth. Power has noted that the satisfactory pace of industrialization in Pakistan was accompanied by some import substitution but also by stagnant exports, saving and per capita income.[24] He was particularly impressed by the relative constancy of the rate of saving over the period; and he has ventured the view that 'the rise in the relative share of non-agricultural value added has depended too much on rising productivity in nonagriculture and too little on shifting labour from lower to higher productivity employment' (that is, from agriculture to industry).[25]

Power's thesis is that Pakistan's 'frustrated take-off' can be explained by the character of its industrialization process, namely, the emphasis on import substitution in the consumption goods sector. Import controls allegedly encouraged investment there rather than in intermediate and investment goods industries. This meant 'scattering thinly scarce capital, foreign exchange and technical and organizational talent...[to produce] a little bit of a lot of things'.[26] As a result, output levels in manufacturing have been bloated by inefficiencies and diseconomies of scale. Power also claims that with the emphasis on consumer import substitution, the early momentum of industrial development may peter out once the take-over of existing markets is completed. This could be avoided if productivity – and therefore real income – gains were to spur the propensity to invest, if the substitution process were to spill into the other sectors, or if foreign demand made it possible to increase the scale of production in consumer goods industries. Finally, Power argues that import substitution in consumer goods carried with it an automatic 'decontrol of consumption',[27] which has tended to drag down the saving rate.

[24] Power, 'Industrialization in Pakistan'.   [25] *Ibid.* p. 198.
[26] *Ibid.* p. 201.   [27] *Ibid.* p. 203.

This line of reasoning has been challenged by Stephen Lewis and Ronald Soligo. For them, it is 'difficult to accept the widely held hypothesis about the distorted nature of industrial growth in Pakistan up to now'.[28] Their position rests on an analysis of sectoral growth rates derived from tax returns and the Census of Manufacturing Industries. These estimates show: that there is an extremely wide range of growth rates for different industries; that there has been a general deceleration in the *rate* of growth of most industries; that consumer goods industries have been growing at relatively slower rates than either intermediate or investment goods industries.[29]

Table 45. *Percentage increases in Pakistan's gross value of output, 1954–64*

Sector	Fiscal years 1955–60	Fiscal years 1960–4
Consumption goods	111	62
Intermediate goods	419	62
Investment goods	208	125

SOURCE: S. R. Lewis, Jr. and R. Soligo, 'Growth and Structural Change in Pakistan's Manufacturing Industry, 1954–64', *Pakistan Development Review*, Spring 1965, p. 101.

It has been found, also, that there are substantial growth differences 'before and after 1959/60, due to fundamental changes in that year in economic policy, the flow of foreign aid, the level of investment and other magnitudes of importance... Beginning in 1959/60, development expenditures were accelerated, and there was a rapid increase in the inflow of foreign capital with a corresponding "liberalization" of imports.'[30] As shown in Table 45, 'industries producing primarily intermediate and capital goods grew at a much more rapid *rate* relative to the "protected" consumer goods industries in the first period [1954–60] than in the second period [1960–4]'.[31] According to Lewis and Soligo, it is not surprising that the supposedly unprotected sectors should have grown so rapidly before 1959/60 since the degree of effective protection of the consumer goods industries was 'nullified by the enormous excess demand for imports and disequilibrium in the foreign exchange markets'.[32] Likewise, they are not surprised by the deceleration of growth rates in the intermediate and

---

[28] S. R. Lewis, Jr. and R. Soligo, 'Growth and Structural Change in Pakistan's Manufacturing Industry, 1954–64', *Pakistan Development Review*, Spring 1965, p. 111. See also S. R. Lewis, Jr., *Economic Policy and Industrial Growth in Pakistan* (London, 1969).

[29] With respect to the last point, Gustav Papanek contends that the Lewis–Soligo growth rates may understate actual growth in the consumption goods industries and overstate it in the intermediate and investment goods sectors; their figures are based on output series valued at market prices and there is some evidence that consumer goods prices have risen much more slowly than those of intermediate and capital goods. G. F. Papanek, 'Growth and Structural Change in Pakistan's Manufacturing Industry: A Comment', *Pakistan Development Review*, Winter 1965, p. 659.

[30] Lewis and Soligo, 'Growth and Structural Change', pp. 95, 99.

[31] *Ibid.* p. 102.

[32] *Ibid.* p. 111.

capital goods industries after 1959/60; indeed, it was noteworthy that those sectors grew as fast as aggregate output.

Lewis and Soligo do not infer that the import liberalization made possible by increased commodity aid inflows slowed down the structural transformation of Pakistan's economy. What they do find is that a different mix of forces was generating growth after 1960: domestic demand was dominant in the consumer and investment goods industries, while import substitution and export growth were significant only in the intermediate goods sector. They also point out that the 'intermediate and investment goods industries...present the greatest scope for further import substitution since imports are a larger proportion of the total supply of these goods'.[33] And they stress that Pakistan's tariff structure has distorted its production by favouring consumer goods over the intermediate and investment goods industries.[34]

Impact on economic policy in Pakistan

It is appropriate, now, to consider the impact of commodity aid on the policies of the Pakistan government – in the broadest sense, the modulation of aid by donor countries so as to induce, bribe or threaten the recipient country into changing its foreign policy or its development strategy.[35]

At the outset, it should be noted that the leverage exerted through commodity aid programmes is only one element of aid diplomacy – albeit a substantial, and perhaps preponderant, one for Pakistan. Development grants and loans have not proved to be pure income transfers, nor have they tended over the years towards the allocative neutrality considered desirable in terms of economic welfare. The average foreign aid grant or loan is conditional; this may be deplored, but it would be naive to ignore it.

However, the concern here is not with the explicit terms of foreign assistance to Pakistan, except insofar as is necessary to distinguish between 'project' and 'programme' (or commodity) aid. Nor will there be any treatment of the impact of aid on the foreign policy of Pakistan. International resource transfers are viewed basically as an instrument of economic development rather than of foreign policy. The prime focus is on the use of commodity aid as a political lever in the development process.

[33] *Ibid.*

[34] Lewis adds that 'aid in the form of increased commodity imports provided greater flows of imports to existing manufacturing industries, and enabled them to utilize installed capacity at a much higher rate than had been possible in the 1950s. The greater availability of foreign exchange also aided in releasing more resources for imports of capital goods, which flowed increasingly into industries producing intermediate and investment goods.' Lewis, *Economic Policy*, p. 160.

[35] See White, *Pledged to Development*, for an interesting discussion of this process in relation to several developing countries including Pakistan. And see A. Carlin, 'Project Versus Programme Aid: From the Donor's Viewpoint', *Economic Journal*, March 1967; also J. M. Nelson, *Aid, Influence, and Foreign Policy* (New York, 1968).

Anatomy of the 'lever' function

Commodity assistance would seem to be a far more flexible and comprehensive instrument of political leverage than project aid. By definition, project loans or grants are 'lumpy', all-or-nothing, once-and-for-all transfers of resources. A project is either acceptable or not; and for purposes of acceptability, its technical or financial feasibility tends to overshadow its place in the overall development strategy. Commodity aid, by contrast, is a flow that can be increased or reduced, not merely interrupted. Decisions affecting the magnitude of the flow can be reversed quickly, according to the degree of compliance with the donor's 'advice'. The modulation of such aid is, therefore, less likely to lead to a deadlock between donor and donee. In short, commodity aid provides a powerful and continuing instrument of leverage on the development process.

Furthermore, the impact of commodity aid is typically spread broadly through the economy of the recipient country, rather than being confined to a particular sector. Consequently, it lends itself much more to a general review of performance or to a reconsideration of broad policies. For example, it is much more difficult to relate a hydro-electric dam than a broad range of industrial materials to import policies or to the degree of reliance on private entrepreneurship in the course of industrialization.

By the same token, whereas project assistance involves only particular choices or, at best, the decision-making process in a given sector, commodity aid can modify the parameters of private and social entrepreneurship throughout the developing country. That is to say, it does not merely reduce the technical and administrative gaps in a given sector; it frees the entrepreneur – be it the individual business man or the state – from economy-wide constraints on growth. Broad policy changes, such as a shift from administrative to fiscal and monetary controls, are therefore more likely to be induced through aid flows which are not tied to particular projects, supplies or suppliers.

In the last analysis, though, the efficiency of commodity aid as a means of influencing economic policy depends on three basic requirements. First, the flow of commodity aid must be large enough so that a substantial reduction will not endanger the political or economic stability of the recipient country, and yet not so predominant that the act of withholding funds or prolonging negotiations could be interpreted as a threat to the entire aid programme.[36] This condition was amply met in the case of Pakistan. Perhaps for the first time in the history of foreign aid, external financing adequate to the needs of a comprehensive development plan was provided through the Pakistan Consortium – about \$2.4 billion over the second plan period, of which roughly a third was non-project aid. At one time, in fact, the objectives of the Plan were over-pledged in the sense that credits made available surpassed Pakistan's absorptive capacity.

[36] Very large commitments of commodity aid can build up donee expectations of a continuous inflow which may then become difficult to change. See US AID, *Principles of Foreign Economic Assistance* (Washington, D.C., 1965), p. 35.

Clearly, a government cannot, in such circumstances, avoid giving close scrutiny to its own performance.[37]

Secondly, the modulation of commodity aid, to be effective, must not impair the working relationship between donor and donee. This requires that the political leverage exerted by the donor be part of a dialogue, a process of mutual interaction; for the constraints to which a recipient country responds by inefficient policies are usually quite real and often created – wittingly or unwittingly – by the donor countries themselves. Again, this condition seems to have been satisfied by Pakistan during much of the 1960s. The attitude of President Ayub's government towards the inquiries and promptings of Western donors was not characterized by the mistrust felt by many developing countries. This may have been due in part to closer contacts between Pakistani and Western officials – through the very large US AID Mission, for example, and the influential Harvard Advisory Group. Then, too, the government of Pakistan had unusually wide scope to argue its case and explain its economic position.

Thirdly, the government of a developing country will be more tolerant of pressures exerted through commodity aid flows if it is in general sympathy with the economic philosophy of the donor country. Whenever this is the case, violent clashes of opinion are likely to be avoided; charges of the violation of sovereignty and of neo-colonialism will be levelled less frequently; and negotiations will focus on administrative or political feasibility and on the probable impact of measures advocated by the donor. Pakistan appears to have adopted a kind of ideological neutrality towards such contentious issues as private entrepreneurship, the use of market mechanisms and the relative priorities of agricultural and industrial development. Unlike India, it did not have a large, well-developed intellectual elite which could articulate a national ideology of development; this has proven to be an advantage with respect to aid diplomacy.

Channels of impact

But if circumstances were favourable to the use of commodity aid as a device for influencing economic policies in Pakistan, it is rather difficult to quote actual instances of pressure and response. One is dealing with the most sensitive aspect of a most sensitive phenomenon – power relations. Rigorous proof would have required access to correspondence and conversations among the officials involved; needless to say, such access was not provided. Consequently, use has been made of secondary sources, and inferences have been drawn from discussions with senior officials of relevant agencies in Pakistan and the United States.

There is at least one clear case of direct political pressure through aid flows: the drastic US reduction of aid commitments to Pakistan (and India) in 1966, to express American disapproval of resource diversion to the military sector in the aftermath of the Indo-Pakistan War. In the fiscal year 1965, AID's

---

[37] General surveillance along these lines is, of course, not inconsistent with laxity in relation to specific uses of aid. Indeed, such instances were not unknown during the Second Plan.

commodity assistance to Pakistan stood at $181 million and had been more or less steadily increasing since 1960; in 1966 it dropped to $115 million.[38]

However, the main locus of pressure has been the Pakistan Consortium. And the chief sources of pressure within the Consortium have, not unexpectedly, been the US government and the World Bank.

It was IBRD which induced the government of Pakistan to undertake a skilful revision of its Second Five-Year Plan – a revision, more of presentation than substance, that ultimately secured the necessary pledges from donor countries. In particular, by redefining maintenance support and non-development imports as commodity aid, Pakistan reassured aid-givers who feared 'landing themselves with an unlimited commitment to fill an ever-widening foreign exchange "gap"'.[39]

The Consortium was gradually led to scrutinize the implementation of Pakistan's plan following these very considerable pledges – in fact, the over-pledging of objectives which took place in 1962. There is little doubt that serious difficulties with Pakistan would have arisen if the Consortium had discussed implementation without first settling the question of the volume of aid. 'The shift of emphasis – from promises of aid to a critical examination of the ways in which aid was to be used – took place because the Consortium itself had created the conditions which made this the natural next move, and one that was acceptable to the recipient.'[40]

This raises an interesting point of strategy. Papanek argues that 'the sensible policies and programs adopted by Pakistan were the major reasons for the increase in resources available. In large part, causality runs from improved policies and performance to increased aid, not vice versa.'[41] The proceedings of the Pakistan Consortium give grounds for questioning this view. What seems more likely is that 'the attitude of the Government of Pakistan was both cause and effect;... that a one-way flow of communication simply was not the pattern of the liberalization programme; [and that] the manipulation of the aid relationship was successful precisely because it was never clear who was doing the manipulating'. In other words, there appears to have been 'simultaneous communication at several levels and in several directions. The participants responded to a situation. Because their communications were in good order, their responses were in accord with each other, and interacted with each other.'[42]

A further point is worth making in this connection. Jacoby notes that the US AID Mission in Taiwan was often used by the local authorities as a 'whipping

---

[38] Essentially, what occurred was a suspension of new commitments for a five-month period; the aid pipeline continued to provide standard monthly disbursements, and the suspension was not used as a bargaining lever for any specific goal. But given the general uncertainty then prevailing, it is difficult to overstress the symbolic importance of the US action.

[39] White, *Pledged to Development*, p. 75. The World Bank Group has itself done relatively little financing through programme loans. Only IDA has extended such credits to Pakistan in recent years. And IBRD has apparently interpreted its Articles of Agreement as limiting them to exceptional cases.   [40] *Ibid.* p. 70.

[41] G. F. Papanek, *Pakistan's Development: Social Goals and Private Incentives* (Cambridge, Mass., 1967), pp. 222–3.

[42] White, *Pledged to Development*, pp. 70, 83.

boy' to overcome the opposition to policy changes which they deemed desirable.[43] To some extent, the same phenomenon can be observed in Pakistan: the Planning Commission 'often had reason to regard [the aid-givers] as allies in its approaches to domestic government departments'.[44] Also, in 1963 the Minister of Finance, personally convinced of the need to liberalize import controls, found a convenient opportunity to do so in the context of the Consortium shift from pledging to appraisal. The experience with import controls merits special attention.

The case of import liberalization

In the decade preceding 1964, virtually all imports to Pakistan were subject to licensing. Once the Foreign Exchange Committee (FEC) had allocated the available resources between the public and private sectors, import licences were processed through three different channels.

In the public sector, the requirements of the various agencies, after approval by FEC, were handled by the Department of Investment Promotion and Supplies in the Ministry of Industries. Import licensing of capital goods requirements in the private sector was ancillary to the broad industrial policy of the country, as reflected in the Industrial Investment Schedule. The Chief Controller of Imports and Exports (CCIE) automatically issued licences for investment projects previously authorized by the Central Investment Promotion and Coordination Committee (CIPCC) under the chairmanship of the Minister of Industries, by one of the provincial Directorates of Industries, or by one of the industrial development banks (PICIC and IDBP).

These two licensing systems have remained outside the liberalization programme.

In fact, in recent years there has been an attempt to rationalize and extend direct controls over capital goods imports, since this area of investment allocation is considered central to the whole planning process. It is in the third import licensing system, controlling essentially consumer goods, raw materials, and spare parts, that a significant degree of import liberalization has occurred.[45]

Under the authority of the CCIE, the third system handled about 70 per cent of private imports and approximately half of total imports. Established following the 1952 foreign exchange crisis, it introduced detailed physical control of imports – with the government determining the total value of licences to be issued and their manner of allocation. While this simplified the management of foreign exchange resources, it also imposed serious distortions on the Pakistan economy. This was to be expected: 'When such controls persist for a long time, they do not keep pace with basic changes in the economy, black markets develop, corruption and bribery increase, and the goals of the control system are subverted.'[46]

[43] N. H. Jacoby, *United States Aid to Taiwan: A Study of Foreign Aid, Self-Help, and Development* (New York, 1966), p. 131.   [44] White, *Pledged to Development*, p. 59.
[45] P. S. Thomas, 'Import Licensing and Import Liberalization in Pakistan', *Pakistan Development Review*, Winter 1966, pp. 503–4. Unless otherwise noted, the import liberalization figures cited below are derived from this source.   [46] *Ibid.* pp. 504–5.

According to Philip Thomas, the third system of import licensing had four main economic weaknesses: through discriminatory protection, it led to over-emphasis on domestic consumer goods industries to the detriment of the export and producer goods industries;[47] it aggravated the disparities in growth and income between East and West Pakistan, since import licences were granted to the main importers in the base period January 1950–June 1952, when most of them happened to be operating in West Pakistan; in the face of an overvalued exchange rate, arbitrary licensing intensified domestic inefficiency because foreign prices confronting importers were lower than the true opportunity cost of imports; new monopoly positions were created, and this brought mis-allocation of resources as well as strong resentment among excluded potential importers.

Impressed by the growing criticism, the government of Pakistan began to liberalize its import policy in 1959. The Export Bonus Scheme introduced in that year reduced and streamlined the administrative controls over imports, thereby permitting actual market demand to be more clearly reflected in the granting of licences. Early in 1960, the government also introduced a new Open General Licence Scheme (OGL), which admitted newcomers, particularly industrial users, to the import trade and provided for automatic granting of repeat licences upon proof of the exhaustion of initial licences. By 1963, about half the imports licensed by CCIE were being processed under the Export Bonus and OGL schemes.

The most important step towards import liberalization was taken in January 1964 when, under Consortium pressure from the World Bank and the US government, Pakistan introduced a so-called 'free list', allowing four iron and steel items to be imported from the United States without licences and with a minimum of other restrictions. The free list was expanded to fifty-four items in July–December 1964, and to fifty-eight in July 1965. While the bulk of the free list imports continued to be financed by foreign aid, Pakistan committed its own foreign exchange resources to twenty-two of the items, including the important spare parts. In addition, a variety of fiscal and monetary devices were introduced to replace, in some degree, the direct licensing controls that were being removed: a 'regulatory duty', ranging from 5 to 20 per cent ad valorem, was imposed on all free list imports; a 'defence surcharge' of 25 per cent of the existing tax rates was levied on both import duties and sales taxes; importers were required to make a 25 per cent deposit when opening a letter of credit in payment for goods purchased; they were not permitted to borrow more than 60 per cent of import value.

The 1959–65 path towards import liberalization was neither straight nor simple. To some extent, new direct controls were superimposed on old ones, and even the free list was hedged in by administrative restrictions. But it is clear that Pakistan had 'moved from an import policy relying almost completely on administrative controls to a policy mix which [included] substantial elements

[47] As already noted, there are good statistical grounds for disputing this view (see Lewis and Soligo, 'Growth and Structural Change').

of indirect controls working through the market...[and] that the trend toward liberalization...had favourable effects on prices and mark-ups, and on production and utilization of capacity'.[48] Nor can there be much doubt that Consortium leverage through commodity aid provided a significant inducement to this liberalizing trend.

There is also good reason to believe that the 1966 resumption of commodity aid flows suspended in 1965 played a strong leverage role in Pakistan's return to the liberalization approach which had lapsed with the Indo-Pakistan War. To be sure, the import system of 1966/7 was more restrictive than the 1964/5 system in several ways: the number of banned items was increased, for example; and measures were introduced to limit the imports of larger firms, as well as to control the pace at which foreign exchange was utilized. But the new scheme was unquestionably more liberal than that which had prevailed in 1965/6. The free list was expanded from thirty-one to sixty-six items, and OGL from nine to eleven.[49] The general surcharge on imports was incorporated into a simplified basic tariff structure. There was an increased reliance on fiscal and monetary instruments to curb excess demand. In consequence, importers were 'faced with prices, taxes, and credit costs which, when taken together, [made] the full cost of imports more closely approximate the true social cost of foreign exchange'.[50]

The return to liberalization was further underscored by the import policy announced in January 1968. Indeed, this may well have been the most important liberalizing move since early 1964. In July 1967 a limited 'cash-cum-bonus' list had been introduced, under which an importer had to purchase bonus vouchers for half of his entitlement in order to get cash licences for the remaining half; this had meant a substantial surcharge on the affected imports. The new list was extended to seventy-one items in 1968, with a resultant near-doubling of many import prices. In addition, a 'price equalization' surcharge was imposed on most free list items financed by aid or barter, so as to bring their effective import prices into line with those obtainable under the cash-cum-bonus system. 'With these price adjustments, it became possible to free over 90 per cent of all raw material imports from administrative restrictions in January 1968.'[51] The Pakistan government had come to accept the proposition that import liberalization was not likely to be viable without significant price increases to siphon off much of the heavy demand on inadequate domestic resources. And that acceptance was doubtless hastened by US leverage exerted in the negotiations for an expanded flow of commodity aid in 1968.[52]

[48] Thomas, 'Import Licensing', p. 525.
[49] Pakistan Planning Commission, *The Mid-Plan Review of the Third Five-Year Plan (1965–70)* (Rawalpindi, 1968), pp. 27–8.
[50] P. S. Thomas, 'The New Import Policy, 1966–67', unpublished mimeo. (US AID, n.p., n.d.), p. 7.
[51] Pakistan Planning Commission, *Annual Plan, 1968–69* (Rawalpindi, 1968), p. 27.
[52] Pakistan's liberalizing trend stalled again in 1968/9, when serious shortfalls in foreign exchange occurred, including a sharp decline in commodity assistance.

11. Foreign aid administration in Pakistan

Reference has been made, in various parts of this study, to certain administrative aspects of foreign economic assistance to Pakistan. The quality of such administration is bound to exert an important influence on the effectiveness of aid; and this is perhaps especially so at the receiving end, where crucial on-the-spot decisions are taken with respect to both the formulation and execution of aid programmes. At this point, therefore, it will be useful to examine Pakistan's system of aid administration in the industrial sphere.[1]

Project aid

Since industrial development programmes are an integral part of the planning process in Pakistan, it seems logical to begin with the way that industrial schemes are launched and approved for inclusion as projects in the overall development effort.[2] There is, in fact, a common planning procedure for the schemes involving foreign aid as well as for those which do not.

Public sector schemes in industry are sponsored by the West Pakistan Industrial Development Corporation (WPIDC), the East Pakistan Industrial Development Corporation (EPIDC), the West Pakistan Small Industries Corporation (WPSIC), the East Pakistan Small Industries Corporation (EPSIC), and the East Pakistan Forest Industries Development Corporation (EPFIDC). In the private sector, schemes are not submitted to the planning authorities, but indirect control is exercised through the licensing system and through the allocation of foreign exchange and other scarce resources; permission to undertake projects is granted only where they fall within the Industrial Investment Schedule, which lists the authorized industries and the investment ceilings in East and West Pakistan.

The initial proposal for any public sector scheme must be submitted on the form 'Planning Commission 1', better known as 'PC 1'. It seeks complete information on the project and consists of several parts. Part A covers summary data and is accordingly called the 'Project Digest'. It includes information on location, total cost, and expected date of commencement and completion; also information on the sponsoring agency with its controlling ministry, and the authorities responsible for consultation, preparatory surveys, feasibility reports

---

[1] Much of the discussion which follows is based on field interviews conducted with senior officials of the central and provincial governments. The literature contains little analysis of foreign aid administration in Pakistan. See, in this connection, A. Waterston, *Planning in Pakistan: Organization and Implementation* (Baltimore, 1963); and Pakistan Planning Commission, *The Mid-Plan Review of the Third Five-Year Plan (1965–70)* (Rawalpindi, 1968).

[2] 'Scheme', as used here, is the term applied by Pakistan to a proposal submitted for approval. Once approval is accorded by the appropriate authorities, the scheme becomes a 'project'. Only projects qualify for foreign assistance.

and plant construction and operation. Part B concerns the nature, purpose, benefits and detailed costs of the project; part C the basis of the cost estimates; part D the financing of the project; part E its manpower, material and other requirements. Part F seeks information on the phasing of the project, the time required for reaching full capacity operation, and a list of related projects which must be completed in time so as not to delay the schedule of work or affect the operation of the project in question.

The total cost of the project determines the level at which it will be scrutinized and approved. Each development scheme costing up to one million rupees is reviewed by a Departmental Working Party of the sponsoring authority. This, in effect, means that there is no external constraint or check if the cost of the scheme does not exceed one million rupees. All schemes above that amount but below Rs. 50 million are considered by a Provincial Development Working Party, and schemes exceeding Rs. 50 million by a Central Development Working Party. The Provincial Development Working Parties are composed of three officials – one each from the Planning and Development Department, the Finance Department and the department or agency sponsoring the project under consideration. The Central Development Working Party is presided over by the secretary of the Planning Commission and contains one representative each from the Ministry of Finance and the ministry or agency sponsoring the project. For projects requiring foreign aid, a representative of the Economic Affairs Division of the President's Secretariat is also included.

The public sector programmes of the five-year plans have been implemented through the Annual Development Programme (ADP).[3] ADP comprises tables on the allocation of financial resources along the following lines: agriculture, water and power, industry, fuels and minerals, transport and communications, physical planning and housing, education and training, health, social welfare, manpower and employment, and the works programme. There is a breakdown of new and ongoing projects, as well as figures on total foreign exchange requirements, project aid available and the balance to be met by Pakistan's own foreign exchange resources. ADP also gives the total estimated cost of each project, the total expenditure to be incurred on it in the relevant plan period, and, if the project has continued from the previous plan, expenditure

[3] In 1968, the Annual Development Programme was replaced by the Annual Development Plan, covering the private sector as well as the public. The Annual Plan 'is intended to provide the mechanism for . . . continuous review . . . on a more systematic basis and represents a new stage in the evolution of the planning process in Pakistan'. Pakistan Planning Commission, *Annual Plan, 1968–69* (Rawalpindi, 1968), p. 1. See also M. Haq, 'Annual Planning in Pakistan', *Journal of Development Planning*, no. 2 (United Nations, N.Y.), 1970; this article appeared after the time of writing. There have, of course, been a number of other organizational changes over the past few years, particularly those arising from the political disturbances of 1968–69. The conversion of West Pakistan into four provinces and the reorganization of the Economic Affairs Division are worth noting in this context. But it is still too early to say whether such changes have materially affected the country's system of foreign aid administration. Furthermore, given the national election results of December 1970, the subsequent political unrest and the serious problems of constitutional revision, it seems pointless to speculate about the shape of administrative things to come.

incurred in the earlier plan. The abstract of the 'industries' programme provides a breakdown according to the major sponsoring agencies, and in terms of particular industries like sugar, chemicals, basic metals, shipbuilding, and paper and hard-board.

This system – whereby the Planning Commission is responsible for preparing annual estimates which form the basis for budgetary allocations – has been very important, because it gives the commission the power and authority to allocate the actual resources known to be available, and not, as in many countries, the task of deciding what resources would in theory be required to reach some arbitrary target. The system also prevents the duplication that would be involved in projects being assessed twice, once by the Planning Commission and then by the Ministry of Finance for inclusion in the annual budget. The net result has been a greater recognition of the Planning Commission's technical competence and an increasingly important role for the commission in the formulation of economic policy.[4]

The machinery of economic policy

The Governors' Conference has been the highest policy-making body in the country. Its chairman is the President of Pakistan, and the provincial governors are the other members. Meetings take place every month or two, often in conjunction with meetings of the National Economic Council, and are attended by ministers and other officials of the central and provincial governments as required. On the basis of papers circulated in advance, the Governors' Conference makes key administrative and policy decisions; discussions frequently include questions affecting implementation of the plan.

The Economic Co-ordination Committee of the Cabinet (ECCC) performs a variety of top-level tasks. These include determination of the future growth pattern of Pakistan's major industries, consideration of urgent economic problems, and co-ordination of economic policies initiated by the various branches of government. ECCC is headed by the central finance minister; its other members are the central ministers of commerce and industries, and the deputy chairman of the Planning Commission.

The NEC is responsible for reviewing the country's economic position, formulating broad development plans, and submitting annual reports to the National Assembly on Pakistan's economic progress.[5] The NEC is also the country's supreme economic advisory body. Among its key members have been: the President of Pakistan as chairman; the governors of East and West

[4] For an illuminating discussion of this role, see M. Haq, *Planning Machinery in Pakistan* (Karachi, 1965). In large part, the growing and recent emphasis on annual planning has been a consequence of rising Pakistani uncertainty as to the availability of foreign aid on the scale required.

[5] The National Assembly has played a minor role in the development of foreign aid policy. This is in sharp contrast with the situation in the aid-giving countries, where (as in the United States) the legislature often spends considerable time on the aid programme proposed by the government.

Pakistan; the central ministers of commerce, finance and industries; the deputy chairman of the Planning Commission; the provincial ministers of finance; the chairmen of WPIDC and EPIDC; and the chairmen of the Water and Power Development Authority in East and West Pakistan. The deputy chairman of the Planning Commission acts as the secretary of NEC, and memoranda for the NEC's consideration are prepared by, or in consultation with, the commission.

NEC operates through an Executive Committee (ECNEC) which approves development projects. The members of ECNEC are the central minister of finance (chairman), the provincial governors or ministers nominated by them, the deputy chairman of the Planning Commission, and the provincial finance ministers. The committee is required to meet at least once every three months, successively in Lahore and Dacca. It may approve or reject a scheme; alternatively, it may defer the scheme and call for further information, or it may accord conditional permission.[6]

The government of Pakistan submits a memorandum to the World Bank Consortium which contains information on the overall and sectoral performance of the economy. It also estimates aid requirements on the basis of total foreign exchange earnings, non-developmental imports and the import content of the development programme.

One important side effect of the major role played by foreign aid in the economic development of Pakistan has been the creation of Planning Commission expertise in formulating, negotiating and implementing aid programmes. The current preference of donor countries and international lending agencies for comprehensive development plans as a basis for their aid or lending operations has also helped to strengthen the Planning Commissions' position. It has, indeed, by now become the most effective government agency in Pakistan. The government entrusts the commission with the task of preparing its presentations for the Consortium and other aid negotiations. Naturally, this has greatly enhanced the Planning Commission's standing with central and provincial operating agencies which need foreign assistance for their projects and pro-grammes.

The Tarbela experience

Recent Pakistani success in persuading Western aid-givers to finance the huge Tarbela Dam bears testimony to the shrewdness of the country's negotiators. The Indus Basin Settlement Plan – culminating in the Indus Waters Treaty of 1960 between India and Pakistan – provided for two dams with supporting services, Mangla on the Jhelum River and Tarbela on the Indus, at an estimated total cost of $1.9 billion. With construction of the Mangla Dam at the half-way point, Pakistan started exerting pressure on the World Bank and the major national contributors to the Indus Basin Fund to commit resources to a

---

[6] There are also Heavy Industry Boards in the Centre and both wings. Relevant schemes are often referred to ECNEC through those boards.

finalized plan for the Tarbela Dam.[7] By then, it had become obvious to Pakistan that unspent resources would be available from Mangla; and that if an agreement could be obtained to divert those resources to Tarbela, it would give Pakistan a favourable position for obtaining the rest of the import require-ments of Tarbela. It also seemed to make sense to begin another big project before the direct income and employment effects of Mangla tapered off. The difficulty, however, lay in the fact that the Indus donor countries, as well as the World Bank, had reservations on both issues because they were sceptical as to the feasibility and soundness of Tarbela. It was planned to be nearly 500 feet high with a storage capacity of 9.5 million acre-feet of water. It would generate 2,000 megawatts of electricity and would bring important benefits to the districts of Hazara, Mardan and Campbellpore. But the fate of the project appeared to be sealed when, towards the end of 1966, the World Bank made it known that, as administrator of the Indus Basin Fund, it was intending to honour the contractural agreement that any surplus money from Mangla could not be transferred to any other project, including Tarbela.

In the context of this unhappy story – with all the elements of another Aswan in the making – the fact of ultimate success seems a remarkable achieve-ment for Pakistani aid diplomacy. The breakthrough undoubtedly came with the voluminous report prepared by Dr Peiter Lieftinck, a Dutch Director of IBRD, which argued forcefully that Tarbela was not only feasible and viable but also entailed more efficient utilization of resources than any other alternative (such as raising the Mangla Dam or sinking more tube-wells).[8]

Pakistan contended, quite rightly, that, given Tarbela's foreign exchange costs of $489 million, the transfer of the unspent $310 million from Mangla would leave a gap of only $179 million which could be easily secured. Accordingly, the government placed a Tarbela contract, the largest of its kind, under offer for competitive bidding. The scramble for a share in this venture meant intense competitive activity, and the aid started flowing. The West Germans offered $100 million conditional on the contract going to a German bidder, with $50 million guaranteed even if Germany failed to get the contract. France offered $30–40 million and Italy $25 million to get a contract for the Franco-Italian Consortium. Canada offered $30 million and Britain $40 million. The United States hesitated until the final hour. At this stage, Pakistan emphasized that the Americans, by their non-participation, were jeopardizing a project of $850 million. When even this had no effect, Pakistan suggested that four countries involved in the Tarbela bidding – Italy, France, the United States and Britain – should match Germany's $100 million conditional offer; or that every bidding country should undertake to provide long-term credit amounting to at least 20 per cent of the orders placed in that country. Both alternatives

[7] The Mangla Dam was completed and began operations in November 1967.
[8] See the published study based on this 1967 report: P. Lieftinck et al., *Water and Power Resources of West Pakistan: A Study in Sector Planning*, 3 vols. (Baltimore, 1968). And see A. A. Michel, *The Indus Rivers: A Study of the Effects of Partition* (New Haven, Conn., 1967).

would have yielded more than the required funds. Pakistan's flexibility and patience proved worthwhile: the United States finally came in on a $75 million 'package deal' with the World Bank (the other bidders providing a total of $99 million).[9]

Aid machinery in flux

As with other recipient countries, initiating, processing, implementing and evaluating foreign aid are a national responsibility in Pakistan. And they have always been under the jurisdiction of a central authority. Until 1958, it was the Ministry of Economic Affairs.

The ministry contained a small unit for processing and administering foreign aid. In addition, it kept a case-by-case record of loans, types of collateral, maturities, terms on which funds could be disbursed, and currencies and conditions of repayment. As the terms and conditions of foreign lending shifted over the years, the ministry developed further machinery to accommodate these changing requirements.

Among the steps taken to expedite aid utilization were the following: efforts were made to finalize allotments of funds well in time; reports on project progress were prepared to remove impediments to efficiency; periodic project reviews were carried out; and special committees were appointed to review the entire aid programme and suggest remedial measures. Also, additional staff was provided to check procurements and clearance of equipment; a Projects Division was set up in the President's Secretariat to oversee the progress of projects and remove bottlenecks; and a senior liaison officer was posted in East Pakistan to ensure that aid for the East Wing was properly and expeditiously processed.[10]

But despite such efforts, the operating results were not impressive. In 1958, a major government reorganization abolished the Ministry of Economic Affairs and established an Economic Affairs Division in the Ministry of Finance. The new division was made responsible for preparing and co-ordinating all foreign aid and technical assistance requests. However, even this arrangement did not work out well, primarily because of a lack of co-operation between the Ministry of Finance and the Planning Commission. The latter found, to its dismay, that it had little or no authority in foreign aid matters, which had become the preserve of a powerful ministry.

[9] The Tarbela Dam, to be completed by 1976, 'will be the largest earth and rock fill dam in the world...[It is] the centerpiece of [a] comprehensive program...for meeting West Pakistan's need for additional supplies of irrigation water and electric power.' IBRD and IDA, *Annual Report 1968* (Washington, 1968), pp. 21–2. IBRD had played an important 'broker's' role in helping to arrange the Tarbela bids and to raise the required external resources.

[10] Then, too, project agreements with the United States provided for periodic review of the status of funds to permit any unutilized balance to be programmed by mutual consultation between the US and Pakistan governments. Unutilized funds were generally re-obligated for agreed projects and purposes requiring urgent financing. This arrangement made it possible to use a substantial amount of aid which would otherwise have been lost.

Since at that point aid inflows were assuming large proportions, the Planning Commission argued that separation of the planning and aid co-ordinating functions was a serious bottleneck in plan implementation. On the advice of the commission, the Economic Affairs Division was moved to the President's Secretariat and was put under the general supervision of the chairman of the Planning Commission. In theory, this amounted to the creation of two divisions of equal status: the Planning Division of the Secretariat (interchangeably called the Planning Commission), and the Economic Affairs Division. In effect, it amounted to a stronger Planning Commission. The commission seems, indeed, to have emerged as the real victor in a power struggle with the State Bank and the ministries of Finance and Economic Affairs; and to have become the 'nerve centre' of economic policy in the government.[11]

Commodity assistance

In the context of US aid, the government of Pakistan submits its annual request for commodity assistance to the AID Mission in Pakistan.[12] A list of essential commodities appropriate for US financing is drawn up, taking into account the needs of the provincial governments, other agencies and private industry. Co-ordination is effected by the Ministry of Commerce and the Economic Affairs Division. The loan agreement and implementation letter are negotiated and signed in Pakistan. Then the Chief Controller of Imports and Exports (or a regional controller) authorizes importation of the items requested; and the Director-General of Supply and Development (or the department concerned) arranges for purchase on the government account.

Funds allocated for the procurement of commodities must be utilized within specified contracting and delivery periods. Because the imports are tied to the United States, importers are often unable to contract for the desired commodities within the prescribed time. In practice, however, these deadlines are extended with great frequency.

But importers must also comply with strict AID regulations in the process of procurement. Some of the important provisions are the following:

SBA notice. Importers who receive authorizations for amounts of $5,000 or more are required to give forty-two days' notice (thirty days for notice and

[11] The Planning Commission's place in the foreign aid system is somewhat less pervasive than such language might imply. For one thing, the Economic Affairs Division retains substantial jurisdiction in aid policy. Secondly, the role of the Planning Commission has been partly a function of personalities rather than structures; there can be little doubt that its strength has varied significantly with the effectiveness of its deputy chairmen. In the latter connection, it is interesting to note that in 1970, after the time of writing, the Commission's prestigious deputy chairman, M. M. Ahmad, became (instead) Economic Adviser to the President and head of a newly separated 'Economic Co-ordination and External Assistance Division'.

[12] Commodity aid is treated separately here because of the peculiarities of its administration. The ensuing discussion is based on the US programme. It has been the dominant one, although other donors have undertaken sizable efforts in recent years. Non-US commodity assistance generally involves less elaborate utilization procedures.

twelve days for exchange of correspondence), along with clear and acceptable specification of their purchases, to the Small Business Administration in the United States.

Pre-check of prices. Commodities must be imported from the cheapest bidders. To ensure this, a 'price-check unit' was created in the Pakistan Office of the Chief Controller of Imports and Exports. The importer, after obtaining quotations, applies to the office for a 'price-check certificate'. The Chief Controller verifies the selected prices by comparing them with other quotations. If a cheaper source is discovered, the relevant information is passed on to the importer for reconsideration. Finally, a certificate is issued and this enables him to open a letter of credit with the appropriate bank.

Shipping requirement. This stipulates that at least 50 per cent of every consignment must be shipped on US flag vessels. Where US ships are not available, AID gives the importer an exemption; and except for certain specified vessels, he can have the entire consignment sent on any ship. In such cases, the government of Pakistan must arrange the cost of freight; that is to say, AID will not finance freight for shipment on non-US vessels. The Pakistan government is responsible for enforcing the '50 per cent' rule, and it keeps quarterly accounts of shipments so that necessary corrective action can be taken in time.

Commodity use. Utilization of commodities by the importer is subject to a check in order to determine whether it is in accordance with the terms of the agreement and the purposes for which the commodities were imported. Much of the utilization has been satisfactory in these terms, but many violations have occurred. For example, prices charged and profits earned by importers have exceeded permissible or otherwise reasonable limits; authorizations, in some cases, have been secured for demands which were not fully justified; proper records of the use of imported goods have not always been produced or maintained; goods other than those permitted have been imported; discounts or commission not allowed under AID regulations have been received by importers; prices paid by importers have sometimes not been competitive. AID claims a refund when the aid is not used in accordance with prescribed regulations; the Economic Affairs Division reviews the position and if a satisfactory explanation is furnished, the claim is withdrawn.

As distinct from general commodity loans, surplus agricultural products have gone to Pakistan under Title I of US Public Law 480. These very large transactions have been arranged through specific agreements negotiated from time to time between aid representatives of the two countries. Local currency sale proceeds are accumulated in a US account in Pakistan and are used for one or more of the following purposes: to help develop new markets for US agricultural commodities on a mutual benefit basis; to procure military, strategic and critical materials; to finance the purchase of other goods and services in Pakistan; to promote balanced economic development and multilateral trade; to pay US obligations; to finance educational exchanges with Pakistan.

Under Title II of PL 480, Pakistan receives surplus agricultural commodities as relief grants for floods and other natural calamities. The costs of transport are borne by the United States, and local distribution is supposed to be free. Sale proceeds, if any, are deposited in a separate account and used for relief or employment purposes. The grants are made in response to requests by the Pakistan government, after scrutiny by the AID Mission and a careful assessment of actual relief needs.

Grants of surplus agricultural commodities have also been made to Pakistan under Title III of PL 480. These transfers are channelled through US relief agencies.

Evaluation

The evaluation process constitutes the weakest link in the planning system of Pakistan. This applies equally to foreign-aided and purely domestic projects and programmes. The former, particularly those undertaken with Consortium assistance, have fared slightly better in this respect since the Consortium normally meets at least once a year to review economic progress in the country before committing additional assistance. Furthermore, the World Bank keeps in direct touch with developments through its general missions to Pakistan, as well as through special missions which examine and report thoroughly on a particular sector; in 1966, for example, an Industrial Mission of IBRD prepared a comprehensive report on developments in the industrial field.[13]

Originally, evaluation was entrusted to the Planning Commission. However, the commission believed that detailed progress reporting should be done by a separate body; and a Projects Division was, accordingly, created in the President's Secretariat. But the division did not measure up to expectations. Its project materials were generally incomplete and out of date. This was primarily due to inadequate reporting by the operating departments, ministries and agencies. The executing bodies rarely followed instructions; reports were vague and exaggerated progress; there was a natural hesitancy in reporting delays and mistakes. In addition, the elaborate forms and the multiplicity of required reports created apathy towards progress reporting. In short, the Projects Division was viewed by most of the agencies as a sort of impersonal overlord and never received the co-operation which was essential for its success.

In August 1961, the division was abolished and its staff and functions were absorbed by the Planning Commission. This experiment fared no better than the first one. The evaluating function was then moved outside the Planning Commission; 'progress cells' were established in the Development Departments of East and West Pakistan, on the ground that expediting and implementation were incompatible with the advisory role of the Planning Commission. More recently, the commission has again been entrusted with the task of evaluation

---

[13] Also, the AID Mission maintains close on-the-spot contact with US-aided projects and programmes (see Chapter 6).

and implementation, but the provincial 'progress cells' have not been abolished.[14]

There is no doubt that evaluation is a difficult function, but it is vital to any planning system. The absence of an effective evaluation unit in a development programme the size of Pakistan's is, therefore, a wide gap which needs to be filled. Nor is it only a matter of project evaluation. The fact is that, despite the existence of appropriate machinery, little is known in Pakistan about the impact of the massive commodity aid on the country's industrial development; once the initial allocations and related procedures are completed, the Pakistan authorities virtually cease to be concerned with the process and results of commodity aid absorption into the economy.[15]

It is small consolation to recognize that the complex task of running a huge aid programme drains away scarce time and manpower which might otherwise be available for progress reporting and evaluation. The gap is there nonetheless; and vigorous efforts to narrow it – in terms of domestic as well as foreign resources – could make the difference between weak and solid economic performance.

[14] In June 1965, the central government again decided to establish a Projects Division in the President's Secretariat, under the supervision of the Planning Commission's deputy chairman. However, the actual creation of the new division was delayed, and in 1966 a Projects Wing began operating within the Planning Commission.

[15] The donor countries have not done much, if any, better in this regard. Even US follow-through on commodity aid is very limited.

12. Conclusions

It is now time to 'take stock' – to look over the ground covered by this study, to highlight its basic findings, and to reflect on the implications of Pakistan's experience for international aid policy in the years ahead.

Let it be underscored, at the outset, that there is a wide variety of topics to which the study has not given in-depth treatment. Merely to list some of them is to sense the breadth of this gap: technical and military assistance; foreign aid flows to Pakistan's agricultural sector; the differential impact of foreign assistance on East and West Pakistan; the social and political effects of foreign economic aid on Pakistan. Such topics involve issues that have a significant bearing on the country's past and future development. Indeed, it could reasonably be argued that problems of regional inequality and social injustice are at the heart of the matter as far as Pakistan is concerned.

But very complex questions arise as to the appropriate framework for examining foreign aid in relation to the whole spectrum of domestic forces underlying a recipient country's progress. Even if the framework were complete, it would still be necessary to ask whether this kind of analysis was manageable within the confines of a single study. And even then, one would have to be satisfied that the relevant empirical data were sufficiently available and reliable to make the full-blown analysis worthwhile. The central judgment made here is that serious conceptual and measurement difficulties militate against such global coverage; and that Pakistani industry – virtually non-existent at the time of Partition, as well as highly dynamic almost continuously ever since – provides a solid testing ground for aid impact on economic development.

And yet, there is no escape from the fact that a large number of important foreign aid issues receive little or no attention in this study. In essence, these 'empty boxes' stand as a call for extensive continuing research on foreign financing in Pakistan. They also impose an overriding sense of modesty about any conclusions drawn from the foregoing analysis.

A summary of findings

The intended role of foreign economic assistance may differ considerably between the recipient and the donors, and also among the donors. This makes for great complexity in judging the success of an aid programme. But in general terms, both recipient and donor seek a higher growth rate and increased industrialization in the aid-receiving country. And it is clear that foreign aid, given its resource base, tends to promote these broad objectives. The crucial question, though, is how far aid does so relative to other factors, and whether it has been as effective as possible in the context of existing social, political and administrative constraints.

There is no short-cut for avoiding a country-by-country approach to these issues. Nor is it convincing to argue that capital is *the* key to economic development, not just one of several major elements in the growth process. Focusing on Pakistan, the difficulties are great indeed – compounded, as they are, by the East–West division and by an enormous variety of sources and types of assistance. But one thing is certain: expansion of Pakistani industry – and of the economy as a whole – would have been severely restricted and retarded by a forced heavier reliance on domestic resources.[1]

If this measure of foreign aid impact is very broad and imprecise, it is no less real. A central ingredient of success has been communication and co-ordination between donor and recipient. While time, energy and money have undoubtedly been wasted in the process of aid-giving to Pakistan, such leakages are far less serious than they might have been, and much less so than in relation to many other recipient countries. In the main, this close working relationship has been fostered by the Pakistan Consortium. And the dynamic role of the Consortium has been chiefly a function of World Bank and United States initiative, coupled with a remarkable flexibility on the part of Pakistan's planners. Of the end results there can be no doubt: a highly constructive airing of foreign aid problems, and a significant increase in the effectiveness of aid as an instrument for supplementing domestic savings and relieving major bottlenecks.

A review of the overall dimensions of foreign economic assistance to Pakistan helps to explain why its effects have been so marked. As of March 1967, the aid total stood at US $4.7 billion (excluding PL 480 assistance under Title I). Loans aggregated $3.4 billion, and grants $1.3 billion; total project aid exceeded $2.5 billion, and non-project assistance amounted to roughly $1.5 billion. By 1960, gross foreign aid inflows had reached some 38 per cent of total development expenditure and 3.4 per cent of GNP; in 1967 the corresponding ratios (including PL 480 and Indus Basin outlays) were 38 and 5.7 per cent, respectively.[2] The United States has been the predominant donor, providing more than three-quarters of total grants and nearly half of all loans; four other donors together accounted for about a third of total aid to Pakistan, namely, the World Bank Group (16 per cent), West Germany (6 per cent), Canada (5 per cent), and the United Kingdom (5 per cent). Over one-third of total assistance went to the industrial sector between 1950 and 1967 – about 40 per cent in project support and the rest in the form of general purpose commodities.

Even if one examines the 'discounted present value' of these aid flows, they remain substantial. In terms of real cost to donors, total assistance to Pakistan

---

[1] 'The availability of [aid-financed] imports goes far to explain the very rapid growth of Pakistan private industry, and [its] high rate of profits and...savings propensities...go far to explain the sizable increase in the aggregate domestic savings coefficient...[Furthermore, Pakistan's higher] level of aid per capita...made industrial development substantially easier than in India...' E. S. Mason, *Economic Development in India and Pakistan* (Cambridge, Mass., 1966), p. 64.

[2] Net aid inflows amounted to Rs. 3.02 billion in 1967. These comprised 34 per cent of total development expenditure and 5.2 per cent of GNP.

was about 60 per cent of its nominal value. The United States, Canada, Sweden, Australia, New Zealand and the socialist countries have been relatively generous in their aid terms, while World Bank loans have provided very little concessionary treatment. For many donors, the real cost of aid ranges between a tenth and a third of nominal value. The ranking of leading donors changes somewhat when the real cost criterion is used: IDA rises from third to second place, Canada from fifth to third, and the United Kingdom from sixth to fourth; West Germany, on the other hand, declines from fourth to fifth, and IBRD from second to tenth; the United States remains solidly in first place.

In these terms, too, the benefits of aid to Pakistan have presumably exceeded its cost to the donors: given the comparative shortages of capital, the general return on investment is probably higher in Pakistan than in the main donor countries; and its cost of borrowing in private capital markets would undoubtedly be higher than the cost actually incurred. But this does not alter the fact that the nominal aid values clearly overstate the real transfers of resources which have been made. And real cost falls even more when the tying of aid is taken into account. Most donors tie their aid to domestic goods and services. While the results will naturally vary according to particular tying patterns, the extent of overvaluation can be very large. In the case of iron and steel products, for example, Pakistan's increased cost due to tying is estimated to have ranged from 41 to 111 per cent.

The aid inflows were heavy nonetheless, and especially so during the Second Five-Year Plan. Some 60 per cent of total foreign loans and 26 per cent of all grants were concentrated in the years 1960–5. This may well explain much of the impressive achievement recorded during that period, including the first appreciable increases in per capita real income. To be sure, the First Plan, unrealized targets aside, had set vital infra-structure in place. But it was the Second Plan which brought economic growth at an unprecedented pace – with the industrial sector in the forefront, and with massive foreign aid to Pakistani industry a major driving force throughout the period. Even so, the forward surge was too brief to be viewed as a self-sustaining process. And indeed, Pakistan's balance-of-payments position worsened in the face of the rapid expansion; while foreign indebtedness rose sharply, and prospects for an early export breakthrough were something less than bright.

This is the context in which the trend of recent aid inflows has become clouded, and in which foreign grants have virtually disappeared. The change began with the suspension of US assistance during the Indo-Pakistan War, continued with only partial resumption of aid in the aftermath of hostilities, and seems now to be reflecting a general malaise in international aid-giving to the underdeveloped world. It is difficult to see how Pakistani growth and efficiency could escape serious harm from extension of this trend into the 1970s. In fact, strong pressures for extreme import substitution are already being felt – not for reasons of long-run economic gain, but out of sheer necessity imposed by scarce foreign resources, and out of deep uncertainty over the future supply of assistance. Rapid and sustained increases in aid to

Pakistan could ease the inward-looking pressures, encourage a more effective use of domestic resources, and improve export and balance-of-payments performance.

But while such aid increases *could* produce these results, there is, of course, no guarantee that they *would*. Much would depend on the types and financial terms of the aid, on the skill with which it was allocated to top priority uses, and on the efficiency of aid administration and appraisal. A closer backward look at aid to Pakistani industry should prove very instructive in this connection. Not surprisingly, the picture that emerges from the present study is a mixed one.

On the donor side, it is worth repeating that while some of the leading aid-givers, notably US AID, Canada and IDA, have been generous in concessionary terms, others – in particular, IBRD and West Germany – have attached rather stringent financial conditions to their assistance. While the World Bank Group has extended only untied credits to the industrial sector (as elsewhere), nearly all the other donors have tied most of their aid to their own supplies of commodities and services. While the United States and the Bank Group have developed sophisticated techniques for assessing the likely cost–benefit effects of their aid, other leading donors have not; and the very sophistication of US and World Bank appraisal has often meant prolonged delays between the submission and execution of aid requests. Though the major Western donors have shown a substantial concern with Pakistan's overall development programme (especially in the Consortium setting), the Soviet Union and China appear to view industrialization as almost exclusively a matter of building heavy industry in the country's public sector; US AID and the World Bank Group have confined their industrial loans almost entirely to the private sector. While the value of industrial non-project aid has been increasingly recognized in Western programmes, it plays little or no part in the aid-giving of most socialist countries. There is, finally, the fact that although virtually all donors pay lip service to the importance of thoroughgoing follow-up procedures for aid appraisal, none has yet developed machinery adequate to this task.

In large measure, these are the programme features which have shaped Pakistan's experience with foreign assistance to industry. Within Pakistan itself, they have been reinforced in both positive and negative ways – positively, by an evolving system of aid administration, by a resourceful Planning Commission standing at the centre of the national 'development' stage, and by a considerable talent for flexibility in accommodating to the realities of international aid diplomacy; negatively, by a propensity for bureaucratic delays and lapses in decision-making, by a conspicuous absence of evaluative follow-up on aid projects and programmes, and by an acute shortage of trained manpower for effective aid policy. This combination of factors was bound to have both favourable and adverse consequences for project as well as commodity assistance. In the event, it is the shortcomings which typically proved more striking in the project field, and the achievements on the commodity aid front.

With regard to project aid, a sample of case studies drawn from both East and West Pakistan reveals a variety of serious problems. Public sector projects seem to have experienced the larger share of the difficulties. These include weak project planning (for example, the Khulna newsprint mill), politically motivated pressures on plant location (the Kushtia and Rajshahi sugar mills), faulty operation and maintenance (the Fenchuganj fertilizer factory), slow processing of high priority projects (the Pak-American fertilizer factory at Daudkhel), and project selection based more on reasons of prestige than on considerations of economic benefit (the initial plans for the Karachi steel mill). Confusion and conflict among imported 'experts' have been particularly disruptive (the high cost penicillin factory at Daudkhel). And smooth project execution has been nullified by uneconomic size of plant (the under-optimum scale Chittagong steel mill).

Private sector projects have had their troubles too. There are instances of very damaging delays arising from political instability and uncertainty (Karnaphuli paper mills, for example). There are also cases of poor planning, ineffective co-ordination and slow progress (the West Pakistan industrial estates project and much of the Cooley loan programme). On the other hand, one can readily cite examples of well-conceived and successful private business ventures (notably Packages Ltd, jointly owned and operated by Pakistani and Swedish interests). And there is clear evidence of dynamic stimulus to private industry through foreign-aided lending institutions (especially the IBRD-favoured PICIC, but also to some extent the small-business-oriented IDBP).

Having gone this far with the case studies, it is important to recognize that they cannot easily be carried further. For one thing, the sample of projects is not entirely satisfactory: although chosen with care, it might well have been larger and more representative, given wider access to the relevant data. Secondly, if public sector projects seem the more prone to serious problems, this may be substantially due to the fact that they are often undertaken in circumstances considered too hazardous for private initiative. But perhaps the most telling point to be made here is that the complexity of most case histories makes it virtually impossible to set up precise general rules for ranking prospective projects. Indeed, it has been argued that secondary or indirect effects – sociopolitical as well as economic – usually turn out to be so ambiguous that the project analyst 'cannot even pretend to classify uniformly, for purposes of decision making, the various properties and probable lines of behavior of projects, as either advantages or drawbacks, benefits or costs, assets or liabilities'.[3] However, this states the issue in the most extreme terms; for if 'each project turns out to represent a unique constellation of experiences and consequences, of direct and indirect effects',[4] then there would be little use in analysing projects at all. It is very difficult to sustain such a position. While the jump from the micro to the macro level can never be a simple one, in practice it must be attempted, and though it is questionable to lay down fixed principles of project selection, it is not futile to search out past experience for rough guidelines to project aid policy in the future.

[3] A. O. Hirschman, *Development Projects Observed* (Washington, D.C., 1967), p. 188.
[4] *Ibid.* p. 186.

The above summary of specific case study findings should be viewed from this perspective. And the same is true for the generalized critical comments that follow: industrial projects are frequently ill-conceived, and aid requests little more than shopping lists; there is often an inordinate waste of effort, financing and time before progress, if any, is recorded; friction in aid negotiation seems all too common; feasibility studies rarely advise against the adoption of a project; costs tend to be underestimated, and demand analysis neglected; ongoing projects typically take precedence over new proposals, regardless of merit; scant attention is paid to the training of Pakistani technicians and managers on the project level; progress reporting is woefully inadequate. Perhaps the most pressing need is for closer integration of project aid into the overall planning process.

Integration is, in fact, at the heart of the difference between project and commodity assistance. Given its wider coverage, industrial commodity aid has come to serve general planning objectives and to be more readily co-ordinated with them. It has a strong potential for increasing the use of manufacturing plant and equipment – all the more so where (as in Pakistan) the import-intensive industries are found in the lower ranges of capacity utilization. It can directly relieve balance-of-payments pressures in the receiving country, and facilitate management of the external accounts. It can sharply accelerate the process of moving the industrial structure towards self-sustained growth – by broadening and deepening the recipient country's capital goods base.[5] Commodity aid can also be a powerful instrument of leverage in the hands of a donor seeking the adoption of sound economic policies by the recipient.

There can be little doubt that the Pakistan economy has reaped substantial gains from foreign non-project aid in industrial commodities. In both wings, production increases exceeding 50 per cent were widely reported for single-shift plant operations during the crucial last two years of the Second Plan; these appear to have paralleled frequent increases in the number of working shifts per plant. Between 1955 and 1964, non-food commodity assistance enabled Pakistan to acquire about 16 per cent more of total imports than would otherwise have been possible, and it continues to provide sizable balance-of-payments relief, as well as added flexibility in the use of foreign resources. Commodity aid has also underpinned a marked shift in Pakistan's imports away from consumer goods, and has thereby contributed to a considerable increase in investment and output in the intermediate and capital goods industries. Perhaps most important of all, the United States – by far the chief commodity donor – and the World Bank have so modulated such aid as to persuade, if not coerce, the government of Pakistan to carry out the import liberalization and other

[5] Two qualifying comments are in order here. Structural change is, in principle, no less related to project aid than to commodity assistance, though Pakistan's experience suggests that the former is likely to be more uneven and less pointed in its impact. Furthermore, there is no guarantee that aid-financed commodity imports will not distort the industrial structure towards greater dependence on foreign resources, though the thesis of frustrated take-off in Pakistan has yet to be proved.

kinds of de-control that have played such an important part in its record of economic performance.

This, of course, is not to say that industrial commodity aid to Pakistan was as effective as it could have been in relation to its size and pattern of transfer. The truth is that the available information does not permit a judgment either way on this issue: donor and recipient follow-up evaluation are no better than in the case of project aid; and the relevant data on end uses are still too fragmentary or elusive to warrant more detailed analysis of commodity aid impact on the industrial sector. Nor should the relative success of commodity aid be construed as an argument for large-scale displacement of project assistance. That success owes much to the fact that massive commodity aid came on the Pakistan scene at a time of great unused capacity caused partly by overemphasis on project assistance. Clearly, there is an appropriate mix of both types of aid, depending on the prevailing circumstances; and an excess of one or the other could have serious detrimental effects on the receiving country's economy.

Some closing reflections on aid policy

An all-purpose model of foreign aid impact has not yet been formulated, and there is still no precise measure of either the relative importance of aid in Pakistan's development or the actual effects of aid in comparison with its Pakistan potential. But an analytical door has been opened here; and there is ample scope for others to build on the conclusions already drawn.

It remains only to ask how far those conclusions are a product of just one aid recipient's experience, and how far they can be projected beyond Pakistan. There are, indeed, impressive elements of uniqueness in Pakistan's experience, notably those associated with the fact of Partition: virtually no industry in the new state; two wings separated by sharp cultural and physical differences, and by about 1,000 miles of Indian territory; an enormous diverted demand for domestic goods and services; an intense economic and political rivalry with India; early assurance of heavy aid inflows through close military alignment with the United States. Such factors argue for a cautious approach to any extension of lessons from the Pakistan story.

But the case for considerable extension seems overwhelming nonetheless. Some of the particular Pakistan elements are by no means immutable; heavy aid flows, for example, are man-made and therefore subject to the broadest policy control. Also, the donor programmes contain many important features – on aid-tying, progress reporting, and so on – which apply across the board vis-à-vis the developing countries. Then, too, Pakistan was responding to problems of aid absorption – mounting indebtedness, sectoral imbalance, excess productive capacity – common throughout the less-developed world.

The outer limits of generalization may well be very wide. Suffice it, here, to make the following points: Large and sustained flows of aid, when combined with Consortium-type communication and flexible policy in the receiving country, are powerfully equipped to produce rapid and continuing economic development. A sudden shrinkage in aid flows is likely to push the recipient's growth strategy excessively inward (via import substitution), and so bring gross inefficiencies into the industrial structure.[6] Aid-induced foreign indebtedness can develop quickly and dangerously from a negligible base, thereby leaving a drastic and costly shift to domestic resources as the only alternative to cheaper or greatly increased assistance. The real cost of aid to donors is apt to be materially lower than its nominal cost, and the real need of aid to recipients is longer-lasting than they or the donors are prepared to recognize. Given markets and raw materials in the developing country, substantial aid should be allocated to the manufacturing sector, because it tends to be a dynamic force promoting domestic savings and self-generated growth, quite apart from, and fully consistent with, the pervasive role of agriculture in the industrialization process. Local lending institutions, soundly conceived, provide a most promising outlet for external financing of industrial expansion in less-developed countries. Finally, donor programmes could be much improved by closer integration into the recipient's planning system, a more judicious admixture of project and commodity assistance, the abandonment of preconceived views as to the merits of private or public sector encouragement, and more vigorous and more scientific evaluation of aid effects in the receiving countries.

In short, foreign aid can be a major influence for economic growth or stagnation in the underdeveloped world. Both its direction of impact and duration of need will be largely a function of the size and types of assistance available, as well as the skill with which it is utilized. Even more important, in the long run, will be the particular developing country's own capacity for solving its fundamental economic problems. This leads back, full circle, to the case of Pakistan – with its significant combination of achievement and challenge.

The improved functioning of the economy attracted greater foreign resources and made it possible to absorb them. In turn, the availability of foreign resources helped make possible increased efficiency by underwriting steps to reduce direct controls...
[but] serious economic problems remain. For one, a process of significant growth has barely begun; it can still be aborted. At best, Pakistanis will remain among the poorest people in the world during the next couple of decades. Further, the growth process has allowed serious economic inequalities to remain between areas and groups...The shift from direct to indirect controls remains incomplete and subject to reversal. Economic inefficiency remains a problem.[7]

As Pakistan prepares to implement its Fourth Five-Year Plan, the challenge seems, indeed, to be overshadowing the achievement.

Real industrial wages actually declined during the 1960s. Some 75 per cent of all Pakistani households continue to subsist on incomes of less than $500

[6] This is not to overlook the possibility that a modest reduction in aid inflows might, in some circumstances, yield increased efficiency through a more selective effort in agriculture and the export industries.

[7] G. F. Papanek, *Pakistan's Development: Social Goals and Private Incentives* (Cambridge, Mass., 1967), pp. 238–40.

a year. The daily calorie intake is approximately 2,100 per person, as compared with the minimum international standard of about 2,600 calories. There are still more than one million families in the cities without decent shelter. The literacy rate remains well below 20 per cent. It is estimated that 1.5 million new jobs per year will have to be created during the early 1970s if an increase in the already high backlog of unemployment is to be avoided. Despite massive and sustained remedial efforts, economic growth in East Pakistan continues to lag far behind that of West Pakistan. Only about one-fifth of total private investment is currently taking place in the East Wing, while the annual growth rate of East Pakistan agriculture, which accounts for roughly two-thirds of the province's total income, was about 3 per cent during the 1960s, as compared with over 5 per cent in West Pakistan.[8]

It is clear that the serious political disturbances of 1968/9 stemmed, in large part, from the failure of social progress to match the record of broad economic growth – and from deep public concern over widespread corruption and restricted participation in basic decision-making. Not surprisingly, the fall of the Ayub regime has had sobering implications for Pakistan's success. It has also spurred new doubts as to the role of foreign assistance in the development process.

In this context, it is necessary to recognize that under some circumstances, foreign aid 'may fragment the economy, introduce monopoly elements into the society, discourage the development of a native entrepreneurial class, lower the domestic savings ratio, raise the capital–output ratio and cause subsequent balance of payments problems'.[9] But this does not refute the basic point that foreign assistance can be a significant positive force in economic development; nor does the Pakistan case support the view that the net effects of aid on a recipient country are likely to be negative.

It is feasible, of course, to construct a more sweeping argument: 'development requires economic reforms; economic reforms are impossible without institutional change; foreign aid tends to strengthen institutions and thereby inhibit change; hence aid tends to retard development'.[10] But such reasoning cannot prove that foreign aid is incompatible with domestic reform. What is really at stake is the assumption that drastic institutional change without aid would produce greater economic benefits than modest reforms with aid; and again, the Pakistan experience affords little basis for this view. The 'reform' thesis turns out to be

---

[8] The above paragraph is based on Planning Commission estimates contained in Pakistan Planning Commission, *Socio-Economic Objectives of the Fourth Five-Year Plan (1970–75)* (Islamabad, 1968), pp. 2, 11, 13, 18. See also A. R. Khan, 'What Has Been Happening to Real Wages in Pakistan?', *Pakistan Development Review*, Autumn 1967; S. R. Bose, 'Trend of Real Income of the Rural Poor in East Pakistan, 1949–66', *Pakistan Development Review*, Autumn 1968. And see S. R. Lewis, Jr., 'Notes on Industrialization and Income Distribution in Pakistan', Research Memorandum no. 37, unpublished mimeo. (Williamstown, Mass.: Williams College, Center for Development Economics, September 1970 [after the time of writing].)

[9] K. Griffin, *Underdevelopment in Spanish America: An Interpretation* (London, 1969), p. 148.

[10] K. B. Griffin, 'Financing Development Plans in Pakistan', *Pakistan Development Review*, Winter 1965, p. 623.

not an argument for eliminating foreign assistance, but rather for gearing it more effectively to institutional change in the receiving countries.

From the very broad perspective of nation-building, it is, indeed, open to question whether foreign aid has come close to its full potential in Pakistan. But as already noted, this raises other complex questions – notably, whether nation-building is an appropriate standard of assessment for aid performance; and if this is so, how one proceeds to carry out such an evaluation. This much seems clear: in terms of the present study, foreign assistance accelerated both economic growth and industrial development in Pakistan, especially during the 1960s; but in some degree, the country's recent crises and frustrations are a product of that growth process. By the same token, foreign aid donors will bear a substantial burden of responsibility for the outcome of Pakistan's struggle in the years ahead. But the heaviest burden will rest on Pakistan itself; for in the final analysis, it is mainly domestic policy and domestic effort which determine success or failure in economic development.

APPENDICES

Appendix 1
A note on the real transfer of resources to developing countries*

The appropriate definition of aid and the measurement of its flows have been discussed extensively in the economic literature.[1] This interest is of fairly recent origin, dating back little more than a decade. Earlier, it was the flow of private capital, the conditions under which it moved, and its impact on capital-exporting and capital-importing countries that had received major attention.[2]

The UN stimulus

This shift is, perhaps, most clearly reflected in the debates which have taken place in the United Nations regarding international capital movements. In 1952, the General Assembly requested an analysis of the international flow of private capital, including its volume, types and direction, as well as the reasons for its continued inadequacy in the light of the growth needs of the developing countries.[3] In 1954, the General Assembly decided that the Secretariat should prepare annual reports on this flow, its contribution to economic development, and the measures taken by governments to affect the flow.[4] A series of such reports appeared over the years, with special emphasis on the legal, fiscal and institutional factors influencing private capital movements abroad.[5]

But in the meantime, the balance-of-payments position of many developing countries had become critical. Investment programmes with a high import content and a declining value of exports created a widening trade gap. Efforts to expand the flow of private capital, so as to bridge this gap, did not meet with appreciable success. Accordingly, the question of how to finance ever-increasing balance-of-payments deficits became a central concern of international economic policy.

This concern with international assistance, as against the flow of private foreign capital, produced a number of General Assembly resolutions, and these led to a

---

* The authors wish to acknowledge the valuable comments made on this appendix by Professor S. Lanfranco of McMaster University, Hamilton, Canada.
[1] See, for example, F. Benham, *Economic Aid to Underdeveloped Countries* (London, 1961); I. M. D. Little and J. M. Clifford, *International Aid* (London, 1965); G. Ohlin, *Foreign Aid Policies Reconsidered* (Paris, 1966); R. F. Mikesell, *The Economics of Foreign Aid* (Chicago, 1968).
[2] In this connection, see A. K. Cairncross, 'Did Foreign Investment Pay?', *Review of Economic Studies*, October 1935; H. W. Singer, 'The Distribution of Gains Between Investing and Borrowing Countries', *American Economic Review*, May 1950; R. Nurkse, 'International Investments in the Light of Nineteenth Century Experience', *Economic Journal*, December 1954.
[3] UN General Assembly, Resolution 622C (VII), New York, 1952.
[4] UN General Assembly, Resolution 512B (XVII), 1954.
[5] UN, *Economic Development of Under-developed Countries: The International Flow of Private Capital, 1953–60*, annual (New York, 1956–60). For a recent comprehensive analysis by the UN, see *Foreign Investment in Developing Countries* (New York, 1968).

series of reports dealing specifically with foreign economic aid.[6] With the trade gap a major constraint on economic growth and the flow of private capital both low and unresponsive to attempts to expand it, the focus of international attention shifted towards the use of inter-governmental loans and grants. The General Assembly urged that 'the flow of international assistance and capital [to developing countries] should be increased substantially so as to reach, as soon as possible, approximately 1 per cent of the combined national incomes of the economically advanced countries'.[7] It further recommended that both developed and developing countries take such measures as might be appropriate to accelerate the flow of aid and to ensure its effective utilization. The one per cent target was included as one of the basic objectives of the 'Development Decade', so designated in 1961, and was later reaffirmed at the first United Nations Conference on Trade and Development.[8]

This new focus on international assistance, along with the one per cent target, underscored the need for meaningful measures of resource transfer. More specifically, the fact that bilateral aid flows would continue to play a key role, coupled with the fact that the objective was one per cent of the *combined* national incomes of the developed countries (and not one per cent of the national income of *each* country), meant that the individual bilateral flows must be measured in such a way as to be comparable. This was necessary in order to obtain an estimate of the overall volume of aid and to assess the distribution of the burden among donor countries. In addition, the United Nations was committed to making annual reviews of progress towards attainment of the stated goals.

Indeed, the decisions taken in the United Nations marked a turning point in donor attitudes towards joint responsibility for the transfer of resources to the developing countries. Those decisions did not, of course, imply an end to bilateral transfers, nor even a massive multilateralization of aid. But they did reflect a new consensus on the vital importance of a global strategy for resource transfer to promote international development.

Problems of aid valuation

Aid transfers have been effected in a great variety of ways. There are the outright grants in untied, freely convertible foreign exchange. There are the loans subject to differing degrees of constraint as to the form, place and manner in which they can be converted into real resources; interest rates and repayment periods vary, loans are tied or untied, and they are repayable sometimes in domestic currency and sometimes in foreign exchange. And there are the movements in kind, in terms of commodities and skills, which are normally valued at the price determined by the exporting or donor countries.

Obviously, determining the total flow of assistance in the case of untied grants of convertible currency offers no difficulties. But the measurement of loan transfers with

---

[6] See UN General Assembly, Resolution 1034 (XI), 1957, and Resolution 662A (XXIV), 1957; also UN, *International Economic Assistance to the Under-developed Countries, 1956–57* and *1960* (New York, 1958, 1961).

[7] UN General Assembly, Resolution 1522 (XV), 1960, p. 13.

[8] UN General Assembly, Resolution 1710 (XVI) and Resolution 1711 (XVI), 1961; UN Conference on Trade and Development, *Final Act and Report*, v. 1, annex A. IV. 2 (New York, 1964).

different interest rates and repayment periods involves the special problem of calculating the present value of future flows. And the most serious valuation problems are those associated with tied aid, and with commodity and technical assistance. In the commodity case, for example, at what price should food aid – which normally comes from government surplus stocks – be valued? Should it be the price at which the food was acquired or the price prevailing in the world market? And would not the world price itself change if such commodities were offered for sale in the international market? As for technical assistance, what would be a realistic wage structure for purposes of converting the value of the technical experts' services into monetary terms?

A growing volume of literature on the burden-sharing problems of defence alliances and economic aid programmes has sought to overcome the deficiencies of ad hoc cost allocation by measuring the burden of alternative forms of payment and by applying the principles of 'equity' or 'ability to pay' in determining the appropriate burden.[9] In the aid context, the United States has often taken the position that it is shouldering an undue share of the burden.[10]

All this has intensified efforts to bring the size and composition of national aid programmes under international scrutiny. The United Nations has dealt with the problem of the real transfer of resources in several publications.[11] The Development Assistance Committee of OECD (DAC) has conducted an annual review of the amount, terms and effectiveness of each member country's aid programme since 1962.[12] OECD defines total official aid as the sum of the following elements: contributions to international organizations for development purposes: bilateral grants; bilateral loans payable in the lender's currency; bilateral loans payable in the borrower's currency; transfers of resources through sale for the recipient's currency.[13] The UN, on the other hand, includes under aid only outright grants and net long-term lending, for non-military purposes, by governments and international organizations. Quite apart from such problems of aid classification, a number of writers have attempted to make international comparisons more rigorous by separating out the concessionary elements of capital transfer.

[9] See, in particular, League of Nations, *Financial Administration and Apportionment of Expenses* (Geneva, 1928); T. C. Schelling, *International Cost-Sharing Arrangements*, Essays in International Finance, no. 24 (Princeton University, September 1955); E. S. Mason 'The Equitable Sharing of Military and Economic Aid Burdens', in *Proceedings of the Academy of Political Science*, May 1963; I. B. Kravis and M. W. E. Davenport, 'The Political Arithmetic of Burden Sharing', *Journal of Political Economy*, August 1963; J. A. Pincus, *Trade, Aid and Development: The Rich and Poor Nations* (New York, 1967).

[10] See, for example, President Kennedy's Message to Congress, 6 February 1961, in *U.S. Congressional Record*, 87th Cong., 1st Session, v. 107, parts 1–2 (Washington, D.C.), pp. 1791–4.

[11] See, for instance, UN, *Measurement of the Flow of Long-term Capital and Official Donations to Developing Countries: Concepts and Methodology* (New York, 1965), and *The Measurement of the Flow of Resources from the Developed Market Economies to the Developing Countries* (New York, 1966).

[12] See OECD, *Development Assistance: Efforts and Policies of the Members of the Development Assistance Committee, 1969 Review* (Paris, 1969).

[13] As of 1969, OECD distinguishes between 'official development assistance' and 'other official flows' – the former confined to items that are both concessional and development-oriented. *Ibid.* annex I.

Real cost measures

John Pincus, for example, has adjusted the 1961 and 1962 aid contributions of the members of DAC by discounting the loan component at four different rates of interest, namely: the domestic long-term rate in the lending country, the highest average lending rate of DAC members (7 per cent), an international lending rate represented by the prime rate of the World Bank, and a 10 per cent rate taken as an approximation of expected yields from private investment in developing countries.[14] The difference between the nominal value of aid and the discounted value based on the lender's domestic rates measures the net financial cost of the transaction to the donor country. The difference between the nominal value and the value based on the average yield of capital in developing countries measures the net benefit accruing to the recipient country.[15]

Wilson Schmidt uses a similar 'present value' technique to analyse the comparative merits of grants and loans, and to point up the conditions under which loans are 'cheaper' than grants and vice versa. He argues that 'on purely economic grounds, the benefactors should choose between loans and grants according to which imposes the minimum cost on the benefactor for a given benefit to the recipient'.[16]

In a more recent study, Pincus has further developed the 'real cost' and 'real benefit' measures of the flow of international resources.[17] The real cost of capital flows for a capital exporter is defined as the income foregone through the outflow in the light of alternative possible uses of the same funds. For a capital importer, the real benefit is the net increase in income made possible by investing the capital inflow, as compared with investing the same amount of capital from other sources. The weighting problem for the various types of aid is handled by using the concept of a 'grant equivalent'. A grant is taken to have a 100 per cent grant equivalent. In the case of loans, annuity tables give the net present value of the flows generated by repayment; the difference between the amount of the loan and the present value is the grant equivalent.[18] That is to say, the grant equivalent of a loan measures the difference between the rate of return in the best alternative market and the return on the actual loan. The grant equivalent will be a higher proportion of the face value of a loan, the more the market rate of interest exceeds the interest rate on the

[14] J. A. Pincus, 'The Cost of Foreign Aid', *Review of Economics and Statistics*, November 1963, and *Economic Aid and International Cost Sharing* (Baltimore, 1965).

[15] The IBRD rate and the 7 per cent rate do not lead to such a straightforward interpretation. They are used to express loans on a common basis for purposes of comparison. For further use of Pincus' approach, see Little and Clifford, *International Aid*, ch. 2; H. G. Johnson, *Economic Policies toward Less-Developed Countries* (Washington, D.C., 1967), ch. 4.

[16] W. E. Schmidt, 'The Economics of Charity: Loans Versus Grants', *Journal of Political Economy*, August 1964, p. 389. Schmidt's formula for the present value of the donor's cost of loans is $L[1 - (p/y)][1 - (1+y)^{-n}](1+z)$, where L = the face value of the loan, p = the interest rate on the loan, y = the domestic rate of return on capital in the benefactor nation, n = the duration of the loan, and z = the effect on real income through changes in the terms of trade per dollar of receipt or payment (p. 394).

[17] J. A. Pincus, *Costs and Benefits of Aid: An Empirical Analysis*, UNCTAD New Delhi Conference, TD/7/Supp. 10 (New York, 26 October 1967).

[18] Industrial firms, banks and insurance companies make wide use of annuity tables to find the net present value of future cash flows. See P. M. Hummel and C. L. Seeback, *Mathematics of Finance* (London, 1956); A. J. Merrit and A. Sykes, *The Finance and Analysis of Capital Projects* (London, 1963); *Capital Budgeting and Company Finance* (London, 1966).

loan, and the longer the loan's grace and amortization periods. If the market rate of interest is equal to the loanr ate, then the present value will be equal to the amount of the loan and the grant equivalent will be zero. If the market rate of interest is lower than the loan rate, then the cost to the lender is negative, although the benefit to the borrower may be positive.

In terms of this technique, Pincus calculates the real cost of aid to donors as the sum of the following items: grants, including technical assistance, at nominal value; loans (on whatever terms and conditions) valued at the difference between nominal value and the present value of repayment, with the discount rate reflecting the market rate of return on long-term capital investment; PL 480 transfers valued at world market prices; other sales or loans repayable in non-convertible currency, valued as grants. For purposes of discounting, three rates of interest are used: the lender's domestic long-term interest rate, ranging from 4.9 to 8 per cent; the IBRD borrowing rate, ranging from 4.0 to 5.6 per cent; and the rate of return which private investors in the lending country demand in order to make equity investments in developing countries, a rate assumed to be 10 per cent.[19]

It remains to note some of the main limitations of the real cost approach to aid measurement. For one thing, there is considerable arbitrariness in the rate of discount assumed for the donor and the recipient; in the extreme case, some countries might not be able to attract lenders on any terms. Secondly, while the real cost approach takes into account differences in interest rates, it overlooks the real value of foreign exchange; and differences in foreign exchange value may well be far more significant than those in interest rates. Thirdly, the tying of aid may also be a much more significant factor than interest rate differences; and aid-tying could mean a drastic reduction in real cost to the donor.[20]

In short, recent efforts to measure the real transfer of resources to developing countries have made solid progress. However, there is much room for improvement and refinement. It is very clear that the real transfers have, in fact, been less than the nominal ones; but the techniques for precise measurement have yet to be developed.

[19] Goran Ohlin uses a slightly different approach to estimate the 'grant element'. For long-term loans with a grace period, he employs the following formula:

$$s = \left(1 - \frac{i}{q}\right)\left(1 - \frac{e^{-qG} - e^{-qT}}{q(T-G)}\right),$$

where s = the grant element as a share of the face value, i = the rate of interest, q = the rate of discount, G = the grace period, and T = maturity. Ohlin, *Foreign Aid Policies*, pp. 101–5. See also OECD, *The Flow of Financial Resources to Less-Developed Countries, 1961–1965* (Paris, 1967), ch. 6 and annex 1; *Development Assistance: Efforts and Policies of the Members of the Development Assistance Committee, 1968 Review* (Paris, 1968), annex II, and *1969 Review*, pp. 76–80 and annex v.

[20] Pincus takes tied aid into account in calculating real benetfi to the recipient, but not in real cost to the donor. Pincus, *Costs and Benefits of Aid*, pp. 32–7.

Appendix 2
Trends in output of selected manufacturing industries in Pakistan, 1950-65

SOURCES: Pakistan Ministry of Finance, *Pakistan Economic Survey, 1965–66* (Rawalpindi, 1966), statistical section, pp. 2, 3, 18–20; Pakistan Central Statistical Office.

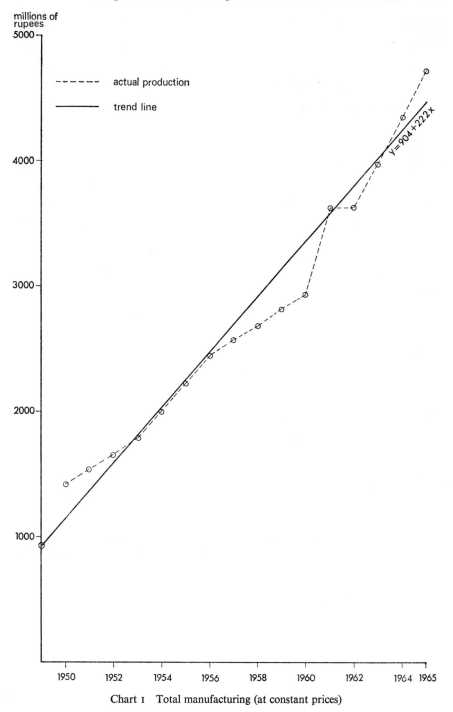

Chart I   Total manufacturing (at constant prices)

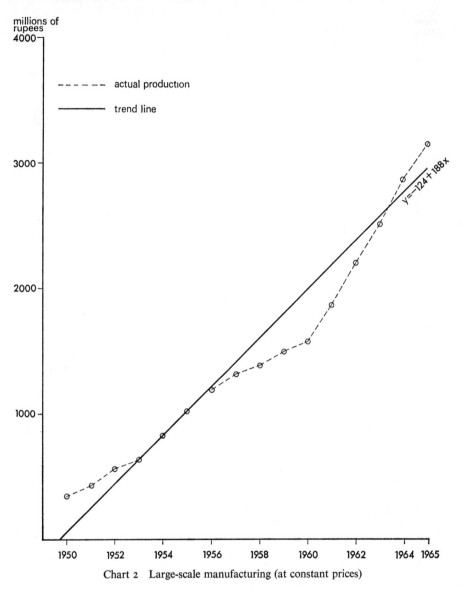

Chart 2   Large-scale manufacturing (at constant prices)

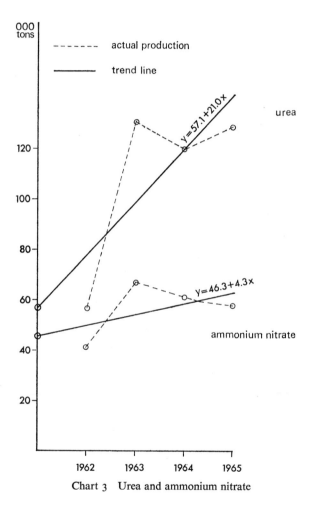

Chart 3   Urea and ammonium nitrate

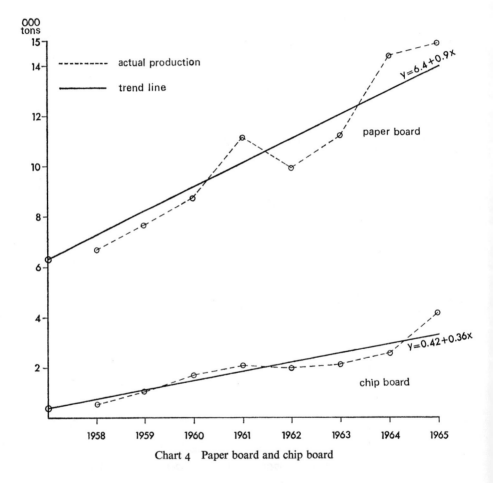

000
tons

actual production

trend line

$y=6.4+0.9x$

paper board

$y=0.42+0.36x$

chip board

Chart 4   Paper board and chip board

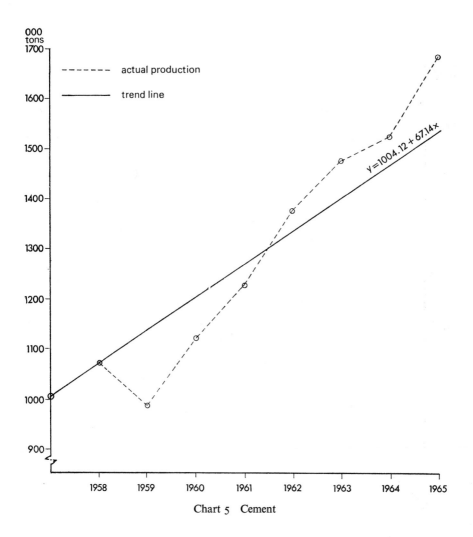

Chart 5   Cement

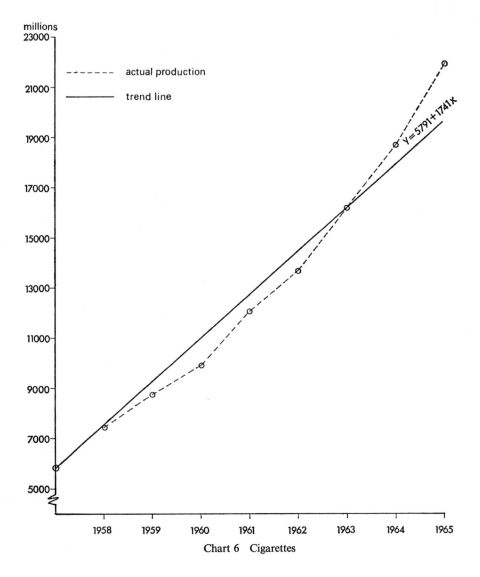

Chart 6   Cigarettes

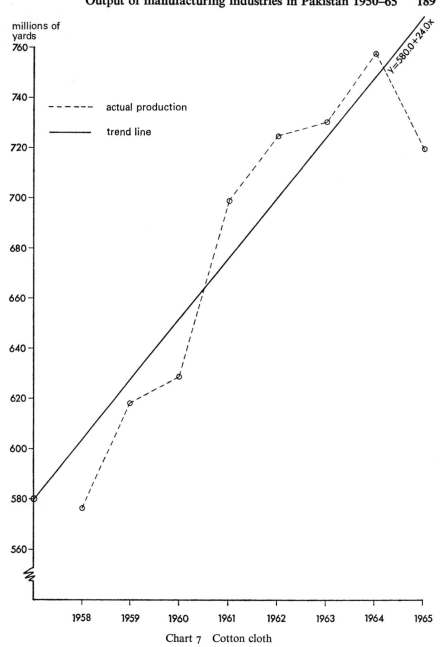

Chart 7   Cotton cloth

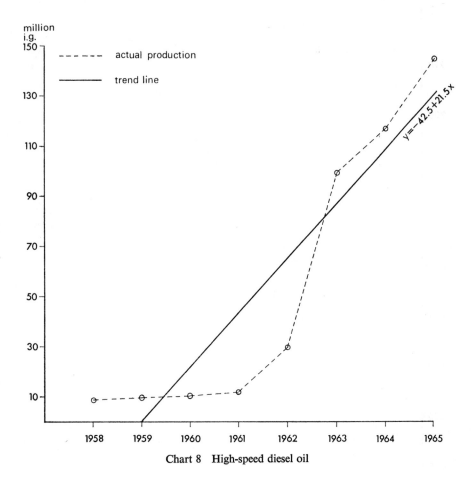

Chart 8   High-speed diesel oil

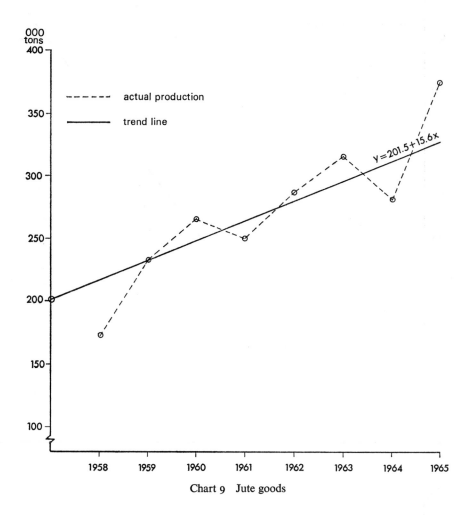

Chart 9   Jute goods

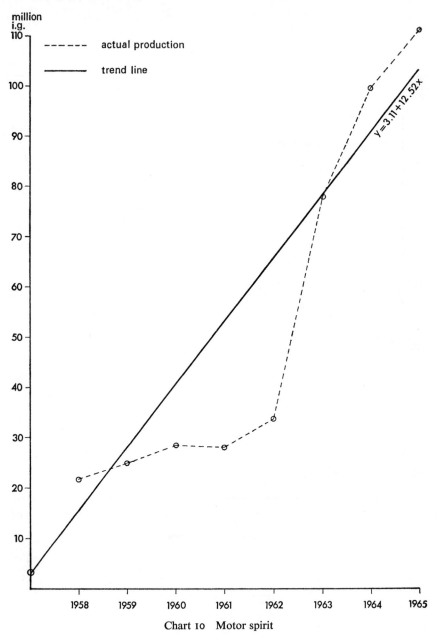

Chart 10   Motor spirit

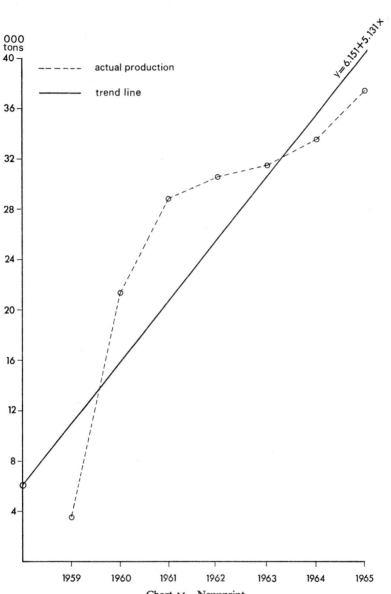

Chart 11   Newsprint

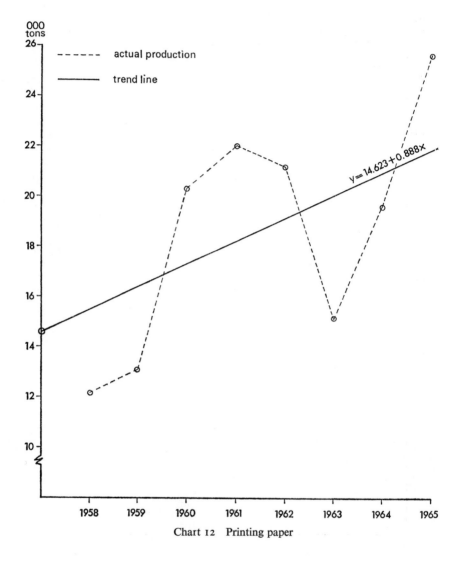

Chart 12   Printing paper

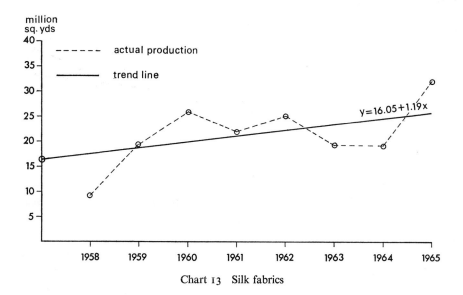

Chart 13 Silk fabrics

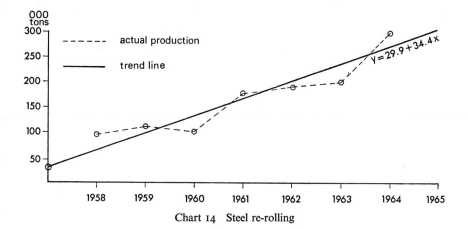

Chart 14 Steel re-rolling

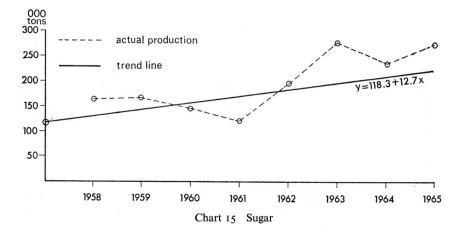

Chart 15   Sugar

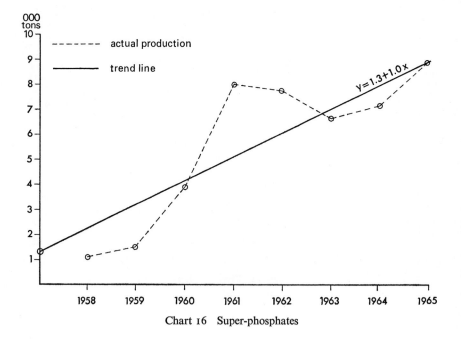

Chart 16   Super-phosphates

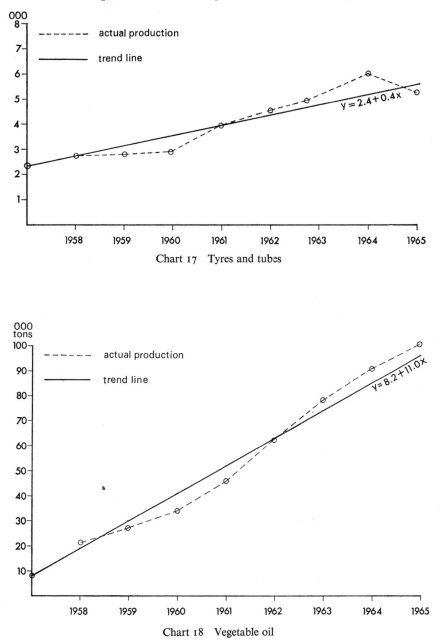

Chart 17   Tyres and tubes

Chart 18   Vegetable oil

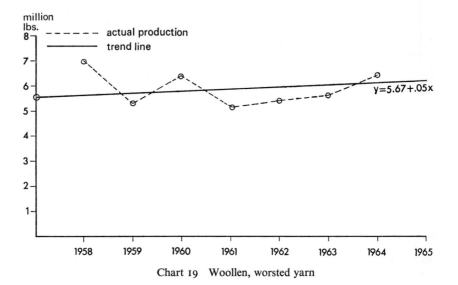

Chart 19   Woollen, worsted yarn

Appendix 3
Foreign aid requirements: a critique of aid projections with special reference to Pakistan*

It has become fashionable, during the past decade, to study the problem of foreign aid in terms of projection of aid requirements. Foreign aid is typically justified in the donor countries as a commitment to achieve a specific development objective having a finite cost. For the developing countries, on the other hand, the 'requirements' approach helps to focus attention on the inadequacy of the existing levels of foreign aid and gives concrete shape to their demands for more assistance.[1]

While projections have served a useful purpose by indicating the broad orders of magnitude of aid requirements and suggesting some criteria for aid allocation, they are, by their very nature, based on a number of simplifying assumptions about the behaviour of certain key relationships in the economy. Savings, import substitution and the choice of technology cannot really be treated as independent of the volume and form of foreign assistance. The limitations of aid projections, which generally do so, are obvious to those who make them and those who use them. Justification for the continuing interest in such estimates lies in the *ceteris paribus* assumption so commonly made in economic analysis. By the same token, one must exercise substantial caution in drawing policy conclusions from those estimates.[2]

It is, indeed, worth underscoring the fact that projection results vary a great deal, depending on the methodology used and on assumptions regarding the basic parameters of the economy. This appendix surveys the application of various methodologies of aid projection to the specific case of Pakistan. The analysis shows that long-term projections help in charting the course of development and highlight key elements in the economic situation which would maximize the return on aid flows from the donor's and recipient's point of view (given an identity of interests). But such projections are usually couched in terms of net inflows and so ignore the disturbing influence of debt servicing; gross flows required are so large that projected net inflows become somewhat unreal. Moreover, recent experience in Pakistan confirms that the 'aid requirements' concept has to be interpreted very flexibly with respect to policy variables which are assumed constant in most of the models. Curtailment of aid in the latter part of the 1960s has produced a Pakistan response which is not directly in accord with expectations resting on the aid requirements approach. The decline

---

* Dr Moin Baqai, Joint Secretary of the Pakistan Economic Co-ordination and External Assistance Division, has contributed extensively to this appendix and shares the responsibilities of co-authorship. However, the views expressed here are in no way related to his official position.
[1] Typically, aid projections include private foreign investment as part of total foreign assistance required by developing countries. These totals are misleading to the extent that such investment moves in response to profit or market incentives.
[2] For a cogent criticism of aid projections, see J. A. Pincus, *Trade, Aid and Development: The Rich and Poor Nations* (New York, 1967), pp. 297–305.

in aid flows has not led to a decline in the rate of growth, but rather to a change in the strategy and sectoral balance of development. Although it is by no means certain that the long-range effects of reduced investment will be entirely offset by a permanent improvement in the capital–output ratio, this opens up a whole new dimension in the discussion of foreign aid.

General approaches to aid projection

The estimates of foreign aid requirements made thus far can be classified as follows: global, regional or national estimates in terms of the 'savings–investment gap';[3] projections based on 'absorptive capacity';[4] and measures of the 'trade gap'.[5] There have also been efforts to combine the different approaches in a 'development stages' analysis,[6] and through concentration on the 'dominant gap'.[7]

More specifically, aid requirements are often projected in terms of a savings–investment gap which is related to a target growth rate corrected for special problems in the foreign trade sector. The target growth rate is set in the light of alternative assumptions regarding absorptive capacity. Investment needs of the economy are worked out for the target growth rate on the basis of explicit or implicit assumptions about capital–output ratios. Savings are projected on the basis of historical or policy-determined behaviour of the marginal rate of savings. The amount by which projected savings fall short of projected investment indicates the gap which foreign assistance is required to fill, that is, the aid requirements inherent in the target growth rate. Problems of foreign exchange are assumed away, since in a simple Keynesian model there is an identity between the savings–investment and export–import gaps.

This ex post identity of the two gaps is, of course, a mere tautology. The ex ante difference between the gaps can be bridged by a process which frustrates the basic objective of maximum growth. Despite the equality of the two gaps in an accounting sense, therefore, it is important to distinguish between them for purposes of economic

---

[3] This is the earliest approach and can be attributed to work done for and by the United Nations; see, for instance, UN, *Measures for the Economic Development of Underdeveloped Countries* (New York, 1951). For more recent formulations, see P. N. Rosenstein-Rodan, 'International Aid for Underdeveloped Countries', *Review of Economics and Statistics*, May, 1961; J. Tinbergen, *Shaping the World Economy* (New York, 1962).

[4] M. F. Millikan and W. W. Rostow, *A Proposal, Key to An Effective Foreign Policy* (New York, 1957). Absorptive capacity is no longer regarded as a major constraint, except in fixing the target growth rate. 'Competent observers suggest that only a minority of developing countries are growing at the maximum rates which their absorptive capacity could permit.' UNCTAD, *Trade Prospects and Capital Needs of Developing Countries* (New Delhi, 1968), pp. 1–2.

[5] B. Balassa, *Trade Prospects for Developing Countries* (Homewood, Ill., 1964). For obvious reasons, this approach has been of major importance in the two UNCTAD Conferences and throughout the family of UN organizations. See also UN, *World Economic Survey, 1962* (New York, 1963).

[6] H. B. Chenery and A. M. Strout, 'Foreign Assistance and Economic Development', *American Economic Review*, September 1966.

[7] The 'dominant gap' has been used by US AID (Summer Project). UNCTAD considers it the most desirable approach but finds it impracticable in view of the limitations of data; instead, UNCTAD aggregates the trade gaps of individual countries – producing a total which is somewhat smaller than the sum of the dominant trade and saving gaps (UNCTAD, *Trade Prospects*). For a recent estimate based on the dominant gap analysis, see Institute of Asian Economic Affairs, *Intra-Regional Cooperation and Aid in Asian Countries* (Tokyo, 1968).

policy. In fact, there is little or no ground for believing that domestic and foreign resources are perfectly interchangeable, and that domestic savings are readily convertible into productive capacity either directly or through foreign trade.

Critics of the 'two-gap' theory point out that an export–import gap persistently larger than the savings–investment gap implies permanence of domestic inflationary pressures. However, this line of argument ignores the structural problems of the balance of payments in a dynamic context, as well as the imperfections of international trading relations. Assuming a small domestic capacity for producing capital goods, savings (in terms of foregone consumption) can be converted into capital goods only through international trade, and then only – for many developing countries – through less favourable terms of trade. Low demand and supply elasticities for a sizable portion of their exports render it unlikely that the required adjustment in balance of payments would be completed without restricting growth. In other words, 'the equality of the two gaps is likely to be bought at the price of economic contraction. If there is an import surplus without inflation, some domestic producers are losing money and will have to cut back if the surplus persists. Therefore,...projections of the trade gap that diverge from the savings gap simply present a realistic view.'[8]

There is, then, considerable justification for projecting aid requirements on the basis of a trade gap which is higher than the savings gap – except, perhaps, in the case of oil-exporting countries. This is also consistent with giving a unique role to foreign aid in the process of development. If aid is to be regarded as a unique factor of production, the need for it cannot be projected merely by concentrating attention on the savings–investment gap. On the other hand, it is important to realize that divergence between the savings and trade gaps may be at least partly amenable to policy manipulation within the developing country. The exchange rate, the level of domestic savings, the allocation of investment to different sectors – all of these are subject to internal influence, and all can affect the degree of divergence between the two gaps. To accept the numbers emerging from fixed relationships would be to frustrate a major purpose of foreign aid projection, namely, the encouragement of remedial policies in the developing countries.

Hollis Chenery and Alan Strout have attempted to fit the gap analysis into an integrated model.[9] They distinguish between three stages of economic growth in terms of broad constraints on the development process: the stage where low levels of skill and organizational ability act as the prime constraint; the stage where a shortage of domestic savings limits growth; and the stage in which the export–import gap is the limiting factor. This model can help to guide the evolution of a developing country's policies over time. It is especially relevant for Pakistan, where the Perspective Plan appears to have been moulded by the 'stages' system.

[8] Pincus, *Trade, Aid and Development*, p. 301. See also R. F. Mikesell, *The Economics of Foreign Aid* (Chicago, 1968), pp. 91–7. For a sceptical view of the two gaps, see H. J. Bruton, 'The Two Gap Approach to Aid and Development: Comment', *American Economic Review*, June 1969. But see H. B. Chenery, 'The Two Gap Approach to Aid and Development: A Reply to Bruton', *American Economic Review*, June 1969.

[9] Chenery and Strout, 'Foreign Assistance'. For a critical review of the Chenery–Strout model, see J. C. H. Fei and G. Ranis, 'Foreign Assistance and Economic Development: Comment', *American Economic Review*, September 1968.

The Perspective Plan

Any discussion of aid requirement projection for Pakistan must start from an analysis of the Perspective Plan.[10] It represents the first authoritative national effort to fix definite long-run growth targets and to project aid requirements in terms of a 'dual-gap' model.

The plan aimed at quadrupling national income over the twenty-year period 1965–85 by setting the target growth rate at 7.2 per cent per annum – a significant acceleration over the 5.4 per cent realized during the Second Five-Year Plan and the 3.5 per cent over the period 1950–65. Investment was to change only gradually in relation to GNP, from 18.4 per cent in 1965 to 22.9 per cent in 1985. The capital–output ratio was assumed virtually constant, showing only slight variations around 2.9. These parameters made sense in terms of the fact that investment in 1965 included sizable expenditures on the Indus Basin Replacement Works. After these infra-structure projects were completed, gross investment would reflect a larger advance in national production. The capital–output ratio could, therefore, be kept low – bearing in mind the self-imposed investment constraint that reliance on foreign aid be eliminated by 1985.

The savings–investment gap was to be bridged by 1985 through a high marginal rate of savings. Estimated at 22 per cent of GNP for the base period, incremental savings would climb to 28 per cent by 1980; this was construed more as a policy directive than as a simple projection. Between 1980 and 1985, the marginal savings rate would decline to 25 per cent, as the foreign exchange constraint would operate to restrict investment.

Foreign exchange requirements would grow in absolute terms up to 1970 and would reach a plateau at the level of Rs. 4 billion (1965 prices) in the early seventies, falling sharply after 1975. As a ratio of GNP, the net inflow of foreign resources would begin declining by the end of the sixties; this would mark a reversal of the trend between 1958 and 1965, when aid inflows had risen from about 4 per cent to 8 per cent of GNP. In summary terms:

'Up to the end of the Second Plan the gap between imports and exports was increasing, necessitating an increase in the flow of foreign assistance. From the Third Plan period the gap will start narrowing and the need for foreign assistance will start diminishing. The strategy for achieving this shift will be to increase exports at a rate faster than imports. Over the Perspective Plan period, exports are expected to increase at nearly twice the rate of increase in imports with the obvious implication that Pakistan's own earnings will start financing an increasing proportion of total imports.'[11]

The most distinctive feature of the Perspective Plan is its self-imposed constraint that dependence on aid should be eliminated over a pre-determined period without any sudden or abrupt shock to the growth process. In this sense, the plan presents a blueprint for 'minimum aid requirements' or 'maximum austerity'.

Interestingly enough, the plan has been criticized both for its emphasis on an

[10] Pakistan Planning Commission, *The Third Five-Year Plan, 1965–70* (Karachi, 1965), pp. 17–37.
[11] *Ibid.* p. 23. The growth of exports was projected at 7.9 per cent per annum, as against a 4.2 per cent increase for imports.

early termination of foreign aid and for its reliance on too much aid over the twenty-year period. The former line of criticism is based on welfare criteria, while the latter stems from deep concern with the problem of debt-servicing. Hollis Chenery and Arthur MacEwan – applying a modified version of the more general Chenery–Strout model to Pakistan – point out that Pakistan's planners are sacrificing economic welfare by means of a self-imposed constraint on foreign aid.[12] Anisur Rahman, on the other hand, has emphasized the debt-servicing legacy which the Perspective Plan would leave even with the self-limiting demand for foreign aid.[13]

The Chenery–MacEwan model

Chenery and MacEwan approach the optimum pattern of aid and growth as a problem in linear programming. The objective is to maximize a social welfare function incorporating the benefits (consumption) and costs (capital inflow) of economic growth. The constraints are stated in terms of policy goals and of definitional, structural and behavioural relationships for each time period.

GNP (V_t) and investment (I_t) are disaggregated into 'regular production' and 'trade improvement' sectors. Foreign aid, defined as the net inflow of external resources (F_t), is used to fill the trade gap determined by the excess of demand for 'traditional imports' over the sales of 'traditional exports' adjusted for the output of the trade improvement sector. Traditional exports are assumed to grow at an exogenously determined rate and can be produced at the capital–output ratio of regular production. However, production for trade improvement requires a higher capital–output ratio. The requirements of traditional imports are determined by a base year import level and marginal import rates related to income and investment levels. The savings rate is determined by base year savings and the marginal savings ratio. While recognizing the influence of public policy on the marginal rate of savings and marginal import rates, the model assumes both as given.

The model thus seeks to determine the requirements of foreign assistance by maximizing the general welfare function:

$$W = \sum_{t=1}^{T} \frac{C_t}{(1+i)^t} + \eta V_t - \gamma \sum_{t=1}^{T} \frac{F_t}{(1+i)^t},$$

where

$$\eta = \delta(1-\alpha) \sum_{t=1}^{\infty} \frac{(1+\rho)^t}{(1+r)^{T+t}}$$

and i is the discount rate during the Perspective Plan, r the discount rate after the plan, α the marginal savings rate, ρ the post-plan self-sustaining rate of growth, and γ the price of foreign capital. The first term of the function indicates the discounted sum of consumption (C) prior to the terminal year (T) of the Perspective Plan. The second term shows the discounted value of consumption in all years after the plan, with a variable weight (δ) attached. And the final term (with the minus sign) represents the discounted sum of total capital inflows weighted by the price of foreign capital.

[12] H. B. Chenery and A. MacEwan, 'Optimal Patterns of Growth and Aid: The Case of Pakistan', *Pakistan Development Review*, Summer 1966.

[13] See, for example, M. A. Rahman, 'The Pakistan Perspective Plan and the Objective of Elimination of Dependence on Foreign Assistance', *Pakistan Development Review*, Autumn 1967. For a more general treatment of the debt service implications of foreign assistance, see G. Ohlin, *Aid and Indebtedness: The Relation between Aid Requirements, Terms of Assistance and Indebtedness of Developing Countries* (Paris, 1966).

Table 3.1. *Projections of net capital requirements for Pakistan (in billions of rupees at 1965 prices)*

	Chenery–MacEwan basic solution	Perspective Plan		Chenery–MacEwan basic solution	Perspective Plan
1963	1.41	—	1974	7.18	—
1964	1.67	—	1975	8.21	4.00
1965	1.97	3.69	1976	9.37	—
1966	2.30	—	1977	9.44	—
1967	2.68	—	1978	7.55	—
1968	3.11	—	1979	5.67	—
1969	3.59	—	1980	3.78	2.50
1970	4.15	4.19	1981	1.89	—
1971	4.77	—	1982	—	—
1972	5.48	—	1985	—	2.00
1973	6.28	—			

SOURCES: H. B. Chenery and A. MacEwan, 'Optimal Patterns of Growth and Aid: The Case of Pakistan', *Pakistan Development Review*, Summer 1966, p. 241; Pakistan Planning Commission, *The Third Five-Year Plan, 1965–70* (Karachi, 1965), p. 19.

The supply constraint is specified in a number of ways. In the 'basic solution', it takes the form of either the price of foreign capital or its terminal date $(T-n)$ being specified. In an alternative presentation, an upper limit is fixed on the total quantity of aid to be received. Still another set of solutions is based on the constraint that capital inflow cannot exceed a given proportion of GNP (5 per cent). Subsequent discussion refers largely to the basic solution.

The model projects 1962 data (averages derived from 1957–62) to 1965 for purposes of comparison with the Perspective Plan. Aid flows provide the major difference in base year estimates: the Chenery–MacEwan figure is Rs. 1.97 billion (1965 prices), as against the plan estimate of Rs. 3.69 billion. There is a corresponding difference in total investment, but the other variables are quite close. The marginal propensity to import is assumed to be 0.10, as against the plan's 0.06, for 1965–85; by contrast, the assumed rate of export growth is 4.9 per cent, as against 7.9 per cent in the plan; the other parameters are not significantly different.

Chenery and MacEwan suggest a sharp acceleration in aid inflow up to 1975. Starting with a 1965 level of foreign assistance about half that of the plan, they project the same ratio of aid to GNP by 1970, namely, 7 per cent; this, of course, represents a deceleration from the 1965 plan figure of 8 per cent. The model suggests a further rise to 10 per cent by 1975, while the plan projects a continued decline to 4 per cent. In the final decade, there is a sharper drop in the model than in the plan: 'This pattern of rising and then falling aid is a logical consequence of the high value of early increases in investment, income and saving for future growth. [Indeed,] if the restriction on the rate of increase in investment were not imposed, the peaking of aid in the early years would be even more pronounced.'[14]

The Chenery–MacEwan and Perspective Plan estimates of net capital inflow are

[14] Chenery and MacEwan, 'Optimal Patterns of Growth and Aid', p. 226.

compared in Table 3.1. Total aid needs are higher in the model because it assumes that 'trade improvements will require substantially more capital than is indicated by the marginal coefficient of 3.0 that has been experienced recently'.[15]

An interesting conclusion drawn from the model is that the optimal growth strategy in the first phase – that is, when investment is rising most rapidly – is not dependent on the total aid to be provided. For the specific case of Pakistan, 'optimum policy until 1969 would be the same either with the aid expected in the Basic Solution or with half that much'.[16]

Thus the main task in the first phase is to ensure that an economy expands at the rate permitted by its absorptive capacity. This condition for optimization is independent of the total availability of aid. Growth strategy in the early years, therefore, should stress short-term criteria rather than those of a long-run nature. It is in subsequent years that total aid becomes crucial; and it should depend on performance, as reflected in the marginal rate of savings. Chenery and MacEwan criticize Pakistan not only for imposing a terminal date on aid inflow, but also (implicitly) for seeking an earlier deceleration of aid than would be warranted by economic criteria.

Rahman and the cost of foreign aid

Rahman has examined the aid implications of both the Chenery–MacEwan model and the Perspective Plan.[17] The two major issues that emerge from his analysis are the impact of aid availability on domestic savings and the debt-servicing legacy left by foreign assistance.

In the models discussed earlier, it is assumed that aid-receiving countries will make maximum use of domestic savings. Rahman questions this assumption. Given the availability of foreign assistance at an interest rate below the economic rate in the recipient country, demand for foreign aid will, he argues, far exceed minimum requirements. Under such conditions, aid will be used not only to speed up economic growth, but also directly to increase consumption; hence the lack of proper emphasis on savings effort in domestic policies. One must recognize this as a possibility, even though foreign assistance is often provided under institutional arrangements which link the aid flow with domestic savings effort; and despite the fact that most of the aid models have been developed with a view to establishing the basic need for relating foreign assistance to domestic performance.[18] Rahman uses the argument about savings to emphasize an alternative strategy: once the costs of foreign aid are deemed too high (and it is to be relied upon less than the optimum solution of Chenery–MacEwan or the more restrained Perspective Plan suggests), the only way out for the developing country is to make a more concerted effort to increase domestic savings.

[15] *Ibid.* p. 234.

[16] *Ibid.*

[17] See particularly M. A. Rahman, 'Foreign Capital and Domestic Savings: A Test of Haavelmo's Hypothesis with Cross-Country Data', *Review of Economics and Statistics*, February 1968.

[18] There seems little doubt that the quantum of total aid per capita, or as a proportion of GNP, in the receiving country has generally been determined more by political relations between donor and recipient than by the recipient's economic performance. On the other hand, Pakistan's experience in the 1960s points to a close positive correlation between domestic savings and foreign aid inflows; see L. B. Pearson et al., *Partners in Development: Report of the Commission on International Development* (New York, 1969), p. 314.

Debt-servicing is implicitly included in the earlier models since aid inflows are treated there on a net basis. But as already noted, the result is a distorted picture of aid requirements. The need to service foreign debt is a cost of aid flows which is considered explicitly in Rahman's model. In part, this is motivated by a non-economic concern with national pride and with the power that dependence on foreign aid places in the hands of donor countries.

Retaining the Perspective Plan's assumption that net aid inflows would cease by 1985, Rahman derives an estimate of gross aid inflow required at that time merely to service the accumulated debt. Assuming, further, that foreign loans will be available throughout the plan period at the concessional interest rate of 3 per cent per annum, he projects total external indebtedness in 1985 at Rs. 103.9 billion. Gross capital inflow would have to rise from Rs. 4 billion in 1965 to about Rs. 8 billion in 1985, mainly to allow continued debt-servicing. If the terms of assistance prove less favourable during the plan period, the required gross inflow in 1985 would be even larger.

Rahman finds such capital inflows particularly objectionable in the light of the non-economic costs of foreign aid.

'Assuming the United States will continue to be, as it is today, the major supplier of foreign assistance for a significant period after the present Perspective Plan terminates, it is important to understand that a continuous dependence on United States foreign assistance should be expected to require from the recipient country pursuance of national and international economic and political policies that agree with the United States *official* views on *United States* social interest. This may or may not agree with the social interests of the recipient country. For Pakistan in particular a commitment of its future indefinitely to aid from the United States or for that matter from any great power may mean the surrender of significant areas of economic and political policy in which it might want to retain its autonomy. Even if the present society considered such price worth paying, it should be debated whether it is ethical to bind, by the bequest of a liability of the magnitude in question, future societies to the same set of values as ruling today.'[19]

Accordingly, the Rahman view is that from the recipient country's standpoint, it is better to plan for 'self-assured growth' (SAG) than for 'self-sustaining growth' (SSG).

He constructs a linear two-sector model, similar to Chenery–MacEwan, in order to derive the terminal (consistency) conditions which must be satisfied if an economy is to reach the state of Self-Assured Growth at the end of a 'Perspective Plan' of T years. SAG differs from SSG mainly in terms of the total absence of debt-servicing liability at the termination of the plan. While there is no net inflow of foreign resources in SSG, the country would require considerable borrowing to repay the debt in the years following termination of the plan. SAG, by contrast, requires a country to emerge as a net exporter of capital before the termination of the plan; that is to say, the net inflow of foreign assistance has to be terminated earlier than for SSG.

Rahman notes that SAG does not necessarily mean complete stoppage in the flow of foreign capital. While concessional foreign finance would be discontinued, 'there is no reason why a continuous further flow of foreign finance at prevailing market

[19] M. A. Rahman, 'Perspective Planning for Self-Assured Growth: An Approach to Foreign Capital from a Recipient's Point of View', *Pakistan Development Review*, Spring 1968, p. 5.

terms should not be considered as a purely business proposition'.[20] Such financing would be appropriate as long as it was offered at a rate of return not exceeding the marginal output–capital ratio in import substitution; and provided that an appropriate proportion of the additional investment was allocated to the import substitution sector.

In fact, import substitution plays a crucial role in the Rahman model. It is desirable to use foreign assistance beyond a certain stage only if opportunities for profitable import substitution exist; and the need for such opportunities arises earlier than in the other models. By the same token, this model is highly restrictive in cases where the size of the market limits profitable investment in import substitution.

Be that as it may, Rahman is questioning the entire approach of projecting aid requirements on the basis of welfare maximization through discounted consumption flows. Borrowing early is very productive in the Chenery–MacEwan model; but to Rahman it has a large legacy of financial indebtedness and social cost.

In these terms, substantial constraints on 'aid requirements' are necessary for Pakistan if the debt burden is to be kept within tolerable limits at the end of the twenty-year perspective plan period. And the plan's more modest aid projections are to be preferred to those of the Chenery–MacEwan model.

Pakistani planners have never made their reasons for self-restraint explicit. There must be a subjective element which Rahman associates with the 'psychic disutility' of aid or national pride; probably, there is also a concern for 'inter-generational equity'.[21] But the most compelling reason for restraint may well be a sense of realism.

Rahman argues that the gross flow of assistance required to smooth out the net flow in $T21$, the year after the Perspective Plan is completed, will be too large to be easily available. However, the gross flow needed in that year would not be much larger than in year $T20$ or $T19$. If the gross aid flow during the plan period is sufficient to meet the net aid requirements of the plan, then post-plan requirements of assistance are also likely to be met. The real question is whether aid of the magnitude projected in the plan and in the other models is realistic. None of them faces directly up to this issue.

Nevertheless, there appears to be a growing desire, in Pakistan's planning circles, for a self-imposed constraint in the form of maximum debt-servicing liability – that is, a growing readiness to cut the demand for aid if its price is not reduced. This is a stronger constraint than that imposed in the Perspective Plan. While the plan assumed a perfectly elastic supply of foreign aid, this no longer seems to be the prevailing official view in Pakistan.[22]

The Tims model

The projection of aid requirements by Wouter Tims differs in important respects from the other attempts discussed in this appendix.[23] In fact, Tims is not specifically

[20] *Ibid.* p. 17.
[21] M. A. Rahman, 'The Welfare Economics of Foreign Aid', *Pakistan Development Review*, Summer 1967, pp. 142–7.
[22] For a grim assessment of the international climate for foreign assistance, see Pakistan Planning Commission, *Socio-Economic Objectives of the Fourth Five-Year Plan (1970–75)* (Islamabad, 1968), pp. 14–15.
[23] W. Tims, *Analytical Techniques for Development Planning: A Case Study of Pakistan's Third Five-Year Plan (1965–70)* (Karachi, 1968). See also A. R. Khan, '"Analytical Techniques for Development Planning": A Review of Tims' Multisector Model for Pakistan's Third Plan (1965–70)', *Pakistan Development Review*, Summer 1968.

measuring aid requirements in his model. This is only part of a more comprehensive planning exercise which allows him to vary the composition of investment and growth, and to manipulate aid requirements accordingly. Foreign aid needs are projected on the basis of a more concrete approach than is possible in global studies. The time horizon, however, is limited to five years; Tims could not go beyond that period and still derive meaningful results within the comprehensive structural and policy framework he adopted.

Tims' estimates reflect many of the key assumptions and policy variables which have influenced Pakistan's own projections of its aid requirements. These estimates also point up significant questions that are not considered in long-term aid projections. Use is made of the dual-gap analysis, but the ex ante gaps are not accepted as final; policy measures are suggested for bridging the difference between them.

The national product is disaggregated into seven groups of commodities and services, and Tims specifies a set of consistent inter-industry relations among production, consumption and trade in each of the sectors. He also determines the levels of GNP, gross investment, exports, imports, and external assistance corresponding to each solution. Then, given the aggregate and detailed figures for 1964/5, he poses the question what changes must occur in Pakistan by 1969/70 if the targets of the Third Five-Year Plan are to be achieved.

On the assumption that GNP increases as projected in the plan and that a known fraction of this income is saved, an estimate of gross domestic savings is obtained. The savings–investment gap is calculated by measuring the difference between the resources needed and those available domestically. Assuming that the plan's targets for agricultural production will be realized, Tims deducts the domestic absorption of these goods from total production to derive the exportable farm surplus; total export earnings are obtained by adding the plan's estimate of exports for the other sectors. Total imports are calculated as the sum of import requirements for consumption, intermediate and capital goods. The foreign exchange or trade gap measures the difference between earnings and requirements of foreign exchange.

By solving the simultaneous equations of the model, Tims obtains a savings–investment gap of Rs. 3.7 billion and a trade gap of Rs. 5.3 billion in 1969/70. He then works out the amount of extra import substitution which must be undertaken to equalize the two gaps.

Tims treats the question of import substitution in considerable depth. 'The Third Plan model itself does not provide any help in this respect, as its only outcome is a total import-substitution requirement to be realized by 1970. Since the feasibility of the development plan as a whole depends to such a large extent on the degree to which it can be demonstrated that a sufficient level of import substitution can be achieved, it was considered necessary to study this problem in much greater detail.'[24] A modified version of Tinbergen's semi-input–output method is used to determine the feasibility and cost of the required import substitution. This implies, as a first step, the determination of all final demand autonomously. Production requirements in all sectors are then determined. No selection of sectors for import substitution is made at this stage; they all expand in parallel fashion without it. The choice of sectors is carried out as the next step, on the basis of the composition of intermediate goods imports projected for 1970.

[24] Tims, *Analytical Techniques*, p. 141.

Through a process of elimination in terms of technical possibilities and the time span and scale of operation required for constructing domestic production units, Tims comes to the conclusion that there are three major industries with sizable import substitution potential, namely, cement, oil refining and iron and steel. He is able to demonstrate that the needed substitution is feasible without creating extra demand for investment. 'This is, however, to a considerable extent the result of a specific composition of the import bill, where a small number of commodities have a large share in the total foreign-exchange costs.'[25] Import substitution over a longer period might not present the same economic possibilities. Priority would have to be given to the development of industries which provide substantial economies of scale.

The UNCTAD II projections

For its 1968 New Delhi Conference, UNCTAD projected global aid requirements on the basis of a series of individual country studies including Pakistan.[26] The estimates focus on the trade gap, although it is acknowledged that in a number of developing countries (notably in Africa) the savings gap is more important at the present stage of development.

The period of projection extends to 1975, and the basic relations are derived from trends up to 1963. The low assumption for the target growth rate is 5.2 per cent per annum, and the high assumption 6.1 per cent; these growth rates determine the level of imports required over the period. For the export projections, growth rates in the developed countries are assumed to be between 4.2 and 4.7 per cent.

The trade gap of the developing countries (measured in 1960 prices) is projected at between $17 billion and $26 billion in 1975, depending upon the various combinations of high and low assumed growth rates in the developed and developing countries. The gap arises largely from payments on account of investment income; net payments of the developing countries are projected to reach $12 to $14 billion by 1975, or roughly between half and three-quarters of the total gap.

UNCTAD notes that part of the gap could possibly be reduced by policy adjustments, within the developing countries, to accelerate import substitution and export expansion. However, given the strong constraints on both export growth and import substitution, not more than $8 billion can be expected to be available through such measures. The required inflow of foreign capital is, therefore, placed at $18 billion, of which $5 billion can be expected from private investment; this leaves $13 billion as the level of foreign assistance needed by 1975.

For Pakistan, the UNCTAD projections are made in terms of a low growth rate of 5.0 per cent and a high rate of 5.7 per cent; these derive from historical coefficients based on the country's experience from 1957 to 1963. By contrast, the growth assumptions of the Perspective Plan and other Pakistan projections take into account the experience of 1960–5. Those second plan years were different enough from the earlier period to lend support to the belief of some observers that a break in the trend occurred at the end of the 1950s. However, it is difficult to judge, on the basis of such limited experience, whether a higher or lower growth rate is more realistic. Suffice it to note

[25] *Ibid.* p. 165.
[26] UNCTAD, *Trade Prospects*, especially annex IV, p. 24; *Trade Prospects and Capital Needs of Developing Countries* (New York, 1968), pp. 356–65.

that the UNCTAD projections assume no acceleration over the growth rates already attained in Pakistan.

With the low growth rate of 5 per cent, the savings–investment gap turns out to be quite small – $91 million. Even on the higher growth assumptions, the savings gap would be only $422 million, indicating the possibility of reduced Pakistani dependence on foreign aid as against the levels prevailing in the mid-1960s. But the import–export gap would be much larger: import requirements are projected on the basis of a marginal propensity to import of 0.21, and the export growth rate is assumed to be 7.1 per cent per annum; the resulting import surplus is $1.2 billion to $1.5 billion (Rs. 5.8 billion to Rs. 7.0 billion).

This UNCTAD trade gap excludes net factor income payments (like debt-servicing). The aid requirement figures are thus in terms of net inflow and are comparable with the projections discussed earlier (except Rahman's). Adjusting the figures to 1965 prices, the higher estimate is close to the Chenery–MacEwan projection for 1975, and much higher than Pakistan's own estimates.[27]

Concluding comments

To sum up, Pakistan's requirements of foreign assistance have been projected in a variety of ways. Most of the estimates are surprisingly close, ranging from $1.2 billion to $1.7 billion for 1975. Pakistan itself has proposed to restrict its need for aid to about half that level. This lower estimate is based partly on an assumed improvement in basic parameters as suggested by the behaviour of the economy in 1960–5; the other estimates rely on earlier experience. However, to a large extent, the difference lies in the rather heroic assumptions made in the Perspective Plan about import substitution and export growth. The truth probably lies somewhere in between these two sets of projections.[28]

In any event, recent developments in international aid relations have diverted the attention of Pakistan's planners from the rather abstract aid requirement projections to a more practical programming of available assistance. The requirements approach, it is argued, is no longer realistic in view of the pressures developing in major aid-giving countries to reduce aid commitments irrespective of needs. Since the amounts which can be justified on requirements criteria are not forthcoming and since the aid actually available does not have to be justified in terms of specific need, the real problem of aid management is to make the maximum use of available resources. A certain degree of fatalism about the future of foreign assistance is combined with a determination

[27] In *Intra-Regional Cooperation*, pp. 149–50, the Institute of Asian Economic Affairs projects the same level of aid requirements as UNCTAD, namely, $1.2 to 1.5 billion for 1975. Target growth rates assumed by the institute are higher (5.40 per cent and 6.73 per cent per annum), while the marginal propensity to import is lower (0.18).

[28] The implications of alternative Pakistan projections have been discussed in detail by the Expert Group on the Uses of Analytical Techniques, established in December 1964 by the DAC of the OECD. The Expert Group does not seem to have made any independent projections on aid requirements. Its deliberations on particular countries are unpublished and have had a restricted circulation. See, for example, OECD Development Assistance Committee, 'A Trial Application of the Uses of Analytical Techniques in Framing Assistance Policies (Case Study of Pakistan): Proceedings of a Joint Meeting of the Working Party on Assistance Requirements of the Development Assistance Committee and of its Expert Group on the Uses of Analytical Techniques, 9th and 10th December, 1965', unpublished mimeo. (Paris, 25 November 1966).

to protect the growth of the economy from the adverse effects of declining aid flows.

Even year-to-year projections are made for the Consortium with a 'tongue-in-cheek' approach. Needs are first presented on the basis of commodity aid requirements as determined by input–output relationships and an assumed growth rate; fertilizer for agriculture figures prominently at this stage; projects are then listed, and this typically pushes total aid requirements above $600 million. However, in the final presentation, the request is scaled down to a level which is considered realistic and which leaves some margin for aid diplomacy. In this context, while shortfalls in fresh aid pledges are shown against plan needs, longer-term aid requirements are seldom even mentioned.

Prime emphasis now appears to be placed on projections of debt-servicing liability. This may be only a reflection of the current mood of despondency regarding prospects for foreign assistance. However, the belief seems to be developing that continued borrowing on present average terms could force Pakistan into a position where default on debt service became inevitable. Hence, if aid terms are not improved, there should be greater self-restraint in seeking fresh loans from abroad. In any case, after two or three years of seeking to replace concessional assistance from the Consortium by export credit-type loans from Eastern Europe, there appears to be a growing concern with aid content rather than with the volume of aid flows.

An alternative solution to the debt-servicing problem is, of course, an acceleration of the gross flows of assistance. While such an approach has not been considered seriously for some time, the McNamara plan for a World Bank initiative seems to attempt just that.[29] A massive increase in IBRD lending at interest rates determined by borrowing rates in the developed countries' markets would be tantamount to shelving the debt service problem in favour of maintaining the volume of assistance. That is to say, the problem of debt service would be postponed to a later stage. Pakistan may have to reconsider its thinking on net aid flows and debt-servicing in the light of such developments.

In the meantime, changes in domestic policies have been initiated which confirm the view that the parameters on which aid requirements are based are also variable within a range. The new priority for agriculture and a much greater emphasis on better utilization of industrial capacity are manifestations of this new strategy. As a result, the capital–output ratio is no longer regarded as fixed; it becomes a variable function of domestic policy and growth strategy. The Planning Commission is quite explicit on the new approach: 'The main focus of these revisions in the [Third] Plan priorities is to secure the desired acceleration in the growth of the economy with a lower level of total investment.'[30]

To be fair, it cannot be uncritically assumed that Pakistan would not have given added weight to agriculture in a more favourable aid climate. Emphasis had, in fact, been shifting towards agriculture since the early 1960s, when the discovery of sweet sub-soil water opened up possibilities of rapid growth in West Pakistan based on tube-well irrigation. The discovery of 'miracle seeds' for wheat and rice extended

[29] Address to the Annual Meeting of the World Bank (30 September 1968), *The New York Times*, 1 October 1968, p. 58. See also the *Pearson Report*.

[30] Pakistan Planning Commission, *Revised Phasing, Sectoral Priorities and Allocations of the Third Five-Year Plan (1965–70)* (March 1967), appended to *The Third Five-Year Plan, 1965–70* (Karachi, 1965), pp. 2–3.

this opportunity"of spreading growth impulses from cash crops to foodgrains. While the rate of advance of the new food technology may have been influenced at the margin by the aid squeeze, there is every reason to believe that its adoption was not chiefly a response to the availability of less foreign assistance. At the same time, it must be pointed out that a short-term decline in the capital–output ratio is not a guarantee that long-term functional relationships between foreign aid, domestic investment and economic growth have changed. There is, indeed, evidence to suggest that certain sectors of Pakistan's economy have been denied needed resources in the process of adjustment to restricted aid flows; and that capital–output ratios may well rise in the next phase of development.

Much of the adjustment has been healthy, to be sure. While the official (overvalued) exchange rate has not been altered, the pricing of foreign currency has been made more realistic. In fact, the weighted average of exchange rates in use under the multiple exchange rate system has changed significantly in recent years. The combined effect of additional taxes on imports, remissions on exports, and improvements in the bonus voucher system has been a substantial correction of the Pakistan rupee's external value.

Where the applicable exchange rate is still high (as in the import of capital goods), arbitrary 'shadow pricing' is used to economize in imports and to encourage import substitution. During the second plan period, the private sector had been allowed to set up industrial capacity to the extent determined by private profitability; and both profitability and excess capacity were induced by an overvalued rate of exchange. During the Third Plan, sanctions for setting up additional capacity in the private sector have been more selectively linked with export and agricultural growth targets; industries are ranked in terms of their impact on the balance of payments, and priorities are redefined in accordance with this objective.

But the increasing emphasis on import substitution may involve considerable cost. In the short run, as Tims has pointed out, there is wide scope for relatively efficient displacement of imports; large concentrations of demand are available in cement and petro-chemicals, for example. However, in the long run, the burden of forced import substitution is likely to be heavy in terms of both the cost of actual development and the growth potential remaining unutilized. This would be especially so to the degree that such substitution is carried out at the expense of more efficient production for export.

Nor is this all. A large number of pressing current problems are bound to persist well into the future – wide regional economic disparities, inadequate human resource development, a highly unequal distribution of income, to name only a few. Coping with such problems will be no less difficult than urgent.

It seems reasonable, nonetheless, to conclude that with the 'house-cleaning' carried out during the period of foreign aid restriction, Pakistan is better equipped today to make efficient use of aid than ever before. Aid requirements can probably be projected on the assumption of more favourable parameters. A given volume of assistance can now be more productive. But continued growth of aid and better terms appear vital if the pace of advance is to be maintained and its economic cost to be minimized.

Appendix 4
Detailed statistics on foreign aid to Pakistan, 1950–67

Table 4.1. *Aid commitments to Pakistan during the Second Five-Year Plan (millions of dollars)*

Country/aid-giving agency	1960/1	1961/2	1962/3	1963/4	1964/5	Total[b]	% Contribution
United States[a]	115.4	95.9	211.9	223.1	252.6	898.9	45.6
West Germany	17.4	34.0	94.5	42.0	28.1	216.0	10.9
IDA	—	21.0	11.5	142.7	32.3	207.5	10.5
Japan	20.6	20.0	37.9	30.0	35.0	143.5	7.3
United Kingdom	22.4	19.6	32.9	19.2	30.2	124.3	6.3
IBRD	15.0	—	43.0	62.0	—	120.0	6.1
Canada	17.4	18.8	16.9	14.4	14.6	82.1	4.2
USSR	30.0	—	—	11.0	—	41.0	2.1
Yugoslavia	—	—	4.8	10.3	15.0	30.1	1.5
France	—	—	—	7.8	17.6	25.4	1.3
Netherlands	—	—	—	1.1	10.8	11.9	0.6
Switzerland	—	—	—	10.0	—	10.0	0.5
IFC	—	4.0	—	—	5.5	9.5	0.5
Denmark	—	—	—	—	7.4	7.4	0.4
Australia and New Zealand	1.3	1.4	1.4	1.8	0.6	6.5	0.3
Italy	—	—	—	3.0	1.6	4.6	0.2
TOTAL	239.5	214.7	454.8	579.3	451.3	1938.7	98.3[c]

SOURCE: Pakistan Planning Commission, *Memorandum for the Pakistan Consortium, 1966–67* (Karachi, 1966), pp. 108–10.

[a] Includes Export–Import Bank but excludes PL 480 assistance.
[b] Includes project and commodity aid but excludes contributions to Indus Basin Development Fund.
[c] The remaining 1.7 % is accounted for by suppliers' credits, which bring total aid commitments to $1,972,000,000.

Table 4.2. *Selected aid flows to Pakistan, 1950–67: sectora allocations (US dollars)*[a]

Donor	Agriculture[b]	Power and irrigation	Communication and transportation	Natural resources	Health, welfare and education	Industry	Commodities[c]	Multi-purpose
United States								
DLF	—	128,112,821	44,045,348	—	3,771,537	26,322,727	—	17,941,545
AID	—	139,980,000	108,299,574	250,000	14,454,848	—	656,810,715	18,000,000
Cooley		—				14,469,630		
Grants	25,950,000	150,311,000	35,427,000	7,755,000	83,205,000	28,598,800	15,000,000	19,456,000
Eximbank			29,910,413			23,293,200		88,000,000
Canada								
Loans		64,140,426			—	5,765,016	—	
Grants		67,498,896	2,669,556	10,389,505	1,977,919	7,709,237	100,919,136	
United Kingdom	6,447,901	34,472,796	63,911,100		3,622,236	86,622,546	38,621,650	478,171
France		16,087,075	3,333,630	1,568,616		40,521,794		
West Germany		48,661,768	108,026,467			119,133,747	37,750,000	
Japan		10,471,298	15,936,267	839,996		185,128,095	19,541,029	
USSR	19,116,603	13,531,751	8,750,911			5,887,089		
Yugoslavia		15,779,243	21,383,151	30,000,000		21,327,781		
China							36,932,432	30,000,000
IBRD	3,000,000	170,669,780	138,126,259			113,006,240		
IDA	46,200,000	87,790,000	82,735,648		57,750,000	6,500,000	50,000,000	
IFC						14,099,705		
TOTAL	100,714,504	947,506,854	662,555,324	50,803,117	164,781,540	698,385,607	955,574,962	173,875,716

SOURCES: Pakistan, *Report of the Working Group on Debt Burden* (Islamabad, 1968), pp. 99–151; US AID Information Office, *Fact Sheet* (Karachi, 1965); US AID, *Pakistan's Economic Development and United States Assistance* (Karachi, 1967); K. Spicer, *A Samaritan State? External Aid in Canada's Foreign Policy* (Toronto, 1966); CIDA, *Annual Review, 1967–68* (Ottawa, 1968). Also, unpublished data provided by: Overseas Development Institute Ltd, London; IBRD, IDA and AID, Washington, DC.

[a] Some grants are not included because information on their allocation by sectors is incomplete. Also, sectoral lines are often difficult to draw.

[b] Excludes US assistance under PL 480.

[c] Non-project aid going mainly to the 'industry' sector.

Sectoral flows (by specification)

Table 4.3. *Agriculture* (*US dollars*)

	Date of agreement	Commitment
United States – grants		
Acquisition and Distribution of Fertilizer	30. vi. 1952	10,565,000
Locust Control	15. iv. 1953	58,000
Ground Water Exploration	27. vi. 1953	188,000
Soil and Water Conservation, range and pasture	25. xii. 1953	53,000
Ground Water Survey – West Pakistan	28. ii. 1954	4,399,000
Agriculture Workshops	10. iii. 1954	1,026,000
Soil and Water Conservation (Baluchistan and Solba)	27. iii. 1954	77,000
Modern Storage of Foodgrains	30. iv. 1954	125,000
Agriculture Development	30. vi. 1954	2,301,000
Plant Protection	30. vi. 1954	753,000
Soil and Water Conservation	30. vi. 1954	494,000
Agricultural Development	25. xi. 1954	2,286,000
Agriculture Research and Demonstration	31. iii. 1955	1,012,000
Water Resources Advisory Services	19. iv. 1955	134,000
Soil Mechanics and Hydraulic Laboratory	23. iv. 1955	163,000
Agriculture and Production	31. vii. 1959	607,000
Animal Husbandry	21. vii. 1960	17,000
Agriculture Extension	31. vii. 1960	272,000
Agriculture Organization – East Pakistan	1. vii. 1963	760,000
Agriculture Area Development – West Pakistan	1. vii. 1964	660,000
	Total (US)	*25,950,000*

Table 4.3. (*cont.*)

	Date of agreement	Commitment
United Kingdom – credits		
Grow More Food Scheme (GOP)[a]	2. iii. 1954	8,400
Heavy Earth-moving Machinery for Reclamation of Land in West Pakistan (WPWAPDA)	27. ii. 1959	644,049
Mechanical Cultivation and Power Pump Irrigation (EPADC)	27. ii. 1959	1,383,965
Pesticide Spraying and Dusting Equipment (GOP)	27. ii. 1959	1,589,858
Reorganization of Horticulture in West Pakistan (GOWP)	27. ii. 1959	21,629
East Pakistan Tube-wells Project (EPWAPDA)	28. xii. 1960	2,800,000
	Total (UK)	*6,447,901*
USSR – export credits		
Import of Heavy Earth-moving Machinery and Rotary and Drilling Machine (WPADC)	17. vi. 1964	11,000,000
Soan Valley Land Improvement Project (WPADC)	25. viii. 1965	1,680,000
Bull-dozers for Land Development in West Pakistan (GOWP)	11. iv. 1966	6,436,603
	Total (USSR)	*19,116,603*
IBRD – loan		
Punjab Agricultural Machinery Project (GOWP – TDA)	13. vi. 1952	3,000,000
IDA – credits		
Development of Agriculture (ADB)	30. vi. 1965	27,000,000
Foodgrain Storage Project, East Pakistan (GOEP – Food Department)	10. ii. 1966	19,200,000
	Total (IDA)	*46,200,000*

[a] The name of the organization receiving the loan or credit appears in parentheses throughout this appendix.

Table 4.4. *Power and irrigation (US dollars)*

	Date of agreement	Commitment
United States – US DLF		
High Tension Grid (WPWAPDA)	18. ii. 1959	11,838,206
Waterlogging and Salinity (SCARP 1) (WPWAPDA)	18. ii. 1959	14,963,315
Secondary Transmission Line (WPWAPDA)	29. vi. 1959	21,681,488
Sui Gas Transmission (1st) (SGTC)	19. ii. 1960	1,993,694
Indus Basin Scheme (WPWAPDA)	19. ix. 1960	70,000,000
Dredger Fleet (EPWAPDA)	14. vi. 1961	2,300,000
Quetta Thermal Power Station (WPWAPDA)	14. vi. 1961	5,336,118
	Total (DLF)	*128,112,821*

Table 4.4. (*cont.*)

	Date of agreement	Commitment
United States – AID loans		
Power Distribution (EPWAPDA)	22. x. 1962	8,600,000
Karachi Power Station 'C' (KESC)	2. xi. 1962	18,900,000
Waterlogging and Salinity (SCARP No. 2-A) (WPWAPDA)	22. iii. 1963	10,800,000
Coastal Embankment (EPWAPDA)	15. viii. 1963	4,330,000
Mechanical Equipment Organization (EPWAPDA)	20. xi. 1963	1,500,000
Machinery Pool Organization (EPWAPDA)	9. xii. 1963	5,000,000
SCARP No. 1 – Operations and Maintenance (GOWP)	31. i. 1964	750,000
Lyallpur Power Station (WPWAPDA)	10. vii. 1964	18,000,000
Sui Gas Purification Plant (3rd)	16. vii. 1964	2,700,000
Sidhirganj Power Station (EPWAPDA)	28. viii. 1964	8,500,000
Karnaphuli (3rd unit) (EPWAPDA)	4. ix. 1964	3,800,000
Two Transmission Lines (WPWAPDA)	17. ix. 1964	2,800,000
Urban Water Supplies (DPH)	17. ix. 1964	3,600,000
Karachi Power Distribution (KESC)	16. x. 1964	7,200,000
Machinery Pool (2nd) (WPWAPDA)	9. xii. 1964	6,000,000
Power Distribution (WPWAPDA)	30. xii. 1964	12,500,000
Mangla Dam Transmission Lines (WPWAPDA)	19. i. 1966	8,200,000
Sui Gas (4th)	21. ii. 1966	2,700,000
SCARP No. 2-B (WPWAPDA)	30. xii. 1966	14,100,000
	Total (AID)	*139,980,000*
United States – grants		
Bolan Dam	1. iv. 1953	75,000
Ganges Kabadak Irrigation	30. i. 1954	1,978,000
Taunsa Barrage	22. ii. 1954	5,894,000
Makhi Dand Reclamation	29. iii. 1956	820,000
Indus Basin	1956–1966	138,000,000
Multan Power Transmission	30. vi. 1957	3,365,000
Power Commission	28. v. 1962	176,000
Karachi Electric Supply Corp.	1. vii. 1964	3,000
	Total (grants)	*150,311,000*
	Total (US)	*418,403,821*

Table 4.4. (*cont.*)

	Date of agreement	Commitment
Canada – loans (US dollars)		
Isolated Power and Distribution (EPWAPDA)	12. vi. 1963	5,550,000
Isolated Power and Distribution (EPWAPDA)	9. viii. 1965	4,902,500
Karachi Nuclear Power Station (PAEC)	29. xii. 1965	44,437,926
East-West Interconnector (EPWAPDA)	17. iii. 1967	9,250,000
Total (loans, US dollars)		*64,140,426*
Canada – grants (Cdn dollars)		
Warsak Hydro-electric and Irrigation Project	1952–9	37,757,518
Shadiwal Hydro-electric Power Development	1953–8	3,126,820
Ganges-Kabadak Project, Thermal Plant for Irrigation Pumps	1954–5	2,592,963
Dacca–Chittagong–Karnaphuli Transmission Line	1954–9	5,769,620
Goalpara Thermal Station, Khulna	1955–6	2,062,610
Bheramara–Ishurdi–Goalpara Transmission Line	1957–63	4,400,000
Sukkur Thermal Power Plant	1958–64	11,415,000
Comilla–Sylhet Transmission Line	1961–3	5,100,000
Sangu Multi-purpose Scheme	1961–3	355,000
Total (grants, Cdn dollars)		*72,579,531*
Total (grants, US dollars)		*67,498,896[a]*
Total (Canada, US dollars)		*131,639,322*

[a] All sectoral grant totals for Canada were converted at the current rate of exchange. This represents an understatement of the US value of Canadian grants, since over most of the period covered the Canadian dollar had a higher external value than it did at the time of writing.

Table 4.4. (*cont.*)

	Date of agreement	Commitment
United Kingdom – credits		
Dergai Hydro-electric Station (WPWAPDA)	2. iii. 1954	453,600
Ghulam Mohammad Barrage (WPWAPDA)	2. iii. 1954	252,000
Guddu Barrage (WPWAPDA)	2. iii. 1954	1,033,200
Irrigation Works in Sind Food Growing Areas (GOP)	2. iii. 1954	14,000
Lyallpur Thermal Station (WPWAPDA)	2. iii. 1954	728,000
Malakand Hydro-electric Station (WPWAPDA)	2. iii. 1954	2,800
Montgomery (Sahiwal) Power House (WPWAPDA)	2. iii. 1954	84,000
Other Electricity Schemes (GOWP)	2. iii. 1954	652,400
Rasul Hydro-electric Station (WPWAPDA)	2. iii. 1954	44,800
Ravi–Marala Links (WPWAPDA)	2. iii. 1954	36,400
Sidhirganj Thermal Station	2. iii. 1954	2,497,600
Warsak Hydro-electric Power Station (WPWAPDA)	2. iii. 1954	358,400
West Pakistan Grid (WPWAPDA)	2. iii. 1954	61,600
Chattak Gas Transmission Line and Equipment (EPIDC)	27. ii. 1959	31,064
Colonization of Ghulam Mohammad Barrage (WPADC)	27. ii. 1959	2,447,578
Lower Sind (Hyderabad) Thermal Scheme (WPWAPDA)	27. ii 1959	97,444
Machinery Pool – Ghulam Mohammad Barrage (WPWAPDA)	27. ii. 1959	1,160,467
Secondary Transmission (EPWAPDA)	27. ii. 1959	1,624,059
Sui Multan Gas Distribution (WPIDC)	27. ii. 1959	33,630
Sukkur–Guddu Reclamation Project (Salinity Control and Waterlogging in Sind) (WPWAPDA)	27. ii. 1959	664,738
Thal Development Project (WPADC)	27. ii. 1959	1,024,216
Electric and Machinery Workshops (EPWAPDA)	8. i. 1962	700,000
Machinery Pool (WPWAPDA)	8. i. 1962	1,400,000
Lower Sind Thermal Scheme (WPWAPDA)	5. xi. 1962	2,699,200
Electric Traction between Lahore and Khanewal Link (PWR)	19. ii. 1965	131,600
Railway Electrification (PWR)	23. vi. 1966	16,240,000
	Total (UK)	*34,472,796*

Table 4.4. (*cont.*)

	Date of agreement	Commitment
France – export credits		
Consultancy Agreement for Power Distribution in Kushtia and Khulna (EPWAPDA)	1. x. 1963	93,578
Installation of Oil Tanks at Chittagong, Pakistan National Oils Ltd (IDBP)	x./xi. 1963	2,779,116
Power Distribution in Kushtia and Khulna (EPWAPDA)	24. vi. 1964	32,813
Two 15,000 KW Gas Turbines at Kotri, Hyderabad (WPWAPDA)	11. vi. 1966	3,436,073
Four 15,000 KW Gas Turbines for Shahjibazar Power Station, Sylhet (EPWAPDA)	30. vii. 1966	7,675,185
Khulna and Kushtia Power Distribution Project (EPWAPDA)	4. viii. 1966	1,520,627
Supplementary Contract	21. i. 1967	549,683
	Total (France)	*16,087,075*
West Germany – capital aid		
Salinity Control and Reclamation of Lower Thal (WPWAPDA)	25. v. 1965	6,750,000
Multan-Lyallpur 2nd Circuit (WPWAPDA)	8. ii. 1966	1,625,000
Ashuganj Power Station (EPWAPDA)	13. x. 1966	17,000,000
West Germany – export credits		
Multan Power Station (WPWAPDA)	31. xii. 1960	16,246,250
Tube-wells (EPWAPDA)	27. iii. 1962	4,504,000
Tube-wells (EPWAPDA)	28. i. 1965	2,536,518
	Total (Germany)	*48,661,768*
Japan – yen credits		
Electric Equipment Pool (EPWAPDA)	13. xi. 1961	1,999,864
Electric Equipment Pool (EPWAPDA)	15. iii. 1963	2,198,955
Electric Equipment Pool (EPWAPDA)	5. x. 1964	806,958
Turbo Generator for Karachi Nuclear Power Plant (PAEC)	5. x. 1964	666,667
Mangla Power Generation (WPWAPDA)	6. vi. 1966	2,100,000
Turbo Generator for Karachi Nuclear Power Plant (PAEC)	6. vi. 1966	2,698,854
	Total (Japan)	*10,471,298*

Table 4.4. (*cont.*)

	Date of agreement	Commitment
USSR – export credits		
Equipment for EPWAPDA Projects	3. xii. 1965	735,015
110 MW Natural Gas Power Station, Ghorasal (EPWAPDA)	3. vi. 1966	12,796,736
	Total (USSR)	*13,531,751*
Yugoslavia – export credits		
SCARP No. III, Lower Thal Doab, Alipur Unit (WPWAPDA)	30. vi. 1965 and 19. xi. 1966	2,651,937
Rural Electrification (EPWAPDA)	21. vi. 1966	5,752,056
Rural Electrification (EPWAPDA)	16. ii. 1967	4,498,102
Construction and Electrification of 580 Tube-wells Project (WPWAPDA)	21. vi. 1967	2,877,148
	Total (Yugoslavia)	*15,779,243*
IBRD – loans		
Pipeline – Sui Gas Transmission Co. (SGTC)	2. vi. 1954	14,000,000
Karachi Power Project (KESC)	20. vi. 1955	13,776,585
Karachi Power Project (KESC)	23. iv. 1958	13,995,946
Karachi Power Project (KESC)	13. viii. 1959	2,397,249
Indus Basin Replacement Works (WPWAPDA)	19. ix. 1960	90,000,000
Northern Gas Pipeline (SNGP)	14. v. 1964	15,000,000
Karachi Power Generation and Distribution (KESC)	15. iii. 1967	21,500,000
	Total (IBRD)	*170,669,780*
IDA – credits		
Dacca–Demra Irrigation Project (EPWAPDA)	19. x. 1961	1,000,000
Salinity Control and Reclamation, Khairpur Area (WPWAPDA)	29. vi. 1962	18,000,000
Brahmaputra Flood Project (EPWAPDA)	26. vi. 1963	5,000,000
Chandpur Irrigation Project (EPWAPDA)	26. vii. 1963	5,250,000
Indus Basin Project (WPWAPDA)	21. vii. 1964	58,540,000
	Total (IDA)	*87,790,000*

Table 4.5. *Communication and transportation (US dollars)*

	Date of agreement	Commitment
United States – DLF		
1st Railways Loan (PWR)	18. ii. 1959	9,019,400
Improvement of Chittagong Port (1st) (CPT)	10. vii. 1959	1,890,759
East Pakistan Inland Waterways – Navigational Aids (IWTA)	12. ix. 1959	1,719,994
Karachi Jet Runway (DGCA)	11. xi. 1959	3,045,130
2nd Railways Loan (PER/PWR)	16. i. 1960	21,870,695
3rd Railways Loan (PWR)	14. vi. 1961	6,499,370
	Total DLF	*44,045,348*
United States – AID loans		
4th Railway Loan	10. ix. 1962	30,290,125
Airport/Airways Service Equipment (DGCA)	22. iii. 1963	1,779,449
Chalna Anchorage Project (DGP & S)	22. iii. 1963	3,600,000
Telecommunication Facilities (T & T)	23. x. 1963	4,700,000
5th Railway Loan	20. xi. 1963	14,500,000
Chittagong Port Project (GOEP/CPT)	14. x. 1964	3,400,000
Dacca–Aricha Road (GOEP)	11. i. 1965	14,000,000
Railway Improvements (PER)	16. iv. 1965	8,700,000
Improvement of Railways (PWR)	23. iv. 1965	7,530,000
PWR Diesel Locomotives (PWR)	22. i. 1966	4,800,000
Lahore–Multan Road (C & WS)	4. v. 1966	15,000,000
	Total AID	*108,299,574*
United States – grants		
East Pakistan Roads Development	17. iii. 1952	1,331,000
Aviation Ground Facilities	28. ii. 1955	5,204,000
Baluchistan State Union Road Development	31. iii. 1955	763,000
West Pakistan Diesel Locomotive School	9. iv. 1955	134,000
Development of Civil Air Transport	30. iv. 1955	4,512,000
Highway Research and Development	30. vi. 1955	140,000
Aircraft Overhaul and Maintenance	20. iv. 1956	261,000
Development of North Western Railway Production Shop	1. v. 1956	26,000
East Pakistan Diesel Locomotive School	31. v. 1956	85,000
Pakistan Regional Transit Facilities	30. vi. 1956	7,566,000
Rehabilitation of Pakistan Railways	30. vi. 1956	14,672,000
Transport Survey – East Pakistan	30. vi. 1960	371,000
Transport Survey – West Pakistan	30. vi. 1961	354,000
Improvement of Pakistan Highway	30. vi. 1965	8,000
	Total (grants)	*35,427,000*
United States – Eximbank		
Aircraft (PIA)	31. i. 1958	2,827,000
Boeing 720-B Aircraft (PIA)	10. iv. 1962	12,100,000
Railway Improvements (PER/PWR)	16. xi. 1962	11,900,000
Helicopters (PIA)	24. viii. 1963	3,083,413
	Total (Eximbank)	*29,910,413*
	Total (US)	*217,682,335*
Canada – grants (Cdn dollars)		
Railway Ties	1951–2	2,770,490
Karachi Port Trust Equipment	1963–4	100,000
	Total (Canada, Cdn $)	*2,870,490*
	Total (Canada, US $)	*2,669,556*

Table 4.5. (*cont.*)

	Date of agreement	Commitment
United Kingdom – credits		
Chittagong Port (CPT)	2. iii. 1954	2,937,200
Railway Improvements (PWR)	2. iii. 1954	14,014,000
Roads (GOP)	2. iii. 1954	509,600
Replacement of Old Ships (IDBP)	27. ii. 1959	5,203,500
Improvement of Railways (PER/PWR)	16. iii. 1961	8,400,000
Buses (WPRTC)	8. i. 1962	2,100,000
Dredger (KPT)	8. i. 1962	2,884,000
Telegraph and Telephone Department Stores (T & T)	8. i. 1962	700,000
Buses (EPRTC)	5. xi. 1962	439,600
Improvement of Railways (PER)	5. xi. 1962	5,460,000
Replacement of Old Ships (NSC)	5. xi. 1962	4,398,800
Improvement of Railways (PER)	25. ii. 1964	48,440
Railway Improvements (PWR)	25. ii. 1964	4,750,760
Railway Improvements (PWR)	25. ii. 1964	800,800
Replacement of Old Ships (NSC)	25. ii. 1964	2,940,000
Special (Ships) Credit (PICIC)	13. x. 1964	7,840,000
M.G. Carriages and Wagon Shop at Hyderabad (PWR)	23. xii. 1964	336,000
M.G. Carriages and Wagon Shop at Hyderabad (PWR)	12. viii. 1966	42,000
Equipment in connection with Electric Traction Project (T & T)	11. iv. 1967	106,400
	Total (UK)	*63,911,100*
France – export credits		
Off-shore Oil Terminal Chittagong (CPT)	17. ii. 1965	2,594,459
Storage and Distribution of Petroleum Products (IDBP)	2. iii. 1966	49,185
Instrument Landing System (DGCA)	14. i. 1967	689,986
	Total (France)	3,333,630
West Germany – capital aid		
Improvement of Railways (PER/PWR)	10. viii. 1962	13,065,000
Telecommunication Stores (T & T)	10. viii. 1962	6,200,000
East Pakistan Ferries (IWTA)	30. viii. 1962	2,750,000
Transport Buses for West Pakistan (WPRTC)	4. ix. 1962	2,500,000
Improvement of Railways (PER/PWR)	19. vi. 1963	9,360,000
Coastal Vessels (IWTA)	16. vii. 1963	4,500,000
Airport and Airways Equipment (DGCA)	3. ix. 1963	625,000
Landing Stages for Ferries (IWTA)	3. ix. 1963	1,000,000
Improvement of Railways (PER/PWR)	25. v. 1964	8,000,000
Repair Yard for Ferries (IWTA)	25. v. 1964	1,750,000
Telegraph and Telephone Stores (T & T)	25. v. 1964	3,500,000
Improvement of Railways (PWR/PER)	6. v. 1965	1,332,750
Telecommunication Equipment (T & T)	25. v. 1965	3,300,000
Special Credits for 3 New Ships (NSC)	30. xi. 1966	1,875,000
Telecommunication Equipment (T & T)	30. xi. 1966	7,742,250

Table 4.5. (*cont.*)

	Date of agreement	Commitment
West Germany – export credits		
Coaxial Cable (T & T)	15. ii. 1961	3,218,779
Railways (PER/PWR)	1. iii. 1962	6,447,112
Coaxial Cables (T & T)	21. iii. 1964 and	
	8. iv. 1964	1,023,838
Two Second-hand Ships (M.V. Padma and Karnaphuli) (NSC)	14. viii. 1964	3,167,500
One New Ship (M.V. Aziz Bhatti) (NSC)	28. xii. 1964	3,752,500
One New Ship (M.V. Sarfaraz Rafiqui) (NSC)	15. ix. 1965	3,810,625
88 Carriages (PWR)	4. iv. 1966	5,506,100
Telephone Industries of Pakistan, Haripur (T & T)	10. vi. 1966	1,679,075
Three Dry Cargo Motor Vessels (NSC)	12. vii. 1966	10,877,188
One Old Ship (M.V. Mellum) (NSC)	19. i. 1967	1,043,750
	Total (Germany)	*108, 026,467*
Japan – yen credits		
Self-propelled Floating Crane (KPT)	13. xi. 1961	1,101,997
T. & T. Department Equipment (T & T)	13. xi. 1961	2,151,230
T. & T. Department Equipment (T & T)	15. iii. 1963	500,110
T. & T. Department Equipment (T & T)	21. ix. 1963	1,899,966
Narayanganj Dockyard (EPIDC)	5. x. 1964	260,000
Pak-Nepal Tropospheric Scatter Microwave Line (T & T)	5. x. 1964	1,214,000
Telecommunication Equipment (T & T)	5. x. 1964	3,319,964
Two Television Stations (M/I & B)	5. x. 1964	2,400,000
Narayanganj Dockyard (EPIDC)	24. ii. 1967	49,000
Railway Sidings for Mymensingh and Shyamapur Sugar Mills (EPIDC)	24. ii. 1967	630,000
Telecommunication Equipment (T & T)	24. ii. 1967	2,410,000
	Total (Japan)	*15,936,267*
USSR – export credits		
Development of Airports (DGCA)	20. viii. 1965	3,105,967
Equipment for E.P. Roads and Highways (GOEP)	2. xii. 1965	3,096,670
Helicopter and Aviation Equipment (GOP)	30. xii. 1966	1,948,828
Purchase of Spares for Helicopter	28. v. 1967	599,446
	Total (USSR)	*8,750,911*
Yugoslavia – export credits		
Construction of a Ship at Karachi Shipyard and Engineering Works (WPIDC)	31. i. 1964	1,358,000
M.V. Chenab (NSC)	19. iii. 1964	2,958,340
Chittagong Shipway and Workshop (CPT)	30. vi. 1965	1,266,131
Construction of a Ship at Karachi Shipyard and Engineering Works (WPIDC)	21. v. 1966	1,600,200
Four New Ships (NSC)	25. x. 1966	14,200,480
	Total (Yugoslavia)	*21,383,151*

Table 4.5. (*cont.*)

	Date of agreement	Commitment
IBRD – loans		
Improvement of Railways (PER/PWR)	27. iii. 1952	27,000,000
Karachi Port Trust Wharves Project (KPT)	4. viii. 1955	14,700,754
Improvement of Railways (PER/PWR)	18. x. 1957	30,967,887
Improvement of Railways (PER/PWR)	30. xi. 1959	12,372,207
Improvement of Railways (PER/PWR)	14. ix. 1962	17,835,411
Improvement of Railways (PER/PWR)	14. ix. 1962	4,750,000
Karachi Port Improvements (KPT)	14. v. 1964	17,000,000
Improvement of Railways (PWR)	26. v. 1967	13,500,000
	Total (IBRD)	*138,126,259*
IDA – credits		
Inland Ports Project (IWTA)	22. xi. 1961	1,985,648
East Pakistan Highway Project (GOEP)	11. vi. 1964	22,500,000
West Pakistan Highway Project (GOWP)	11. vi. 1964	17,000,000
Improvement of Pakistan Eastern Railways (PER)	24. vi. 1964	10,000,000
Improvement of Pakistan Western Railways (PWR)	24. vi. 1964	25,000,000
Inland Water Transport Project (IWTA)	26. viii. 1964	5,250,000
Highway Engineering Project (GOWP – C & W Dept)	22. viii. 1966	1,000,000
	Total (IDA)	*82,735,648*

Table 4.6. *Natural resources (US dollars)*

	Date of agreement	Commitment
United States – AID loans		
Extraction and Conversion of Timber in Chittagong Hill Tracts (FIDC)	23. x. 1963	250,000
United States – grants		
Chittagong Timber Extraction	30. vi. 1952	650,000
Forestry Development	30. vi. 1952	725,000
Karachi Fish Harbour	9. iii. 1955	472,000
East Pakistan Fisheries Development	16. iii. 1955	177,000
West Pakistan Fisheries Development	16. iii. 1955	560,000
Mineral Exploration and Development	31. iii. 1956	3,648,000
Mkerwal Collieries	30. vi. 1956	1,022,000
Pakistan Fisheries Development	30. v. 1960	98,000
Forest and Range Management	1. vii. 1964	204,000
Forest Products – East Pakistan	1. vii. 1964	199,000
	Total (grants)	7,755,000
	Total (US)	*8,005,000*

Table 4.6. (*cont.*)

	Date of agreement	Commitment
Canada – grants (Cdn dollars)		
Thal Experimental Farm	1951–2	196,745
Aerial Resources Survey	1951–8	3,355,990
Pest Control – Aircraft, Trucks, Spray Equipment, Pesticides	1952–64	2,193,950
Hatching Eggs and Incubator	1954–5	3,106
Biological Control Station, Rawalpindi	1954–8	55,383
Equipment for Tractor Training School	1955–6	17,250
Tarnab Farm Workshop Equipment	1957–8	2,277
Aerial Survey and Forest Inventory	1960–1	625,000
Data-processing Equipment for Agricultural Census	1961–2	271,810
Chittagong Hill Tracts (Land-use Study)	1963–4	500,000
Fishing Equipment	1963–5	3,950,000
	Total (Canada, Cdn $)	*11,171,511*
	Total (Canada, US $)	*10,389,505*
France – export credits		
Expansion of Coal Production (WPIDC)	5. vii. 1963	264,862
Expansion of Coal Production (WPIDC)	13. v. 1964	24,858
Expansion of Coal Production (WPIDC)	3. ix. 1964	154,390
Expansion of Coal Production (WPIDC)	31. iii. 1965 and 18. v. 1965	426,062
Expansion of Coal Production (WPIDC)	2. ix. 1965	147,711
Expansion of Coal Production (WPIDC)	3. iii. 1966	111,431
Quarrying and Mining Equipment for Limestone Deposits (EPIDC)	29 viii. 1966	169,738
Mining Equipment for Sore-Range and Legari Units (WPIDC)	27. ix. 1966 and 30. ix. 1966	269,564
	Total (France)	*1,568,616*
Japan – yen credits		
Degari Coal Mines (WPIDC)	5. x. 1964	839,996
USSR – loan		
Oil Exploration (O. & G.D.C.)	4. iii. 1961	30,000,000

Table 4.7. *Health, welfare and education* (*US dollars*)

	Date of agreement	Commitment
United States – DLF		
Water and Sewage (KDA)	30. vi. 1958	3,771,537
United States – AID loans		
Malaria Eradication (1st) (DPH)	28. ii. 1963	2,554,848
Public Health Engineering Consultants (GOEP)	9. xii. 1963	1,500,000
Malaria Eradication (2nd) (DPH)	25. ii. 1965	10,400,000
	Total (AID)	*14,454,848*

Table 4.7. (*cont.*)

	Date of agreement	Commitment
United States – grants		
Community Development, Housing and Social Welfare	1956–66	1,589,000
Education	1956–66	11,709,000
Health and Sanitation	1956–66	6,107,000
Public Administration and Public Safety	1956–66	13,587,000
Community Development and Housing		
Village Aid	30. vi. 1952	5,254,000
Community Development – Housing	3. iii. 1955	49,000
Social Welfare Administration	30. vi. 1955	4,000
Housing Research and Demonstration	9. iii. 1956	70,000
Education		
Inter-College Exchange	30. vi. 1954	10,684,000
General Education Advisory Services	23. iv. 1955	95,000
Senior Education Leader Training	8. xii. 1958	5,000
Teachers Training Institute	1. x. 1959	1,831,000
Agriculture University – West Pakistan	30. vi. 1964	1,140,000
Assistance to Peshawar University	30. vi. 1964	360,000
East Pakistan Universities	30. vi. 1964	903,000
Health and Sanitation		
Mass Disease Control	17. v. 1952	1,096,000
East Bengal T.B. Hospital	23. iv. 1953	73,000
Karachi Water Supply	30. vi. 1954	5,493,000
Nursing Education and Facilities	28. ii. 1955	647,000
Rural Health Development	28. ii. 1955	1,819,000
Fenestration Surgery	30. vi. 1955	5,000
Massachusetts Contracts, Contract Services for Medical Personnel	1. i. 1956	1,135,000
Basic Nursing Education	29. iii. 1956	62,000
Undergraduate Medical Education	27. vi. 1956	76,000
Medical Instrument Repair	30. vi. 1956	57,000
Municipal Water Supply	30. vi. 1956	77,000
Village Water Supply	30. vi. 1956	955,000
Postgraduate Medical Center	31. i. 1957	2,079,000
Dacca–Chittagong Water Supply	30. vi. 1961	1,243,000
Cholera Research Laboratory	30. vi. 1962	730,000
Malaria Eradication	30. vi. 1963	206,000
Community Water Supply, Regional Project	n.a.	56,000
Labour		
Industrial Disputes	30. vi. 1955	5,000
Labour Relations Training	30. vi. 1958	206,000
Skilled Labour Training	30. vi. 1958	1,366,000
Improvement of Labour Relations	30. vi. 1964	26,000
Technical Training Pilot Project – East Pakistan	15. vi. 1965	35,000

Table 4.7. (*cont*).

	Date of agreement	Commitment
Public safety and Public Administration		
Balance of International Payments Study	30. vi. 1955	8,000
Bank Inspection	30. vi. 1955	15,000
Budget Procedure Study	30. vi. 1955	3,000
Industrial Economics	30. vi. 1955	6,000
Procurement and Supply Training	30. vi. 1955	18,000
Supervision of Banking and Industry Finance	30. vi. 1955	3,000
Techniques of Economic Control	30. vi. 1955	5,000
Business Administration	30. iv. 1957	2,047,000
Statistical Services	30. iv. 1957	1,332,000
Public Administration	31. x. 1957	3,303,000
Public Safety	30. iv. 1958	4,387,000
Assistance to Planning Institute	30. vi. 1962	572,000
Government Management	30. vi. 1963	666,000
Tax Administration	n.a.	6,000
	Total (grants)	*83,205,000*
	Total (US)	*101,431,385*
Canada – grants (Cdn dollars)		
Mobile Dispensaries	1955–65	11,795
Books on Cost Accounting (Pakistan Institute of Industrial Accounting)	1959–60	15,000
Equipment for Rawalpindi Veterans Hospital	1963–4	25,000
Cobalt Beam Therapy Units	1963–4	75,000
Lahore Refugee Housing Scheme	1963–4	2,000,000
	Total (Canada, Cdn $)	*2,126,795*
	Total (Canada, US $)	*1,977,919*
United Kingdom – credits		
Karachi Water Supply (KDA)	2. iii. 1954	1,741,600
Karachi Water Supply (KDA)	27. ii. 1959	1,880,636
	Total (UK)	*3,622,236*
IDA – credits		
Chittagong Water Supply and Sewerage (CWASSA)	16. viii. 1963	14,000,000
Dacca Water Supply and Sewerage (DWASSA)	16. viii. 1963	16,000,000
East Pakistan Education Project (GOEP)	25. iii. 1964	4,500,000
West Pakistan Education Project (GOWP)	25. iii. 1964	8,500,000
East Pakistan Education Project (GOEP – Education Dept)	17. vi. 1966	13,000,000
Lahore Water Supply and Sewerage Project (GOWP – B.D. & L.G. Dept)	12. v. 1967	1,750,000
	Total (IDA)	*57,750,000*

Table 4.8. *Industry (US dollars)*

	Date of agreement	Commitment
United States – DLF		
Development of Private Industry (PICIC)	4. xii. 1958	4,200,000
Development of Private Industry (PICIC)	15. i. 1960	9,903,279
Development of Private Industry (PICIC)	12. v. 1961	7,500,000
Wah Factories (WOFB)	24. iv. 1962	4,719,448
	Total (DLF)	*26,322,727*
United States – Cooley Fund loans (in thousands of rupees)[a]		
Production Facilities for Pharmaceuticals – Warner Lambert (Warner Lambert Pharmaceuticals Co.)	17. iv. 1959	1,000
Pharmaceutical Plant Facilities – Abbott Laboratories (Abbott Labs.)	18. ii. 1960	2,000
Pfizer Eastern Corp. – Dumex Pakistan Ltd (Chas. Pfizer & Co.)	4. iv. 1960	2,000
Working Capital for Pharmaceutical Plant – Lederle Laboratories (American Cyanamid Co.)	15. vii. 1960	1,000
Working Capital and Jute-bagging Plant – Pakistan Fabric Co. (Belton Bagging Co.)	7. iii. 1961	2,000
Equity in Pakistan Services Hotel Chain – Intercontinental Hotels Corp. (Pan American World Airways)	27. iii. 1961	4,667
For Pharmaceutical Production – Wyeth Laboratories (American Home Products Corp.)	14. ix. 1961	1,800
Construction of Pharmaceutical Plant – Parke, Davis & Co. (Parke, Davis & Co.)	11. x. 1961	2,075
Construction of Hotel in Karachi – Pakistan Service Ltd (Pan American World Airways)	16. vii. 1962	5,743
Working Capital and Jute-bagging Plant – Pakistan Fabrics Co. (Belton Bagging Co.)	14. viii. 1962	1,000
Working Capital for Distribution of Locally Manufactured Sewing Machines – Singer Sewing Machine Co. (Singer Mfg. Co.)	29. ix. 1962	5,000
Construction of Tyre and Tube Plant – General Tyre and Rubber Co. (General Tire and Rubber Co.)	18. iv. 1963	7,113
Expansion of Pharmaceutical Plant – Merck, Sharp and Dohme (Merck & Co.)	12. viii. 1963	1,500
Equity in Pakistan Services Hotel Chain – Intercontinental Hotels Corp. (Pan American World Airways)	26. xi. 1963	3,500
Construction of Bulk Storage Terminal – Pakistan-American Liberty Tank Terminals (American Liberty Tank Terminals)	4. ii. 1964	476
Construction of Hotel in Dacca – Pakistan Services Ltd (Pan American World Airways)	24. viii. 1964	4,477
Pharmaceutical Plant Construction – Carter Wallace (Carter Products Inc.)	1. x. 1964	1,000
Fruit-juice Processing – Shezan International (Ambor Corp.)	4. xii. 1964	2,375

[a] These loans are made from the local currency proceeds of the sale of surplus PL 480 commodities. The name of the US partner is in parentheses.

Table 4.8. (*cont.*)

	Date of agreement	Commitment
Working Capital and Jute-bagging Plant – Pakistan Fabrics Co. (Belton Bagging Co.)	4. ii. 1965	2,300
Working Capital and Capital Assets for Poultry-breeding Farm – Arbor Acres Pakistan Ltd (Arbor Acres Farm, Inc.)	5. ii. 1965	875
Corn-processing – Rafhan Maize Products Co. Ltd (Corn Products Co.)	4. vi. 1965	5,000
Construction of Hotel in Lahore – Pakistan Services Ltd (Pan American World Airways)	10. xi. 1965	3,903
Expansion of Foundry and Machine Shop – Singer Industries Ltd (Singer Co.)	17. i. 1966	2,250
Construction of Hotel in Rawalpindi – Pakistan Services Ltd (Pan American World Airways)	22. iii. 1966	3,449
Construction of Modern Dairy Plant – Sunshine Farms Ltd (Bresler Ice Cream Co.)	24. iii. 1966	600
Construction of Pharmaceutical Plant – Johnson & Johnson Pakistan Ltd (Johnson & Johnson)	28. iii. 1966	1,800
Total (Cooley Fund loans, thousands of rupees)		*68,903*
(US $)		*14,469,630*
United States – grants		
Fertilizer Factory – Daudkhel	28. v. 1952	12,804,000
Industrial Technical Assistance Centre	30. iv. 1954	2,269,000
Industrial Research and Development	30. vi. 1954	892,000
Industrial Development Survey	18. iii. 1955	437,000
Industry and Transport Advisory Service	4. iv. 1955	40,000
Administration Oil Companies	30. vi. 1955	5,000
Manufacture of Industrial Alcohol	30. vi. 1955	3,000
Offset Printing	30. vi. 1955	800
Engineering Services for Projects	1. ii. 1956	1,847,000
Industrial Productivity Centre	30. vi. 1956	263,000
Survey of Industrial Ordnance Factory	26. iv. 1957	34,000
Fertilizer Plant	21. vi. 1957	10,000,000
Industrial Productivity	n.a.	4,000
Total (grants)		*28,598,800*
United States – Eximbank		
Cotton-ginning and Pre-cleaning Machinery (IDBP); Exhibits in the Pakistan International Industrial Fair (IDBP)	4. iv. 1961	6,400,000
Intercontinental Hotel, Karachi (IDBP)	1. vii. 1962	3,462,800
Construction of General Tyre and Rubber Co. Factory, Karachi (IDBP)	19. iv. 1963	800,000
Development of Private Industry (IDBP)	10. xii. 1963	2,500,000
Intercontinental Hotel, Dacca (IDBP)	24. viii. 1964	3,348,500
Intercontinental Hotel, Lahore (IDBP)	12. x. 1965	2,081,000
Intercontinental Hotel, Rawalpindi (IDBP)	21. iii. 1966	2,200,900
Development of Private Industry (IDBP)	10. v. 1967	2,500,000
Total (Eximbank)		*23,293,200*
Total (US)		*92,684,357*

Table 4.8. (*cont.*)

	Date of agreement	Commitment
Canada – loan (Cdn dollars)		
Khulna Newsprint Extension (EPIDC)	23. xi. 1962	6,232,500
Canada – grants (Cdn dollars)		
Maple Leaf Cement Plant (Daudkhel)	1953–7	6,439,502
Khulna Hard-board Plant	1961–3	1,850,000
	Total (Canada, Cdn $)	*14,522,002*
	Total (Canada, US $)	*13,474,253*
United Kingdom – credits		
Jauharabad Sugar Mills (WPIDC)	2. iii. 1954	1,265,600
Leiah Sugar Mill (Thal Development Authority)	2. iii. 1954	1,265,600
Cold Storage Plant for Potato Seeds (IDBP)	27. ii. 1959	178,870
Cotton-ginning Machinery (IDBP)	27. ii. 1959	687,652
Jute Looms (EPIDC)	27. ii. 1959	4,851,366
Khyber Tobacco Plant (IDBP)	27. ii. 1959	43,242
Kushtia and Rajshahi Sugar Mills (EPIDC)	27. ii. 1959	124,796
Mechanized Fisheries Project (IDBP)	27. ii. 1959	854,614
Sulphur-refining Plant (IDBP)	27. ii. 1959	66,966
Jute Mills Machinery (EPIDC)	28. xii. 1960	9,800,000
Textile Machinery (IDBP)	28. xii. 1960	1,400,000
Jute Mills Machinery (EPIDC)	8. i. 1962	11,816,000
Development of Private Industry (IDBP)	5. xi. 1962	3,869,867
Development of Private Industry (PICIC)	5. xi. 1962	2,479,200
Jute Mills Machinery (EPIDC)	5. xi. 1962	8,653,333
Kushtia, Rajshahi and Thakurgaon Sugar Mills (EPIDC)	18. vi. 1963	4,876,640
Jute Mills Machinery (EPIDC)	25. ii. 1964	7,392,000
Development of Private Industry (IDBP)	23. xii. 1964	1,008,000
Jute Mills Machinery (EPIDC)	23. xii. 1964	8,456,000
Kushtia, Rajshahi and Extension of Thakurgaon Sugar Mills (EPIDC)	23. xii. 1964	1,568,000
Development of Private Industry (IDBP)	12. viii. 1966	506,800
Jute Mills Machinery (EPIDC)	12. viii. 1966	9,578,000
Jute Machinery (EPIDC)	4. iv. 1967	3,799,158
Jute Machinery (PWSR)	4. iv. 1967	2,080,842
	Total (UK)	*86,622,546*
France – export credits		
Cinecolour Laboratory Ltd, Karachi (IDBP)	20. ii. 1963	304,714
Plastiko Industries Ltd, Karachi (IDBP)	7. vii. 1963	148,183
Pahartali Textile and Hosiery Mills No. 2, Chittagong (IDBP)	7. viii. 1963	337,416
DDT Factory, Barabkunda, Chittagong (EPIDC)	13. ix. 1963	1,078,262
Four Sugar Mill Distilleries (PICIC)	20. x. 1963	1,515,811
Distillery for Hyesons Sugar Mills, Khanpur (PICIC)	9. xii. 1963	483,790
Conforce Ltd, Lahore (IDBP)	22. i. 1964	288,209
Phosphate Fertilizer Factory, Chittagong (EPIDC)	13. ii. 1964	810,199
Oil Refinery for Eastern Refinery Ltd, Chittagong (PICIC)	4. iii. 1964 and 5. ix. 1966	15,955,784
Insecticide Factory, Lahore (PICIC)	13, 20. v. 1964	1,333,992

Table 4.8. (*cont.*)

	Date of agreement	Commitment
Two Beet-refining Plants (PICIC)	29. v. 1964 and 3. vi. 1964	1,093,643
Air-conditioning Equipment for Satrang Textile Mills, Dacca (IDBP)	25. ix. 1964	101,037
Expansion of Lyallpur Chemical and Fertilizer Factory (WPIDC)	10. xii. 1964	238,930
Super-phosphate Fertilizer Factory, Chittagong (EPIDC)	22. ii. 1965	1,114,000
Expansion of Pak-American Fertilizer Factory, Daudkhel (WPIDC)	3. xii. 1965 and 20. xii. 1965	2,509,292
North Bengal Paper Mills, Paksey (EPIDC)	25. iii. 1966	1,994,863
Engineering Services for Streptomycin Factory, Chittagong (EPIDC)	3. v. 1966	1,235,553
Machine Tools Factory, Karachi (WPIDC)	16. vi. 1966	212,405
Cement Factory, Chittagong (EPIDC)	27. viii. 1966	2,059,120
Two Gas Generators for Zeal-Pak Cement Factory, Hyderabad (WPIDC)	5. ix. 1966	3,270,775
Auxiliary Machinery for Jute Mills (EPIDC)	27. iii. and 28. iv. 1967	785,608
Machine Tools Factory, Karachi (WPIDC)	15. vii. 1966 to 5. vi. 1967	3,650,208
	Total (France)	*40,521,794*
West Germany – capital aid		
Manghopir Cement Factory (PICIC)	25. v. 1962	3,500,000
Development of Private Industry (IDBP)	30. viii. 1962	15,000,000
Development of Private Industry (PICIC)	30. viii. 1962	17,500,000
Development of Private Industry (IDBP)	17. x. 1962	750,000
Development of Private Industry (PICIC)	19. vi. 1963	5,000,000
Manghopir Cement Factory (PICIC)	26. vii. 1963	2,000,000
Development of Private Industry (IDBP)	19. viii. 1963	5,000,000
Development of Private Industry (IDBP)	24. iii. 1964	1,000,000
Development of Private Industry (PICIC)	24. iii. 1964	2,500,000
Development of Private Industry (PICIC)	1. ix. 1965	2,500,000
Development of Private Industry (IDBP)	17. iii. 1966	1,250,000
Development of Private Industry (IDBP)	12. iv. 1967	2,500,000
West Germany – export credits		
Zeal-Pak Cement Factory, 4th Kiln, Hyderabad (WPIDC)	13. ii. 1961	1,149,965
Soda Ash Factory, Gharo (IDBP)	7. vi. 1961	5,457,640
Acetate Rayon Plant, Karachi (IDBP)	27. vii. 1961	19,537,500
Polythene Plant, Karachi (IDBP)	29. x. 1962	9,838,750
Cement Factory, Hattar (IDBP)	21. v. 1963	3,375,000
Sugar Mills, Badin (WPIDC)	11. vii. 1963	2,875,683
Sugar Mills, Bannu (WPIDC)	21. vii. 1963	2,803,116
Cement Factory, Hattar (IDBP)	22. vii. 1963	3,125,000
Zeal-Pak Cement Factory Agreement (Supplementary for Sapres) (WPIDC)	18/21. viii. 1964	135,218
North Bengal Paper Mills, Paksey (EPIDC)	25. iii. 1966	6,250,000
Electric Wire and Cable Factory, Khulna (EPIDC)	10. vi. 1966	2,445,150
Diesel Plant, East Pakistan (EPIDC)	10. xii. 1966	1,695,725
Natural Gas Fertilizer Factory, Multan (WPIDC)	2. iii. 1967	1,945,000
	Total (Germany)	*119,133,747*

Table 4.8. (*cont.*)

	Date of agreement	Commitment
Japan – yen credits		
Chittagong Steel Mills (EPIDC)	13. xi. 1961	4,405,882
Development of Private Industry (IDBP)	13. xi. 1961	3,264,102
Development of Private Industry (PICIC)	13. xi. 1961	4,968,939
Karnaphuli Rayon and Chemicals Ltd, Chittagong (PICIC)	13. xi. 1961	2,000,000
Chittagong Steel Mills (EPIDC)	15. iii. 1963	8,000,000
Consumable Material and Spare Parts for Chittagong Steel Mills (EPIDC)	15. iii. 1963	3,999,601
Development of Private Industry (IDBP)	15. iii. 1963	986,548
Development of Private Industry (PICIC)	15. iii. 1963	2,474,849
Karnaphuli Rayon and Chemicals Ltd, Chittagong (PICIC)	15. iii. 1963	4,000,000
Mymensingh and Shyamapur Sugar Mills (EPIDC)	15. iii. 1963	1,300,000
Chittagong Steel Mills (EPIDC)	21. ix. 1963	12,405,000
Development of Private Industry (IDBP)	21. ix. 1963	838,064
Development of Private Industry (PICIC)	21. ix. 1963	3,000,000
Extension of Chittagong Steel Mills (EPIDC)	21. ix. 1963	500,000
Karnaphuli Rayon and Chemicals Ltd, Chittagong (PICIC)	21. ix. 1963	3,000,000
Mymensingh and Shyamapur Sugar Mills (EPIDC)	21. ix. 1963	2,748,041
PVC Plant, Karachi (IDBP)	21. ix. 1963	3,971,000
Alloys Steel Plant, Karachi (PICIC)	5. x. 1964	6,584,000
Chittagong Steel Mills (EPIDC)	5. x. 1964	5,744,674
Development of Private Industry (IDBP)	5. x. 1964	985,115
Extension of Chittagong Steel Mills (EPIDC)	5. x. 1964	3,000,000
Jetty Material for Chittagong Steel Mills (EPIDC)	5. x. 1964	616,067
Karnaphuli Rayon and Chemicals Ltd, Chittagong (PICIC)	5. x. 1964	1,695,372
Natural Gas Fertilizer Factory, Ghorasal (EPIDC)	5. x. 1964	412,520
Sulphation Plant for the Pak-American Fertilizer Factory, Daudkhel (WPIDC)	5. x. 1964	1,454,667
Alloys Steel Plant, Karachi (PICIC)	6. vi. 1966	5,920,000
Development of Private Industry (IDBP)	6. vi. 1966	1,000,000
Development of Private Industry (PICIC)	6. vi. 1966	5,000,000
Extension of Chittagong Steel Mills (EPIDC)	6. vi. 1966	1,500,000
Natural Gas Fertilizer Factory, Ghorasal (EPIDC)	6. vi. 1966	1,601,146
Two Cement Factories, West Pakistan (GOWP)	6. vi. 1966	1,180,000
Ammonium Sulphate Plant – Fenchuganj Fertilizer Factory (EPIDC)	24. ii. 1967	704,000
Caustic Soda Plant (IDBP)	24. ii. 1967	700,000
Chittagong Steel Mills (EPIDC)	24. ii. 1967	1,000,000
Development of Private Industry (IDBP)	24. ii. 1967	2,500,000
Development of Private Industry (PICIC)	24. ii. 1967	3,500,000
Expansion of Fauji Sugar Mills (IDBP)	24. ii. 1967	1,000,000
Ghorasal Fertilizer Factory (EPIDC)	24. ii. 1967	3,236,000
Two Cement Factories (GOWP)	24. ii. 1967	5,320,000

Table 4.8. (*cont.*)

	Date of agreement	Commitment
Japan – suppliers' credits		
Natural Gas Fertilizer Factory, Fenchuganj – Kobe Steel Works (EPIDC)	31. v. 1958	20,566,124
Thermal Power Station for Natural Gas Fertilizer Factory, Fenchuganj – Mitsubishi Heavy Industries (EPIDC),	24. x. 1959	4,644,402
Textile Machinery (IDBP)	3. xi. 1960	20,646,878
Textile Machinery (IDBP)	9. viii. 1962	12,918,650
Textile Machinery (IDBP)	20. v. 1965	9,836,454
	Total (Japan)	*185,128,095*
USSR – export credits		
Equipment for East Pakistan Building Directorate (GOEP)	2. xii. 1965	3,135,079
Equipment for EPSIC	2. xii. 1965	208,754
Equipment for EPIDC Projects	3. xii. 1965	1,748,261
Flour Mill Machinery, Aziz Flour Mills, Multan (IDBP)	27. i. 1967	102,384
Machinery for Ittefaq Foundry and Workshop, Lahore (IDBP)	31. i. 1967	147,000
Karachi Shipyard and Engineering Works (WPIDC)	10. iii. 1967	456,369
Machinery for Karimi Industries (IDBP)	24. iv. 1967	89,242
	Total (USSR)	*5,887,089*
Yugoslavia – export credits		
M.V. Bagh-e-Karachi; M.V. Abasin (IDBP)	9. xi. 1962	5,949,854
Slaughter House, Karachi (IDBP)	9. iv. 1963	1,490,160
Slaughter House, Islamabad (IDBP)	13. iii. 1964	291,200
M.V. Bagh-e-Dacca (IDBP)	19. iii. 1964	2,907,083
Flour Mills, Karachi, Haji Allah Baksh (IDBP)	15. ix. 1964	130,622
Brick-making Plant, Hyderabad Abdul Ghani Kala Khan (IDBP)	16. xii. 1964	154,211
Chittagong Dry Dock and Heavy Steel Structural Works (EPIDC)	27. ii. 1965	8,555,949
Slaughter House, Dacca (IDBP)	20. vi. 1965	682,920
Slaughter House, Lahore (IDBP)	26. vi. 1965	1,165,782
	Total (Yugoslavia)	*21,327,781*
IBRD – loans		
Karnaphuli Paper Mills Project (PIDC)	4. viii. 1955	4,200,000
Development of Private Industry (PICIC)	17. xii. 1957	4,085,377
Development of Private Industry (PICIC)	25. ix. 1960	9,935,833
Development of Private Industry (PICIC)	27. vi. 1961	14,785,030
Development of Private Industry (PICIC)	13. ii. 1963	20,000,000
Development of Private Industry (PICIC)	30. vi. 1964	30,000,000
Development of Private Industry (PICIC)	9. vii. 1965	30,000,000
	Total (IBRD)	*113,006,240*
IDA – credit		
Small Industrial Estates (WPSIC)	2. xi. 1962	6,500,000

Table 4.8. (*cont.*)

	Date of agreement	Commitment
IFC – investments		
Adamjee Industries Ltd	29. x. 1958	749,705
Steel Corp. of Pakistan Ltd	9. vii. 1959	630,000
Ismail Cement Industries Ltd, Gharibwal (PICIC)	7. ix. 1961	4,000,000
Ismail Cement Industries Ltd (PICIC)	3. viii. 1964	1,260,000
Crescent Jute Products Ltd (PICIC)	24. xi. 1964	1,950,000
Packages Ltd, Lahore (PICIC)	18. xii. 1964	2,310,000
Pakistan Paper Corp. Ltd (PICIC)	5. vi. 1967	3,200,000
	Total (IFC)	*14,099,705*

Table 4.9. *Commodities (US dollars)*

	Date of agreement	Commitment
United States – AID loans		
Commodities (Iron and Steel) (1st) (C.C.I. & E.)	11. v. 1962	88,339,925
General Commodities (2nd) (C.C.I. & E.)	31. viii. 1962	40,742,724
General Commodities (3rd) (C.C.I. & E.)	27. iii. 1963	29,536,182
General Commodities (4th) (C.C.I. & E.)	28. ix. 1963	68,191,884
General Commodities (5th) (C.C.I. & E.)	13. vii. 1964	100,000,000
General Commodities (6th) (C.C.I. & E.)	21. xii. 1964	140,000,000
General Commodities (7th) (C.C.I. & E.)	4. v. 1966	50,000,000
General Commodities (8th) (C.C.I. & E.)	17. viii. 1966	70,000,000
General Commodities (9th) (C.C.I. & E.)	9. iii. 1967	70,000,000
	Total (AID)	*656,810,715*
United States – Eximbank		
Wheat	17. ix. 1952	15,000,000
	Total (US)	671,810,715
Canada – grants (Cdn dollars)		
Food	1952–67	51,508,200
Other	1954–67	57,007,000
	Total (Canada, Cdn $)	*108,515,200*
	Total (Canada, US $)	*100,919,136*

Table 4.9. (*cont.*)

	Date of Agreement	Commitment
United Kingdom – credits		
Chandpur Electric Supply Co. (C.C.I. & E.)	2. iii. 1954	39,200
Inland Water Transport, East Pakistan (C.C.I. & E.)	27. ii. 1959	1,888,708
Tea Machinery (C.C.I. & E.)	27. ii. 1959	1,018,782
Marine Diesel Engines (C.C.I. & E.)	18. vi. 1963	723,360
Steel Billets for CDA (C.C.I. & E.)	25. ii. 1964	840,000
Tea Machinery and Artificial Irrigation Equipment (C.C.I. & E.)	25. ii. 1964	812,000
Auto Spares (C.C.I. & E.)	23. xii. 1964	1,008,000
Drugs and Medicines (C.C.I. & E.)	23. xii. 1964	2,240,000
Car Components (C.C.I. & E.)	23. xii. 1964	448,000
Chemicals (C.C.I. & E.)	23. xii. 1964	1,624,000
Printing Press, Islamabad (Industries Division)	23. xii. 1964	1,008,000
Reactive and Dyes (C.C.I. & E.)	23. xii. 1964	960,400
Tyres and Tubes (C.C.I. & E.)	23. xii. 1964	1,008,000
Tractors (C.C.I. & E.)	23. xii. 1964	2,016,000
Wheels, Tyres and Axles (PWR)	23. xii. 1964	588,000
Cables for Mangla Unit iv (WPWAPDA)	12. v. 1966	168,000
Cables for Railway Electrification (T & T)	12. v. 1966	103,600
Drugs and Medicines (C.C.I. & E.)	12. v. 1966	999,600
Pesticides (AD-GOWP)	12. v. 1966	450,000
Radio Equipment for (T. & T.) Dept (T & T)	12. v. 1966	700,000
Reactive and Dyes (C.C.I. & E.)	12. v. 1966	4,001,200
Spares for Earth-moving Machinery (WPWAPDA)	12. v. 1966	859,600
Tea Machinery (C.C.I. & E.)	12. v. 1966	999,600
Tractors (C.C.I. & E.)	12. v. 1966	2,917,600
Ammonium Sulphate (WPADC)	20. x. 1966	280,000
Drugs and Medicines (C.C.I. & E.)	20. x. 1966	1,500,000
Dyes and Chemicals (C.C.I. & E.)	20. x. 1966	5,150,000
Marine Diesel Engines (C.C.I. & E.)	20. x. 1966	420,000
Pesticides (Ministry of Agriculture)	20. x. 1966	210,000
Printing Press, Islamabad	20. x. 1966	400,000
Raw Material and Packing Material for Pharmaceutical Industries (EPIDC)	20. x. 1966	750,000
Spares for Earth-moving Machinery (WPADC)	20. x. 1966	300,000
Tractors (C.C.I. & E.)	20. x. 1966	2,090,000
Vehicles CHD (WPRTC)	20. x. 1966	100,000
	Total (UK)	*38,621,650*
West Germany – capital aid		
Commodities (C.C.I. & E.)	10. viii. 1962	6,000,000
Commodities (C.C.I. & E.)	18. iii. 1964	5,500,000
Commodities (C.C.I. & E.)	21. i. 1965	6,250,000
Commodities (C.C.I. & E.)	23. vi. 1966	7,500,000
Commodities (C.C.I. & E.)	24. v. 1967	12,500,000
	Total (Germany)	*37,750,000*

Table 4.9. (*cont*).

	Date of agreement	Commitment
Japan – yen credits		
Machine Tools and Workshop Equipment (C.C.I. & E.)	21. ix. 1963	369,992
Power Tillers (EPIDC)	21. ix. 1963	220,137
Spare Parts and Consumable Material for Chittagong Steel Mills (EPIDC)	21. ix. 1963	999,900
Cables (T & T)	6. vi. 1966	1,200,000
Fertilizers (EPADC)	6. vi. 1966	800,000
Four-Wheel Drive Vehicles and Spares (C.C.I. & E.)	6. vi. 1966	1,000,000
Pesticides (EPADC/AD) (GOWP)	6. vi. 1966	1,000,000
Trucks and Spares (C.C.I. & E.)	6. vi. 1966	5,000,000
Cables and Cable Boxes (WPWAPDA)	24. ii. 1967	210,000
Dyes and Chemicals (C.C.I. & E.)	24. ii. 1967	1,000,000
Fertilizers (EPADC)	24. ii. 1967	6,630,000
Marine Diesel Engines (C.C.I. & E.)	24. ii. 1967	611,000
Power Tillers (C.C.I. & E.)	24. ii. 1967	500,000
	Total (Japan)	*19,541,029*
China – loans		
1st Loan, for Import of Commodities	18. ii. 1965	30,000,000
2nd Loan, for Import of Foodgrains	17. i. 1967	6,932,432
	Total (China)	*36,932,432*
IDA – credits		
Commercial Road Vehicles Project (I.P. & S.)	13. i. 1966	25,000,000
Industrial Imports (C.C.I. & E.)	23. xii. 1966	25,000,000
	Total (IDA)	*50,000,000*

Table 4.10. *Multi-purpose* (*US dollars*)

	Date of agreement	Commitment
United States – DLF		
Karnaphuli Multi-purpose Project (EPWAPDA)	18. ii. 1959	17,941,545
United States – AID loans		
Feasibility Studies (EAD)	27. iii. 1963	2,000,000
Services of General Consultants (EPWAPDA)	15. viii. 1963	4,400,000
General Consultants (WPWAPDA)	20. xi. 1963	5,600,000
General Investigation and Consulting Services (WPWAPDA)	27. vi. 1966	6,000,000
	Total (AID)	18,000,000
United States – grant		
Karnaphuli Multi-purpose Project	30. vi. 1954	19,456,000
United States – Eximbank		
Mutual Security Project and Non-Project Loan	16. iii. 1955	20,000,000
Mutual Security Project and Non-Project Loan	13. vii. 1956	26,000,000
Mutual Security Project and Non-Project Loan	28. vi. 1957	42,000,000
	Total (Eximbank)	*88,000,000*
	Total (US)	*143,397,545*
United Kingdom – credit		
Old Contracts Financed prior to the Approval of the List of Schemes	27. ii. 1959	478,171
China – loan		
1st Loan, for Projects	18. ii. 1965	30,000,000

Appendix 5
Foreign project loans and credits to Pakistan industry
(as of 1967)

Public sector[1]

Belgium
  Pak-American fertilizer factory, Dandkhel (WPIDC)
Canada
  Khulna newsprint extension (EPIDC)
China
  Various projects, including a heavy machinery plant at Taxila
Denmark
  White cement plant (WPIDC)
  Zeal-Pak cement factory, Hyderabad (WPIDC)
France
  Acid plant (EPIDC)
  Cement factory, Chittagong (EPIDC)
  DDT factory (EPIDC)
  Lyallpur chemical and fertilizer factory (WPIDC)
  Machine tools factory, Karachi, 45 credits (WPIDC)
  North Bengal paper mills, Paksey (EPIDC)
  Pak-American fertilizer factory, Dandkhel, 2 credits (WPIDC)
  Phosphate fertilizer factory, Chittagong, 2 credits (EPIDC)
  Streptomycin factory, Chittagong (EPIDC)
  Zeal-Pak cement factory, Hyderabad (WPIDC)
Germany, West
  Diesel plant (EPIDC)
  Electric wire and cable factory, Khulna (EPIDC)
  Natural gas fertilizer factory, Multan (WPIDC)
  North Bengal paper mills, Paksey (EPIDC)
  Sugar mills, Badin (WPIDC)
  Sugar mills, Bannu (WPIDC)
  Zeal-Pak cement factory, Hyderabad, 2 credits (WPIDC)
Italy
  Machine tools factory, Karachi (WPIDC)
  North Bengal paper mills (EPIDC)
  Pak-American fertilizer factory, 2 credits (WPIDC)
Japan
  Chittagong steel mills, 10 credits (EPIDC)
  Fenchuganj fertilizer factory, 3 credits (EPIDC)

---

[1] Sectoral classification here is according to final destination of funds, not by guarantor; the State Bank of Pakistan uses the latter approach.

Ghorasal fertilizer factory, 3 credits (EPIDC)
Mymensingh and Shyamapur sugar mills, 2 credits (EPIDC)
Pak-American fertilizer factory (WPIDC)
Two cement factories, 2 credits (GOWP)
Netherlands
Natural gas fertilizer factory, Multan (WPIDC)
Panchagarh sugar mills (EPIDC)
Sugar mills, 1 loan, 6 credits (EPIDC)
  Poland
Lumber-processing complex, Kaptai (EPFIDC), and wood-treating and seasoning
  units, Chittagong (EPFIDC)
Sweden
Zeal-Pak cement factory, Hyderabad (WPIDC)
Switzerland
East Pakistan machine tools factory, Dacca, 47 credits (EPIDC)
Machine tools factory, Karachi, 45 credits (WPIDC)
United Kingdom
Jauharabad sugar mills (WPIDC)
Jute looms, 2 credits (EPIDC)
Jute machinery (PWSR)
Jute machinery, 7 credits (EPIDC)
Kushtia, Rajshahi, and Thakurgaon sugar mills, 3 credits (EPIDC)
Leiah sugar mills (Thal Development Authority)
USSR
Equipment for East Pakistan Building Directorate (GOEP)
Equipment for EPIDC projects
Equipment for EPSIC
Karachi shipyard and engineering works (WPIDC)
Yugoslavia
Chittagong dry dock and heavy steel structural works (EPIDC)

Private sector

Czechoslovakia
  Hussain sugar mills (PICIC)
Denmark
  Dairy plant (PICIC)
  Development of private industry (IDBP)
France
  Cinecolour laboratory (IDBP)
  Conforce Ltd (IDBP)
  Crescent sugar mill (PICIC)
  Eastern refinery (PICIC)
  Frontier sugar mill, 2 credits (PICIC)
  Habib sugar mill (PICIC)
  Hyesons sugar mill (PICIC)
  Insecticide factory (PICIC)
  Pahartali textile mill (IDBP)

Plastiko industries (IDBP)
Premier sugar mills, 2 credits (PICIC)
Satrang textiles (IDBP)
Germany, West
Acetate rayon plant (IDBP)
Cement factory, Hattar, 2 credits (IDBP)
Development of private industry, 6 loans (IDBP)
Development of private industry, 4 loans (PICIC)
Manghopir cement factory, 2 loans (PICIC)
Polythene plant (IDBP)
Soda ash factory (IDBP)
Italy
Cigarette-manufacturing plant (IDBP)
Embroidery plant (IDBP)
Flour mill machinery, 3 credits (IDBP)
Furniture-manufacturing plant (IDBP)
Pen-manufacturing plant (IDBP)
Shahtaj sugar mills (PICIC)
Silk mill machinery (IDBP)
Textile machinery, 2 credits (IDBP)
Three flour-milling plants (IDBP)
Two cold storage plants (IDBP)
Japan
Alloys steel plant, 2 credits (PICIC)
Caustic soda plant (IDBP)
Development of private industry, 6 credits (IDBP)
Development of private industry, 5 credits (PICIC)
Fauji sugar mills (IDBP)
Karnaphuli Rayon and Chemicals Ltd, 4 credits (PICIC)
PVC plant (IDBP)
Textile machinery, 3 credits (IDBP)
Poland
Bahawalnagar sugar mills (PICIC)
Switzerland
Textile machinery, 5 credits (IDBP)
United Kingdom
Cold storage plant for potato seeds (IDBP)
Cotton-ginning machinery (IDBP)
Development of private industry (PICIC)
Development of private industry, 3 credits (IDBP)
Khyber tobacco plant (IDBP)
Mechanized fisheries project (IDBP)
Sulphur-refining plant (IDBP)
Textile machinery (IDBP)
United States
Cotton-ginning machinery (Eximbank–IDBP)
Development of private industry, 2 credits (Eximbank–IDBP)

Development of private industry, 3 loans (PICIC)
General Tyre and Rubber Co. (Eximbank–IDBP)
Intercontinental Hotels, Dacca, Karachi, Lahore, Rawalpindi (Eximbank–IDBP)
Wah factories (WOFB)[2]
USSR
  Flour mill machinery (IDBP)
  Foundry machinery (IDBP)
  Machinery for Karimi industries (IDBP)
Yugoslavia
  Brick-making plant (IDBP)
  Flour mills (IDBP)
  Slaughter houses, Dacca, Islamabad, Karachi, Lahore (IDBP)
IBRD
  Development of private industry, 6 loans (PICIC)
  Karnaphuli paper mills (PIDC)
IDA
  Small industrial estates (WPSIC)
IFC
  Adamjee Industries Ltd
  Crescent Jute Products Ltd (PICIC)
  Ismail Cement Industries Ltd, 2 loans (PICIC)
  Packages Ltd (PICIC)
  Pakistan Paper Corp. Ltd (PICIC)
  Steel Corp. of Pakistan Ltd

[2] This item includes the public sector production of ammunition.

SOURCE: Pakistan, *Report of the Working Group on Debt Burden* (Islamabad, 1968), pp. 99–151. See also State Bank of Pakistan, *External Debt Servicing Liability* (Karachi, 1965), pp. 53–6.

Appendix 6
United States commodity assistance to Pakistan, 1953–66

AID and predecessor agencies: commodity assistance to Pakistan, fiscal years 1953–66 (thousands of dollars)[a]

Commodities	1953	1954	1955	1956	1957	1958	1959	1960	1961	1962	1963	1964	1965	1966
TOTAL	15,000	2,999	17,759	49,549	47,719	56,492	76,650	111,967	118,091	112,635	159,229	145,163	181,089	115,064
Foodstuffs	15,000	—	2,501	2,971	6,110	5,988	4,547	1,744	2,021	3,019	18	4	—	—
Bread grains	15,000	—	—	—	—	—	—	—	—	—	—	—	—	—
Rice	—	—	65	—	—	—	577	—	—	—	—	—	—	—
Fats and oils	—	—	4	-4	—	—	—	—	—	-1	—	—	—	—
Sugar and related products	—	—	347	546	—	—	—	—	—	—	21	5	—	—
Dairy products	—	—	2,076	2,424	6,110	5,988	3,967	1,742	2,021	3,021	-4	-1	—	—
Vegetables, fruits, nuts and preparations	—	—	8	5	—	—	—	—	—	-2	—	—	—	—
Miscellaneous edible agricultural products	—	—	—	—	—	—	3	2	—	1	1	—	—	—
Feeds and fertilizers	—	2,999	-46	3,685	132	19	7	3	—	3,093	9,150	-148	819	7,742
Seeds, other than oilseeds	—	—	7	3	2	4	7	3	—	—	—	—	—	—
Fertilizers	—	2,999	-53	3,682	130	15	—	—	—	3,093	9,150	-148	819	7,742
Fuel	—	—	—	2,958	4	226	4,901	7,190	8,452	14,786	6,530	5,430	7,772	2,323
Petroleum and products	—	—	—	2,958	4	226	4,901	7,190	8,452	14,786	6,530	5,430	7,772	2,323
Raw materials and semi-finished products	—	—	7,270	18,948	21,124	18,580	32,565	48,454	55,428	62,642	100,207	92,641	139,292	64,200
Cotton	—	—	—	—	—	—	—	1	1	1	—	—	—	—
Wool and other animal hairs, unmanufactured	—	—	—	516	—	—	2,261	3,257	1,987	—	4	—	—	—
Chemicals and related products	b	—	2,959	8,190	7,038	6,171	9,657	11,517	14,626	4,847	11,295	17,469	6,612	14,179
Coal tar dyestuffs	—	—	—	—	—	—	—	—	3,561	905	3,177	2,479	1,040	137
Miscellaneous fibre products	—	—	—	—	—	—	—	13	11	—	—	—	—	—
Leather and products	—	—	—	—	—	2	—	—	—	—	—	—	—	—
Fabricated basic textiles	—	—	2,817	231	445	219	1,178	236	253	21	1,202	273	3	—
Lumber and manufactures	—	—	12	12	—	19	25	8	8	—	1,083	76	570	—
Pulp and paper	—	—	9	9	33	109	—	—	—	1	58	470	10	—
Non-metallic minerals	—	—	19	64	48	92	411	997	829	20	709	359	488	24
Metallic ores and concentrates	—	—	—	—	—	—	—	2,621	—	—	—	—	—	—
Ferrous scrap	b	b	b	b	17	b	b	b	—	—	—	5	19	—
Iron and steel mill products	b	b	1,153	8,235	10,479	10,835	17,231	28,993	32,845	55,952	82,074	69,009	128,533	49,113
Non-ferrous metals and products	—	—	301	1,690	3,055	1,128	1,800	831	1,305	896	605	2,494	2,012	746

Machinery and vehicles	7,371	18,617	18,052	28,030	30,785	47,808	46,340	26,121	37,706	43,732	29,087	39,996
Machinery and equipment	5,421	12,517	13,862	18,400	18,638	29,300	26,144	15,389	17,765	23,420	15,875	21,340
Motor vehicles, engines and parts	1,689	5,475	3,456	3,711	6,396	9,384	7,605	2,695	11,169	15,625	7,718	10,121
Miscellaneous vehicles, parts, accessories, etc.	b	b	b	b	b	b	1,217	277	203	148	89	132
Aircraft, engines and parts	28	521	637	5	757	1,794	1,190	136	—	1,354	131	19
Railroad transportation equipment	55	82	2	5,479	3,993	7,305	10,182	7,186	8,322	2,957	4,386	8,251
Vessels and equipment	178	21	95	435	—	25	2	438	247	227	888	133
Miscellaneous	664	2,371	2,297	3,654	3,842	6,767	5,851	2,973	5,616	3,504	4,114	804
Miscellaneous inedible animal and vegetable products	—	11	8	—	—	—	—	—	—	—	—	—
Miscellaneous metal manufactures	158	278	—	154	249	288	251	141	2,039	990	892	328
Scientific and professional instruments	276	272	212	492	270	268	116	92	85	220	276	116
Rubber and rubber products	7	860	868	2,182	2,800	4,217	4,709	2,527	3,273	2,262	1,490	246
Miscellaneous industrial commodities	223	957	1,273	826	523	1,993	775	213	219	32	1,456	114
Unclassified commodities and adjustments	—	−64	—	—	—	—	—	—	—	—	—	—

SOURCE: Unpublished data from the United States AID Statistics and Reports Division (Washington, D.C.).

a Excludes PL 480 and Export–Import Bank loans. Totals shown are sums of unrounded figures, and therefore may differ slightly from totals of rounded figures in the table; negative figures are due to adjustments in prior years' records.
  A separate commodity code for this group was established at the beginning of the fiscal year 1961; items purchased were included in the larger group prior to that time

SELECTED BIBLIOGRAPHY

Selected Bibliography

1 Books and monographs

Adelman, Irma, and Morris, Cynthia T. *Society, Politics, and Economic Development: A Quantitative Approach*. Baltimore: Johns Hopkins Press, 1967.

Adler, John H., and Kuznets, Paul W., eds. *Capital Movements and Economic Development*. New York: St. Martin's Press, 1967.

Ahooja-Patel, Krishna, ed. *Development Aid: The Economic and Legal Structure*. Twickenham, England: *Journal of World Trade Law*, Special Issue, March–April 1970.

Akhtar, Abdul Hafiz. *Small and Medium Industries of Pakistan: A Select Bibliography, 1948–62*. Karachi: Pakistan Institute of Development Economics, September 1963.

Akhtar, S. M. *Pakistan – A Developing Economy*. Lahore: Publishers United Ltd, 1966.

Ali, Chaudhri Muhammad. *The Emergence of Pakistan*. New York: Columbia University Press, 1967.

Ali, Tariq. *Pakistan: Military Rule or People's Power?* London: Jonathan Cape, 1970.

Andrus, J. Russell, and Mohammed, Azizali F. *Trade, Finance, and Development in Pakistan*. Stanford, Calif.: Stanford University Press, 1966.

Areskoug, Kaj. *External Public Borrowing: Its Role in Economic Development*. New York: Praeger, 1969.

Arnold, H. J. P. *Aid for Development: A Political and Economic Study*. London: The Bodley Head, 1966.

Asher, Robert E. *Development Assistance in the Seventies: Alternatives for the United States*. Washington, D.C.: Brookings Institution, 1970.

Grants, Loans and Local Currencies: Their Role in Foreign Aid. Washington, D.C.: Brookings Institution, 1961.

Avramovic, Dragoslav, et al. *Economic Growth and External Debt*. Baltimore: Johns Hopkins Press, 1964.

Baker, James C. *The International Finance Corporation: Origins, Operations, and Evaluation*. New York: Praeger, 1968.

Baldwin, David A. *Economic Development and American Foreign Policy, 1943–62*. Chicago: University of Chicago Press, 1966.

Baqai, Moin. *Pakistan's Economic Progress: Possibilities of a Take-Off*. Occasional Paper no. 4. Montreal: McGill University, Centre for Developing-Area Studies, 1969.

Barna, Tibor, ed. *Structural Interdependence and Economic Development: Proceedings of an International Conference on Input–Output Techniques, Geneva, September 1961*. London: Macmillan, 1963.

Benham, Frederic. *Economic Aid to Underdeveloped Countries*. London: Oxford University Press, 1961.

The Colombo Plan and Other Essays. London: Oxford University Press, 1956.

Beringer, C., and Ahmad, I. *The Use of Agricultural Surplus Commodities for the Economic Development of Pakistan*. Monograph no. 12. Karachi: Pakistan Institute of Development Economics, 1964.

Berliner, Joseph S. *Soviet Economic Aid: The New Aid and Trade Policy in Under-developed Countries*. New York: Praeger, 1958.

Bhagwati, Jagdish N. *Amount and Sharing of Aid*. Monograph no. 2. Washington, D.C.: Overseas Development Council, 1970.

The Tying of Aid. UNCTAD/TD/7/Supp. 4. Geneva: 1 November 1967.

Bhagwati, Jagdish, and Eckaus, Richard S., eds. *Foreign Aid: Selected Readings* Middlesex, England: Penguin Books Ltd, 1970.

Billerbeck, Klaus. *Soviet Bloc Foreign Aid to the Underdeveloped Countries: An Analysis and Prognosis*. Hamburg: Archives of World Economy, 1960.

Bognár, József. *Economic Policy and Planning in Developing Countries*. Budapest: Akadémiai Kiadó, 1968.

Braibanti, Ralph. *Research on the Bureaucracy of Pakistan: A Critique of Sources, Conditions, and Issues, with Appended Documents*. Durham, N.C.: Duke University Press, 1966.

Briant, P. C. *Canada's External Aid Program*. Montreal: Canadian Trade Committee, Private Planning Association, 1965.

Bruton, Henry J., and Bose, Swadesh R. *The Pakistan Export Bonus Scheme*. Monograph no. 11. Karachi: Pakistan Institute of Development Economics, 1963.

Cairncross, A. K. *Factors in Economic Development*. London: Allen & Unwin, 1962.

Callard, Keith. *Pakistan: A Political Study*. London: Allen & Unwin, 1957.

Chandrasekhar, Sripati. *American Aid* and *India's Economic Development*. New York: Praeger, 1965.

Clay, Lucius L., et al. *Report to the President of the United States from the Committee to Strengthen the Security of the Free World*. Washington, D.C.: U.S. Government Printing Office, March 1963.

Davenport, Robert W. *Financing the Small Manufacturer in Developing Countries*. New York: McGraw-Hill, 1967.

Degras, Jane, and Nove, Alec, eds. *Soviet Planning: Essays in Honour of Naum Jasny*. London: Blackwell, 1964.

Falcon, Walter P., and Papanek, Gustav F., eds. *Development Policy II: The Pakistan Experience*. Cambridge, Mass.: Harvard University Press, 1971.

Fei, John C. H. *An Analysis of the Long-Run Prospects of Economic Development in Pakistan*. Monograph no. 9. Karachi: Pakistan Institute of Development Economics, 1962.

Frank, Charles R., Jr. *Debt and Terms of Aid*. Monograph no. 1. Washington, D.C.: Overseas Development Council, 1970.

Frank, Charles R., Jr., and Cline, William R. *Debt Servicing and Foreign Assistance: An Analysis of Problems and Prospects in Less Developed Countries*. AID Discussion Paper no. 19. Washington, D.C.: US AID, June 1969.

Friedmann, Wolfgang G., et al. *International Financial Aid*. New York: Columbia University Press, 1966.

Fulbright, J. William. *The Arrogance of Power*. New York: Random House, 1967.

Geiger, Theodore. *The Conflicted Relationship: The West and the Transformation of Asia, Africa and Latin America*. New York: McGraw-Hill, 1967.

Ghouse, Agha M., ed. *Pakistan in the Development Decade: Problems and Performance: Proceedings of the Third Economic Development Seminar, Karachi, March 30–April 2, 1968*. Lahore: Government of West Pakistan, 1968.

Goldman, Marshall I. *Soviet Foreign Aid.* New York: Prager, 1967.

Goldwin, Robert A., ed. *Why Foreign Aid?* Chicago: Rand McNally, 1963.

Goulet, Denis. *The Cruel Choice: A New Concept in the Theory of Development.* New York: Atheneum, 1971.

Goulet, Denis, and Hudson, Michael. *The Myth of Aid: The Hidden Agenda of the Development Reports.* Maryknoll, N.Y.: Orbis Books, 1971.

Gray, Clive S. *Resource Flows to Less-Developed Countries: Financial Terms and Their Constraints.* New York: Praeger, 1969.

Griffin, Keith. *Underdevelopment in Spanish America: An Interpretation.* London: Allen & Unwin, 1969.

Hannah, J. A. *International Developmental Assistance: A Statement by the Task Force on International Developmental Assistance and International Education.* Washington, D.C.: National Association of State Universities and Land-Grant Colleges, January 1969.

Haq, Mahbub ul. *Planning Machinery in Pakistan.* Karachi: Planning Commission, 1965.

  The Strategy of Economic Planning: A Case Study of Pakistan. Karachi: Oxford University Press, 1963.

Haq, M., and Khanam, Khadija. *Deficit Financing in Pakistan, 1951–60.* Monograph no. 3. Karachi: Pakistan Institute of Development Economics, 1964.

Harwood, W. F., et al. *Encouraging the Growth of Small Industry in Pakistan.* Stanford, Calif.: Stanford Research Institute, 1963.

Hasan, Parvez. *Deficit Financing and Capital Formation: The Pakistan Experience, 1951–59.* Karachi: Pakistan Institute of Development Economics, 1963.

Hayter, Teresa. *Effective Aid.* London: Overseas Development Institute, 1967.

  French Aid. London: Overseas Development Institute, 1966.

Hirschman, Albert O. *Development Projects Observed.* Washington, D.C.: Brookings Institution, 1967.

Hirschman, Albert O., and Bird, Richard M. *Foreign Aid – A Critique and a Proposal.* Essays in International Finance, no. 69. Princeton, N.J.: Princeton University, July, 1968.

Hogan, Warren P. *Capacity Creation and Utilisation in Pakistan Manufacturing Industry.* Economic Development Report no. 84. Cambridge, Mass.: Harvard University, Center for International Affairs, September 1967.

Holbik, Karel. *The United States, the Soviet Union and the Third World.* Hamburg: Hamburg Institute for International Economics, 1968.

Holbik, Karel, and Meyers, Henry A. *West German Foreign Aid, 1956–1966: Its Economic and Political Aspects.* Boston: Boston University Press, 1968.

Islam, Nurul. *Imports of Pakistan: Growth and Structure – A Statistical Study.* Statistical Paper no. 3. Karachi: Pakistan Institute of Development Economics, 1967.

Jackson, Robert Sir. *A Study of the Capacity of the United Nations Development System.* DP/5. 2 vols. Geneva: United Nations Development Programme, 1969.

Jacoby, Neil H. *United States Aid to Taiwan: A Study of Foreign Aid, Self-Help, and Development.* New York: Praeger, 1966.

Johnson, Harry G. *Economic Policies toward Less-Developed Countries.* Washington, D.C.: Brookings Institution, 1967.

Kahnert, F., et al. *Agriculture and Related Industries in Pakistan: Prospects and Requirements until 1975*. Paris: OECD, 1970.

Kaplan, Jacob J. *The Challenge of Foreign Aid: Policies, Problems, and Possibilities*. New York: Praeger, 1967.

Keenleyside, Hugh L. *International Aid: A Summary with Special Reference to the Programmes of the United Nations*. New York: James H. Heineman, 1966.

Kim, Seung Hee. *Foreign Capital for Economic Development: A Korean Case Study*. New York: Praeger, 1970.

Kindleberger, Charles P. *Power and Money: The Economics of International Politics and the Politics of International Economics*. New York: Basic Books, Inc., 1970.

King, John A., Jr. *Economic Development Projects and Their Appraisal: Cases and Principles from the Experience of the World Bank*. Baltimore: Johns Hopkins Press, 1967.

Kirdar, Üner. *The Structure of United Nations Economic-Aid to Underdeveloped Countries*. The Hague: Martinus Nijhoff, 1966.

Krassowski, Andrzej, ed. *British Development Policies: Needs and Policies 1970*. London: Overseas Development Institute, 1970.

Lachman, Alexis E. *The Local Currency Proceeds of Foreign Aid*. Paris: OECD, 1968.

Lambe, James, ed. *British Development Policies: Needs and Prospects 1969*. London: Overseas Development Institute, 1969.

Lewis, Stephen R., Jr. *Economic Policy and Industrial Growth in Pakistan*. London: Allen & Unwin, 1969.

Pakistan: Industrialization and Trade Policies. London: Oxford University Press, 1970.

Lieftinck, Pieter, et al. *Water and Power Resources of West Pakistan: A Study in Sector Planning*. 3 vols. Baltimore: Johns Hopkins Press, 1968.

Little, I. M. D., and Clifford, J. M. *International Aid*. London: Allen & Unwin, 1965.

MacEwan, Arthur. *Contradictions in Capitalist Development: The Case of Pakistan*. Economic Development Report no. 159. Cambridge, Mass.: Harvard University, Center for International Affairs, July 1970.

Development Alternatives in Pakistan: A Multisectoral and Regional Analysis of Planning Problems. Cambridge, Mass.: Harvard University Press, 1971.

Maddison, Angus. *Social Development of Pakistan, 1947–1970*. Economic Development Report no. 169. Cambridge, Mass.: Harvard University, Center for International Affairs, June 1970.

Madhava, K. B., ed. *International Development 1969: Proceedings of the Eleventh World Conference of the Society for International Development, New Delhi, November 1969*. Dobbs Ferry, N.Y.: Oceana Publications, 1970.

Mahmud, K. *Trade Unionism in Pakistan*. Lahore: University of the Punjab, Department of Political Science, 1958.

Markham, Jesse W., and Papanek, Gustav F., eds. *Industrial Organization and Economic Development: In Honor of E. S. Mason*. Boston: Houghton Mifflin, 1970.

Mason, Edward S. *Economic Development in India and Pakistan*. Occasional Papers in International Affairs, no. 13. Cambridge, Mass.: Harvard University Press, 1966.

Foreign Aid and Foreign Policy. New York: Harper & Row, 1964.

Maung, Mya. *Burma and Pakistan: A Comparative Study of Development*. New York: Praeger, 1971.

Meier, Gerald M. *The International Economics of Development: Theory and Policy*. New York: Harper & Row, 1968.

Michel, Aloys A. *The Indus Rivers: A Study of the Effects of Partition*. New Haven, Conn.: Yale University Press, 1967.

Mihaly, Eugene B. *Foreign Aid and Politics in Nepal: A Case Study*. London: Oxford University Press, 1965.

Mikesell, Raymond F. *The Economics of Foreign Aid*. Chicago: Aldine, 1968.

Public International Lending for Development. New York: Random House, 1966.

Millikan, Max F., et al., eds. *The Role of Popular Participation in Development*. M.I.T. Report no. 17. Cambridge, Mass.: Massachusetts Institute of Technology, Center for International Studies, March 1969.

Montgomery, John D. *Foreign Aid in International Politics*. Englewood Cliffs, N.J.: Prentice-Hall, 1967.

The Politics of Foreign Aid: American Experience in Southeast Asia. New York: Praeger, 1962.

Moomaw, I. W. *The Challenge of Hunger: A Program for More Effective Foreign Aid*. New York: Praeger, 1966.

Müller, Kurt. *The Foreign Aid Programs of the Soviet Bloc and Communist China: An Analysis*. New York: Walker, 1967.

Myrdal, Gunnar. *Asian Drama: An Inquiry into the Poverty of Nations*. 3 vols. New York: Twentieth Century Fund, 1968.

Nelson, Joan M. *Aid, Influence, and Foreign Policy*. New York: Macmillan, 1968.

Norbye, O. D. K. *Development Prospects of Pakistan*. Development Research Monographs. 3 vols. Bergen, Norway: Chr. Michelson Institute, 1965.

Ohlin, Goran. *Aid and Indebtedness: The Relation between Aid Requirements, Terms of Assistance and Indebtedness of Developing Countries*. Paris: OECD, 1966.

Foreign Aid Policies Reconsidered. Paris: OECD, 1966.

O'Leary, Michael K. *The Politics of American Foreign Aid*. New York: Atherton Press, 1967.

Papanek, Gustav F. *Aid, Foreign Private Investment, Savings and Growth in Less Developed Countries*. Economic Development Report no. 195. Cambridge, Mass.: Harvard University, Center for International Affairs, June 1971.

Comparative Development Strategies: India and Pakistan. Economic Development Report no. 152. Cambridge, Mass.: Harvard University, Center for International Affairs, December 1969.

Pakistan's Development: Social Goals and Private Incentives. Cambridge, Mass.: Harvard University Press, 1967.

ed. *Development Policy – Theory and Practice*. Cambridge, Mass.: Harvard University Press, 1968.

Pearson, Lester B., et al. *Partners in Development: Report of the Commission on International Development*. New York: Praeger, 1969.

Perera, Phillips. *Development Finance: Institutions, Problems, and Prospects*. New York: Praeger, 1968.

Peterson, Rudolph A., et al. *U.S. Foreign Assistance in the 1970s. A New Approach: Report to the President from the Task Force on International Development*. Washington, D.C.: U.S. Government Printing Office, 4 March 1970.

Phillips, Hiram S. *Guides for Development: Institution-Building and Reform.* New York: Praeger, 1969.

Pincus, John. *Costs and Benefits of Aid: An Empirical Analysis.* UNCTAD/TD/7/Supp. 10. Geneva: 26 October 1967.

    Economic Aid and International Cost Sharing. Baltimore: Johns Hopkins Press, 1965.

    Trade, Aid and Development: The Rich and Poor Nations. New York: McGraw-Hill, 1967.

Prebisch, Raul. *Change and Development: Latin America's Great Task.* Washington, D.C.: Inter-American Development Bank, July 1970.

Rahman, M. Anisur. *East and West Pakistan: A Problem in the Political Economy of Regional Planning.* Occasional Papers in International Affairs, no. 20. Cambridge, Mass.: Harvard University Press, 1968.

Ranis, G., and Nelson, J. M. *Measures to Ensure the Effectiveness of Aid.* AID Discussion Paper no. 12. Washington, D.C.: US AID, September 1966.

Rao, V. K. R. V., and Narain, Dharm. *Foreign Aid and India's Economic Development.* Bombay: Asia Publishing, 1963.

Research Committee on Foreign Aid. *Foreign Aid: A Symposium, A Survey and an Appraisal.* Calcutta: Indian Council on Current Affairs, 1968.

Robock, Stefan H. *Brazil's Developing Northeast: A Study of Regional Planning and Foreign Aid.* Washington, D.C.: Brookings Institution, 1963.

Rockefeller, Nelson A. *Quality of Life in the Americas: Report of a U.S. Presidential Mission for the Western Hemisphere.* Washington, D.C.: US AID, August 1969.

Roosa, Robert V., et al. *Economic Growth: Balance of Payments.* New York: American Bankers Association, 1962.

Sayeed, Khalid B. *The Political System of Pakistan.* Boston: Houghton Mifflin, 1967.

Sen, Sudhir, *United Nations in Economic Development – Need for a New Strategy.* Dobbs Ferry, N.Y.: Oceana Publications, 1969.

Shaffer, Harry G., ed. *The Soviet Economy: A Collection of Western and Soviet Views.* 2nd ed. New York: Appleton-Century Crofts, 1969.

Singer, Hans W. *International Development: Growth and Change.* New York: McGraw Hill, 1964.

Soper, Tom. *Aid Management Overseas.* London: Overseas Development Institute, 1967.

Spicer, Keith. *A Samaritan State? External Aid in Canada's Foreign Policy.* Toronto: University of Toronto Press, 1966.

Stern, Joseph J., and Falcon, Walter P. *Growth and Development in Pakistan, 1955–1969.* Occasional Papers in International Affairs, no. 23. Cambridge, Mass.: Harvard University Press, 1970.

Strout, Alan M., and Clark, Paul G. *Aid, Performance, Self-Help, and Need.* AID Discussion Paper no. 20. Washington, D.C.: US AID, July 1969.

Tansky, Leo. *U.S. and U.S.S.R. Aid to Developing Countries: A Comparative Study of India, Turkey, and the U.A.R.* New York: Praeger, 1966.

Thorp, Willard L. *The Reality of Foreign Aid.* New York: Praeger, 1971.

Tims, Wouter. *Analytical Techniques for Development Planning: A Case Study of Pakistan's Third Five-Year Plan (1965–70).* Karachi: Pakistan Institute of Development Economics, 1968.

Vanek, Jaroslav. *Estimating Foreign Resource Needs for Economic Development: Theory, Methods and a Case Study of Colombia.* New York: McGraw-Hill, 1967.

Vassilev, Vassil. *Policy in the Soviet Bloc on Aid to Developing Countries.* Paris: OECD, 1969.

Von Vorys, Karl. *Political Development in Pakistan.* Princeton, N.J.: Princeton University Press, 1965.

Walters, Robert S. *American and Soviet Aid: A Comparative Analysis.* Pittsburgh: University of Pittsburgh Press, 1970.

Ward, Barbara, et al., eds. *The Widening Gap – Development in the 1970's.* New York: Columbia University Press, 1971.

Waterston, Albert. *Planning in Pakistan: Organization and Implementation.* Baltimore: Johns Hopkins Press, 1963.

Weaver, James H. *The International Development Association: A New Approach to Foreign Aid.* New York: Praeger, 1965.

Weisskopf, Thomas E. *The Impact of Foreign Capital Inflow on Domestic Savings in the Underdeveloped Countries.* Economic Development Report no. 156. Cambridge, Mass.: Harvard University, Center for International Affairs, July 1970.

White, John. *German Aid: A Survey of the Sources, Policy and Structure of German Aid.* London: Overseas Development Institute, 1965.

Japanese Aid. London: Overseas Development Institute, 1964.

Pledged to Development: A Study of International Consortia and the Strategy of Aid. London: Overseas Development Institute, 1967.

Wilcox, Wayne A. *Pakistan: The Consolidation of a Nation.* New York: Columbia University Press, 1963.

Wolf, Charles, Jr. *Foreign Aid: Theory and Practice in Southern Asia.* Princeton, N.J.: Princeton University Press, 1960.

Ziring, Lawrence. *The Ayub Khan Era: Politics in Pakistan, 1958–1969.* Syracuse: Syracuse University Press, 1971.

2   Articles

Adelman, Irma, and Morris, Cynthia T. 'Performance Criteria for Evaluating Economic Development Potential: An Operational Approach'. *Quarterly Journal of Economics,* May 1968.

Adler, John H. 'Aid and Investment'. *International Targets for Development.* Edited by Richard Symonds. New York: Harper & Row, 1970.

Aggarwal, R. M. 'Technical Aid to South East Asia'. *Muslim Economist,* 30 June 1950.

Alsop, M. H. 'American Recession and Sydney Conference: Far-Reaching Repercussions on Pakistan's Development Plan'. *Enterprise,* 16 February 1954.

'Progress Report on the Colombo Plan'. *Economic Observer,* 16 September 1952. Also in *Pakistan Business News & Views,* 15 July 1952.

Anstey, Vera. 'The Colombo Plan with Special Reference to India and Pakistan'. *Economics and Commerce,* June 1952. Also in *Economia Internazionale,* February 1952.

Arnold, Percy. 'Australian Aid to Pakistan under the Colombo Plan'. *Pakistan Trade,* May 1955.

'Britain's Role in Pakistan's Economic Development'. *Economic Observer,* July 1956.

Ayoob, Mohammed. 'U.S. Economic Assistance to Pakistan, 1954–1965'. *India Quarterly*, April–June 1967.

Ball, R. J. 'Capital Imports and Economic Development: Paradoxy or Orthodoxy?'. *Kyklos*, vol. xv, fasc. 3, 1962.

Balneaves, E. 'Is Pakistan Wasting Foreign Aid?' *New Commonwealth*, 13 June 1955.

Bell, John O. 'American Aid and the Agricultural Crisis in Pakistan'. *Enterprise*, 16 February 1957. Also in *Economic Observer*, February 1957.

'Pakistan's Development and American Aid'. *Economic Observer*, February 1957.

Benham, F. C. 'Canada's Assistance to Pakistan under Colombo Plan'. *Weekly Bulletin*, 25 February 1954. Also in *Pakistan Trade*, March 1954.

Bergan, Asbjorn, 'Personal Income Distribution and Personal Savings in Pakistan: 1963/64'. *Pakistan Development Review*, Summer, 1967.

Berrill, Kenneth E. 'Foreign Capital and Take-Off'. *The Economics of Take-Off into Sustained Growth. Proceedings of a Conference held by the International Economic Association*. Edited by W. W. Rostow. London: Macmillan, 1963.

Bhagwati, Jagdish. 'Alternative Estimates of the Real Cost of Aid'. *Unfashionable Economics: Essays in Honour of Lord Balogh*. Edited by Paul Streeten. London: Weidenfeld & Nicolson, 1970.

Bird, Richard M. 'The Influence of Foreign Aid on Local Expenditures'. *Social and Economic Studies*, June 1967.

'What's Wrong with the United States Foreign Aid Programme?' *International Journal*, Winter 1969–70.

Bose, Swadesh R. 'Trend of Real Income of the Rural Poor in East Pakistan, 1949–66'. *Pakistan Development Review*, Autumn 1968.

Braibanti, Ralph. 'External Inducement of Political-Administrative Development: an Institutional Strategy'. *Political and Administrative Development*. Edited by Ralph Braibanti. Durham, N.C.: Duke University Press, 1969.

Bruton, Henry J. 'The Theory of Foreign Aid'. *Indian Economic Journal*, January 1961.

'The Two Gap Approach to Aid and Development: Comment'. *American Economic Review*, June 1969.

Carlin, Alan. 'Project Versus Programme Aid: From the Donor's Viewpoint'. *Economic Journal*, March 1967.

Carlson, V. D. 'International Assistance to Meet the Social Needs of Pakistan with Special Reference to Priority'. *Proceedings of the 3rd Session of the Pakistan Conference on Social Welfare*. Lahore, 1959.

Central Statistical Office. 'Estimation of National Income in Pakistan'. *Pakistan Development Review*, Winter 1961.

Chenery, Hollis B. 'The Two Gap Approach to Aid and Development: A Reply to Bruton'. *American Economic Review*, June 1969.

Chenery, Hollis B., and MacEwan, Arthur. 'Optimal Patterns of Growth and Aid: The Case of Pakistan'. *Pakistan Development Review*, Summer 1966.

Chenery, Hollis B., and Strout, Alan M. 'Foreign Assistance and Economic Development'. *American Economic Review*, September 1966.

'Foreign Assistance and Economic Development: Reply'. *American Economic Review*, September 1968.

Cohen, Benjamin I. 'Relative Effects of Foreign Capital and Larger Exports on Economic Development'. *Review of Economics and Statistics*, May 1968.

'Colombo Plan and Foreign Aid Effect on Our Development'. *Karachi Commerce*, 10 May and 17 May 1952.

'Colombo Plan and Pakistan'. *MCC Trade Journal*, 24 October 1953.

'Colombo Plan Report Explains Increase in Income and Industrial Production in Pakistan'. *Enterprise*, 19 January 1957.

'Development Assistance: Changing Needs and Problems'. *OECD Observer*, October 1968.

'Economic and Technical Aid from U.S.A.' *Pakistan Trade*, June 1957.

'Economic Development of Pakistan under the Colombo Plan'. *Economic Digest* (Pakistan), February 1958.

Fei, John C. H., and Paauw, Douglas S. 'Foreign Assistance and Self-Help: A Reappraisal of Development Finance'. *Review of Economics and Statistics*, August 1965.

Fei, John C. H., and Ranis, G. 'Foreign Assistance and Economic Development: Comment'. *American Economic Review*, September 1968.

Fisher, Franklin M. 'A Theoretical Analysis of the Impact of Food Surplus Disposal on Agricultural Production in Recipient Countries'. *Journal of Farm Economics*, November 1963.

'Foreign Aid and Its Utilization'. *Pakistan Trade*, January 1957.

'Foreign Aid and Its Utilization in Pakistan'. *Economic Observer*, December 1956.

'Foreign Aid and Pakistan's Development'. *Karachi Commerce*, Annual no. 1955.

'Foreign Aid and Technical Assistance'. *Weekly Bulletin*, 6 September 1956.

'Foreign Aid for Pakistan's Agriculture'. *Pakistan Business News & Views*, 1 October 1953.

'Foreign Economic Aid to Pakistan'. *Economic Digest* (Pakistan), 30 December 1956.

'Foreign Economic Aid to Pakistan'. *Weekly Bulletin*, 15 August 1959.

'Foreign Economic Aids in East Pakistan'. *East Pakistan Information*, 3 September 1958.

'Foreign Economic Assistance to Pakistan.' *Pakistan Trade*, January 1955.

Friedman, Milton. 'Foreign Economic Aid: Means and Objectives.' *Yale Review*, June 1958.

Galbraith, John Kenneth. 'A Positive Approach to Foreign Aid'. *Foreign Affairs*, April 1961.

'Underdevelopment: An Approach to Classification'. *Fiscal and Monetary Problems in Developing States: Proceedings of the Third Rehovoth Conference*. Edited by David Krivine. New York: Praeger, 1967.

Geiger, Theodore, and Hansen, Roger D. 'The Role of Information in Decision Making on Foreign Aid'. *The Study of Policy Formation*. Edited by Raymond A. Bauer and Kenneth J. Gergen. New York: The Free Press, 1968.

Gilbert, R. 'Role of Foreign Aid in the Development Programmes'. *Seminar on Planning and Development, Lahore, March 26–28, 1962*. Lahore: Government of West Pakistan, 1962.

Glassburner, Bruce. 'The Balance of Payments and External Resources in Pakistan's Third Five-Year Plan'. *Pakistan Development Review*, Autumn 1965.

Griffin, Keith B. 'Financing Development Plans in Pakistan'. *Pakistan Development Review*, Winter 1965.

'Foreign Capital, Domestic Savings and Economic Development'. *Bulletin of the Oxford University Institute of Economics and Statistics*, May 1970.

Griffin, K. B., and Enos, J. L. 'Foreign Assistance: Objectives and Consequences'. *Economic Development and Cultural Change*, April 1970.

Habibullah, M. 'How Economic Aid Has Helped Pakistan'. *European–Atlantic Review*, Spring 1960.

'Role of Foreign Capital and Aid in the Economic Development of Pakistan', and 'Financial Institutions and Economic Development'. *Pakistan Economic Journal*, July–September 1960.

Hagen, Everett E., and Hawrylyshyn, Oli. 'Analysis of World Income and Growth, 1955–1966'. *Economic Development and Cultural Change*, October 1969.

Haq, Khadija, and Baqai, M. 'Savings and Financial Flows in the Corporate Sector, 1959–63'. *Pakistan Development Review*, Autumn 1967.

Haq, Mahbub ul. 'Annual Planning in Pakistan'. *Journal of Development Planning*, no. 2 (United Nations), 1970.

'Tied Credits – A Quantitative Analysis'. *Capital Movements and Economic Development*. Edited by John H. Adler and Paul W. Kuznets. New York: St Martin's Press, 1967.

Hashmi, S. S. 'Main Features of the Demographic Conditions in Pakistan'. Country background paper presented at the Asian Population Conference, New Delhi, 10–20 December 1963. Karachi: Pakistan Central Statistical Office, November 1963.

Holzman, Franklyn D. 'The Real Economic Costs of Granting Foreign Aid'. *Journal of Development Studies*, April 1971.

Horowitz, David. 'Narrowing the Gap through International Aid'. *Fiscal and Monetary Problems in Developing States: Proceedings of the Third Rehovoth Conference*. Edited by David Krivine. New York: Praeger, 1967.

Horvath, Janos. 'Economic Aid Flow from the USSR: A Recount of the First Fifteen Years'. *Slavic Review*, December 1970.

Islam, G. 'Foreign Aid, Its Anatomy and Effects'. *Enterprise*, 21 June 1958.

Islam, Nurul. 'Comparative Costs, Factor Proportions, and Industrial Efficiency in Pakistan'. *Pakistan Development Review*, Summer 1967.

'Foreign Aid and Economic Development'. *Social and Economic Studies*, September 1959.

'International Economic Assistance in the 1970's – A Critique of Partners in Development'. *Pakistan Development Review*, Winter 1970.

Issawi, Charles, et al. 'Foreign Assistance: Objectives and Consequences: Comments and a Reply'. *Economic Development and Cultural Change*, October 1971.

Joshi, Vijay. 'Saving and Foreign Exchange Constraints'. *Unfashionable Economics: Essays in Honour of Lord Balogh*. Edited by Paul Streeten. London: Weidenfeld & Nicolson, 1970.

Kennedy, Charles, et al. 'Foreign Capital, Domestic Savings and Economic Development: Three Comments and a Reply'. *Bulletin of the Oxford University Institute of Economics and Statistics*, May 1971.

Khan, Azizur Rahman. 'Import Substitution, Export Expansion and Consumption Liberalization: A Preliminary Report'. *Pakistan Development Review*, Summer 1963.

'What Has Been Happening to Real Wages in Pakistan?'. *Pakistan Development Review*, Autumn 1967.

Khan, N. M. A. 'The Impact of American Aid on Pakistan'. *Pakistan Horizon*, December 1959.

Khan, Taufiq M., and Bergan, Asbjorn. 'Measurement of Structural Change in the Pakistan Economy: A Review of the National Income Estimates, 1949/50 to 1963/64'. *Pakistan Development Review*, Summer 1966.

Killen, J. S. 'Pakistan's Economic Development and American Aid'. *MCC Trade Journal*, September 1958.

Kumar, R. 'The Balance of Payments Problem and Economic Development'. *Indian Economic Journal*, April 1961.

Lakdawala, D. T. 'Development and Foreign Aid'. *Indian Economic Journal*, January–March 1968.

Levitt, Malcolm S. 'The Allocation of Economic Aid in Practice'. *Manchester School of Economic and Social Studies*, June 1968.

Lewis, Stephen R., Jr. 'Aspects of Fiscal Policy and Resource Mobilization in Pakistan'. *Pakistan Development Review*, Summer 1964.

'Domestic Resources and Fiscal Policy in Pakistan's Second and Third Plans'. *Pakistan Development Review*, Autumn 1965.

Lewis, Stephen R., Jr., and Khan, Mohammad Irshad. 'Estimates of Noncorporate Private Saving in Pakistan: 1949–1962.' *Pakistan Development Review*, Spring 1964.

Lewis, Stephen R., Jr., and Soligo, Ronald. 'Growth and Structural Change in Pakistan's Manufacturing Industry, 1954–64'. *Pakistan Development Review*, Spring 1965.

McAuley, Alistair, and Matko, Dubravko. 'Soviet Foreign Aid'. *Bulletin of the Oxford University Institute of Economics and Statistics*, November 1966.

MacEwen, Arthur. 'Pakistan, Economic Change and Social Scientists'. *Bulletin of Concerned Asian Scholars*, no. 4 (San Francisco), May 1969.

Matin, Abdul. 'Role of Foreign Aid in the Economic Development of Pakistan'. *Seminar on Planning and Development, Lahore, March 26–28, 1962*. Lahore: Government of West Pakistan, 1962.

McKinnon, Ronald I. 'Foreign Exchange Constraints in Economic Development and Efficient Aid Allocation'. *Economic Journal*, June 1964.

Morgenthau, Hans J. 'A Political Theory of Foreign Aid'. *American Political Science Review*, June 1962.

Naqvi, Syed N. H. 'The Balance-of-Payments Problem and Resource Allocation in Pakistan – A Linear Programming Approach'. *Pakistan Development Review*, Autumn 1963.

Naseem, H. A. 'International Aid and Economic Growth of Pakistan'. *NIPA Reporter*, August and September 1962.

Papanek, Gustav F. 'Economic Survey – Pakistan'. *The Far East and Australasia, 1970: A Survey and Directory of Asia and the Pacific*. London: Europa Publications Ltd, 1970.

'Growth and Structural Change in Pakistan's Manufacturing Industry: A Comment'. *Pakistan Development Review*, Winter 1965.

'Industrial Production and Investment in Pakistan'. *Pakistan Development Review*, Autumn 1964.

Pincus, John A. 'The Cost of Foreign Aid'. *Review of Economics and Statistics*, November 1963.

Power, John H. 'Development Strategy for Pakistan'. *Pakistan Development Review*, Autumn 1963.

'Industrialization in Pakistan: A Case of Frustrated Take-Off?'. *Pakistan Development Review*, Summer 1963.

Prest, A. R., and Turvey, R. 'Cost–Benefit Analysis: A Survey'. *Economic Journal*, December 1965.

Qayum, A. 'Long Term Economic Criteria for Foreign Loans'. *Economic Journal*, June 1966.

Qureshi, D. M. 'Effective Utilization of Foreign Aid'. *Seminar on Planning and Development, Lahore, March 26–28, 1962*. Lahore: Government of West Pakistan, 1962.

'Role of Foreign Aid in the Economic Development of Pakistan'. *Economic Observer*, August 1955. Also in *Pakistan Trade*, August 1955.

Rab, Abdur. 'Pakistan's Economic Interest in Relation to the Sterling Area.' *Pakistan Economic Journal*, July–September 1959.

Rahman, M. Anisur. 'Foreign Capital and Domestic Savings: A Test of Haavelmo's Hypothesis with Cross-Country Data'. *Review of Economics and Statistics*, February 1968.

'The Pakistan Perspective Plan and the Objective of Elimination of Dependence on Foreign Assistance'. *Pakistan Development Review*, Autumn 1967.

'Perspective Planning for Self-Assured Growth: An Approach to Foreign Capital from a Recipient's Point of View'. *Pakistan Development Review*, Spring 1968.

'The Welfare Economics of Foreign Aid'. *Pakistan Development Review*, Summer 1967.

Rosenstein-Rodan, P. N. 'International Aid for Underdeveloped Countries'. *Review of Economics and Statistics*, May 1961.

Schmidt, Wilson E. 'The Economics of Charity: Loans Versus Grants'. *Journal of Political Economy*, August 1964.

Sharif, M. R. 'Foreign Aid Utilization in Pakistan, Its Problems'. *Finance and Industry*, July 1962.

'Some Aspects of Foreign Aid'. *Economic Observer*, December 1956.

'Technical Aid to Pakistan'. *Weekly Bulletin*, 8 September 1955.

'Technical and Economic Assistance from Abroad'. *Pakistan Trade*, April 1956.

'Total Foreign Aid to Pakistan'. *MCC Trade Journal*, January 1957.

'U.S. Aid and Pakistan Economy'. *Karachi Commerce*, 13 March 1954.

Singer, Hans W. 'External Aid: For Plans or Projects?'. *Economic Journal*, September 1965.

Stern, Robert M. 'International Financial Issues in Foreign Economic Assistance to the Less Developed Countries'. *Economic Development and Structural Change*. Edited by Ian G. Stewart. Edinburgh: Edinburgh University Press, 1969.

Thomas, Philip S. 'Import Licensing and Import Liberalization in Pakistan'. *Pakistan Development Review*, Winter 1966.

Tokman, Victor E. 'An Evaluation of Foreign Aid: The Chilean Case'. *Bulletin of the Oxford University Institute of Economics and Statistics*, May 1969.

Ul-Haque, Irfan. 'Foreign Finance in the Third Five-Year Plan of Pakistan'. *Journal of World Trade Law*, March–April 1970.

Wilcox, Clair. 'Pakistan'. *Planning Economic Development*. Edited by Everett E. Hagen. Homewood, Ill.: Richard D. Irwin, 1963.

Winston, Gordon C. 'Consumer Goods or Capital Goods – Supply Consistency in Development Planning'. *Pakistan Development Review*, Autumn 1967.

Wolf, Charles, Jr. 'Institutions and Economic Development'. *American Economic Review*, December 1955.

3 Documents

Canada

Canadian International Development Agency. *Annual Review, 1967–68*. Ottawa: Queen's Printer, 1968.

Department of External Affairs. *International Development: Foreign Policy for Canadians*. Ottawa: Queen's Printer, 1970.

External Aid Office. *Annual Review, 1966–67*. Ottawa: Queen's Printer, 1967.

General Agreement on Tariffs and Trade

Trade of Less-Developed Countries – Development Plans: Study of the Second Five-Year Plan of Pakistan. Geneva: GATT, 1962.

World Bank Group

International Bank for Reconstruction and Development. *Suppliers' Credits from Industrialized to Developing Countries*. Washington, D.C.: IBRD, 1967.

IBRD and IDA. *Annual Report, 1966/67*. Washington, D.C.: IBRD, 1967.

IBRD, IFC and IDA. *The World Bank Group in Pakistan*. Washington, D.C.: IBRD, [1965].

International Finance Corporation. *Annual Report, 1966/67*. Washington, D.C.: IFC, 1967.

International Monetary Fund

Staff Report on Pakistan. Washington, D.C.: IMF, 19 April 1968.

Organization for Economic Co-operation and Development

Development Assistance: Efforts and Policies of the Members of the Development Assistance Committee. Paris: OECD, Annual, 1964–70.

'Development Assistance: 1967 and Recent Trends'. Mimeographed. Paris: OECD, 4 July 1968.

The Flow of Financial Resources to Countries in Course of Economic Development, 1955–1959. Paris: OECD, 1961.

The Flow of Financial Resources to Less-Developed Countries, 1956–1963. Paris: OECD, 1964.

The Flow of Financial Resources to Less-Developed Countries, 1961–1965. Paris: OECD, 1967.

Geographical Distribution of Financial Flows to Less Developed Countries, 1960–1964. Paris: OECD, 1966.

Quantitative Models as an Aid to Development Assistance Policy: Report by the Expert Group on the Uses of Analytical Techniques. Paris: OECD, 1967.

Resources for the Developing World: The Flow of Financial Resources to Less-Developed Countries, 1962–1968. Paris: OECD, 1970.

Pakistan

Central Statistical Office. *20 Years of Pakistan in Statistics, 1947–1967.* Karachi: Manager of Publications, 1968.

Ministry of Economic Affairs. *Critical Report on Operations of Economic Aid to Pakistan from U.S.A.* Karachi: Manager of Publications, 1957.

Ministry of Finance. *The Budget in Brief, 1966–67.* Rawalpindi: Manager of Publications, 1966.

The Budget in Brief, 1968–69. Islamabad: Manager of Publications, 1968.

Economy of Pakistan, 1948–68. Islamabad: Manager of Publications, 1968.

Foreign Economic Aid: A Review of Foreign Economic Aid to Pakistan. Rawalpindi: Manager of Publications, 1962.

Pakistan Economic Survey, 1965–66. Rawalpindi: Manager of Publications, 1966.

Pakistan Economic Survey, 1967–68. Islamabad: Manager of Publications, 1968.

Planning Commission. *Annual Plan, 1968–69.* Rawalpindi: Manager of Publications, 1968.

Annual Plan, 1969–70. Islamabad: Manager of Publications, 1969.

Evaluation of the First Year (1965–66) of the Third Five-Year Plan, 1965–70. Rawalpindi: Manager of Publications, 1967.

Evaluation of the Third Five-Year Plan (1965–70). Islamabad: Manager of Publications, 1971.

Final Evaluation of the Second Five-Year Plan (1960–65). Karachi: Manager of Publications, 1966.

First Five-Year Plan: Preliminary Evaluation Report. Karachi: Manager of Publications, 1960.

The First Five-Year Plan, 1955–60. Karachi: Manager of Publications, 1958.

The Fourth Five-Year Plan, 1970–75. Islamabad: Manager of Publications, 1970.

Industrial Policy and Import Liabilities. Rawalpindi: Manager of Publications, 1967.

Memorandum for the Pakistan Consortium, 1966–67. Karachi: Manager of Publications, 1966.

Memorandum for the Pakistan Consortium, 1967–68. Rawalpindi: Manager of Publications, 1967.

Memorandum for the Pakistan Consortium, 1968–69. Rawalpindi: Manager of Publications, 1968.

Memorandum for the Pakistan Consortium, 1969–70. Islamabad: Manager of Publications, 1969.

The Mid-Plan Review of the Third Five-Year Plan (1965–70). Rawalpindi: Manager of Publications, 1968.

Outline of the Third Five-Year Plan, 1965–70. Karachi: Manager of Publications, 1964.

Preliminary Evaluation of Progress during the Second Five-Year Plan. Karachi: Manager of Publications, 1965.

The Second Five-Year Plan (1960–65). Karachi: Manager of Publications, 1960.

Socio-Economic Objectives of the Fourth Five Year Plan (1970–75). Islamabad: Manager of Publications, 1968.

The Third Five-Year Plan, 1965–70. Karachi: Manager of Publications, 1965.

State Bank of Pakistan. *External Debt Servicing Liability.* Karachi: Manager of Publications, 1965.

Working Group on Debt Burden. *Report of the Working Group on Debt Burden.* Islamabad: Manager of Publications, 1968.

United Nations

Department of Economic and Social Affairs. *Export Credits and Development Financing: Part One – Current Practices and Problems.* U.N./E/4274. New York: 1966.

Export Credits and Development Financing: Part Two – National Export Credit Systems. U.N./E/4274/Add. 1. New York: 1967.

The External Financing of Economic Development: International Flow of Long-term Capital and Official Donations, 1962–1966. Report of the Secretary-General. U.N./E/4438. New York: 1968.

The External Financing of Economic Development: International Flow of Long-term Capital and Official Donations, 1963–1967. Report of the Secretary-General. U.N./E/4652. New York: 1969.

The External Financing of Economic Development: International Flow of Long-term Capital and Official Donations, 1964–1968. Report of the Secretary-General. U.N./E/4815. New York: 1970.

International Development Strategy: Action Programme of the General Assembly for the Second United Nations Development Decade. U.N./ST/ECA/139. New York: 1970.

Economic and Social Council. *Committee for Development Planning: Report on the Sixth Session, 5–15 January 1970.* U.N./E/4776. New York: 1970.

Economic Commission for Asia and the Far East. *Industrial Development: Asia and the Far East.* 4 vols. U.N./E/CONF. 54/R.B.P./2. New York: 1966.

UN Conference on Trade and Development. *Growth and External Development Finance.* UNCTAD/TD/7/Supp. 1. Geneva: 17 October 1967.

Growth, Development Finance and Aid (Synchronization of International and National Policies): Issues and Proposals. UNCTAD/TD/7. Geneva: 11 October 1967.

The Outlook for Debt Service. UNCTAD/TD/7/Supp. 5. Geneva: 31 October 1967.

UN Industrial Development Organization. *Industrial Development Survey,* UNIDO/ID/CONF. 1/46*. Vienna: 1 September 1967.

United States

Agency for International Development. *Gross National Product: Growth Rates and Trend Data by Region and Country.* Washington, D.C.: US AID, 1968.

Pakistan Briefing Book. Lahore: US AID, 15 November 1966.

Pakistan's Economic Development and United States Assistance. Karachi: US AID, 1967.

Principles of Foreign Economic Assistance. Washington, D.C.: US AID, 1965.

Statistical Fact Book: Selected Economic and Social Data on Pakistan. Karachi: US AID, June 1966.

A Study on Loan Terms, Debt Burden and Development. Washington, D.C.: US AID, April 1965.

U.S. AID in East Pakistan. Dacca: US AID, 1966.

Committee for Economic Development. *Assisting Development in Low-income Countries: Priorities for U.S. Government Policy.* New York: September 1969.
Development Assistance to Southeast Asia. New York: July 1970.
National Planning Association. *A New Conception of U.S. Foreign Aid.* Special Report no. 64. Washington, D.C.: March 1969.
US Senate. Special Committee to Study the Foreign Aid Program. *The Foreign Aid Program: Compilation of Studies and Surveys.* Washington, D.C.: Government Printing Office, July 1957.

Unpublished material

Carlin, Alan. 'An Evaluation of U.S. Government Aid to India'. Unpublished Ph.D. dissertation, Massachusetts Institute of Technology, 1964.
Fontaine, F., et al. 'CIDA Policy Review'. 8 vols. Mimeographed. A series of papers on Canada's foreign aid programme, tabled in the House of Commons, 13 January 1970. Ottawa: CIDA Information Division, 1970.
Lewis, Stephen R., Jr. 'Notes on Industrialization and Income Distribution in Pakistan'. Research Memorandum no. 37. Mimeographed. Williams College, Center for Development Economics, September 1970.
Loutfi, Martha F. 'An Analysis of the Cost of Foreign Aid to the Donor Country: The Case of Japan'. Unpublished Ph.D. dissertation, University of California at Berkeley, 1970.
Mohammed, Azizali F. 'Some Aspects of the Impact of Foreign Aid on an Under-developed Country: The Case of Pakistan'. Unpublished Ph.D. dissertation, George Washington University, 1958.
Papanek, Gustav F., and Jakubiak, Susan C. 'Aid and Development'. Paper presented at the Dubrovnik Conference of the Development Advisory Service of Harvard University, June 1970.
Perkins, James A., et al. 'Development Assistance in the New Administration: Report of the President's General Advisory Committee on Foreign Assistance Programs'. Mimeographed. Washington, D.C., October 1968.
Sayeed, Khalid B. 'The Performance Profile of the Government of Pakistan'. Mimeographed. McGill University, Centre for Developing-Area Studies, 1971.
Smith, J. Graham. 'External Assistance, Industrialization and Economic Development: A Case Study of Medium-Term Finance and Suppliers' Credit to Ghana, 1957–1966'. Mimeographed. McGill University, Centre for Developing-Area Studies, 1968.
Tims, W., and Stern, J. 'Pakistan Inter-Industry Flow Table (Revised), 1963–64'. Mimeographed. Harvard University, Center for International Affairs, 1967.

Index